THE UNION
OF THE CANADAS

THE GROWTH OF
CANADIAN INSTITUTIONS

A HISTORY OF CANADA IN EIGHTEEN VOLUMES

The Canadian Centenary Series is a comprehensive history of the peoples and lands which form the Dominion of Canada.

Although the series is designed as a unified whole so that no part of the story is left untold, each volume is complete in itself. Written for the general reader as well as for the scholar, each of the eighteen volumes of *The Canadian Centenary Series* is the work of a leading Canadian historian who is an authority on the period covered in his volume. Their combined efforts have made a new and significant contribution to the understanding of the history of Canada and of Canada today.

W. L. Morton, Vanier Professor of History, Trent University, is the Executive Editor of *The Canadian Centenary Series*. A graduate of the Universities of Manitoba and Oxford, he is the author of *The Kingdom of Canada; Manitoba: A History; The Progressive Party in Canada; The Critical Years: The Union of British North America, 1857-1873*; and other writings. He has also edited *The Journal of Alexander Begg and Other Documents Relevant to the Red River Resistance*. Holder of the honorary degrees of LL.D. and D.LITT., he has been awarded the Tyrrell Medal of the Royal Society of Canada and the Governor General's Award for Non-Fiction.

D. G. Creighton, former Chairman of the Department of History, University of Toronto, is the Advisory Editor of *The Canadian Centenary Series*. A graduate of the Universities of Toronto and Oxford, he is the author of *John A. Macdonald: The Young Politician; John A. Macdonald: The Old Chieftain; Dominion of the North; The Empire of the St. Lawrence* and many other works. Holder of numerous honorary degrees, LL.D. and D.LITT., he has twice won the Governor General's Award for Non-Fiction. He has also been awarded the Tyrrell Medal of the Royal Society of Canada, the University of Alberta National Award in Letters, the University of British Columbia Medal for Popular Biography, and the Molson Prize of the Canada Council.

J. M. S. CARELESS

THE
UNION
OF THE
CANADAS

THE
GROWTH OF
CANADIAN
INSTITUTIONS
1841-1857

The Canadian Centenary Series

McClelland and Stewart

© McClelland and Stewart Limited, 1967

Reprinted 1972, 1977, 1979

0-7710-1912-2

The Canadian Publishers
McClelland and Stewart Limited
25 Hollinger Road, Toronto   M4B 3G2

Manufactured in Canada by Webcom Limited

THE CANADIAN CENTENARY SERIES

A History of Canada

W. L. Morton, EXECUTIVE EDITOR

D. G. Creighton, ADVISORY EDITOR

VOLUMES STARRED ARE PUBLISHED

†ALSO AVAILABLE IN PAPERBACK

CONTENTS

_____

The Union of the Canadas

The Canadian Centenary Series

Half a century has elapsed since *Canada and Its Provinces*, the first large-scale co-operative history of Canada, was published. During that time, new historical materials have been made available in archives and libraries; new research has been carried out, and its results published; new interpretations have been advanced and tested. In these same years Canada itself has greatly grown and changed. These facts, together with the centenary of Confederation, justify the publication of a new co-operative history of Canada.

The form chosen for this enterprise was that of a series of volumes. The series was planned by the editors, but each volume will be designed and executed by a single author. The general theme of the work is the development of those regional communities which have for the past century made up the Canadian nation; and the series will be composed of a number of volumes sufficiently large to permit an adequate treatment of all the phases of the theme in the light of modern knowledge.

The Centenary History, then, was planned as a series to have a certain common character and to follow a common method but to be written by individual authors, specialists in their fields. As a whole it will be a work of specialized knowledge, the great advantage of scholarly co-operation, and at the same time each volume will have the unity and distinctive character of individual authorship. It was agreed that a general narrative treatment was necessary and that each author should deal in a balanced way with economic, political and social history. The result, it is hoped, will be an interpretive, varied, and comprehensive account, at once useful to the student and interesting to the general reader.

The difficulties of organizing and executing such a series are apparent: the overlapping of separate narratives, the risk of omissions, the imposition of divisions which are relevant to some themes but not to others. Not so apparent, but quite as troublesome, are the problems of scale, perspective, and scope, problems which perplex the writer of a one-volume history and are magnified in a series. It is by deliberate choice that certain parts of the history are told twice, in different volumes from different points of view, in the belief that the benefits gained outweigh the unavoidable disadvantages.

In this study of the Canadian Union from 1841 to 1857, Professor Careless deals with one of the most formative periods in Canadian history. During the Union, government as British North America had previously known it was thoroughly remodelled, and the primitive forms of colonial rule took on an almost complete resemblance to the Victorian parliament and civil service in England.

The chief feature of the change was responsible government by political party, a change accomplished along parallel lines and with equal vigour in the Maritime Provinces. But Canada saw also the beginning of the institutions of local government and local democracy, the reform of the law to fit Canadian conditions and principles, and the freeing of society from outmoded institutions such as seigneurial tenure and clergy reserves. It was a period of creative change in which the fundamental institutions of modern Canada were formed; French and English Canada were to live by these institutions, and with them English Canada was to endow the new West beyond the Great Lakes. Momentous events – the Irish famine, the repeal of the Corn Laws, and the revolutions of 1848 – disturbed the progress of the Union, and its growth was stimulated by such innovations as the Grand Trunk Railway and the Reciprocity Treaty. It was rich also in such able and constructive men as Robert Baldwin, L. H. LaFontaine, Egerton Ryerson, P.-J.-O. Chauveau, Paul Kane and William Logan. In effect, Mr. Careless's subject is the creation of modern Canada and the certain if unwitting preparation of Confederation; and he has described the events and the men in a manner and with a skill worthy of his theme.

W. L. MORTON,
Executive Editor.
D. G. CREIGHTON,
Advisory Editor.

The Union of the Canadas

The 1840's and 50's in Canada have an interest of their own. They witnessed the emergence of a community in central Canada sufficiently advanced and integrated to provide the basis for expansion across a transcontinental domain. And in this maturing community there was a remarkable growth of institutions that would serve the future Canadian federal state. Not only did the system of responsible cabinet government take shape, but also the party mechanisms to operate it. Not only was a coherent structure of central administrative departments created, but the institutions of municipal government besides. Nor was this all. Within the union formed in 1841 from the two old provinces of Upper and Lower Canada, lasting patterns of public education were established for both French and English-speaking Canadians. The two different school systems constructed became the heritage of the successor provinces of Quebec and Ontario. Universities, both secular and church-connected, made their effective appearance in this era. So did a particularly distinctive Canadian educational institution, the separate school.

This was a time as well of sweeping economic change, when Canada met the loss of the imperial protective trading system and made a vital readjustment in commercial policy, chiefly through opening American markets. It was a time of the coming of the railways, of developing capitalism and business power, of urban and industrial advances which clearly demonstrated that the frontier stage was passing for a large segment of British America. Cultural developments also made that fact plain. Still, the keynote of the period was, above all, institutional growth.

Its most obvious aspect was the achievement of a political system whereby the Canadian communtiy could govern its own internal affairs. There need be no apology for dealing at length once more with responsible government and its politics. So much of the story of the Canadian union centres on the issue of making government responsible to an increasingly self-conscious provincial population. Yet underlying that issue, running through and beyond it, is the deeper theme of the relations of the French and English-speaking peoples within the United Province. The union had bound them together, compelling them to work out new adjustments that were at least as significant as the strains so evident between them. In the later stages of the union, indeed, the province was racked with sectional discord between French and English elements that could only be composed within a greater enterprise, Confederation. But in its day the union of the Canadas evolved the dual French-English political party, with dual ministerial leadership, and brought the two peoples to self-government in partnership. The major features of institutional growth under the union were produced by their joint efforts – as well as by their inability to escape the one really fundamental Canadian Fact, that they had to live together.

I have many persons to thank for help in preparing this volume; first of all, Professor W. L. Morton of Trent University, Master of Champlain College. As Executive Editor of the Canadian Centenary Series he performed his editorial functions with constant patience, understanding and encouragement. Professor D. G. Creighton of the University of Toronto, Advisory Editor of the Series, read the manuscript with equal care and kindness. Professor John Moir, of Scarborough College and the University of Toronto, generously let me see material gathered for a biography of Sydenham; Professor Fernand Ouellet of Carleton University kindly provided several items from his own researches.

I am grateful to Professor William Ormsby of Brock University for lending me his important manuscript on the inception of the Canadian union. And I owe a special debt to Dr Jacques Monet, s.j., of Loyola College for the use of his valuable thesis on French-Canadian politics in the 1840's, shortly to be published. I much appreciate the assistance readily extended at the Public Archives of Canada and at other archives and libraries as well. I must also thank my daughter, Virginia Careless, for helping me gather newspaper material. Finally, I gratefully acknowledge the aid given my researches from the Humanities Research Fund of the University of Toronto.

J. M. S. CARELESS

MAPS

---

1. Province of Canada, 1856

2. Railways, Canals and Towns of United Canada

AUTHOR'S NOTE

The counties of the Province of Canada are shown on the first map as they were in 1856, in order to permit the inclusion of counties established since the union because of the spread of settlement or the redistribution of parliamentary seats, as under the Representation Act of 1853. On the whole, however, the addition of new counties reduced the bounds of older ones by subdivision, without replacing the basic pattern that existed in 1841. Accordingly, parliamentary seats that are mentioned in the text from the inception of the union onward may generally be located from the counties as depicted on the map.

Maps prepared by C. C. J. Bond

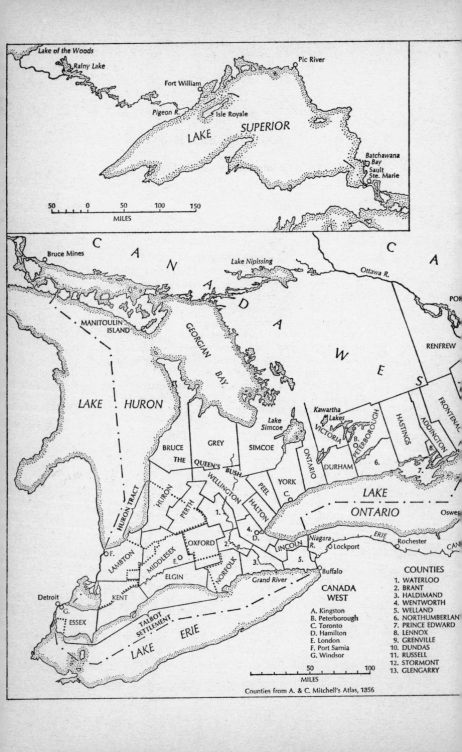

LAKE SUPERIOR

Lake of the Woods
Rainy Lake
Fort William
Pigeon R.
Isle Royale
Pic River
Batchawana Bay
Sault Ste. Marie

50 0 50 100 150
MILES

CANADA

Bruce Mines

MANITOULIN ISLAND

LAKE HURON

GEORGIAN BAY

Lake Nipissing

Ottawa R.

WEST

RENFREW

PORT

BRUCE
THE QUEEN'S BUSH
GREY
SIMCOE
Lake Simcoe

HURON TRACT
HURON
PERTH
WELLINGTON
1.
PEEL
YORK
HALTON
4.
D.
2.
OXFORD
E. O
3.
NORFOLK
LINCOLN
5.

VICTORIA
Kawartha Lakes
PETERBOROUGH
B.
DURHAM
ONTARIO
HASTINGS
6.
ADDINGTON
8.
LENNOX
FRONTENAC
7.

LAKE ONTARIO
Oswego

Niagara R.
Lockport
Buffalo
ERIE
Rochester
CAN

F.
LAMBTON
MIDDLESEX
ELGIN
KENT
Detroit
G.
ESSEX
TALBOT SETTLEMENT
Grand River

LAKE ERIE

CANADA WEST

A. Kingston
B. Peterborough
C. Toronto
D. Hamilton
E. London
F. Port Sarnia
G. Windsor

50 100
MILES

Counties from A. & C. Mitchell's Atlas, 1856

COUNTIES

1. WATERLOO
2. BRANT
3. HALDIMAND
4. WENTWORTH
5. WELLAND
6. NORTHUMBERLAND
7. PRINCE EDWARD
8. LENNOX
9. GRENVILLE
10. DUNDAS
11. RUSSELL
12. STORMONT
13. GLENGARRY

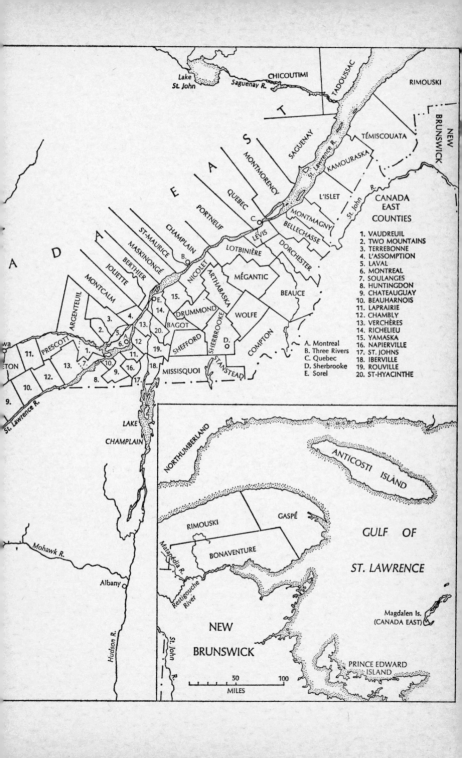

CANADA
EAST
COUNTIES

1. VAUDREUIL
2. TWO MOUNTAINS
3. TERREBONNE
4. L'ASSOMPTION
5. LAVAL
6. MONTREAL
7. SOULANGES
8. HUNTINGDON
9. CHATEAUGUAY
10. BEAUHARNOIS
11. LAPRAIRIE
12. CHAMBLY
13. VERCHÈRES
14. RICHELIEU
15. YAMASKA
16. NAPIERVILLE
17. ST. JOHNS
18. IBERVILLE
19. ROUVILLE
20. ST-HYACINTHE

A. Montreal
B. Three Rivers
C. Quebec
D. Sherbrooke
E. Sorel

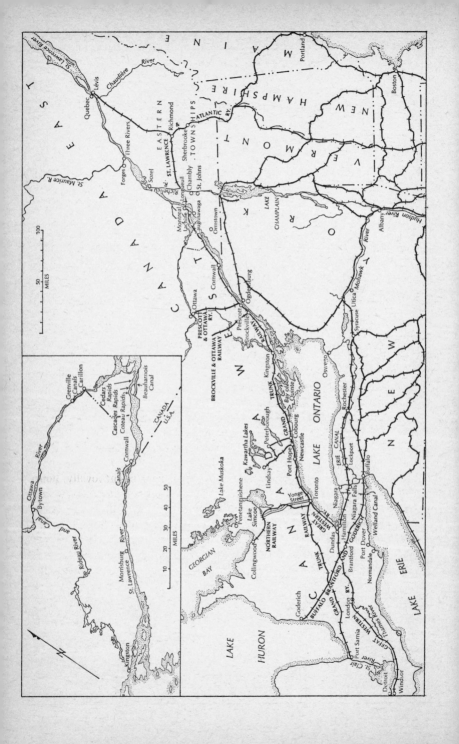

CHAPTER 1

The Pattern of Union

1840–1841

On February 10, 1841, the union of the Canadas uneasily began. The crash of cannon in Toronto and Montreal announced at noon that the separate provinces of Upper and Lower Canada were no more. Henceforth, English-speaking Upper Canadians and predominantly French-speaking Lower Canadians would dwell under one constitution in a single Province of Canada. Within the old limits of Lower Canada a French ethnic majority, an English minority, had lived constrainedly together for half a century already; but now all the English colonists in Great Britain's two most populous American possessions would be combined with the French Canadians in one political unit. Two peoples of diverse origins, cultures, and national aspirations would have to reach a new accommodation, in the sphere of politics and government at least. The fundamental Canadian problem of duality assumed wholly different proportions as this design for the union of the Canadas, precursor of the much broader British North American union of 1867, came formally and soberly into effect.

It was a day of mixed auspices. English Canadians might loyally, hopefully, observe that this was the young Queen Victoria's first wedding anniversary, and the christening-day of her first child as well. French Canadians would be more likely to recall, with painful clarity, that just three years earlier on February 10, 1838, an act of the imperial British parliament had suspended the constitution of Lower Canada, in consequence of the Rebellion of 1837 in the province. Since then they had been under the rule of a nominated Special Council and helpless to prevent the effecting of a union which was designed to submerge and ultimately assimilate them as a people, thus disposing of the French-Canadian "problem" in British North America forever.

The Special Council met in Montreal, commercial metropolis of the Canadas, under the eye of the assiduous governor, Lord Sydenham, who made his residence there in preference to the old Lower Canadian capital city

1

of Quebec. It was in Montreal, therefore, that the ceremonies to inaugurate union in Lower Canada were held. Proclamations in French and English had been posted through the snowy streets to herald the day of union—and had all been ripped down overnight.[1] None the less, at one o'clock in the afternoon of February 10, the judges, the commander of the forces, the mayor and corporation, the lesser civil and military officials, gathered in scarlet, gold and black at the eighteenth-century Château de Ramezay. There they watched as Charles Poulett Thomson, Baron Sydenham of Sydenham in Kent and Toronto in Canada, resplendent in full uniform, was sworn in as first governor-general of the United Province. He was a slight, handsome figure in his early forties, cheerfully vain and cocksure but astute and ever-resourceful, whose particular triumph it was to have carried the project of union forward to this moment of completion. A crowd outside the entrance, entertained by the bands of the Royal Welch Fusiliers and the 85th Light Infantry, heard Sydenham's proclamation read. It made an eloquent, earnest appeal to the loyalty and good feelings of Lower Canadians "of whatever origin" to make the union work: "In your hands rests now your fate."[2] Yet when some three hundred citizens came to pay their respects at the Governor's grand levee afterward, less than fifty French Canadians were among them; and of these one third were officials, and another third clergy.[3]

True, the powerful commercial class of restless Montreal, the leading element in Lower Canada's English-speaking minority, were warmly enthusiastic over the union. It would finally put right the mistake made in 1791, when two separate Canadas had been created out of the old Province of Quebec, and would free them from the weight of a hostile French majority within Lower Canada. It would remove interprovincial barriers from the rich trade which the merchants of Montreal controlled up the great inland waterway of the St Lawrence River, and make a political entity out of what was already a geographic and commercial unit. And it would surely enable work to proceed on canals to conquer natural barriers in the water route, now that the French Canadians who had opposed heavy expenditure on public works could be outvoted in the union legislature. Small wonder that the vigorous commercial tory organ, the Montreal Gazette, hailed "a new era in the history of this great Province," which "every loyal subject in CANADA will have this day celebrated with that hearty joy and cordial gratulation so peculiar to BRITONS."[4]

But down-river in Quebec, still the heart of French Canada, the satirical weekly Le Fantasque noted the "singular coincidence" of the union's being initiated on a Wednesday—mercredi. For, as all should know, mercredi signified the day of Mercury, the god of merchants—and thieves.[5] And the reform oracle, Le Canadien, for years the redoubtable champion of French rights, scorned Sydenham's appeal for unity as an empty pretence, when nothing had been done to ease the jealousies and animosities between French and English. "Le jeu qu'on a fait dans le Bas-Canada pendant un demi-siècle, on va le recommencer sur une plus grande échelle dans les deux Canadas Unis," it darkly predicted.[6] Notably, too, a young teller of the Quebec Bank, François-Xavier Garneau, put aside the major history of the French-Canadian people he had begun the year before, in order to produce for Le Canadien a long and fervent remonstrance against the coming obliteration of the French language and the denial of the genius of France.[7]

There could be no doubt that union was a major measure of British colonial policy aimed largely against the French. Yet the intentions behind it had not been merely negative or reactionary. They had originated with the late Lord Durham, that imperial emissary of boldly advanced views who had been sent from England to inquire into the conditions that had induced armed rebellion in both Canadas in 1837. After five bustling months spent in the country as governor-in-chief and lord high commissioner in 1838, he had set down a host of recommended changes in his famed Report on the Affairs of British North America, issued in 1839, the year before his early death. And something of Durham's brisk reforming spirit had stirred the aging whig government of Lord Melbourne, faced as it was with the grave embarrassment of colonial disorders in the free and improving British nineteenth century.

The Canadian rebellions themselves had been small, localized, and soon put down. Yet in Lower Canada, at least, there had been hard skirmishes and sharp suppression by British forces, and considerable French-Canadian sympathy manifested for the rebel champions of popular rights, Louis-Joseph Papineau and his fellow patriote radicals. Here, in consequence, rebellion's aftermath was acrid with French-English rancour and suspicion. It was scarcely surprising that Durham, centring his attention on this more populous and deeply troubled province, had concluded that the greatest source of Canadian ills was the warring of "two nations," French and English, within one body politic. Hence he had proposed the union of Upper and Lower Canada, to turn the French into a minority in a predominantly English-speaking colony. Then, assuredly, they would abandon their deluded efforts to preserve a backward little French enclave in a vast progressive British empire, and gradually of their own volition embrace the benefits of assimilation. One nation would disappear within the other, and the strain and conflict of duality be gone. So great was a nineteenth-century British liberal's faith in the superiority of English-speaking civilization, with its parliamentary constitution, steam engine, and world-wide industrial leadership.

Of course, to accompany union Durham had urged responsible government, advocated by reformers on both sides of the Atlantic, whereby a colony's government would be held responsible to its elected assembly in the same way that the British cabinet was held responsible to parliament. The extension of this British practice to colonies would break the power of tory oligarchies firmly rooted in the appointed executive and legislative councils beyond the assembly's control—power that had exasperated radical reformers in both Canadas to the point of open revolt. And so it would treat the other great ill that Durham had perceived in British America, the conflict between representative popular institutions and local officials not subject to their will. "The Crown," asserted his Report, "must . . . submit to the necessary consequences of representative institutions; and if it has to carry on the Government in unison with a representative body, it must consent to carry it on by means of those in whom that representative body has confidence.[8] The Melbourne ministry, however, had dismissed the proposal of responsible government as quite unsuitable for colonies, though they did affirm that much might be done in practice to improve relations between government and people in Canada. And above all, they had taken up the idea of union.

The Union Bill they had formulated provided equal representation for the two Canadas within one legislature, even though the upper province then had only some 450,000 inhabitants to 650,000 in Lower Canada. Durham himself had merely envisaged representing the population of the union as a whole, without any such two-part division. He had counted on the combined numbers of the English Lower Canadians and the Upper Canadians to produce a general English-speaking preponderance, which would steadily grow as British immigration continued to fill in the sparsely settled districts of Upper Canada. But the Melbourne government wanted to be sure of English ascendancy from the start of union. This could be established beyond question by giving half the seats in the new legislature to Upper Canada, since the Lower Canadian English element would certainly hold some of the seats in the other half, leaving the French Canadians securely in the minority. In effect, Upper Canada would be over-represented to ensure the maintenance of British rule.

To promote this new imperial scheme the strongest man in the whig cabinet, Lord John Russell, had moved to the post of Colonial Secretary. And another able cabinet member had left the presidency of the Board of Trade to govern the Canadas and prepare the way for union. This was Charles Poulett Thomson, member for Manchester, a highly practical liberal business man, thoroughly skilled in the arts of political management, a compound of calculation, driving ambition and buoyant energy. He took up his task in Canada in October, 1839, and received his peerage in August, 1840, as a mark of his success in negotiating acceptance of the union plan by Upper Canada and at least providing nominal approval for it in Lower Canada through the Special Council. In view of these achievements, the Act of Union was put through the British parliament in the summer of 1840, to take effect in Canada by proclamation the following year. This Act, however, would have consequences quite unlooked-for by its designers. The Canadian union would be hide-bound by its basic principle of equal representation. The differences between the two old provinces would only be perpetuated by the division of the legislature into Upper and Lower Canadian halves. Far from being made a unitary state, Canada would become a quasi-federal union of two distinct sections, functioning within a single legislative framework.[9]

But all this lay in the future. And in 1841, as union was proclaimed in Canada, the French Canadians were bound to regard it not only as having been designed to undermine their national identity, but as magnifying that wrong by decisively under-representing their own section of the country. Furthermore, while English Lower Canadian merchants might recognize (as Durham had) that union offered a far broader base for developing the great St Lawrence transport system, the French saw only that the heavy Upper Canadian debt, largely incurred to build canals, would be charged against the united province as a whole. And this, despite the fact that in Lower Canada the old French-controlled assembly had avoided a similar debt burden by blocking outlays sought by the English business interests. Finally—to cap the series of iniquities—English would become the sole official language of record in the legislature, even though French might still be used in parliamentary debate.

Thus it was that French Canada's antipathy to union varied only in degree; from a lethargy of dejection to fervent demands for repeal. But the strongest former partisans of French political opinion, Papineau and his radical associates, were in exile or scattered and disorganized, although Louis-Joseph's cousin and close colleague, courtly old Denis-Benjamin Viger, a much-venerated figure who had first entered the assembly in 1808, was back in politics after having been released from prison without trial. The most prominent spokesman for the French Canadians at present seemed to be John Neilson, owner of the bilingual *Quebec Gazette*, a veteran constitutional reformer who, despite his British origin, had stoutly identified himself with the cause of Lower Canada's autonomy and now was in the forefront of French agitation for repeal. Neilson, white-haired embodiment of stalwart Scots integrity, had a record of unimpeachable loyalty and moderation during the recent times of violence. Yet he was also a convinced believer in the old Lower Canadian constitution of 1791, and the balanced freedom possible under it, if it were only properly applied. Thus he sought to repeal the Act of Union. Still, he characteristically wrote of it that, for the present, "intimately persuaded as we are that it is founded in error, we are nevertheless bound to submit."[10]

Another leader was emerging in French Canada, however: Louis Hippolyte LaFontaine. He had sat in the Lower Canada assembly for Terrebonne since 1830, when, not twenty-three, he had been an earnest liberal disciple of the great prophet, Papineau. But LaFontaine, deliberate, dispassionate and even aloof by nature, took up his own judicious course. He had broken with the extremists at the outset of rebellion in 1837, insisting still on parliamentary action, and had carried Lower Canada's case to England. He had briefly been imprisoned on his return; but that, indeed, had helped to distinguish him in French-Canadian eyes as one of the heroes of reform, as did his bold appeals to British authorities thereafter on behalf of the political prisoners. Since then he had steadily gained in stature, in the eclipse of older French-Canadian leaders. Now thirty-three, he was coolly reserved but compelling, well over middle height, solid and imposing. He had a remarkable resemblance to Napoleon, which he obviously cultivated in arranging his hair. It was said that during a visit he paid to Napoleon's tomb in Paris, old soldiers of the Emperor crowded about this startling reincarnation of their master.[11]

LaFontaine's manner, tight-lipped and imperious, was Napoleonic too. But his very air of aloof destiny inspired confidence at a dark moment for French Canada, and his shrewd political realism gave good reason for it. While deploring the union, he had come to recognize the futility of seeking outright repeal in the face of set British policy. He was prepared instead to try to function within it, to overcome its worst features through the co-operation of reform forces in both Canadas: he meant to use a British-designed constitution on behalf of the French. To do so, he would have to mould a French-Canadian party in accord with his own purpose. He was a Montreal politician, firmly based there; but in the other chief focus of French political strength, Quebec, he had as well a loyal and able associate, Augustin-Norbert Morin. Furthermore, Etienne Parent, editor of Quebec's Le Canadien and a powerful intellectual influence in French Canada, was in essential agreement. Like LaFontaine, Parent could see the value of working positively with Upper Canada associates in the union, instead of reacting negatively in withdrawal, as would Neilson or the Viger-Papineau elements. There was, in fact, but one real hope for French Canadians: to find allies under the bleak new dispensation.

As for the English Lower Canadians, who in time past had relied on the British oligarchy of officials centred at Quebec, they looked expectantly for continued tory-conservative rule under the new union—but English-speaking rule, in any case. The Moffatts and McGills, Montreal business leaders of the tory "British party" of Lower Canada, no longer need face an unshakable French majority in the assembly. With that in mind, their supporters might well hail the union day with thanksgiving, exclaiming also over the glowing prospects of new commercial progress. Moreover, as if in anticipation, St Lawrence trade had shot up during the previous season, as business recovered from the effects of prolonged world depression. The winter timber cut was promising, too. Quebec shippers expected some seven million feet of white pine to come down the river with the spring of 1841, along with five million of red pine, four million rock elm and four million white oak.[12] Montreal forwarders were no less hopeful.

But the French-Canadian community, largely based on small-scale farming, was still feeling the consequence of a long series of ruinously bad crops in the last decade, of debt and rural unemployment. To these had been added the costs of abortive rebellion: the loss or destruction of property by troops in some localities, and the emotional wounds left by suppression and reprisal, the looting, the arrests and imprisonments. Above all, there was the exile of fifty-eight *patriote* prisoners to the Australian convict settlement of Van Diemen's Land, which a small and clannish people devoted to their homes on the St Lawrence saw with special pain. And yet, if French Canadians, gloomy and disheartened as they were, greeted the union with bitter apprehension—"le mariage forcé," a new symbol of subjection—there was hardening purpose within them still to survive.[13]

II

In Upper Canada in 1841, the inauguration of union at Toronto, the former provincial capital, also brought mixed feelings. Some welcomed it readily enough. In fact, a member of the Toronto Tandem Club (they raced two-horse sleighs on the thick harbour ice) produced a festal ode for the occasion:

> Hail February tenth! auspicious day,
> The harbinger of joys of great account.
> On you our Maiden Queen was given away,
> Our Royal Princess taken to the Font.
> The cannon's roar proclaimed the Union Law
> At noon of you; and then, as I'm a sinner,
> Together the good folks at eve you draw
> By acclamation, to a civic dinner. . . .[14]

Despite the official celebrations, however, the dominant mood in Toronto at union was one of grey February despondency. The city had just learned that an old Upper Canadian rival, Kingston, was to be the seat of government for the United Province, and Toronto's hopes of becoming an even greater capital had come crashing down. The tory Toronto *Patriot* glumly prophesied that property depreciation would be "fearful."[15] Sir George Arthur, the last lieutenant-governor of Upper Canada, reported to his superior, Lord Sydenham at Montreal, that he had done his dutiful best to inaugurate the union properly in Toronto. There had been the royal salute at noon, Signior Blitz, the magician, at Government House in the evening and the public banquet in the Ontario House—through which the Governor had suffered with a sick headache from the noise of the band and thirteen bumper toasts. Yet Arthur admitted wryly, "I had no alternative but this course, or fall in with the prevailing melancholy mood of the City, and fire Minute Guns on the occasion."[16]

Of course, Toronto was a special case, and gloom in the fallen Lake Ontario city was offset by jubilation to the east in Kingston where the frozen lake met the frozen St Lawrence. "We congratulate the citizens of Toronto," said the Kingston *Chronicle and Gazette* in smug delight, "that the Public Records will now be placed in a situation equally secure from foreign invasion on the one hand and from internal insurrection on the other"—a sly reference to American raids on Toronto in 1813 and rebel attack there in 1837.[17] Throughout Upper Canada there were mingled strains of doubt and hope; regrets for the loss of the western province's separate existence, fears that it would be dominated by the more populous eastern community; yet also expectations of far greater economic and political opportunities to be found within United Canada. In the balance, the forces favourable to union were the stronger; for, unlike Lower Canada, Upper Canada had not had its constitution suspended in consequence of the rebellion of 1837, and the union project had been approved by its own provincial legislature.

The limited, ill-organized rising of the Upper Canada radicals under William Lyon Mackenzie had been readily quelled by the colonists themselves, while Mackenzie took refuge in the United States. Whatever their grievances, the mass of Upper Canadians had shown little desire for actual revolt. But the brief Mackenzie outburst had been followed by a series of raids from across the border during 1838, backed by American would-be liberators of Upper Canada. These wildly inept and futile attacks had practically identified the rebel cause with banditry and armed aggression from the United States, keenly remembered from the War of 1812. Radicalism, with its demand for elective institutions on the pattern of American democracy, was thoroughly discredited in Upper Canada. The bulk of reformers held aloof, while tory-conservative partisans of the governing oligarchy dominated a vociferously loyal assembly. Assuredly, there had been no cause to suspend the Upper Canadian constitution.

Furthermore, the Melbourne ministry in England had been concerned to obtain proper colonial acceptance of its union plan, and this had been the first assignment for Sydenham (then Poulett Thomson) when he was sent in 1839 to govern Canada. In Lower Canada, of course, he had only had to pass it through an unrepresentative Special Council; but in Upper Canada he had had to win the support of the legislature. Indeed, Thomson had needed all his lively magnetism and deft persuasion, since the dominant western tories and conservatives were not eager to be yoked with alien, disaffected and presumably backward French. The safeguard of equal representation for Upper Canada had partly brought them around; but economic inducements had done much more for tory interests closely linked with the business community. Union promised that the problem of dividing customs revenues on the St Lawrence would be ended, that the crippling Upper Canadian debt would be taken over, and that the much wider financial resources of a united province could be used to complete the unfinished line of canals on Upper Canada's vital St Lawrence outlet to the sea.

Some of the staunchest tories, however, those most fully identified with the old provincial oligarchy, the Family Compact, had still been notably reluctant to see their established preserve of power absorbed in a larger unit. Hence Thomson had counterbalanced the Compact tories on the government side of the assembly by seeking support from the reform opposition ("truly Her Majesty's," he blithely noted).[18] And he had gained that support; partly because of reforms to be expected from a vigorous governor eager to effect Lord Durham's detailed recommendations for practical improvements; partly for another, more significant reason—because reformers looked for union to achieve what Durham had strongly coupled with it: responsible government.

Apart from union itself, this was the largest single issue now before the Canadas, after two decades of friction between entrenched governing authorities and aspiring popular democracy that had finally issued in rebellion. Could a colony have its government brought under the control of its people and still remain a colony? Were the only possibilities subjugation to central imperial control or total separation, as the American Revolution had seemed to demonstrate? Besides Durham, other liberal imperialists in England had discerned a different possibility: colonial home rule based on the British principle of government responsibility to the representatives of the people. Such men were Charles Buller and Edward Gibbon Wakefield, who had shared in Durham's mission to Canada and in drafting its findings. But the most perceptive advocate of responsible government was the Upper Canadian reformer, Robert Baldwin, who saw it as the very means of maintaining the ties of empire through permitting a colony to manage its own concerns according to British practice and within the imperial system.

Baldwin had put the concept to the Colonial Office in 1836 in a carefully reasoned memorandum. He and his father, Dr William Warren Baldwin, had discussed it with Durham during his stay in Canada, and Durham's Report showed evidence of Robert Baldwin's arguments. Certainly, the "responsible principle" was very much in the air after the Report of 1839, though more as a broadly desired objective than as a well-defined and well-understood technique of government. If the chief remaining British possessions in America could put into effect a principle which would allow the peaceful expansion of colonial liberty and democracy under the British parliamentary constitution, then the consequences not only for Canada, but also for the rest of Britain's empire, would be profound indeed.

The views of the imperial government, however, ran flatly to the contrary. However admirable in Britain, responsible government was logically impossible in a colony, even for the conduct of its internal affairs, all that was then proposed. Durham had held that if imperial concerns such as trade, defence, and constitutional structure were reserved for imperial control, domestic matters could be safely left to colonial hands. But the precise mind of Lord John Russell rejected any possibility of dividing the indivisible, sovereignty. In a dispatch which virtually coincided with Poulett Thomson's arrival in Canada, the Colonial Secretary proved to his own complete satisfaction that a colonial governor could not both follow his instructions from England and act on the advice of councillors responsible to a local assembly. If he did the former, "the parallel of constitutional responsibility entirely fails"; if the latter, "he is no longer a subordinate officer, but an independent sovereign."[19] A colonial executive could not function under two commands. The sheer fact of empire required obedience to the central power in London, not to the dictates of local representatives.

Nevertheless, apart from this allegedly indisputable principle, Russell and the British cabinet had every desire to rule Canada in practice with the support of a colonial majority. Hence the Secretary had earnestly instructed Thomson on becoming governor that "the importance of maintaining the utmost possible harmony between the policy of the legislature and of the executive government admits of no question."[20] The key word was "harmony," noted repeatedly. The governor was to keep control firmly in his own hands, in order to shape and sustain an amicable concord between his executive and the representative body. In this way, indeed, the inadmissible demand for responsible rule could be killed with kindness.

This had remained Thomson's consistent aim, even though he did inform the Upper Canada legislature that the country would henceforth be governed "in accordance with the well understood wishes and interests of the people."[21] Reformers might seize on that; but in Thomson's own mind, the governor would do the understanding. He himself concluded that there were ample grounds for changes in Canadian government. Yet he deemed the ills complained of, and their remedies, essentially practical. In other words an efficiently run administration under his command, freed from old Compact incumbents and representing the main interests in the assembly, would be able to satisfy every real need and silence talk of the responsible principle. Reformers believed instead that practical changes away from old oligarchic rule would inevitably open the way to the responsible system. Holding opposite purposes, they and the Governor could go some distance together, each side assuming it could use the other.

The leaders of Upper Canada reform kept their eyes fixed on the final goal. Most prominent among them now were Robert Baldwin and Francis Hincks, who had played important though not dominant roles in previous years. As in Lower Canada, the older, more radical reform leaders had been ruined by their association with rebellion. Both men would still be described as "advanced" and "ultra" reformers by critics to the right, particularly because they were so insistent on the doctrine of responsible rule. Yet both sought only to work within British constitutional frames; they meant to build a liberal party on the basis of the large number of moderate reformers who rejected radical American-style democracy and tory oligarchy alike; and they could scarcely be deemed disloyal in supporting a principle advocated by a British governor, Durham himself. Aside from their common political tenets, however, the two men were very different.

Baldwin, now thirty-six, was a native Upper Canadian, a Toronto lawyer of impeccable standing in the social élite of "old" families that had ruled the provincial capital, a member of the privileged, official Church of England and a one-time prize pupil of Dr John Strachan, the formidable tory Anglican Bishop of Toronto. Hincks was an Anglo-Irish immigrant of thirty-three, with a strongly nonconformist Protestant background, who after a brief period at Belfast University had spent ten years in Canada as a commission merchant, bank manager, and now a journalist. Baldwin was conservative and aristocratic by temperament; a man of principle acutely, even self-righteously, proud of his integrity, drawn reluctantly into politics by a sense of *noblesse oblige* and an abiding belief in responsible government. Hincks was flexible and adaptable, at home in the rough-and-tumble colonial business world, an ambitious opportunist who saw the realities of power in politics and was eager to use them to achieve effective, popular, entrepreneurial rule. Yet in their very differences they complemented each other.

Baldwin furnished the idea and the moral authority. Not only did he have position and prestige; he conveyed an air of unassailable rectitude that was worth whole regiments of hot radical Mackenzies in this critical era after rebellion. A tall man, whose stature was less apparent because of his round-shouldered stoop, Baldwin's features were rather heavy, his eyes veiled, his manner phlegmatic. In private, he was shy and warmly affectionate. Yet he could command a parliament by the force of his assured dignity and the intellectual power of his arguments. He was anything but a typical Canadian politician, then or now. But no one played a more influential role in pressing the constitutional cause of responsible government against every plan and desire of contemporary British authorities like Russell and Poulett Thomson.

Hincks was the gifted strategist and tactician who provided the staff work for political action to carry Baldwin's idea into effect. Spare, agile, sharp-faced with darting eyes, he had none of Baldwin's commanding presence, and he spoke in a rush of words. Nevertheless, he was a hard, aggressive battler in debate, and as editor of the forceful Toronto *Examiner*, begun in 1838 to revive a party press hard hit by reaction to the rebellion, he was well placed to influence reform opinion and to make his keen political insight felt. Above all, as he appraised the new Canadian union, he saw how it could be used to advance responsible rule. It would make possible a powerful alliance with French-Canadian reformers, to create a party capable of dominating the assembly: ". . . a United Parliament," he argued, "would have an immense Reform majority."[22] If the resolve of the French Canadians to overcome their subordination in the union could be linked with the Upper Canadian demand for responsible government, that measure could be made virtually irresistible.

Since April 1839, therefore, Hincks had been in continual correspondence with the most significant French-Canadian figure in the lower province, LaFontaine, familiarizing him with Baldwin's position, impressing on the influential French-Canadian liberal that the responsible principle would place government under popular control and thereby give the major element in Lower Canada an effective share in directing the union. "I feel certain," Hincks wrote, "that if once we had responsible government as in England . . . we should in a very short time obtain everything we have ever asked."[23] Again and again he had stressed the theme: "You want our help as much as we do yours. . . . Our liberties cannot be secured but by the Union."[24] The French leader had wavered in doubt and indignation as the actual union scheme took shape. But finally Hincks had laid the basis for agreement on the responsible principle that would allow LaFontaine and his associates and Baldwin and his colleagues to work in close collaboration.

And meanwhile in Upper Canada, reform hopes for responsible government had joined with tory and conservative expectations of material benefits to produce the majority for union that Governor Thomson had been seeking with purposes of his own. On the one hand, the Governor managed to bring Robert Baldwin into the Upper Canadian administration in 1840 as Solicitor General. On the other, he worked effectively through William Henry

Draper, the Attorney General, a handsome, urbane lawyer of English origin and noted parliamentary skill; an open-minded conservative who was far from being one of the old Compact tory element. Thomson was even able to use the majority he had gathered in the last legislature of Upper Canada to treat "the one great overwhelming grievance," as he termed it[25]—the clergy reserves, that one-seventh of the public lands allocated to endow the Church of England and repeatedly assailed by non-Anglican inhabitants of the western province as the unjust monopoly of a privileged minority. The Governor skilfully negotiated a measure to apportion among other churches some of the funds from sales of clergy reserves. Although this sectarian compromise settlement of 1840 pleased neither high Anglican tories nor those reformers who had pressed for outright secularization of the reserves, it did offer a *modus vivendi* for the future, and hence was acceptable to a broad middle group.

That, in fact, was the essential response of Upper Canada to the union of February, 1841. There were reasons to doubt its wisdom—but it was a *modus vivendi* that opened a broader, more inviting road ahead than the old paths of extremism which the province had been following. Compact tories might be only sulkily acquiescent, especially in Tory Toronto. Eclipsed radicals might chafe at the failure to achieve a fully elective democratic state. But the majority of Upper Canadians, of both reform and conservative leanings, had turned their backs on extreme opinions, and despite misgivings as union was inaugurated, they were ready to try to make it work. It could only be hoped that the mass of Lower Canadians would come to the same view.

III

The constitutional machinery established under the Act of Union was much the same as that in the two former Canadian provinces. There would again be a legislative council appointed for life on good behaviour, consisting of not less than twenty members; and a legislative assembly, of eighty-four, elected on a wide freehold franchise.[26] Members of the assembly were required to own property worth five hundred pounds; parliament was to meet at least once a year, and to be dissolved for new elections at or before the close of a four-year term. The speaker of the council would be appointed by the governor; the speaker of the assembly would be elected by its members. Above these two houses of the legislature stood the governor-general, representing the Crown, empowered as before to give or withhold assent to the bills that had passed both chambers or to reserve them for imperial judgment in London before they could become law. In further accord with regular colonial practice, he would execute the laws and administer the province with the assistance of an executive council. This was a body with little formal constitution, but significant because it was composed of his chief advisers and administrative officials, who in the past had held their influential posts as virtually permanent appointments. In the Act of Union it was scarcely more than mentioned in passing, being a customary adjunct of the governor rather than part of the statutory scheme; yet again according to regular practice he had to look to it for "advice, consent or concurrence" on various subjects, while on others he could act alone.[27]

The executive council had indeed been the real stronghold of the old provincial oligarchies. If this central organ, the heart of government, could actually be made responsible to the assembly under the union, reformers would have small cause to worry further about the legislative council. In time previous, that appointed upper chamber assuredly had blocked assembly bills; but it could have little strength of its own without an interlocking oligarchy in the government. Consequently, although radicals in former days had sought an elective legislative council as a panacea for the country's political ills, liberals like Baldwin and Hincks had fixed their sights instead on bringing the executive council under assembly control. This would continue to be their objective under the union constitution—to treat the council as a British cabinet responsible as a unit to parliament.

One significant new feature of the Union Act was, of course, the equal sectional division of the assembly. There would be forty-two representatives from each of the two former provinces, an arrangement to be altered only by a two-thirds majority vote in both legislative houses. Another notable new feature was the carefully drawn financial prescription.[28] The duties and other revenues of the two old provinces were to be combined as one "consolidated revenue fund." From this the salaries of the government officials and judges were to be met as a fixed charge, thus constituting a permanent civil list. Otherwise all Crown revenues were surrendered to the consolidated fund and placed at the legislature's disposal. In fact, the crucial control of revenue lay in the assembly's hands, for only the elected body might formulate measures appropriating money from the consolidated fund or imposing new taxes. No appropriation or tax could be initiated, however, without the governor's recommendation. Hence, as in Great Britain, the origination of money bills would lie with the government, not with assembly members, thus helping to prevent extravagance and petty politicking—unless the government indulged in them itself.

The Union Act maintained the rights granted the Roman Catholic Church in Lower Canada under the Quebec Act of 1774, and the Protestant clergy reserves of Upper Canada, first established under the Constitutional Act of 1791 and now altered in the disposition of their income by the settlement measure of 1840. The continuance of these vested ecclesiastical rights was only to be expected. But also expected, yet not included when the final bill reached Canada, was a comprehensive scheme of local government. Thomson, or Sydenham as he was by now, strongly regretted the omission.[29] He had wanted what Durham proposed and he himself strongly endorsed: a comprehensive pattern of municipal institutions, which would provide Canadians with valuable political training, take petty issues and local log-rolling out of provincial affairs, and consequently produce a better quality of parliamentary life. He was able to establish corporate municipal bodies in Lower Canada by ordinance of its Special Council before the Union Act went into effect; but there was not sufficient time left to carry a similar scheme for district councils through the Upper Canada legislature as well. Moreover, significant as Sydenham's own scheme was, it left the local bodies largely under the control of centrally appointed officials. Full municipal self-government still remained a question for the future.

There was another, much larger question for the future; one that really overrode the other issues facing the union of 1841, since it involved the very existence of Canada: the relationship of the province to the British imperial trading system. The country lived esssentially by producing wood and grain; and the British preferential duties on colonial timber, wheat, and flour supplied protected overseas markets for these vital Canadian exports. There was also significant traffic in sawn lumber and agricultural produce across the border with the United States; but thus far the Canadian staple trades were directed above all to the British market overseas, within the framework of the imperial Navigation Acts and the confining, yet shelter-ing, mercantilistic policies of the long-lived "old colonial system." The restrictive side of that system had its drawbacks—for example, it kept foreign shipping out of the St Lawrence trade—but far more important in Canadian economic life was the favourable pattern of imperial duties that offset some of the costs of transportation to far-off British ports.

Great Britain had maintained substantial preferences for colonial timber ever since the Napoleonic Wars had revealed the danger of relying on foreign sources for raw materials vital to a wooden British navy and merchant marine. In wide use now in the British construction industry, Canadian timber entered the United Kingdom almost duty-free, while that from the much closer Baltic region paid substantial charges. Colonial timber production was virtually being subsidized by the British taxpayer in the interest of national security—and in accord with the best precepts of mercan-tilism. As a result, Canadian exports of massive square-hewed timbers, mainly white and red pine, had risen almost steadily to 1841, while Cana-dian deals, heavy planks of sawn lumber, had also taken the lead over the Baltic product in the British market. It was largely because of the imperial differential duties, in fact, that wood had become Canada's most valuable commodity. It formed nearly two-thirds of the value of all her exports to Great Britain.[30]

The preferences available to Canadian cereal exports had not operated quite so satisfactorily. Since the British Corn Law of 1828, Canadian grain exports had at least been sure of admission to the mother country's market on payment of an import duty much below the protective rates levied against foreign bread-stuffs. Yet, because of transatlantic shipping costs, poor Canadian harvests or low British prices could still effectively close off the metropolitan market to the colonists. Another British measure, however, the Colonial Trade Act of 1831, had enabled American wheat and flour to be admitted duty-free to Canada for export via the St Lawrence, thereby adding American to Canadian supplies in the overseas trade. It was in part because of this enactment, together with the lifting of world depression, that the St Lawrence grain trade had strikingly recovered by the time of union. While in 1839 only 249,471 bushels of wheat and flour had gone out the river, 1,739,119 bushels had been exported in 1840.[31] In the latter year, indeed, the waterway had been filled to capacity with supplies of wheat and flour, and expectations for the 1841 season were quite as high.

This sharp upsurge in St Lawrence commerce made the completion of canals along that route almost imperative. Some were built or building, others only projected; but a through line of canals to overcome the rapids in the upper river seemed necessary just to carry the existing traffic.[32] They were all the more necessary in the grand strategy of the St Lawrence commercial interests, to meet the competition of the American Erie Canal route, which tapped the Great Lakes hinterland at Buffalo and other points and drew off much of its trade southward to New York. In fact, the future development of Canadian commerce appeared to rest on three prerequisites: canalization of the upper St Lawrence beyond Montreal, continued preferences in the British market for St Lawrence exports, and ease of trade across the inland United States border, to tie in as much western territory as possible to the great river route. The union of the Canadas could help markedly, by eliminating separate provincial jurisdictions on the river and, of course, by providing improved revenues and credit for constructing the canals. The other requirements for the economic development of the union, however, were beyond Canadian control. On one hand, Canada's business interests looked for the maintenance and even extension of British differential duties under the imperial protective system. On the other, they sought to trade as freely as possible with the American midwest. But this Canadian commercial design—free-trade in the interior, protectionist without—was threatened by countercurrents on either side.

In the United States, a low-tariff Democratic régime had just been replaced by a Whig administration strongly backed by protectionist business elements. The Whigs were more likely to raise trade barriers than lower them; and there was considerable American animosity towards the British provinces in any case, largely the result of border troubles after the Canadian rebellions. The support shown in the border states for the cause of the fugitive rebels—Mackenzie, Papineau and their comrades—and the "Patriot" attacks that had followed from the United States, had not only roused Canadian anger but also brought reprisal in the raiding and burning of Mackenzie's supply ship, *Caroline*, on the American side of the Niagara River. The worst of these strains had passed by 1841; yet soldiers still watched along the ice-sheathed Niagara, and the case of the Canadian, Alexander McLeod, recently arrested in the United States for supposed participation in the *Caroline* raid, had stirred up old acrimonies anew. Certainly the United States would not be disposed to treat Canadian trading interests with much benevolence.

In Canada's crucial British market, the idea of free trade was steadily gaining ground. The liberal economists of England had long been confuting the old teachings of mercantilism. Powerful British industry, looking to world markets and low production costs, pressed for the reduction of import duties. A rising movement led by industrialists urged the repeal of the Corn Laws protecting British agriculture; laws, they charged, which kept cheap bread from labouring classes and benefited only the landed aristocracy. Furthermore, radicals in the parliament at Westminster were continually pouring scorn on the antiquated structure of the old colonial system —and on the folly of keeping up the burdens of empire at all. Richard Cobden, leading figure in the influential Manchester School that combined the laissez-faire interests of industrialism with the economic gospel of free trade, denounced not only the ridiculously unsound colonial preferences but also the cost of defending possessions around the world. They meant only waste, weakness and the peril of wars to England, whose vast factories were the true key to her wealth and power. Views so sweeping were still not widely accepted in imperial Britain. Yet they did denote a trend that scarcely augured well for colonial interests deeply committed to a protective imperial system.

Moreover, the mass of people in both Canadas still looked for imperial military protection against the United States. When that country was still far from friendly, when the surge of American expansionism and the claims of "manifest destiny" projected continental limits for the fast-developing republic, both English and French Canadians relied on the interposition of British power as their best guarantee of survival against the aggressively confident strength of the United States. Too exposed, poor and underpopulated to defend their long land frontier alone—with only a "paper" militia system that made every able-bodied male nominally liable to serve in war time—the Canadian communities had, since the War of 1812, thoroughly grown into the habit of depending on British garrisons of regulars for their defence.[33] And the garrisons had been considerably reinforced in the critical period following the outbreak of rebellion in 1837, until there were 13,000 regulars in British North America: nineteen infantry battalions instead of nine, together with two battalions of Guards, a cavalry regiment, and auxiliary forces locally raised but under British pay.

Most of the local corps had been disbanded in 1839, but the imperial military establishment in the Canadas was still sizable and expensive: a fit subject for free-trade Cobdenite strictures on "peace, retrenchment, and reform."[34] And while the immediate threat of American border raids seemed to have lifted, there was still a critical dispute continuing between Britain and the United States over the precise line of the border between Maine on the one side and the provinces of New Brunswick and Lower Canada on the other. The diplomatic contest over the border had come close to actual war in 1839, and might do so again. In Upper Canada there was tension over events in the McLeod case, going on across the boundary in New York State. Early in February 1841, only a few days before the union of the Canadas was declared, a violent armed mob of five hundred had prevented bail being given for McLeod at the jail in Lockport, New York, near the Niagara frontier.[35] The legal clash, as British authorities sought his release and American authorities refused, might yet become a *casus belli* directly involving Canada in another embroilment with the United States. Neither in its imperial nor in its American relations was the new province of Canada free from the prospect of grave problems.

Thus underlying the whole political, constitutional, and economic pattern of the union of the Canadas was the question of its relationship to the broader pattern of empires: the maritime British and the continental American. It was a fundamental question. And yet, however fundamental, this issue had not become clearly visible to Canadians in the wintry months of early 1841. Far more apparent to them then were the other issues that confronted the new united province: the assimilation or survival of French Canada, the responsible principle sought by Baldwin, LaFontaine and Hincks *versus* the reign of "harmony" under a judicious British governor like Sydenham; the ever-present problem of canals and material development generally, the deep-seated cultural differences in Lower Canada, the sectarian disputes over reserves in Upper Canada. These drew the attention of the colonists far more as they entered into union.

Union, in the last analysis, they recognized for what it was: a linking of two continuing communities, French and English, rather than the fusion of two former provinces. Despite the aim of assimilation behind it, they did not lose their awareness of its duality. Nor were expressions of goodwill entirely absent regarding the future relationship of the two peoples of Canada. Said one paper in the Niagara region, near the strained American border:

> We shall be happy indeed to find both strive for their mutual benefit, and that, whenever a blow may be struck at British liberty, we may see both French and English shoulder by shoulder in the field, and thereby proclaim to our vaunting neighbours that though we *have had* unfortunate differences, they are now hushed. . . . Hurrah then! for the British—hurrah for the Canadian French! and nine times nine cheers for their union![36]

CHAPTER 2

The World of United Canada

The new-made Province of Canada stretched for more than a thousand miles from the fretted, grey Atlantic cliffs of Gaspé to the wilderness of rock and deep green forest above the head of Lake Superior. Beyond, to the north and west, lay Rupert's Land, the huge and lonely domain of the fur-trading Hudson's Bay Company, its one little settlement at Red River on the open plains more than four hundred miles from Fort William at the lakehead. Southward, the Great Lakes and upper St Lawrence River marked the border between Upper Canada and the United States. It was guarded by defence works at critical points but could still be easily crossed, as it could also in that region of Lower Canada south of the St Lawrence and east of Montreal known as the Eastern Townships. Farther eastward, however, the rising line of rugged Appalachian Mountains effectively isolated the St Lawrence Valley from American New England, and from the British Atlantic provinces in the corner of the continent as well. Hemmed in on the north by the wilds of the vast and ancient granite mass, the Precambian Shield, on the south by the Appalachians and the American boundary, the settled lands of Canada ran in a narrow belt of farms and villages down the long valley of the St Lawrence from the shores of the Great Lakes, broadening out only in the fertile inter-lake peninsula of southwestern Upper Canada and in the hills of the Eastern Townships.

Well over a million people lived in the Province of Canada in 1841: 670,-000 in the Lower Canadian half, now denominated Canada East; 480,000 in the Upper Canadian half, now Canada West. And the St Lawrence - Great Lakes waterway linked them not only to each other but to the transatlantic British metropolis at one end and the core of the great republic at the other. The Canadian hinterland was supplied and shaped by both: British trade, immigration and political structure expressed the transatlantic connection; American-style enterprise, ways of life and social outlook, the influence of the continent. Remote as the world of Canada might seem, rimmed as it was by interminable forests and the timeless emptiness of the north, its people were still in decisive contact with the far wider worlds of Britain and the United States.

In Canada East, settlement now extended well down the south shore of the St Lawrence below Quebec through the county of Kamouraska. Here the French-Canadian villages, clustered around their church spires about six miles apart, gave a peaceful agricultural prospect in sharp contrast with the wild, dark north shore across the river.[1] Between Quebec and Montreal the continuous village "street" that travellers had so often noted spread out along both banks, where trim whitewashed houses stood at the fronts of narrow farms in the old seigneurial domains, which reached back in long bands from the water's edge. Yet not far behind them there were only rough bush clearings, except where the seigneuries had spread up tributary rivers like the Chaudière, the St Maurice, and especially the Richelieu. The greatest density of settlement lay in the district of Montreal, in the rich plain about the city and in the well-occupied Richelieu valley. Unlike other areas generally, counties here had more acreage under cultivation than remained wild. In Chambly county in the early forties the ratio rose to nearly four to one.[2]

Smaller concentrations of French-Canadian farming population were focussed on Quebec and on Three Rivers, while predominantly English-speaking settlement was advancing in the Eastern Townships. There the British American Land Company was striving to plant British immigrants on its eight hundred thousand acres of wild land, and Sherbrooke, the company's headquarters, was rising as a commercial centre for the region. A British traveller who surveyed the Townships, just before the union, found "several good stores and genteel houses" in Sherbrooke. He judged it "possibly destined in no great number of years to become large and populous."[3] And while the farm frontier was spreading in the Eastern Townships it was also moving westward up the Ottawa River into the lumbering region around Hull (or Wright's Village, as it was then called).

As for the towns, Montreal, with some 40,000 inhabitants, had now passed Quebec, which had about 35,000. Three Rivers came far behind with 3,000; places like Sherbrooke, Sorel and Hull were virtually still villages, though they had a more commercial existence than the little farming hamlets beneath their gleaming tin-clad spires. But Montreal was the economic heart of Canada, living primarily by moving the crops of the interior out by the St Lawrence and in return importing overseas products and British manufactures for the inland country. It was the chief terminus and transshipment point in the river trade because it lay at the limit of ocean-going navigation, where vessels found their further way upstream barred by the first in the series of rapids that broke the upper St Lawrence into swirling reaches of white water as it poured downward from Lake Ontario. In the shipping season, before winter closed the water route, Montreal's harbour was thronged with tall-masted sailing craft from Liverpool and the Clyde, big paddle-wheelers in the Montreal-Quebec service, smaller steamboats, barges and Durham boats of the up-river trade.

Above the city, the great tributary of the Ottawa joined the St Lawrence to supply an alternative route westward, used since early fur-trade days, and opened the way to the vast timber resources of the upper Ottawa Valley. Furthermore, from Bytown on the Ottawa the Rideau Canal route led through a chain of locks, lakes and streams to Kingston on Lake Ontario, thus providing a back way into Canada West and the lands of the Great Lakes. The Rideau Canal, with its substantial masonry locks, was a notable piece of engineering. Yet its effectiveness was restricted by smaller locks that formed a bottleneck on the lower Ottawa itself. Moreover, completion of canals on the upper St Lawrence would cause the longer, more circuitous Rideau route—built and maintained by Great Britain as a military link with Upper Canada safely distant from the American border—to lose most of its commercial significance. For the time being, however, much of the freight upbound from Montreal went by way of the Rideau to avoid the swift currents in the turbulent St Lawrence. Numbers of British immigrants to Canada West also travelled via the Rideau route, as did quantities of sawn lumber from the region.[4] It provided a three-day steamboat journey from Montreal to Kingston; six days, if barges were being towed.[5]

On the other hand, the bulk of the downbound traffic from the West moved by the upper St Lawrence, since despite the breaks in navigation, grain and flour from Canada West or adjacent American states could still go to Montreal for export more quickly and cheaply by this direct route than by way of the Rideau. In the early forties, besides, it was possible to journey by steamer and stage-coach from Montreal up to Kingston in twenty-six hours as compared to twenty-four for the trip downward.[6] Yet the need for completing the St Lawrence canals was obvious. Just west of Montreal, the eight-mile Lachine Canal, open since 1825, did pass the first set of rapids, although its depth was only five feet. Farther onward, the Cascades, Cedars and Coteau rapids produced a total drop of eighty-three feet in the river that it would require the Beauharnois Canal, eleven miles in length, to overcome; but work had not even begun. Still farther on, in Canada West above Cornwall, there were the Long Sault rapids. Here the eleven-mile Cornwall Canal had been under construction since 1832; it was still incomplete in 1841, thanks to the veritable bankruptcy of the old Upper Canadian exchequer. And finally, in the area near Morrisburg a series of shorter canals would be needed, though downbound steamers could shoot the rapids here.[7] In fact, of all the breaks in the long St Lawrence - Great Lakes water highway, only one, far to the west at Niagara Falls, had really been overcome; there the forty wooden locks of the Welland Canal carried schooners between lakes Ontario and Erie.

Whatever the deficiencies in its access to the western hinterland, the aggressive Montreal business community still thrived; and thrived as well from sizable trade with Vermont across the American border to the south. There were dealers in grain, barrel staves and potash, millers who ground American wheat into Canadian flour for export, forwarders and importers who dominated the Upper Canada trade. There were shipbuilders and shipowners with fleets of river vessels, bankers and insurance agents who financed and ministered to the export trades. The central precinct of these mercantile rulers of Montreal was Notre Dame Street, behind the lines of warehouses and solid stone-built docks remarked upon by visitors.[8] Here in 1841 could be found such men as Peter McGill, mayor of the city and president of the Bank of Montreal; George Moffatt, civic magistrate, former executive councillor, and a leader of the British party, a powerful merchant and insurance agent; or John Molson, the wealthy brewer and capitalist, president of the first Canadian railway (the Champlain and St Lawrence, which had opened in 1836) and until recently a member of the Lower Canadian Special Council.[9] But beyond this staid yet vigorous élite, the city displayed a noisy, zestful variety of life: buoyant habitant farmers come to market in queues and *bonnets rouges*, uncertain new Scots immigrants in kilt and plaid, brisk Yankee traders, boisterous Irish labourers. Indeed much of Montreal's interest lay in its lively populace, for visitors found its buildings unappealing; substantial but drab, in sombre stone with frowning iron shutters and doors.[10] The most notable edifice was the big Roman Catholic church of Notre Dame, lately rebuilt in up-to-date Gothic style. From the river it towered over Montreal, while above it loomed the wooded crest of Mount Royal, about a mile behind the town.

Montreal's old rival, Quebec, lacked the wide hinterland and commercial power of the city up the river. Yet it was still the port for larger ocean vessels, since shallows in the St Lawrence above Quebec blocked their voyage onward; and it was the centre of the "emigrant trade," for British immigrants usually preferred to transfer to river steamers here rather than face the delays and uncertainties of continuing on by sail up the channel to Montreal.[11] Above all, the capacious, heavy-laden timber ships sailed from Quebec, making it Canada's chief lumber port. Forty-foot sticks of pine and oak, roughly squared with the broad-axe, were floated this far down-river in giant rafts, often sixty feet in width and two or three hundred feet long. Strongly bound together with saplings, they carried cabins and cook fires for the crew aboard, who guided them with sweeps and sails until Quebec was reached. There the rafts were broken up behind the booms of crowded timber coves, and the great sticks loaded through the wide ports of timber ships for the voyage to England. The unused capacity of these ships on their return voyage provided a cheap and ready means of transporting immigrants, of whom about 25,000 arrived at Quebec each year.[12] It was more profitable to fill empty holds with human cargo than merely to add to the piles of rock dumped in the river by vessels returning in ballast.

Quebec, key to the square timber and immigrant traffic, was also a major shipbuilding centre. Materials came readily to hand in a day when the wooden sailing-ships had scarcely begun to feel the challenge of the steam-ship on the open seas, and certainly not of iron-built vessels. In 1841, in fact, sixty-four ocean-going craft were turned out by Quebec shipyards.[13] Furthermore, though the city was no longer a seat of government it was still a vital military citadel and the religious and cultural capital of French Canada. High on Cape Diamond the guns of Quebec's massive fortifications commanded the passage into Canada. Further along the heights of the Upper Town rose the cupola of the old Catholic cathedral, the stately Bishop's Palace, and the austere complex of buildings that housed the powerful Seminary of Quebec. Here, side by side, were the discipline and ceremonial of a British imperial garrison and the august institutions and traditions of a deep-rooted French Catholic culture. And on the tight-packed strip of shore below the heights there lay another, proletarian, Quebec, a brawling dockside town of seamen, timbermen and shipyard workers.

At the time of union, there were approximately 510,000 French Canadians in Canada East to 160,000 English.[14] Montreal was almost equally divided in its population; more than a third of Quebec's was English-speaking. Otherwise the Eastern Townships held most of the non-French elements—particularly the southern counties of Stanstead, Missisquoi, Shefford and Sherbrooke—although the western lumbering county of Ottawa also had a decisive English-speaking majority, much of it composed of Irish working in rough lumber shanties in the woods. The Irish were also numerous in the working class of Montreal and Quebec. Largely Roman Catholic, they added a special ingredient to the dominant French Catholicism of Canada East. The rest of the English-speaking inhabitants were strongly Protestant: Anglicans, Presbyterians, Methodists and others in that order, composing about seventeen per cent of the total Lower Canadian population. English and Scots blended easily into the business life of the towns, while American ancestry was common in the farming Townships, first opened by settlers from the United States.[15]

If, outside the Townships, the English-speaking minority remained largely commercial and urban, so the French majority continued to be mainly agricultural and rural. There were some French-Canadian petty bourgeois, generally linked with the farming community; storekeepers, local millers and craftsmen. But *grand commerce*, on the whole, remained in English hands.[16] Nevertheless, the growth of an educated professional middle class did provide an urban-centred élite for the French-speaking community; notaries and journalists, doctors like Etienne-Pascal Taché, lawyers like LaFontaine and his colleague, Morin. Developing countries in the present century have often illustrated how an emerging middle class that lacks economic power will seek political power, shaping intellectual and national movements in order to express its own inherent drive for recognition and authority. French Canada in the middle of the last century displayed the same phenomenon. Indeed, the struggle over responsible government in French Canada must be viewed in social terms as the effort of the middle class to achieve power, and the political organization effected by LaFontaine and his associates as the embodiment of the directing skill of this new élite. Political liberals, they were essentially social conservatives, for they sought to defend a stable French culture and society against dynamic English commercial capitalism. In this endeavour they were replacing an older, more aristocratic generation of French political leaders, men like Papineau and Viger, more closely linked with the seigneurial order and the possession of large landed estates.

There was, of course, an older French clerical élite as well. Once the seigneurial landlords had shared the Roman Catholic Church's social prestige in French Canada, as pervasive as its spiritual authority. But seigneurialism was in decline as an agrarian system, and the ranks of the seigneurs had been infiltrated by English merchants buying estates.[17] The church thus stood unrivalled as the guardian of French Canada's past tradition; and a recent challenge from the present, from anti-clerical and even rationalist currents among the French professional group, had been checked with the defeat of political radicalism in 1837-38, with which anti-clericalism had been strongly identified. Widely endowed with lands, its rights and dues guaranteed by the Quebec Act, provider of schools, hospitals, and welfare institutions, the church in French-Canadian society virtually bulked larger than the state. The latter, moreover, was alien in its British origin and imposition. The church was as native as the French language: both served together to delimit and defend a distinctive national culture; the church sustained the language, as the language the church. And under cautious, experienced old Bishop Signay of Quebec, complemented by the zealously energetic Ignace Bourget, Bishop of Montreal since 1840, this great clerical dominion seemed in securely capable hands.

The mass of the French Canadians, however, were not priests, professionals, or seigneurs. They were habitant farmers, secure tenants like their ancestors on family holdings in the seigneuries. The seigneurial system had lost the association it had once had with government colonization policy under old French rule; it was widely regarded by the English as a feudal anomaly from a vanished past; and it was challenged by the spread of English freehold tenure—farm ownership—in the newer settlements. Yet the social stability and family cohesion provided by the long-established patterns of seigneurial farming had helped maintain a distinctive, compact French-Canadian community in America, as British immigration flooded in around it. Hence contemporary descriptions of rural Canada East drew a clear distinction between the "Seigneuries" and the "Townships," the former connoting long, narrow farms and close-knit traditional French-Canadian society; the latter, block farms and a more scattered, fluid, predominantly English-speaking population.[18] There was another distinction, too. Generally, the seigneuries had suffered more acutely in the recent years of agricultural depression. In fact, if seigneurial farming had been socially a mainstay of French Canada, economically it was itself facing a crisis.

Lower Canada had earlier produced considerable quantities of wheat for export, but falling prices and declining yields had gone hand in hand since the 1820's. Infestations by wheat fly and rust, spreading gradually through the province in the thirties, had given obvious reasons for bad harvests. But the cause really lay deeper, in farming practices that were exhausting the soil with wheat production—particularly those of antiquated and wasteful seigneurial agriculture, which was also subject to excessive subdividing, since habitants were reluctant to leave the traditional community and open newer districts. Consequently, French-Canadian lands were undergoing painful readjustments to producing less valuable coarse grains and fodder crops, or even returning to subsistence farming. This agrarian decline was causing emigration to the United States, alarming to French religious and secular leaders; and rural discontent and debt had been clearly reflected in the Rebellion of 1837-38 among the stricken, crowded seigneuries of the Richelieu.[19]

Some 40,000 Canadiens left the country between 1831 and 1844. In consequence, the French population was only growing at the rate of two per cent a year, half the rate of the preceding sixty years.[20] And this while immigration was steadily adding to English numbers. At the same time, while French farmers were in distress—and often blaming the business power of les Anglais, their control of commerce, and their banks—English-speaking settlers in the Townships had seemed in happier condition. In part, this was because their soils had been less drained of fertility by long exploitation; in part, because their farming practices were generally better than those of the highly conservative French agrarian class. The latter did little or nothing to rotate crops, fallow, fertilize, or clear their fields of weeds, and they raised poor breeds of livestock except for excellent horses.[21] None the less, the habitant jealously eyed English appropriation of good land from his ancestral domain, while the English farm-proprietor looked down on the "indolence" of the backward French. In general, agrarian problems only added to ethnic tensions in Canada East.

When the union began, the worst agrarian distress in Lower Canada was ending as the infestations ran out their course, farming became diversified, and prices improved with the passing of world depression. Moreover, lumbering, the second major occupation after farming, had flourished through the bad years; Quebec had even enjoyed a prosperous timber trade.[22] Nevertheless, in good years or bad, the broad differences between the two cultural communities remained all but unaltered. It did not help that the emotional, prejudicial term "race" was freely used by both sides to identify these differences. Indeed, the mystiques of blood, racial character, and divine intention were readily invoked by French and English in the best, or worst, fashion of nineteenth-century romantic nationalism. The one real question now was, would "racial" tensions and cultural differences be eased or amplified within the new world of the union?

II

In Canada West, among a population of some 480,000 at the time of union, less than 14,000 were of French origin and only 6,500 of continental European birth.[23] About half of the overwhelming English-speaking majority were immigrants from Britain; Irish, English, and Scots, in that order. For while some British immigrants continued to settle in Canada East, the mass came on to the western section, where large areas of fertile land, both wild and partly improved, still awaited occupation. Here the Canada Company's Huron Tract invited settlers—a great triangle of one million acres of soaring forest, shadowed clearings, and open blocks of farms, stretching inland from Lake Huron. North of it, the two million acres of the Queen's Bush were just being opened, while southward between the Thames and Lake Erie the Talbot Settlement still had farms to fill. Furthermore, settlement was spreading not only in the western peninsula but also in the central districts north of Toronto, up through the Kawartha Lakes backwoods, and in the east along the Upper Canadian side of the Ottawa Valley.

It was estimated that 1,751,500 acres were being farmed in Canada West in 1842, as against 3,000,000 in Canada East.[24] Since so much of Canada West was still in the frontier stage, uncultivated lands considerably exceeded cultivated in most of its districts. Only in the eastern counties of Prescott and Russell was the reverse true.[25] Urban communities were small, none approaching Quebec or Montreal. Toronto had about 14,000 inhabitants, Kingston, once the larger, some 6,000; Hamilton, at the head of Lake Ontario, 3,400; and London, in the heart of the western peninsula, 2,000.

Numerous market and milling centres were growing steadily, with the expanding farm population in their vicinities, but places like Niagara on the Niagara frontier or Cornwall on the upper St Lawrence would not maintain the same rate of growth, since their older settled districts were fairly full already.

Toronto, no longer a capital, still had a head start from having had that advantage, and seemed likely to remain an important administrative and judicial centre for Canada West. At any rate, it was better placed to deal with the fast-rising western districts than was Kingston, well to the east. And Toronto drew other advantages from its central position and excellent harbour on Lake Ontario, from where steamers left regularly for Kingston or Rochester, Hamilton or Niagara.[26] It could tie in to its markets broad areas to west, north, and east, and deal with the world outside either by way of the St Lawrence to Montreal or through the Welland and Erie canals to New York. Moreover, the route northward from Toronto to Georgian Bay provided a short way to the Upper Lakes. Part of it now was embodied in Yonge Street, the main Upper Canadian highway north, which opened fertile farming country to the city, and rich timber resources beyond.

Yet this future Ontario metropolis had few natural features to commend it, set as it was on a flat lake-shore, a long sand-spit before it, a muddy marsh at one end, and a low line of pine-clad hills behind. A little ill-built town of staring, tasteless brick; so the English traveller and author, Mrs Anna Jameson, had described it a few years earlier.[27] But Sir Richard Bonnycastle, visiting just before the union, deemed Toronto's harbour "spacious and beautiful," and found a remarkable air of bustling affluence in its principal streets. King Street, the main business thoroughfare, promised to be very handsome, with fine shops already exhibiting the "superfluous luxury" of plate-glass windows and brass railings.[28] The public buildings might look more utilitarian than elegant, but Bonnycastle was much more impressed that this city of such evident wealth and enterprise had been a wilderness encampment less than half a century before. And the fact was, that while the "old" local aristocracy of Compact toryism might bemoan Toronto's lost political glories, its new and rising business men—such as the English miller and distiller, William Gooderham, the Scots importer, Isaac Buchanan, and the Ulster Irish wholesale merchant, William McMaster—were looking forward confidently to far greater commercial progress.[29]

Canada West generally was so full of recent immigrants, and so much in the stage of extensive rather than intensive growth, that its social structure was naturally ill-defined. Nevertheless, in the towns one could distinguish an upper class of officials, often sizable landholders (who were in close social contact with the officers of the British garrison, where that existed); a middle class of merchants, shopkeepers and skilled craftsmen, whose wealthy upper ranks might certainly be allied with the office-holders; and a lower class of wage labourers composed largely of immigrants, without the resources yet to farm. Many would never acquire them. Already Toronto and other towns were evincing the presence of the permanent poor, raising local problems of bad housing, sanitation, and winter relief, even in a society presumably characterized by the robust, self-reliant pioneer.[30] There was also brawling and family suffering caused by the "liquor evil," which was endemic in this hard-drinking frontier society but was concentrated in the inns, bars, and squalid dram-shops of towns. In response, a temperance movement was developing. Toronto's temperance society, founded in 1839, had 1,300 members by 1841.[31] Similar societies were being established in Lower Canada, where Roman Catholic *curés* sponsored them for the parish poor.

The upper and lower strata of society were less in evidence in the Upper Canada countryside than in the towns. Small proprietors working their own farms constituted a broad agrarian middle class; though there were, of course, hired men on one hand, and on the other, an element of gentry in the government-appointed magistrates and British half-pay officers who managed to maintain themselves on the land. Moreover, there were differences within the middle class itself, between increasingly prosperous commercial farmers in more advanced districts and settlers in the still primitive backwoods, clearing land for their limited crops and lacking good roads out to market. Yet both groups produced for sale, and were dependent on purchased, imported goods, whether or not barter was the immediate means of exchange at the local mill or general store. The self-sufficient pioneer was largely a creature of myth.[32] Almost from the start the Upper Canadian farmer had been part of a cash economy, specializing in wheat production for outside markets. To this the backwoodsman could add valuable potash from the trees he cleared and burned, while the more developed farmer had hides, meat and other produce to offer from his broader fields. However, those fields were not necessarily well-treated, too much being attempted with too little labour available. Canadian-born farmers and those from the States were frequently the worst land-butchers. Some, indeed, were professional pioneers who made their profit in clearing and selling farms rather than in working them. Lowland Scots or English made better "improving farmers" and the Irish often poor ones.[33]

Wheat, the staple of Upper Canadian agriculture, could still readily be raised, even by the extravagant "soil-mining" methods of extensive farming, because the ground held the stored-up fertility of centuries. And although soils in eastern Upper Canada were already showing signs of depletion, there were abundant lands in its western districts just undergoing settlement; in fact, wheat acreage would increase by 400 per cent in the 1840's.[34] Consequently, Canada West was already producing proportionately larger crops than more populous Canada East, which indeed was faced with a transition away from wheat. Consequently, too, western rural society was plainly wealthier, with relatively more farm stock, local mills and manufactories, and higher tax assessments, despite its pioneering newness.[35] Visitors noted particularly the prosperous, well-kept farms in such vicinities as the Bay of Quinté, Yonge Street, and the Niagara Peninsula, and the neat fields of the German Mennonites in the west around Waterloo.[36]

In many areas of Canada West, lumbering remained an important subsidiary to farming; but in the Ottawa region lumber ruled and agriculture was subsidiary. From the magnificent pine stands of the Ottawa Valley, reaching two hundred feet high, the heavy timbers could be rafted downstream in "cribs" to the St Lawrence, and there combined in larger units, called drams, to be sent on to Quebec for export.[37] On the Ottawa, then, a distinctive lumber community had developed. Some of its members were farmer-lumberers engaged on their own in logging in the winter and farming in the summer. More were simply hired hands, the shantymen, largely Irish or French-Canadian, who passed their lives working in the camps for wages except for wild sprees to town to spend the season's earnings. This forest proletariat grew as the timber trade increased, and the timber-making gangs with their broad-axes and oxen advanced up the Ottawa and its tributaries, tapping the Lake Temiskaming area in the early 1840's.[38] As the Ottawa lumber empire expanded, timber slides were built to improve water transit, towing companies developed on the lower river, and large camp-operators appeared, holding leases to broad timber limits. In short, with growing investment and large-scale operation, the lumber community was exhibiting aspects of emergent capitalism.

It also tended to produce an agriculture of its own to supply the camps. Lumberers paid two or three times the original cost of hay brought in to feed their animals, and shantymen required feeding too.[39] These demands invited farming to follow lumbering up the Ottawa, for even thin forest soils, newly cleared, could produce crops that would sell to camps in the vicinity. More important, the better farmlands along the lower Ottawa developed for the shanty market a diversified kind of agriculture not found elsewhere in Upper Canada's wheat cash-crop economy; the farmers of the area were the only ones enjoying considerable internal trade and not oriented to production for export.[40] Their advantage would be reduced when improved transport by canals, and then railways, enabled farmers in better-endowed regions to compete with them.

The lumber community showed the contrasts and inequalities of the fast-growing forest frontier. It was opulent and powerful on the one hand; crude, ramshackle and unruly on the other. Bytown, its capital, where the

Rideau Canal joined the Ottawa River opposite the mills of Hull, was the scene of frequent riots and head-breakings between rival Irish and *canadien* lumbermen. In the early forties, in fact, a veritable "Shiners' War" raged there, when the Irish element, known as Shiners, sought to drive French Canadians out of the timber trade by force and intimidation, and met reprisals in turn.[41] And yet this rowdy lumber town, later to be rechristened Ottawa, was being blithely urged by a local paper in February, 1841 as a better choice than Kingston for the capital of Canada.[42]

Because of Irish and French predominance in much of the Ottawa Valley, the Roman Catholic faith was strong there. Elsewhere in Canada West there were significant Catholic elements among the Highland Scots of Glengarry on the upper St Lawrence or the Germans of Waterloo county in the western peninsula. In general, however, Catholicism in Upper Canada rested increasingly on Irish settlement, and Roman Catholics still constituted less than fourteen per cent of the total population of Canada West in 1841.[43] Moreover, Irish immigrants from Protestant Ulster outnumbered those from the Catholic south of Ireland.[44] Throughout much of the west, in fact, "Irish" was more likely to connote Belfast and the Orange Order than Dublin and Holy Church, particularly in Toronto. And the Orange Order, ultra-loyal as well as ultra-Protestant, transferred some of the militancy and violence of divided Ireland to Upper Canada, above all at election time.

As for dominant Protestantism in Upper Canada, Anglicans comprised some twenty-two per cent of the total population, Presbyterians nearly twenty, and Methodists seventeen; while Baptists, Quakers, Lutherans and Congregationalists together made up another six per cent.[45] Apart from those not identified by religion in the census returns for 1841 (and a tiny Jewish element of .2 per cent), the rest of the inhabitants were divided among a variety of little Protestant sects, including a few distinctive communal groups like the German-speaking Mennonites of Waterloo county. Of the major Protestant denominations, the Methodists and Presbyterians were themselves divided. Methodism had once been the strongest religious persuasion in Upper Canada, rooted as it was in the original Loyalist and American settlers. Internal divisions, however, and immigration that had enlarged other churches, had somewhat reduced its earlier role. Of course immigration had also brought in British Wesleyans; but the union achieved between them and the Canada Methodists, the main body, had broken down in 1840 and was not to be restored until 1847. There were other lesser Methodist sects as well. Nevertheless, the Methodists were the most fully indigenous or acclimated of all the principal Upper Canadian denominations and their members played an influential role in public affairs.

The Presbyterians, who naturally included the great bulk of Scottish immigrants, were chiefly members of the Church of Scotland, their national church and the established body in the Scottish homeland. But there were smaller Presbyterian sects, besides, who opposed the principle of establishment, and some of this latter element were drawn from Ulster Irish or American backgrounds. The largest single denomination was the Anglican, which still virtually constituted an official church in Canada West, endowed and supported by the state, its clergy closely linked with governing circles. The mighty Bishop Strachan no longer wielded the political power he had exercised in the noonday of the Family Compact. Yet his church still controlled the charter of the provincial university of Upper Canada, and it would still receive much the largest share of the income from the clergy reserves, together with that from the Anglican rectories also authorized under the Constitutional Act of 1791. The partial division of the reserves fund provided for in 1840 had, however, stilled much of the attack on Anglican privilege for the moment. Moreover, the Church of England was steadily gaining adherents from British immigration—English, Anglo-Irish, and some Scots.[46]

The churches in general exerted wide influence on Upper Canadian life. Aside from their religious functions, they were almost the only broad social organizations in a largely amorphous pioneer community. Church membership linked scattered backwoods settlers, provided familiar ties for immigrants; and questions of church and state relations made fervently hot politics. Furthermore, the religious diversity of this western community, so much in contrast with the religious uniformity of French Canada, helped to shape viewpoints on social or political issues which were often widely different from those of the eastern majority. One of the greatest problems of United Canada, in fact, would be the reconciling of the dominant and determined Roman Catholicism of the East with the equally dominant and determined Protestantism of the West.

III

Cultural activity was decidedly limited in the Canadas at union. Yet it was not without interest, both as the expression of a people still close to the frontier era, and as the basis for more rapid growth during the next two decades. Indeed, the older French-Canadian community had already made literary beginnings which, while often imitative of venerable classical models, had a promising vigour of their own. Poetry, satire and belles-lettres had all been manifested in French Canada in the years before the union; in 1837 Philippe Aubert de Gaspé *fils* had written a first novel, *L'Influence d'un livre*. But writing had in the main been strongly political, reflecting the struggle for power waged by the French-controlled assembly in Lower Canada and the *patriote* sentiments thus aroused. Authors were frequently journalists; often active politicians besides. In Montreal, Denis Viger, the veteran reform leader and a wealthy, cultivated lawyer, had produced both poems and a series of scholarly political treatises. The younger reformer, Morin, sensitive and brilliant, had also written verse and political pamphlets, helped draft the Ninety-Two Resolutions of 1834, and edited the influential *La Minerve*, the Montreal French liberal journal. In Quebec, Parent's *Le Canadien* was still more authoritative in moulding French-Canadian opinion. Here, too, Swiss-born Napoléon Aubin conducted the sparkling *Fantasque*, often gaily irreverent, especially where English governors were concerned.

By now the suppression evoked by the rebellion had passed; a time when newspaper offices were shut, Parent and Aubin went to jail, and Morin into hiding. The French press and politico-literary activity were thriving again. Parent, moreover, was arguing significantly in his journal that the British connection and French-Canadian existence were integrally related: that the latter's survival depended on British political institutions, and the former's ability to withstand American republicanism on a strong, satisfied French Canada.[47] Here was a theme for new French leaders of the forties to develop —most notably, Louis LaFontaine. Younger writers were also appearing, like Garneau and Joseph-Edouard Cauchon, both of whom contributed to *Le Canadien*. As if to show his versatility, Cauchon, then a law student, produced a creditable little school physics book in 1841, *Notions élémentaires de la physique*. But his long, colourful career in journalism and politics was only beginning.[48]

In urging the feasibility of assimilating the French Canadians, Lord Durham had described them in his Report as a people without a literature or history. He had not recognized the force of French-Canadian feelings for an identity two centuries old and increasingly finding literary expression. Nor could he have conceived that François-Xavier Garneau would seize on the disparaging description as a challenge, and begin an epic history of French Canada designed to celebrate its own particular national heritage. Furthermore, Durham's assessment had ignored other and not inconsiderable expressions of French-Canadian cultural identity: the characteristic church architecture of the St Lawrence Valley, a handsome blend of baroque with native austerity; the estimable tradition of carved wooden religious sculpture, displayed in the same churches; and the well-established crafts of cabinet-making and silversmithing, whose products had a dignity and distinction all their own.

For English Canada, Montreal and Toronto were the centres of cultural activity. The first was wealthier and more advanced, but the second had a wider potential field in the English-speaking community of Canada West.

Considering both the rawness of the western section and the limited size of the English eastern minority, it is not surprising that English Canada lacked the well-developed cultural patterns exhibited in the older and more closely knit French society. Furthermore, it was inundated by a flow of immigration too large to be quickly absorbed, was bound by close dependent ties to Britain, yet drawn by the great success-example of the neighbouring United States. Such a society—no closed, walled garrison like French Canada—was hardly likely to exhibit a firm character of its own.

What literary activity it did display was mainly associated with newspapers, most of them quite small, but proportionately more numerous than those of French Canadians.[49] The *Montreal Gazette* was both the leading eastern English paper and the chief tory-conservative organ in the Canadas; Toronto's *Patriot* or *British Colonist* could not equal it. On the liberal side, Francis Hincks's *Examiner* had not, perhaps, achieved the same influence as the fiery journalism of William Lyon Mackenzie in the Upper Canada of earlier days, and the reform press had no strong representative in Montreal. Yet local reform papers were appearing more widely in the West by the time of union. Their combats with tory rivals, also proliferating, would make lively reading on contentious issues such as Robert Baldwin's pet principle, responsible government.

A number of books had also appeared in English Canada describing life in the Upper Canadian settlements. They had often been written by British visitors for a homeland public interested in prospective emigration; they varied from conscientious handbooks for intending settlers to anecdotal travellers' tales. But some of the better works were by emigrants themselves, although still directed chiefly at a British audience: products of a small but significant element of cultivated English middle class and gentry who had made new homes in Canada. Among these authors were Catharine Parr Traill and her sister, Susanna Moodie, whose *Roughing it in the Bush* first came out in instalments in the pathfinding little Montreal periodical, the *Literary Garland* (1838-52). There was also Sir Richard Bonnycastle, who retired to Canada, after commanding the Royal Engineers at Kingston, and who produced *The Canadas in 1841* and similar volumes. These "literary pioneers" were virtually in their prime at the time of union,[50] writing for local journals as well as for British publishers. And one local journal, in Brockville, Canada West, was then edited by English Canada's first native-born novelist, the eccentric John Richardson, who wrote *Wacousta* (1832), *The Canadian Brothers*, published in Montreal in 1840, and numerous other works besides.

There was another aspect to the growing cultural activity in Canada: the improvement of educational facilities. Here the united province was on the threshold of a major new development. The scattered and inadequate local schools of the two old Canadas would be replaced by an increasingly effective province-wide structure of public education. Fundamental patterns had been set in both communities. There were already publicly-assisted, non-denominational common schools and district grammar schools in the West; in the East there were parochial or district schools based on "confessional" or religious distinction, either Catholic French or Protestant English.[51] But in each section of the union a general school system maintained and directed by provincial authority would be built on these foundations, in response to widespread popular demand for state-supported education.

Higher education was similarly becoming a reality. At Montreal, McGill University, chartered in 1821, and in 1829 incorporating the first medical school in America with hospital clinical facilities, would begin its teaching in the arts in 1843. Meanwhile French Catholic religious communities were increasingly establishing *collèges classiques*, which trained the rising lay élite of French Canada. In the West, the provincial university of Upper Canada, King's College, chartered since 1827, would finally open at Toronto in 1843. In the meantime, however, the Methodists had founded Upper Canada Academy at Cobourg in 1836; and this became Victoria College in 1841. Victoria's first principal, Egerton Ryerson, the powerful Methodist leader well known to journalism and politics, was to play an authoritative part in shaping the western schools system under the union.

Thanks to improving provisions for education, some of the crudities and cultural limitations of a half-fledged frontier society began to pass away. But the frontier age in any case was passing as a more thickly settled, better-defined community took shape. In Canada East, good land in the Townships was rapidly disappearing, and other new areas looked too remote and rugged to invite ready expansion. Though much fertile wild land remained to be occupied in Canada West, that section, too, was really approaching its limits of good arable soil, as settlement spread along the shores of Lake Huron towards the limestone Bruce Peninsula, or probed inland towards the inexorable rock barriers of the huge Precambrian Shield. The end of the open agricultural frontier would soon have to come.[52] And while this still lay in the future, signs of a maturing, consolidating community were already apparent in Canada by the early 1840's. The constant rise in rural population, the improvement of rough, stump-filled clearings into well-cultivated fields, the transition in many localities from log shanties to farm buildings of sawn lumber—these were all aspects of a spreading social transformation. So were the rise of populated hamlets around sawmill and gristmill sites, and the emergence of flourishing urban communities where once there had only been "four corners" with mill, tavern, general store, and smithy. And throughout the developing western countryside, organized churches with substantial buildings were replacing the periodic meetings held by itinerant missionaries in taverns or barns.

Furthermore, despite the continuing problem of bad roads—mud pits in spring and fall, rutted tracks in summer—internal communications were steadily being developed to knit the community together. Yonge Street had been macadamized (graded with interlocked stone and gravel) nearly to Lake Simcoe by 1841. Governor Sydenham, by ordinance, had sought to improve the winter "snow roads" of Canada East.[53] Wooden plank roads, which could be built for half the cost of macadamized ways, were increasingly being laid down.[54] Traffic moved freely by steamboat or lake schooner along main water routes in open season, while canals would soon be building anew on the St Lawrence. It only remained for the coming of the railway to provide sure, year-round heavy transport and lift the remaining burdens of inland isolation. Already lines were being talked of, charters sought; and a rail route from Toronto north to Georgian Bay had tentatively been surveyed.[55]

Accordingly, the world of the new united province was a world in process of vital change as it moved away from pioneering simplicity. The process, of course, would take years still to work itself out, but essentially the province of Canada was passing from a phase of extensive growth to one of intensive development. Ahead lay a different world, of the railway, steam-powered machinery, and the rising city; and a rural community with its own municipal life, well-developed commercial villages, and increasingly diversified agriculture. With the increase in wealth and population, class lines became more marked as advancing capitalism and the spread of wage-earning affected either end of the social scale. Old officialdom, backwoods egalitarianism in the West, French-Canadian agrarianism in the East, all gave ground before the growing power of middle-class business interests. This mounting bourgeois influence displayed itself in the politics of the union, in the parties of both sections, reform as well as tory. Under Baldwin and Hincks, for example, Upper Canadian reform soon lost its earlier suspicions of banks and large-scale business enterprise. And in Lower Canada, LaFontaine and his associates would successfully mediate between the French rural masses and the English commercial classes of the towns.

In short, while political and economic developments have chiefly commanded attention in this era of the contest for responsible government and the onset of free trade, one must also recognize other crucial changes that were proceeding half unnoticed. For the years of United Canada, in fact, were years of a major social transition.

CHAPTER 3

The Brief Reign of 'Harmony'

1841

While the union was being launched, the indefatigable Governor Sydenham was still hard at work completing its new government in preparation for the election of the first united legislature. His object, of course, was a régime which, unlike the old self-sustaining oligarchies, would remain closely under his own control; yet a government, also, which would represent a wide spectrum of popular interests, so that it could be assured of parliamentary goodwill and support. In this way the reign of harmony between executive and legislature would be secured. To provide for such a system, to free his hand, the Governor had been armed since his arrival with a critically important dispatch from the Colonial Office. This pronouncement actually applied to British colonies generally and was a mark of the policies of imperial administrative reform which Lord John Russell at the Colonial Office was striving earnestly to effect. It dealt with the practice which had developed over the years of regarding the incumbents of public offices in the colonies, appointed during pleasure, as having the equivalent of tenure during good behaviour; in other words, appointment for life.

"You will understand, and will cause it to be made generally known," ran the dispatch of October 16, 1839, ". . . that not only will such officers be called on to retire from the public service as often as any sufficient motives of public policy may suggest the expediency of that measure, but that a change in the person of governor will be considered as a sufficient reason for any alterations which his successor may deem it expedient to make in the list of public functionaries . . ."[1] Only judges and persons in administrative posts not involving "the character and policy of the government" were to be exempt. In short, the day of the permanent office-holding compacts was finished in Canada, even though Compact tories might still continue in politics. The Canadian union would be ruled through something approaching a British ministry, a body of the chief officers of government that changed in membership in accord with the changing dictates of "public policy." Oligarchy had been uprooted at the stroke of a pen, and the basis for a profound political transformation laid.

Sydenham, indeed, worked to establish much of the pattern of a ministry in Canada. Intent on bringing order and efficiency out of administrative jumble, he sought to organize a unified set of government departments, each with its own ministerial head in the executive council. In this he was also carrying out Russell's own views on administrative reform.[2] He adjusted existing offices and functions to establish clear and coherent chains of command. He created new offices and posts, such as those of the Provincial Secretary and President of the Council (the latter a kind of council business manager) to expedite the handling of government affairs.[3] Each executive councillor, moreover, would be required to hold a seat in the legislature.[4] Thus Sydenham shaped his council into a well-knit effective governing instrument, almost a cabinet of ministers, which he would direct and lead in person, virtually as his own prime minister.

Yet this executive was still not to be the equivalent of the ruling British cabinet, responsible as a unit to parliament. A ministry it might loosely be called in Canada, but its members would not be held collectively responsible to the elected house; only individually to the Governor, who saw his council as a body of advisers and department heads "to consult—but no more."[5] Sydenham's very intention, after all, was to outflank the movement for responsible government, so inadmissible in colonies. Besides, the Colonial Secretary had carefully explained that the Canadian government could not be held to depend on majority support in the representative house, as was the case in Britain.[6] It would be eminently desirable to have such support in the Canadian assembly as a matter of practice; but it could not be made a matter of right. The provincial ministry or council had to remain the governor's. He would direct it as far as possible in keeping with the assembly's wishes; yet sometimes his view of the imperial interest might require him to oppose them. Both sides, Russell had said, must exercise "a wise moderation."[7] Again the objective was harmony and good government, not assembly rule and self-government—an administration, one might say, responsive but not responsible to the representatives of the Canadian people.

Nevertheless, Russell and Sydenham had gone a good deal further than they knew in establishing the new system. In the cause of harmony they had, above all, tied the government to the legislative body. Governors under the union would need to choose their executive councillors from among influential men in the legislature, to give them the broadest possible following there. Government policies would have to be presented and championed by councillors sitting in the assembly; and while an adverse vote need not bring the administration down, it well might lead the governor to remake it, in order to strengthen its standing with the house. Indeed, he would have to be his own prime minister in a fully political sense: as leader of a government party which sought to keep control of the elected chamber. Though government was to be directed from above, the principle of harmony really compelled it to function through the assembly.

Consequently, reformers like Baldwin and Hincks could readily conceive of reversing the whole line of control, through capturing the house with a well-organized reform party, so that the governor could only govern on their terms, or else abandon the effort at harmony. Their strategy, therefore, would be to keep attention focused on the principle of responsible government; to claim that the Colonial Office dictum that government officials would be changed to suit the needs of public policy had established the conditions for responsible rule; and to strive for an alliance of eastern and western reform capable of dominating the united assembly. With the last sharply in mind, Hincks had kept up his correspondence with LaFontaine, seeking the French-Canadian support for responsible government that could throw the parliamentary balance of power to reformers. "The Governor may call our theory nonsense if he pleases," Hincks told the Lower Canadian leader, "but if we get a majority of such men as you and I are, we will make him acknowledge that to oppose us will be nonsense."[8]

In contrast, Sydenham counted on controlling the union assembly through a coalition of moderate elements; ". . . the mass of the people are sound," he confidently averred, "moderate in their demands and attached to British institutions, but they have been oppressed by a miserable little oligarchy on the one hand and excited by a few factious demagogues on the other. I can make a middle reforming party, I feel sure, which will put down both."[9] In Upper Canada, assuredly, he had combined both moderate reformers and conservatives to carry the union; and he had even brought staid Robert Baldwin to become Solicitor General, thereby giving the impression that his government might yet move onward to responsible rule. For Sydenham, still ready to use reformers' hopes as far as he could, had stayed cordially vague as to whether his new régime would finally embrace the responsible principle as they understood it. Yet in Lower Canada the French Canadians had remained implacably hostile to his most winsome approaches. He was too thoroughly identified with Durham's aim of "anglification"—and had he not put through the hated union? His efforts to obtain French backing for his government failed. LaFontaine had firmly rejected the offer of an appointment as Solicitor General for Lower Canada.[10]

None the less, the enterprising governor mingled varied party interests and practical administrators in the new executive council named on February 13, three days after the union of the Canadas took effect. Five of its members came from the former Upper Canadian régime: William Henry

Draper, the able, eloquent conservative, in a leading position still as Attorney General for Canada West; Robert Baldwin, now Solicitor General West; two prominent reformers, Samuel Bealey Harrison and John Henry Dunn, as Provincial Secretary West and Receiver General respectively; and the conservative Robert Baldwin Sullivan, his namesake's cousin—wittily clever, not too scrupulous, and somewhat alcoholic—as President of the Council. Three came from the last Lower Canadian government: the Montreal tories Charles Richard Ogden and Charles Dewey Day, Attorney General and Solicitor General East; and Dominick Daly, Provincial Secretary East, a complaisant yet far from incapable bureaucrat who believed in serving constituted authority, whatever its political views. Another councillor of no political affiliation was added a few weeks later; Hamilton Hartley Killaly, jaunty Irishman and skilled engineer, who was to take charge of the government's intended public works program. It was a moderate-toned administration with a good deal of ability; though its double-barrelled western and eastern appointments revealed the inherent duality of the union. Sydenham himself, agent of the imperial policy of assimilation, had had to recognize the practical realities of two different legal and social systems in establishing the pattern of union government.

Almost at the outset, difficulty arose. Following Robert Baldwin's appointment to the new council, that earnest reformer wrote to Sydenham to record his "entire lack of confidence in the entire council except Mr Dunn, Mr Harrison and Mr Daly."[11] He also sent this candid message to Draper, Sullivan, Ogden and Day. It was very like Baldwin, principled to the degree of political piety, and, as he said to Sydenham, filled with "an almost nervous anxiety" lest his own position among former party opponents in the government be misunderstood.[12] Sydenham's reaction was as typical. "Was there ever such an ass!" he scornfully commented to his deputy, Sir George Arthur, who was briefly continuing in office in Canada West.[13] Draper, however, received Baldwin's avowal of lack of confidence, but friendly personal feelings, with his usual aplomb. He could see no reason not to unite "in every measure of practical utility. . . . This field appears to me ample enough for all our exertions without seeking points of difference upon any theory of government."[14]

Yet there was really more to it than that. Baldwin, personally mild and gentle, but undeviatingly "the man of one idea," was serving notice that he could not continue to accept a mixed ministry which the Governor would direct; that he expected it to become a true party cabinet based on the responsible principle. Sydenham, aware of the crucial issue, sought to hold it off by answering Baldwin stiffly that he would apply to his executive council for advice when he considered it expedient. "If they cannot agree, then will be the time for me to decide between their conflicting opinions . . .

and then, as it appears to me, would be the fitting time for any member of the Council to declare his opinions. . . ."[15] For the present the question was passed over. The first task was to win the elections, to shape, as each saw it, the right sort of parliament for the union. Sydenham needed Baldwin to ensure the support of the advanced or "ultra" reformers. Baldwin needed an alliance with the Governor to strengthen the reform cause against tory interests at the polls. As Hincks assured a dubious LaFontaine, ". . . had Baldwin retired now he would have damaged our elections."[16] But even before they began, the decisive issue for the future had again been marked: between the Sydenham system of rule by governor's coalition, and the Baldwin design for rule by responsible party cabinet.

II

The administration formed, writs were issued for elections to be held by early April. But preparations for the contests had been under way for months, since everyone knew a parliament would be called once union had been inaugurated. This would be the first appeal to the people in Upper Canada in five years, the first in six in Lower Canada. It would test the strength of French anti-unionism, of displaced Compact toryism—and the power of the governor-general to combat them. To secure the government party he needed in the legislature, Sydenham meant to manage the elections to the utmost of his ability. Even the year before, his civil secretary, T.W.C. Murdoch, had reported, "All His Excellency thinks about is the forthcoming election. . . . He plans and talks of nothing else."[17] The Governor accordingly had made a triumphal progress through Upper Canada the previous autumn in what was really a campaign tour, rousing public enthusiasm for his leadership, fostering candidates who would follow it in parliament, and arranging that they should always be "displayed prominently" at his side.[18] Western reformers had also been active, seeking to associate themselves with the Governor's evident popularity, while keeping responsible government always in the public eye. Francis Hincks said confidently, "If there is any shampooing in this business, it is we who are 'using' the Moderate party, as they call themselves."[19] But Sydenham was equally counting on his own efforts to ensure wide government support. He remarked to Arthur, ". . . the cry is that I meddle in the Elections! I wish I could do so more effectually."[20]

Preparations in the East were similarly advanced. In French Canada, "le comité canadien de Québec" led by vigorous old John Neilson had been busy since October organizing constituencies for the struggle. The leaders of the church, Bishops Signay and Bourget, were strongly opposed to the union, which they saw as threatening the very existence of the Catholic *nation canadienne*, as inviting the resurgence of radicalism and endangering the established rights of the church—and even the British tie itself, which the clergy had traditionally looked to as the guarantee of those rights. On their own terms, Viger and the erstwhile Papineau radicals were equally opposed to a union which they saw as destroying French national liberties for the dubious benefits of a British constitutional system. With clerical favour on one hand, the support of Viger and the Papineau group on the other, Neilson's committee had drawn up an eloquent *Adresse aux Electeurs de toute la Province* and launched an extensive anti-unionist electoral campaign.[21] Meanwhile LaFontaine had issued his own powerful election address in his constituency of Terrebonne outside Montreal, no less firmly denouncing the sins of the union, but adding significantly, "je suis en faveur de ce principe anglais du gouvernement responsable."[22] And so he opposed the injustices within the union, not union itself, arguing that through it an alliance with Upper Canadian liberals could be achieved to win responsible government and thus regain the rightful liberties of French Canadians: "Notre cause est commune."[23] Neilson, instead, considered responsible government a mere trick of Sydenham's "to humbug the people."[24] But LaFontaine and his Quebec allies, Morin and Parent, were able to avoid a split in the French party between the Neilson-Viger elements and their own supporters, since all could agree on attacking the evils of the existing Act of Union, whatever else they might look for in the future.

At the same time, Lower Canadian supporters of Sydenham and the union—the British party—had also been preparing. In the towns and in counties with a considerable English-speaking population the unionist forces had named their own candidates as 1841 began. But in late February even the naturally sanguine governor only expected them to carry about a dozen of the forty-two eastern seats. From French electors, he was sure, ". . . we shall not have a man returned who does not hate British connection . . . they are altogether in the hands of a little group of Doctors and Lawyers who tell them all sorts of lies which it is impossible to contradict, as they can none of them read, and distrust the Seigneurs as much or more than they would do the British."[25] Accordingly, Sydenham stood ready to do all he could to minimize French influence and throw weight to English voters in Canada East.

By proclamation on March 4, 1841, he defined new boundaries for eastern urban constituencies. In effect, they transferred French-speaking districts of Quebec and Montreal to the surrounding counties, enlarged Sherbrooke to bring English votes together, and limited Three Rivers to cut down French.[26] This deft gerrymander practically assured the town seats of the East to unionist commercial interests. George Moffatt, whom Sydenham had privately described as "the most pig headed, obstinate, ill-tempered brute in the Canadas,"[27] but an influential leader of the British party in the old Lower Canadian legislative council, now agreed to stand in Montreal, while Ogden and other ministerial candidates found similarly safe urban constituencies. The French party's press loudly denounced the step— "another glaring example of the injustice embodied in the policy of Lord Sydenham," according to the *Quebec Gazette*; while *Le Canadien* called for "assez de vertu, de constance, de fermeté, de dévouement pour résister à tant de tyrannie."[28] Tory English papers saw "salvation" in it; though a more thoughtful *Montreal Gazette* considered the move impolitic and unjust.[29] At the same time, Sydenham, "le Grand Electeur,"[30] was looking to counties where, with help, there would be sufficient English-speaking population to give unionists a fighting chance. His chief election agent in the East, his military secretary Major Campbell, carefully chose polling places "most convenient to the loyal inhabitants of the county" and removed from main areas of French settlement.[31] He recommended returning officers for the polls with equal care.[32] Moreover, as events soon showed, any troops that might be dispatched to check election violence would virtually be made available only to one side, that of loyally British friends of union.

Any violence there was, when the polls opened in mid March, occurred in seats poised between those securely English and those incontestably French. Elections then were held by open voting at various dates during several weeks, and polling in each case might take some days. The system itself almost invited violence. The franchise-holder had to step up before a turbulent crowd of friends and foes, establish his right to vote and openly declare his choice, while enemy partisans tried to howl him down or more vigorously discourage him. Consequently electors came in rival bands for protection, and one side or the other might strive to capture the polling place by force, especially to hold a narrow lead or to reverse it. Hotly contested elections thus all too easily degenerated into pitched battles of fists, cudgels and stones—and sometimes gunshots and death. Nearby inns at times were battle headquarters, centres of vote-buying, mob-hiring, and the "treating" evil, where the simple citizen might be plied into fuddled acquiescence or fired to battle lust. And returning officers, if not prejudiced the right way, could be overawed by mob power, unless troops were called out. For even in towns the few police had scant power at election time.

In Vaudreuil, the French party candidate was leading on the second day of voting, when armed supporters of the British candidate attacked and held the poll for unionist electors, killing two men in the process.[33] In Chambly, Louis-Michel Viger—"le beau Viger," not to be confused with the older Denis-Benjamin Viger—had also taken the lead when enemy partisans, "the Irish boys," captured the poll and put up sufficient voters to gain a bare majority of ten. Viger's appeal to Sydenham for troops to prevent intimidation went unheeded. The returning officer declared for his opponent, since, not too surprisingly, no other Viger supporters had come forward.[34] In Beauharnois, on the other hand, troops ringed the poll at Ormstown in the only English-speaking district of the county, where the returning officer, a member of the election committee of the British candidate, turned back French voters who spoke no English and closed the poll after only two days, long before the more distant franchise-holders could come in.[35] Then in Montreal county, a French mob that seized the polling place battered to death two men, one the Irish baker employed by Mayor Peter McGill. Two thousand Irish and other English-speaking citizens came boiling out of the city to seek revenge. James Leslie, a LaFontaine adherent standing in the reform interest, applied to the Governor for troops, again without result, and gave up the contest in order to avoid more violence.[36]

There were other riots and casualties, but one of the most inglorious episodes in the elections in Canada East occurred in LaFontaine's own constituency, Terrebonne. Here the population was overwhelmingly French-Canadian; yet the poll had been placed in the outlying nondescript little hamlet of New Glasgow, a pocket of Scots and Irish settlement, and the returning officer again was a supporter of the British party candidate. The Montreal *Herald* saw the problem very simply. "From the known character of the majority of the electors in Terrebonne," it declared, "we doubt not LaFontaine would be returned if all the votes were polled; but it must be the duty of the loyalists to muster in their strength and keep the poll!"[37] In mid March LaFontaine began to hear ominous news of "stonebreakers" and "Glengarrians" flowing into New Glasgow, canal labourers and men from road gangs hired by the opposing interests.[38] An anonymous correspondent warned him to collect his own forces. "If you can muster 1000 all will be well. You must arrive prepared for action, as I think you will be attacked first."[39] There were other urgent warnings; LaFontaine heeded them. As the voting opened, he marched through the woods into New Glasgow with over eight hundred men of his own, armed with clubs and pitchforks—only to find a better-armed enemy, some six or seven hundred strong and including two hundred bully boys, drawn up strategically in full possession of the polling place.[40] Of course, he appealed for troops. Once more they did not come. To avoid a bloody pitched battle LaFontaine withdrew, conceding the election but, as he did so, proclaiming that the blame lay with Lord Sydenham "for the events in which the LAW OF THE BLUDGEON HAS PREVAILED."[41]

In any case, Terrebonne returned the British candidate, McCulloch, although its French-speaking population outnumbered its English by roughly ten to one. And when the elections closed on April 8, it was clear that in addition to LaFontaine's own defeat his friends had been largely outplayed in the Montreal district by the forces engineered by Sydenham. Neilson's men had done better in the Quebec district, however, which was still more solidly French-Canadian; and it seemed likely that the Neilson-Viger anti-union elements would dominate the French party in the new parliament. Still, LaFontaine had avoided any split in party ranks, while several strong supporters of his responsible-government policy had been elected in the Quebec region: Morin, Parent, and Dr Taché. Yet the real victor in Canada East was undoubtedly Sydenham. He could count some nineteen or twenty supporters of his government returned in Lower Canada. This was nearly half the eastern parliamentary contingent of forty-two, instead of a mere fragment—in no small part a tribute to effective, if unblushing, election management.

The Canada West elections went still better for the Governor. But while there was not the deep cultural and social cleavage over the union in the West, there was violence, nevertheless. Compact toryism still had numerous adherents, and it had vehement partisans also in 20,000 members of Orange lodges.[42] Fearful of the new association with French Catholic Canada and the upsetting of the old governing system, tories and Orangemen were roused to fight a fierce rearguard action for "British connexion." On the other hand, if radicalism was virtually impotent as an independent force, rankling memories of the rebellion period could still stir reform "ultras" to wild election clashes with Orange and tory forces. More moderate elements might generally dominate the contests in Canada West, but violence could readily break through at the polls. There was rioting in many constituencies. Men were killed in Halton West, in Durham, and at Toronto, where a shot was fired from the upper windows of the Orange centre, Allan's Tavern, into a roaring crowd below. Reformers nearly pulled the building apart before the soldiers arrived.[43] In the First Riding of York outside the city, supporters of the reformer, James Hervey Price, wore white armbands and carried pistols to combat the tory followers of John Gamble.[44]

Still, the Sydenham cause was safely in the ascendant in Upper Canada because of its appealing promise of stable, progressive government and escape from the excesses and upheavals of the recent past. Western business men like Isaac Buchanan or William Hamilton Merritt, promoter and builder of the Welland Canal, looked to Sydenham to lead a "commercial and industrial improvement party."[45] Farmers approved the Governor's attempts to check the importation of competing American produce, his efforts to have the imperial duty on Canadian grain repealed, his concern for the building of roads. Reformers found it wise to claim his favour for responsible government, without looking into the matter too closely. Even tory candidates paid lip-service to the magic name.[46] Nevertheless, Sydenham took no chances, and did not fail to organize for the widest possible success.

It was for this reason in particular that Arthur had been kept at his post in Canada West after the union, to carry out his superior's election strategy. Arthur and S. B. Harrison, the Provincial Secretary West, functioned as Sydenham's central agents for the western elections, in much the same way as Campbell and Murdoch served for the eastern. The Governor came to rely especially on the chill sagacity of the all-but-inscrutable Harrison—remarkably silent, but remarkably perceptive. Again the most favourable polling places and returning officers were carefully selected. The latter were required to send daily reports on the voting and make "necessary recommendations."[47] Baldwin submitted his own list of suggested names. When he complained that some had been discarded, Sydenham simply indicated that "Harrison took the people who were recommended by our candidates."[48] The use of patronage, of gerrymander, the sending of troops to the right constituencies, the issuing of land patents when needed to enfranchise new voters—all played a part in the Governor's election tactics for the West. So did the directed voting of those who held places in government services. Public servants, a significant group among urban electors, though essentially derived from the tory past, had it impressed on them that they "should not act at variance" with government policy.[49] The point was driven home by the instant dismissal of the tory clerk of the peace in Hamilton, when he voted there against the Provincial Secretary and moderate reformer, Harrison himself.[50]

These calculated efforts helped bring victory even in a Compact tory stronghold like Toronto, where two moderate reformers, Dunn, the Receiver General, and Isaac Buchanan, won the polls. In Hamilton, it is true, Harrison was defeated by the potent tory champion, Sir Allan MacNab, a local worthy, leader of loyal forces in the late rebellion and the Speaker of the last Upper Canadian house; a bold and boisterous figure, all bluff high-tory squire, combined with sharp-eyed demagogy. Yet Harrison was later found a seat in Kingston, and the other Sydenham ministers were safely elected. Robert Baldwin was returned both in Hastings and in the Fourth Riding of York, north of Toronto. Francis Hincks came in for Oxford in the west. The forces of old Compact toryism took less than ten seats, and only in the eastern old United Empire Loyalist regions of Upper Canada was any significant group of them elected. Some of these might yet support the government, moreover.

In general, when the elections were over in April, it appeared that the ministerial side had triumphed in Canada West, winning twenty-eight or nine of its forty-two seats in parliament.[51] The strongest core of government support lay in the moderate reformers associated with Harrison, and the moderate conservatives associated with Draper. Indeed, it could almost be said that they led a Draper-Harrison ministry backed by a Draper-Harrison party. Yet the ministry and its followers were Sydenham's, above all. And even if six ultra-reformers, including Baldwin and Hincks, were subtracted from the Governor's party, his position over all still looked secure. With his victory in Canada West, his strong showing in Canada East, Sydenham would have a safe working majority in the union parliament as a whole. Whatever the discords sounded in the process, the system of harmony had evidently won its chance to govern in Canada: thanks to the unremitting care and skill of a master politician, who had shown much more ability than scruples throughout the critical first elections of the union.

III

Parliament would not meet till June, largely because Sydenham's prolonged ill-health after the elections, a severe siege of gout, forced its postponement.[52] It would gather in the new capital of the union, Kingston. The little limestone town at the foot of Lake Ontario, where the St Lawrence began, where the route from the Rideau and Ottawa came down, and the powerful mass of Fort Henry loomed above the naval dockyard, had been bustling for months now with eager preparations. Under the superintendence of breezy Hamilton Killaly, a range of substantial stone cottages belonging to the Marine Railway Company had been finished as government offices. Alwington House, the handsome residence of Baron Grant of Longueuil outside the town, had been leased for the governor-general.[53] And the new General Hospital, with its large ward area, had been lavishly refitted to house the legislative chambers. The accommodation, wrote Sydenham, " . . . would be thought magnificent by us Members of the English House of Commons. But the fellows in these Colonies have been spoiled by all sorts of luxuries, large armchairs, desks with stationery before each man, and heaven knows what, so I suppose they will complain."[54]

The Governor General moved from Montreal to his new capital late in May. He arrived by steamer, still pale and none too well, with his left arm in a sling, to be greeted at the wharf by a red-coated guard of honour from the 24th Regiment at Fort Henry, the heads of departments and other government officials, the civic dignitaries and the officers of the St George's, St Andrew's and St Patrick's societies.[55] One of his first acts in early June was to complete the roster of the new parliament by appointing twenty-four members to the legislative council; significantly again, twelve from each half of Canada. Those from the eastern section included English business magnates like Peter McGill and George Pemberton, and six French Canadians of wealth and social standing. Few of the latter, however, could be said to have had much political influence, except perhaps for René-Edouard Caron, the mayor of Quebec. Among those named as legislative councillors from the western section were R. B. Sullivan, the President of the Executive Council, and William Morris, merchant and influential leader of Upper Canadian Presbyterianism. Meanwhile, the elected members of the legislative assembly were arriving, to crowd the inadequate hotel and boarding-house facilities of little Kingston. Prices soared: they were asking $6.00 a week for room and board at one well-established hotel, the British American.[56] Loud complaints went up of "gouging." The talk of frauds and misrepresentations was warmly rebutted in the local *Chronicle and Gazette*, as it retorted that members of the provincial parliament were all too quick to "insolently revile" Kingstonians, and contended (a bit inaptly) that no one had called it gouging when doctors in England had raised their prices twenty times over during a descent of Asiatic cholera.[57]

The legislature was to open on June 13. The day before, however, Robert Baldwin upset the pace of final preparations by precipitating a ministerial crisis. Now that there was a parliament assembling, he moved to put the issue of responsible government to the trial that had been postponed before. Francis Hincks had been busy consulting with their Upper Canada reform friends and with French-Canadian members to plan a joint course of action in the house. It was clear that Baldwin's own role was compromised by his position in the existing government: he would have to make Sydenham play out the hand. Accordingly, he told Hincks that he would advise the Governor to call LaFontaine and other reformers into the administration, and if his advice was declined, he would resign.[58] Yet that decision came only after "anxious and sleepless nights . . . not in bed till four,"[59] since Robert Baldwin earnestly hated trouble, and was driven to it only by the almost neurotic compulsion of his principles. Not for him the aggressive enjoyment of a well-conceived encounter, such as Hincks displayed. On June 12, he wrote to Sydenham to assert that the "United Reform Party" represented the great majority of Canadians, that the four conservative members of the executive council, Draper, Sullivan, Ogden and Day, did not merit their confidence, and that the introduction of Lower Canada reformers into the government was essential.[60]

It was an open challenge by the chief proponent of responsible party government to the Sydenham "mixed" ministerial system. It was also an attempt to realize Hincks's strategic design of controlling the assembly and executive through an Anglo-French reform alliance. Yet in the latter regard there was the danger that moderate western reformers would prefer to stand by Sydenham in any trial of strength, rather than join with notably anti-unionist French Canadians. And there was the further difficulty that the most influential member of the French reform contingent, John Neilson, backed by Viger and his friends, put so little faith in the Hincks-LaFontaine answer for French Canada's troubles, the reform alliance designed to win responsible rule. Still, conceivably, the western moderate liberals might be brought to follow their "advanced" reform brethren; and conceivably, too, the eastern French group would collaborate with them at least to upset the existing administration. Morin, in fact—taking over for LaFontaine while the latter lacked a seat in parliament—had already written to Hincks in May to assure him that "the Reformers of both Provinces must and will act together."[61] It was clear, he said, that immediate repeal of the union was impossible, and that Neilson was "not for violence and for creating difficulties." There was no "practical discrepancy" to prevent eastern and western liberals working profitably together.

Hence Baldwin, striving for the moment to speak for both sections of reform, might at least look for majority backing in the assembly, even if he failed to bring Sydenham to reconstruct the government according to the responsible principle. But he would fail completely. The Governor reacted decisively, with the sense of timing that told him when to act as well as to delay. He was confident that he could dispense with Baldwin and his few "ultras," now that elections were over; he counted on the moderates in the assembly to turn from further constitutional bickering. At Alwington on June 13, he treated Baldwin's letter as tantamount to resignation, and responded that he accepted it "without the least regret."[62] Indeed, Sydenham affirmed his own position by adding a sharp rebuke to his ex-councillor for a "proposal in the highest degree unconstitutional, as dictating to the crown who are the particular individuals whom it should include in the ministry."[63] Then he turned to watch events in parliament, as it convened that very day.

In the house, his closest counterpart in opposition, the manoeuvring Hincks, might try for an initial victory when Austin Cuvillier was put forward for Speaker by the "united reformers," moved and seconded by Morin and Merritt, the latter now a convert to responsible government. But Sydenham simply refused to try a test of confidence so early, and had his supporters indicate their cordial acceptance of Cuvillier: the emphasis was to be on harmony and positive development, not empty quarrelling. The Governor struck that persuasive note in a thoroughly skilled Speech from the Throne, setting forth ministerial policy for the session. Above all, he used it to announce that an imperial guaranteed loan of one and a half million pounds was proposed for the province. This munificent measure, designed to reduce the weight of public debt and to enable work on canals in particular to be renewed, had been planned in principle ever since Sydenham had first come to Canada. He had discussed it with Russell in dispatches; he could have disclosed it sooner, if necessary, to help carry the union or the elections of 1841. Indeed, some imperial financial help had been anticipated; but the full public revelation had been saved till this highly propitious moment.

The Sydenham régime might well have carried parliament in any case; but the imperial loan was a glowing substantiation of its promises to end useless discord and achieve constructive progress.

The debate on the address in reply to the Throne Speech saw Hincks and Baldwin working strenuously to keep the issue of responsible government to the fore, and trying to swing a reform majority behind it. Baldwin strove repeatedly to pin down the Attorney General, Draper, when he talked suavely but cloudily about "the absolute necessity for the preservation of harmony between the government and the people."[64] Did this mean the ministry would resign if it lost a vote of confidence? Draper conceded that he would resign himself, but that the council's final responsibility still lay to the Governor. He proved remarkably adept at telling the moderate reformers in the assembly what they really wanted to hear: namely, that every practicable degree of responsible government was furnished under the benign system of harmony as guided by Lord Sydenham. The vote that followed proved the government's hold. The address in reply was passed by a large majority.[65] Baldwin and Hincks carried only four other western "ultras" with them in opposition, along with the French-Canadian group of nineteen members. The Sydenham system had triumphed in its first parliamentary challenge. Hincks's *Examiner* said gloomily, "We have a Tory ministry as firmly seated in power as any Family Compact. . . ."[66]

In actual fact, of course, the Compact tories led by MacNab formed another element of opposition, at the other end of the political scale. But the divided anti-ministerial forces had so little in common they could seldom come together effectively against the centre. They divided also when, on June 23, Neilson's long-expected motion against the Act of Union was inevitably and conclusively defeated, 50 to 25.[67] On various occasions, indeed, either Upper Canada tories or advanced reformers might vote with the government majority. Only the French party remained solid in its opposition. Consequently, after the opening weeks of excitement and uncertainty, it seemed altogether likely that the ministerial group would steer its way safely through the rest of the session.

It was still true, nevertheless, that alignments in the house were not hard and fast. After all, the ministerial side was a loose coalition of party elements, in which the firmest groups were probably the Lower Canadian British party and the Upper Canadian moderate conservatives. It still required all Sydenham's watchful skill behind the scenes to keep his majority and the system of harmony in being. Western moderate liberals might yet be won over to Robert Baldwin and the party unity he stood for. They might yet combine effectively with Morin and the French Canadians, if they should express LaFontaine's rather than Neilson's views. In short, the cause of responsible government and reform alliance had lost a battle to the Sydenham system, but not the war—even though the Governor General gleefully informed Lord John Russell, "I have got rid of Baldwin and finished him as a public man forever."[68]

IV

Be that as it may, what the *Chronicle and Gazette* at first had called the "do-nothing-but-talk session"[69] now managed to get down to a substantial legislative program. In the field of education, Day, the Solicitor General East, introduced a bill in July to provide a general system of public primary schools for both sections of the province. It established a Chief Superintendent of Education, with an assistant superintendent for each section. They would regulate the system and control the disbursement of the annual provincial grant (to be $80,000 initially for Upper Canada, $120,000 for Lower) which would go to support the common schools along with locally raised rates and pupils' fees. It was a fairly rudimentary measure, soon to be replaced by fuller education acts for each section of Canada. Yet the Day Act was a significant beginning that set a pattern, particularly in regard to its provision for "separate schools," whereby religious minorities in both Canadas were enabled to establish state-aided schools of their own.

This Common School Act of 1841 was passed with little difficulty, and with little awareness of how tangled and emotion-filled a subject public education would become in later years of the union. Yet before it finally went through, parliament had turned to a series of other measures which Sydenham had promised and was eager to effect, to carry out his many-sided plans for modernizing Canada. Acts provided for the buying-out of private interests in the Welland Canal, and for its deepening and enlargement; for the improvement of St Lawrence navigation, and the building of roads and highways. To direct these operations, and particularly to take charge of the great canal-building program planned, the Board of Works was set up for the union as a whole, in the keeping of H. H. Killaly. To deal more effectively with the flow of immigrants an act of 1841 imposed a head tax of five shillings each. The tax was not intended to restrict the flow, but to provide for medical examination at the quarantine station at Grosse Isle below Quebec, and furnish relief and transport to their destinations for those immigrants who arrived destitute. Furthermore, new regulations were enacted to administer the sale or grant of lands to settlers, since the Crown lands of both Canadas had been transferred from imperial to colonial control by the Act of Union. They were placed under a single Commissioner of Crown Lands, who had a seat in the executive council.

With the creation of this post, and that of Chairman of the comprehensive Board of Works, Sydenham completed his reconstruction of the council into a coherent body of ministers, presiding over well-defined departments and responsible, as he said, "both to the Governor and to the Public for their acts."[70] Whatever his intention, one of his greatest gifts to Canada was this administrative reorganization that placed the offices of the permanent public service in ordered array under a set of political heads who could account for them in parliament. For, without this essential provision of a ministerial system, all Baldwin's high talk of the principles of responsible government, and Hincks's more earthly party manoeuvres, could well have remained impractical and empty of achievement. The Governor, moreover, was also training his councillors in the operation of a ministerial system in parliament. He remarked to Russell, ". . . they have none of them the slightest notion of carrying on a Govt. in the House, so I am obliged to be *Leader* myself which as I cannot go there is awkward, and takes up a great deal of time. What between lecturing Members every morning and schooling my Cabinet every day, my hands are therefore pretty full."[71]

Under this useful and necessary training in technique, parliament itself was settling down as a smooth-running mechanism. The public began to find it almost dull. Of perhaps more interest in the hot and droughty summer at Kingston were the visit of the "South African Giraffe or Camel Leopard," proclaimed the first one in captivity, or the building of the first screw-propeller lake steamer at the Marine Railway Company's dock.[72] Nevertheless, Sydenham's program did not succeed completely. He failed with his scheme to establish a bank of issue, which was to provide a sound paper currency for Canada, some of which would be used to implement the building of public works. The plan embodied features of the former Bank of the United States, and of central banking reforms which the financial wisdom of Sir Robert Peel would shortly institute in England. Yet in Canada it met the same kind of fears of financial tyranny and money monopoly that had helped overturn the American bank. Robert Baldwin and the French Canadians here combined with the Upper Canada tories to resist the ministerial bill, and they gained sufficient strength to cause Sydenham to drop it for the time being. With habitual optimism, he informed Russell that the assembly "wished to defer it for this session."[73] But the episode, in fact, showed that his group in parliament was not so solid, after all.

And it showed something else as well: the opening of a rift between Hincks and Baldwin. Hincks was developing a growing appreciation of the policies of Sydenham, a man so like him in many ways. No less pragmatic than the Governor, the western "ultra" was attracted by the immediate value of the ministerial program for economic progress. As a political realist, he concluded that the initial battles of the session had demonstrated that the time was not ripe for a victorious reform alliance, and that the long-range aim of responsible rule must be held in abeyance for the present. Moreover, as an individual with a good deal of financial talent himself, and a background in banking, Hincks was strongly sympathetic to the ministerial scheme for a bank of issue. Because of his understanding of finances, in fact, he had been chosen chairman of parliament's Committee on Currency and Banking, and there his casting vote had carried the measure forward, before it subsequently met defeat in the Committee of the Whole. Baldwin had a hard time trying to explain Hincks's course to a perturbed LaFontaine, while the quite unperturbed Hincks instead grew positively friendly to the Governor General in the pages of the *Examiner*.[74] Still further, he even told Dr Baldwin, Robert's father, that he could no longer oppose Sydenham, since he saw "the Executive Councillors acting in every respect as a ministry . . . we have *practical* responsibility."[75] In short, he had listened to the Governor's siren song of harmony and progress, and was assuming the attitude of moderate reform.

The rift between Hincks and Baldwin became an open party breach on another issue, that of municipal institutions for Canada West. To complement those already established for the East by ordinance of the late Lower Canadian Special Council, Harrison introduced in early August the government's measure for the West, the District Councils Bill. Sydenham was notably relying more and more on Harrison as his principal minister, even to the partial displacement of Draper. The former had proved so compatible and useful during the election dealings, and, besides, was virtual leader of the moderate reformers, a much larger group on the government side than Draper's western conservative associates. Harrison's bill, modelled on the Municipal Ordinance of Lower Canada, would incorporate councils for the Upper Canadian districts, empowered to levy tolls and taxes for local purposes, and to carry out such functions as the administration of justice, the maintenance of local roads and bridges, and the overseeing of local schools and charitable institutions under public authority.[76]

Hitherto the districts, which were the real operating unit for what local government there was, had been scantily managed by appointed justices of the peace, meeting in Quarter Sessions. Townships, the next unit below them, did have some locally elected officers, but their powers were minimal; counties, of which several might lie within a single district, were little more than parliamentary constituencies, without importance in the scheme of local administration. Now Harrison's—or Sydenham's—bill proposed to introduce a significant measure of elective local government. It would establish a council for each district, composed of representatives elected in the townships, and under a warden appointed by the central government. The townships would have elective councils with lesser powers also. It was a notable step towards municipal self-government, one strongly desired by Sydenham both in the interest of sound, economical administration and in order to bring government closer to the people.[77] But it was attacked from both sides; by tories who abhorred this dangerous move towards republicanism and democracy, and by Baldwin and his colleagues who found it by no means liberal enough.

The latter objected sharply to the appointment of the district wardens, treasurers, and municipal clerks by governor-in-council, contending that this simply gave new power and patronage to the central government. Hincks, however, supported the bill as a major improvement which could be carried further later; and after a hard struggle the votes of the government side finally passed it, effectively establishing municipal institutions on a province-wide scale. "Now it is impossible for any Government or any Parliament to prevent the Union Act working well," said Sydenham happily.[78] The District Councils Act was indeed a typical Sydenham compromise between authority above and the rights of the people below; an attempt, one might say, at a system of harmony in the local sphere—which could also open the way there for further, unintended change. But whatever its ultimate consequence, the immediate result was to split Hincks from his former associates. They angrily called him traitor; though Baldwin was more restrained, refusing to sanction the charge that Hincks had deserted true reform.[79] The object of attack fought back fiercely, retorting that events had shown that there was yet no united reform party; that he was as true a reformer as ever, but under the circumstances was necessarily following the dictates of his own conscience. Sydenham, at any rate, might smile, for certainly two of his most dangerous former opponents in the West were left far apart.

Nevertheless, he had still failed to make any inroads on the resolute opposition of the eastern French-Canadian block. Further attempts to detach their leading men had failed, as when Morin was offered a ministerial post, and after careful consultation refused it.[80] Yet the French party faced difficulties of its own. The Neilson-Viger wing were more inclined than ever to policies of withdrawal and "racial" separation. They could well point out that the grand reform alliance with Upper Canadians had proved wholly ineffectual. On the other hand, the LaFontaine-Morin group could equally point to Neilson's defeat in the vote on the union, and the sheer necessity of learning to work within it. There was, however, new doubt and alarm rising in French Canada over an early fruit of the union, Day's School Act.[81] Its philosophy of general public education for the whole province seemed a distinct threat to French and Catholic schooling, so essential to the cultural survival of French Canada. Were *unionnaires* like Morin and Parent forgetting their national values in a one-sided concern for association with Upper Canadian liberals? The classic French-Canadian distrust of the *vendu* arose to suggest that a reform alliance would be only one more form of selling out.

Some telling gesture was vital now, if the LaFontaine policy of survival through co-operation was not to be wholly rejected by the French-Canadian party.

Robert Baldwin supplied it. Since he had been elected both for Hastings and the Fourth Riding of York, he proposed to make the safely liberal Fourth York seat available to LaFontaine in order to bring him into parliament. It would be a dramatic embodiment of the idea of reform alliance, to have its prospective French-Canadian leader returned for an Upper Canadian constituency. And when in mid August Dr Baldwin put the proposal to Fourth York's reform committee, they accepted, asserting their pleasure at "expressing their feelings in this way for their Lower Canadian friends."[82] A surprised Louis LaFontaine gratefully sent Robert Baldwin his "sincere thanks for this mark of confidence in my political principles—I cannot value it too much."[83] Etienne Parent, who came along to follow LaFontaine's victorious campaign among the farmers of North York, gladly made the point clear for his readers in Le Canadien: "Ils élisent M. Lafontaine pour montrer, disent-ils, leur sympathie envers les Bas-Canadiens, et leur détestation des mauvais traitements et des injustices auxquelles nous avons été exposés."[84]

The idea of reform alliance was thus effectively re-confirmed. So was LaFontaine's position in the French party, and also the partnership that was arising between the leading champions of responsible rule in the two Canadas. However, the Fourth York by-election was not over until just after parliament rose in mid September. And before the session concluded, the question of responsible government had once again come up before it. On September 3, Baldwin, seconded by D.-B.Viger, moved a series of six resolutions which were designed to make the assembly and the ministry formulate a definite position on the principle of executive responsibility. Thereupon, Harrison, as Sydenham's mouthpiece among the moderate reformers, moved another series of four amendments. They were obviously an expression of the Governor's own position, and were intended to out-manoeuvre his stubborn antagonist. Remarkably, subtly, close to Baldwin's in general tenor, they nevertheless omitted his important reference to the assembly's right to hold the executive councillors responsible for every government action; and once more they re-affirmed the essential need for harmony between executive and legislature.[85] Baldwin himself felt compelled to support the amended Harrison version, rather than see tories defeat this partial acceptance, at least, of the vital principle of responsible rule.

But the truth was that the scope of Sydenham's tireless ingenuity was nearing its limit at last. Indeed, within a year's time, it would even be assumed that an executive council which could not hold the confidence of the assembly would have to resign; and the indefinitely-worded Harrison-Baldwin Resolutions of 1841 would be interpreted to that very end. Sydenham's tactical victories, his superb managerial skill, all his valuable practical reforms—none of these could really maintain the half-way house of "harmony" which he had occupied with such invincible self-assurance. The issue of self-government was too basic. It had only been postponed. The French Canadians were still obdurately divided from a régime built all too plainly on "English domination," and the Governor's election devices had merely deepened the gulf. Nor was there anything firm in the existing ministerial coalition, however successful it had temporarily been under his skilful guidance. If this was harmony, it was peace in Sydenham's time only; and his time was fast running out.

Never strong, he had worn out his health with constant effort. During the summer he sent in his formal resignation, to take effect in September when parliament had risen, sure that he had completed the essential work of his mission and overcome the fallacy of responsible government. "The great and harassing questions of Clergy Reserves and Responsible Government settled"—so he summed it up to Lord John Russell—"the Offices of Govt. arranged so as to ensure responsibility in those who are at their head and an efficient discharge of their duties to Governor and Public. The Legislature assembled, acting in harmony with the Executive, and really employed in beneficial measures of Legislation . . . . nothing therefore can now prevent or mar the most complete success, and Canada must henceforward go on well except it is most terribly mismanaged."[86]

"I long for September," he wrote, "beyond which I will not stay if they were to make me Duke of Canada and Prince of Regiopolis."[87] Then, on September 4, while pleasantly contemplating his return home in triumph, he was riding in the countryside near Kingston when his horse stumbled and fell, and Sydenham's right leg was badly shattered. At first he went on directing affairs from his sick-bed at Alwington House, but infection set into the wound, gout returned, and he had no strength left to rally. Yet he arranged for the prorogation of parliament, which had wound up a highly productive session with a total of 102 bills passed. By September 18, the Governor's case was clearly hopeless; and parliament was prorogued in his absence by a deputy. The next day he died, in agonies of lock-jaw. He was buried in St. George's Church in Kingston: one of the ablest British governors ever to come to Canada.

He was a careerist, and an opportunist to the point of unscrupulousness. There was a cheerful arrogance about him that let him dismiss the wrongs his methods might inflict with the blandest of ease. The French Canadians never ceased to scorn him; to them Sydenham, or Poulett Thomson, always remained "le Poulet," the strutting cockerel. Yet all his energy and resourcefulness had been given to the betterment of Canada as he saw it. His personal ambitions were devoted to public purposes; his formidable duties were never slighted. To offset his complacent over-confidence and vanity, moreover, there was native shrewdness and warm personal charm. This was no impervious, distant aristocrat, but a down-to-earth, approachable politician, with a genial interest in people. A rising generation of Canadian public men could learn a good deal from Sydenham, the deft practitioner of parliamentary skills, the first real party manager in the country.

But as for his system of harmony, the truth was that it had accomplished almost the opposite of what he had so confidently believed. Thanks to his régime, the Canadian government was now in fact a ministry, dependent for all significant purposes on a majority in the assembly. However much it might also look to the governor, it was an organized group of councillors sitting in parliament, who would be held responsible there. And if a new governor did not keep a parliamentary majority, he might well be compelled to accept ministers who could—just as Baldwin and Hincks themselves had intended. In sum, by striving so diligently for the form of harmony, Sydenham had virtually ended with the substance of responsible rule.

CHAPTER 4

Bagot and Challenge

1842-1843

After Sydenham's death, Canadian affairs were almost quiet during the closing months of 1841. His mixed ministry had survived the session with a deserved reputation for achievement. The Harrison-Baldwin resolutions seemed to have cleared the air on the responsible principle: "The Magna Carta of responsible government is now in the journals of the House," said the conservative *Montreal Gazette*, with some acerbity, "understand it who may."[1] And while the government might also feel relief at having parliament over, it yet had little cause to fear its opponents. Reformers were still divided, with Baldwin pulling one way, Hincks another: indeed, Sydenham had had an appraising eye on the latter, and just before his death had planned to offer him the new post of Inspector General in the administration, virtually that of minister of finance. As for the French Canadians, to all intents they were marking time during the parliamentary intermission, not certain what their policy now should be towards the union, and awaiting a successor to Sydenham who, they felt, would surely not be worse. As for the western tories, closely connected as they were with business activities, they were at least mollified by the thriving state of Canadian commerce. Thanks to high grain prices in England, over two million bushels of wheat and flour were shipped out before the close of 1841, and the timber trade did equally well with 373,000 tons of pine exported and 31,000 tons of oak. As a mark of the good times, receipts from tolls on the Welland Canal for the 1841 season nearly doubled those of 1839.[2]

Accordingly, in this mellow autumn interlude, it was not a matter of great concern that the delays of transatlantic communications left the Province of Canada for some months under a temporary administrator, Sir Richard Downes Jackson, commander-in-chief of the forces. In England, meanwhile, the government had changed—three weeks before Sydenham's death, in fact. The old Melbourne whig ministry had finally collapsed in decrepitude. The tories and conservatives had taken over. They were a much more vigorous group, at least as guided by the new conservative prime minister, Sir Robert Peel, whose considerable talents would be directed towards reforming fiscal and commercial policy, not unaffected by the progress of free-trade ideas in Britain. At the Colonial Office, however, a less diligent if less dogmatic minister had replaced Russell. This was Edward Geoffrey, Baron Stanley, heir to the great earldom of Derby, who was moderate-minded and intelligent but tended to treat his official role as an aristocratic avocation rather than a full-time career in itself. The new British régime duly considered the question of finding a governor-general for Canada, as Stanley advised Peel that the man must be able to work "the soothing system," not be "squeezable," and have parliamentary experience.[3]

In this regard, Peel also received advice from Charles Buller in a letter setting forth his own views of the qualifications for the post. Though Buller was on the other side of politics, his disinterested judgement had to be taken seriously, for he was both a leading advocate of colonial reform at Westminster and Durham's former secretary on the great mission to Canada. Buller stressed the need for integrity and political impartiality in any candidate, and continued, "He must be a humane just man who will have the liberality and good sense to raise up those whom we have been forced to put down in Canada. I allude especially to the French."[4] And to this point Peel significantly pencilled on the margin of the letter, "I entirely agree." Immediately afterwards he wrote to Buller, concurring in all his opinions and informing him of the choice the government had made. Peel observed, "You say 'The Governor General of Canada will in fact among his Duties have in great measure those of Ambassador to the United States.' This consideration and the knowledge that he was one of the most popular ambassadors ever accredited to the United States induced Lord Stanley and me to propose the appointment of Sir Charles Bagot."[5]

Bagot was appointed in late September. When the news reached Canada in October, it was greeted with mingled doubt and approval: doubt because, after all, Sir Charles had had no experience of dealing with legislatures and had no known constitutional views; approval because he did indeed have a commendable record in diplomacy for high character, impartiality and sound common sense. At the little Canadian capital, the *Chronicle and Gazette* voiced a widespread sentiment when it declared itself prepared to support the new governor-general if he would work to the one end, "Canada's prosperity," regardless of party.[6] But it was some time before the province could find out. Bagot's sailing from England was delayed till November by violent autumn gales in the English Channel. He then had a long and stormy passage to the nearest ice-free winter port, New York, reached it late in December, and came on overland. It was not till January 10, 1842, that he finally arrived in Kingston, travelling bundled in furs by sleigh across the frozen St Lawrence from the American side, and escorted by some two hundred other sleighs, hoofs crunching on the crisp snow-cover of the river ice.[7]

This new governor was obviously very different from his predecessor. Tall, erect and courtly, he was sixty, not forty-two; of old landed family, not the city business world; at home in the embassies of St Petersburg, The Hague or Washington, not in cabinet offices or party committee-rooms. He was the nephew of the great tory Duke of Wellington, now government leader in the House of Lords. He was a man of wit and cultivation, of easy charm in conversation, but, again, scarcely acquainted with the rattle and bang of politics. Yet Bagot's cool detachment, prudence and tact had served him very well in diplomatic negotiations, and might do so again in the uncertain balance of Canadian affairs. He had been British minister to Washington in the hard years following the War of 1812. That, in fact, was a strong reason for his appointment now to Canada, since differences with the United States still loomed so large. There was discord left from the time of the "Patriot" border raids; there were disputed boundary claims to both east and west; and the case of Alexander McLeod itself had taken the shape of an international incident. There seemed special need of a Bagot, who, as Peel recorded, "had accommodated himself to American Society, and made himself extremely acceptable to the American people."[8]

Actually, between the time of Bagot's appointment and his ultimate arrival, the McLeod case had finally been settled. McLeod, deputy sheriff of the Niagara District, had been arrested during a trip to New York State in November, 1840, and charged on highly dubious evidence with murder and arson committed during the Upper Canadian attack on the *Caroline*. He had remained in jail nearly a year while a diplomatic and legal battle was fought over him. The British minister in Washington protested against the arresting of a private citizen for a public act. The United States government first sought to fix British responsibility for the *Caroline* raid, and then, since Britain seemed to have conceded that there had indeed been a public act, tried with little success to have McLeod released from the jurisdiction of the New York state courts. Neither side by any means looked to war, yet the impasse that developed when the New York supreme court insisted on proceeding with McLeod's trial could have had disastrous consequences.[9] But when at length, in October 1841, the prisoner came to trial at Utica, the testimony against him proved so plainly specious, and the evidence that he had been nowhere near the *Caroline* so convincing, that the jury speedily threw out the charges. With his acquittal, at least one serious Anglo-American irritant was removed.

The others were looked into when, in February 1842, Peel sent a special commissioner to Washington to deal with outstanding issues between Great Britain and the republic: Lord Ashburton, member of the great London banking house of Baring. In the ensuing months Ashburton, who had already had years of business experience in America, opened negotiations on a variety of topics with the Whig Secretary of State, Daniel Webster. A Canadian-American extradition agreement was drawn up. Britain reasserted that the *Caroline* attack had been necessary in view of piratical raids on Canadian territory, but expressed regret for the violation of neutral rights. This the Americans were ready to treat as an apology, and waived claims for reparation. The uncertain western boundary line between Lake Superior and Lake of the Woods was also settled at the cost of four million acres of the British claim, including Isle Royale in Lake Superior. But by far the most serious problem was the eastern Canadian and New Brunswick border with Maine, undetermined ever since the peace treaty after the American Revolution had been notably vague about the area where a line drawn northward from the St Croix was to meet the height of land between the Atlantic and the St Lawrence. At length, a compromise boundary was arrived at, which left five-twelfths of the disputed region in British possession and kept the Americans back from the slopes overlooking the St Lawrence.[10] In view of the conflicting claims presented by either side in a so-called "battle of the maps," the line achieved was probably not too unreasonable, although the northward reach of Maine would bar the most direct lines of land communication henceforth between Canada and the Maritime Provinces. At any rate, the Ashburton Treaty, finally signed in August 1842, did mark a settlement of rankling Anglo-American disagreements. And in the meantime, the conducting of the negotiations eased strains for Canada. Accordingly, that province and its new governor, Sir Charles Bagot, had lessening reason to watch warily southward, and could concentrate on internal concerns instead.

In governing Canada, Bagot's basic aim was that of Sydenham before him. He meant to carry on the system of harmony; the instructions he received from Stanley to that effect were unchanged in essence from those Sydenham had had from Russell. He was to choose as his advisers "the ablest Men, without reference to distinction of local party." Stanley even used words of Sydenham's in enjoining Bagot to turn the legislature and people "from the discussion of abstract and theoretical questions . . . to the calm and dispassionate consideration of practical measures. . . ."[11] Certainly the tories and conservatives in England were no less determined than the whigs to maintain the imperial authority of the governor against any colonial claim for responsible government, and to uphold a union designed to keep the British element securely in the ascendant, even if the French might be shown more attention now. Bagot himself was a British tory in background and upbringing. He could have little sympathy with the "ultra" notions of a Baldwin or the separate national aspirations of the French Canadians. If anything, he tended privately to incline toward the Compact tory faction, as evinced in a confidential appraisal of the Canadian scene which he sent to Stanley in February 1842, after he had been six weeks in the province.[12]

"The Country has never during the past five years, been in so tranquil and prosperous a state as at present," he asserted. While not presuming that the discords in the union were over, he considered that the government could safely meet the next parliamentary session without encountering serious obstacles to its program. All seemed to indicate, Bagot said, the wisdom of the instructions he had received to discourage party sentiment and bring the ablest men of all parties into his government. He approved of Sydenham's coalition ministry; sought only to strengthen it. And he believed that the existing "unnatural alliance" among the opposition forces, of French Canadians, ultra-reformers (who apart from Baldwin had little influence) and Compact tories, could be broken up before the next session. As for the tories, he was sure that they had been taught to "mitigate those exclusive views" which had earned them such distrust, and that "their loyalty and attachment to British connection will have convinced them that a factious opposition can profit them nothing." As for the French, he thought they showed a more amenable spirit: moreover, "Surrounded and outnumbered by a race of British descent . . . the French Canadians can scarcely avoid seeing that their natural Post is an alliance with the government, and that by such an alliance alone can they hope to maintain their peculiar laws and privileges."

It was a mixture of insight, insufficient knowledge, and wishful thinking. Bagot's views would change markedly over the next few months as he acquired knowledge, and as his own calm clarity of mind led him to discard wishful thinking. He would face realities of party feeling and cultural division which Sydenham, for all his skill, had merely manoeuvred around.

II

Bagot undoubtedly worked hard, both to acquaint himself with the two sections of Canada and to exploit the "better feeling" he believed he could discern.[13] Undoubtedly, too, he did produce a good impression in French Canada, where he made it his special charge to try to restore the regard of the people for the representative of the Crown. His distinguished bearing, polished manners and cordial courtesy—besides his fluent French—won him favour on viceregal progresses to Montreal and Quebec. And he gave more substantial reason for goodwill in the number of official positions now offered to French Canadians: district judgeships (including one to Morin), numerous clerkships (including one to Taché), municipal appointments, and places in the customs service. In this, it is true, the Governor was confirming and enlarging lists already drawn up by Sir Richard Jackson as administrator. Yet it was a valuable gesture of conciliation, intended by Bagot to give French Canadians their fair share of public posts through the judicious use of patronage. Nevertheless, he had to record in March, "The French Canadians are still sulky and will always be troublesome if they can be by mere force of habit. . . . It is despairing to see how they always take justice and kindness only as instalments of their own unreasonable pretensions."[14]

The Governor General did not give up; he went further. In May, he appointed two deputy superintendents of education for Canada East and West respectively, under a nominal superintendency in the executive council: Jean-Baptiste Meilleur, a French Roman Catholic physician and scholar, and Robert Murray, an Upper Canadian Presbyterian minister. Consequently, the two Canadian sections could evolve their own differently conceived educational systems; and consequently, too, French Canadians were relieved of their fears of absorption in a general, secular, and English school system under the Day Act of 1841.[15] The appointment of Dr Meilleur, a capable academician in close touch with the clergy, went far to assure the *Canadiens* of Bagot's good intentions; though he could scarcely have foreseen that through the control of their own education, the French had gained a powerful means of maintaining their own identity, and thus of thwarting the union's very purpose of assimilation.

Similarly with regard to law: Bagot's desire for conciliation led him to defer (permanently, as it turned out) the proclamation of an ordinance of the old Special Council reorganizing Lower Canadian court procedures on the lines of English common law. Again the anglicization of institutions intended by the union was prevented, as French Canada kept its own legal system. Yet one might question whether Bagot was subverting basic policy here for a short-term advantage, or recognizing the far more basic fact of duality, and the unwisdom of trying to impose English patterns on French judicial practice virtually as a punitive measure this late in the day. At any rate, by his actions the Governor General gained a greatly improved opinion for himself among French Canadians. And at the same time he gained a broader understanding of their position under the union.

Meanwhile Bagot had been busy in Canada West as well, using the interval to deal with "a great scandal," as he called it—the fact that, though chartered for fifteen years, the provincial university of Upper Canada, King's College, had still not begun teaching.[16] It had been bogged in repeated wrangles between tory defenders of the Anglican control of its endowment and reform critics who urged the interests of other denominations, or even a non-denominational university. Then financial mismanagement, depression, and fruitless arguments over whether to build or teach first, had continued the delay. But Bagot, with his own warm interest in cultural pursuits, moved to bring action at last. He worked through Draper, the

Attorney General West, an Anglican and a Toronto man, quite capable of dealing with the crusty Bishop of Toronto, old John Strachan. Bagot himself adroitly urged Strachan along.[17] The result was an agreement to start the construction of a university building at Toronto immediately, to appoint a staff, and begin teaching in temporary quarters in a year's time. Thus, on April 21, the Governor came to Toronto by steamer from Kingston for the ceremony of laying the cornerstone for King's College. The university site was in the fields beyond the city to be known as Queen's Park, and in the sunny spring day the crowd was beaming with good humour and goodwill. Said Bagot, "I never saw a thing or heard a word which could have led anyone to imagine that there were two parties in the Town."[18]

But now the Governor General turned to a far larger problem, that of reconstructing his executive council to strengthen it and make it more fully his own. He was already working closely with Draper, for whom he felt more affinity than for Sydenham's erstwhile mainstay, the aloof Harrison. But he wanted to broaden the basis of his ministry, and carry out his instructions to bring in the ablest members of all parties, by adding men to either side of Draper and Harrison: the prominent Kingston tory, J. S. Cartwright, and the advanced reformer, Francis Hincks, already marked by Sydenham for Inspector General. Early in June, Hincks accepted that office, proclaiming that he did so "without the slightest compromise of my wellknown political principles"[19]—while the angry Baldwinite press predicted, ". . . nothing can come of it but disgrace, infamy, confusion and misgovernment."[20] Cartwright, however, refused the Solicitor Generalship West, still vacant since Baldwin's resignation, precisely because Hincks had been offered a place. The staunch Compact tory would not sit beside the former "ultra." It took all Draper's smoothest persuasion (he was not called "Sweet William" for nothing) to bring in Henry Sherwood, the tory mayor of Toronto, instead.[21]

In any case, Bagot had not really assured the support of the tories in the opposition; nor, above all, of their strongest and most obstreperous spokesman, Sir Allan MacNab, for a scheme to soothe him with the adjutantgeneralship of the militia broke down.[22] If anything, moderate tories or conservatives on the government side might even be led away to the Compact tory forces in opposition, now that the unequalled managerial skill of Sydenham was no longer there to hold the ministerial coalition together.[23] At the same time, moderate or ministerial reformers were also growing restive. Evidently Robert Baldwin's firm call for liberal party unity was having some influence upon them, including Harrison himself.[24] Plainly, Baldwin's cause was waxing again, despite the defection of Hincks. He gained a further supporter in a by-election, while LaFontaine's previous return and that of another French Canadian meant that the government side in any case had effectively lost three seats in parliament. In short, by midsummer, Bagot's earlier confident belief that his ministry could safely meet the house had lost a good deal of its validity. Instead it became a matter of holding off parliament until he could improve his council. He worked with growing concern. The facade of Sydenham unity and harmony was fast breaking down.

But the crux of the problem was the French Canadians. Their solid group might swing the balance of power, whether they moved with newly rallying tories or increasingly vigorous Baldwinites. Stanley and Bagot each wanted to secure French participation in the administration, believing it was necessary both for a strong "all-parties" government and to appease the French Canadians in regard to the union. The aim, of course, was to detach individual *Canadiens*, to "multiply *vendus*," as Stanley candidly called it.[25] But the French party, as an embattled cultural minority, had a cohesion that was hard to break. They were very different from the English-speaking tories and reformers who had party elements both within and without the ministry: restless, factious elements, moreover, so that Hincks's appointment tended to weaken conservative government backing, and Sherwood's to upset Harrison and the ministerial reformers, rather than to bring any new support. The power of the French block in opposition, therefore, was a major threat to Bagot's insecure administration. He became more and more worried about the problem that the French Canadians posed, and more and more aware of how inadequately, or even disastrously, his predecessor had dealt with them in the scheme of union.

To Stanley he wrote: "The means which Lord Sydenham had resorted to, in order to carry and complete the measure, may have been absolutely necessary—but they involved a public, and something very like a private quarrel on his part with the whole mass of the French inhabitants of Lower Canada —and it would have been totally impossible for *him* ever again to conciliate them, or indeed ever again to have met, with any prospect of success, another Parliament in this country."[26] At the same time Bagot's two most capable ministers, Harrison and Draper, told him in July that the French Canadians had to be brought in. "There is no disguising the fact," said Harrison bluntly, "that the French members possess the power of the Country.[27] Draper, more circumspect, "could not conceal from Your Excellency my strong apprehension that . . . the government cannot be carried on in the House of Assembly." He foresaw that the French would probably be tied to Robert Baldwin, and expressed his own readiness to resign his post, in the "unhesitating opinion that the opportunity of securing the French party ought not to be lost upon any question affecting merely an individual officer of the government."[28] "What is then to be done?" Bagot asked Stanley anxiously. "Are we to bide our time and wait till immigration hems in and overwhelms French population and French Power? This must happen some day or other—but in the meanwhile I may lose my majority in the Legislature, and we may then have to begin all over again."[29]

The Governor had not really changed his mind about the ultimate and natural assimilation of the French Canadians within the union. But he had come to perceive the need of changing policy to win them over now, if "harmony" was to go on functioning in Canada. He sought to place French Canadians in the higher posts of dignity and authority, naming more of them among new appointments to the legislative council, and making the eminent Vallières de Saint-Réal Chief Justice of the Montreal District. His own view of the French—"a proud and courteous people"—deepened and improved.[30] And, as he subsequently told Stanley, he recoiled from the thought of trying to carry through the next session by "the unscrupulous personal interference of Lord Sydenham, combined with practices that I would not use, and your Lordship would not recommend. . . ."[31] Those methods had been exhausted. They had only brought on the day of reckoning which he must meet, when parliament convened before autumn. Yet always he faced the fact that efforts to bring leading French politicians into the ministry itself did not succeed. He could not, for example, find a French Canadian to take the post of Solicitor General East, made vacant through Day's appointment to the judicial bench. And if he had, he knew now, "I should have got nothing but the individual man—his influence over the French Canadians is gone from the moment that he takes office. He is then immediately in their eyes, 'Le Vendu' and 'Le Vendu' he remains."[32]

Both Draper and Harrison advised him of the inescapable conclusion: the French would have to be taken in as a body, a party in their own right —which probably meant their ally, Robert Baldwin, also. Bagot still hoped to avoid the latter consequence with its wholly unpleasant concomitant, Baldwin's responsible-government doctrine. But at the end of July he sent a plain warning to Lord Stanley that he perceived no answer but to admit the French to power on their own terms, as a party in themselves.[33] He assured the Colonial Secretary that he would not act without his advice, then hopefully awaited an answer before he had finally to open parliament.

None came. Stanley in August forwarded Bagot's message to Peel, expressing his own fear that if the French and radicals were let in as a party group, "the union is a failure and the Canadas are gone."[34] But the Colonial Secretary himself had "gone to the North"—it was the grouse season; and transatlantic communications were too slow for any reply to reach the Governor General in time.[35] The legislature was called for early September. Bagot would have to deal with the almost certain crisis, when it gathered, upon his own decision. In fact, he confronted the most serious challenge yet to the system of harmony. Could he respond to it, somehow remake his council satisfactorily with the French Canadians, and still not yield to Robert Baldwin's rival design for responsible party government?

III

When parliament opened on September 8, it grew clear beyond doubt that the administration was not going to command a majority. LaFontaine was there now, buoyed by recent by-election victories in Lower Canada, the dominant figure in the French party. Baldwin was near at hand, the two of them working closely as they planned the tactics for bringing down the council and instituting the responsible system.[36] Tories had plans of their own. Allan MacNab—"intriguing, slippery, unprincipled," said Bagot[37]— was himself wooing the French Canadians for an alliance of convenience, to defeat the government in a joint attack on the union. The Speech from the Throne was innocuous enough; but the storm would inevitably begin when the debate upon it was launched. In the moment before it started, Bagot made his own move. He approached the French party, to see if they would enter into a reconstruction of the ministry before it was brought down. On September 10 he sent for Louis LaFontaine, to inform him confidentially that the French Canadians would be invited into the government; but not as individuals—as spokemen for their party, bringing with them "not only their own talents . . . but the good will and attachment of their race."[38]

It was a triumphant moment for the grave French Canadian with the impressively Napoleonic face and manner. He had only just taken his seat in the union parliament; and yet he had been the recipient of the offer to admit his people into power. For thanks to his skill in party organizing, along with powerful press support, notably from Parent's Le Canadien, LaFontaine had all but united the French members behind his policies of reform alliance and working within the union. No doubt, as well, he had been aided by Bagot's own efforts at conciliation, which had put the union in a better light for the French Canadians and given them new hope for its future. On the other hand, the Governor had recognized LaFontaine's stature for several months past, and had seen him as the man through whom negotiations could be opened with the French as a body. Moreover, the fact that he stood for the maintenance of union was vitally important from Bagot's point of view. For that reason, as well as his strength in his party, LaFontaine had obviously been the right man to approach.

He was Napoleonic, too, in knowing how to exploit a breach. He staggered Sir Charles by asking, in reply, for four places in the government— one of them for Robert Baldwin. The alliance Hincks had projected, which Baldwin had confirmed in the Fourth York by-election, was in decisive operation. On Baldwin's part, the trust he inspired had done much to make it so effective now. He had stressed to LaFontaine that "Everything depends on the Lower Canada reformers" playing their part in government; that he wanted to see the French "in a position to give the most complete refutation to the imputation of their being *impracticable.*"[39] He would do anything, he said, to see that end achieved, whether by joining or by supporting the French Canadians in government. LaFontaine returned the favour. If the Governor General wanted the *Canadiens*, he would have to take Baldwin, the arch-exponent of the responsible system, with them.

Negotiations wavered, as Bagot strove to avoid the full price; started and stopped again. And at this juncture, on the night of September 12, the Governor's own council held a critically important meeting, in which Draper particularly played a leading role.[40] The ministers decided that under the Harrison-Baldwin resolutions they would be bound to resign if the government was beaten in the house. Their advice to Bagot was a veritable ultimatum. LaFontaine had to receive a definite offer. Draper would retire; Ogden, absent in England, would be forced out; Day's place was still empty; Sherwood could be removed. This would provide the places for the French and Baldwin. And if Sir Charles could not agree, the ministers, "after great deliberation," must resign.[41] Here was crisis within crisis. Challenged on every hand, the Governor had little choice of action left.

Nevertheless, the veteran of many a conference table still did his unflustered best. He rejected a brash approach from MacNab, who offered him, on conditions, a quite inadequate sixteen tory votes. On September 13, by letter to LaFontaine, Bagot agreed to provide four places and to accept Baldwin's inclusion in the council, "upon the express understanding that he was to consider himself as brought in by the French Canadian party."[42] In short, he was to be merely their appendage; Bagot still strove to prevent the emergence of a party government based on the accession of a reform alliance, as such, to power. He still hoped to govern through a mixed ministerial coalition and break up any single party front. And so his letter also sought to retain some of his tory-conservative ministers, and to secure pledges of pensions for those who would resign. But LaFontaine returned, plainly upset, to decline the terms as too constricting.[43] The negotiations collapsed again, while Baldwin increased the pressure with a no-confidence motion in parliament. Now the Governor faced not only the imminent defeat or resignation of his ministry, but also the dire probability that afterward he would have no other recourse but to call on LaFontaine and Baldwin to form a new and wholly reform administration.

The old diplomat moved rapidly to avert this total loss of his control. Through Draper, who maintained his statesmanlike readiness to resign himself in order to bring in the French Canadians, the Governor disclosed to the assembly his letter setting forth the definite offer to LaFontaine. A fiercely explosive debate followed; but, as Bagot shrewdly calculated, the sweep of the change proposed made a decisive impression on the house. The mood changed, as heat ebbed and hope grew. Though MacNab was "exceedingly bitter and violent," Bagot had saved his ministry.[44] Now negotiations were successfully renewed for its reconstruction: an additional Upper Canadian place was to be made available for an associate of Baldwin, and the matter of pensions was left for later decision. By September 20, the crisis at last was over. Baldwin withdrew his no-confidence motion. Bagot's government received resounding support in the assembly from all but the unconverted Neilson, the much discomfited MacNab, Cartwright, and two other tories.[45]

In the reconstituted council, LaFontaine replaced the conservative Ogden as Attorney General East, while Morin was appointed Commissioner of Crown Lands. Thomas Aylwin, a leading Quebec lawyer and supporter of LaFontaine, became Solicitor General East. And Etienne Parent was named Clerk of the Council, giving up his assembly seat and editorship of Le Canadien, as his new office was a non-political, civil-service position. In the Upper Canadian half of the government, Baldwin became Attorney General West in place of Draper, who cheerfully resigned, and James Small, a Baldwin man, succeeded the protesting Sherwood as Solicitor General West. Otherwise the western ministers remained; the moderate liberals Harrison, Dunn and Hincks, the conservative Sullivan, and the non-partisan Killaly. So also did the non-partisan provincial secretary for the eastern section, that amiably permanent bureaucrat, Dominick Daly. Thus, although much more a reform council than before, this was still mixed coalition government.

Bagot had managed not to succumb to the principle of a one-party ministry. Nor had he been compelled to dissolve his government and make a new one in response to an assembly vote. He thought, indeed—in relief and satisfaction—that he had snatched victory out of defeat. Yet the truth was that he had only been able to meet challenge by retreat, and by a yielding of strategic terrain that would have sharply distressed Sydenham. To all intents this reconstructed council was a reform-dominated ministry. It became more so, as Baldwin and Hincks gradually healed their rift, as Harrison and Dunn acted more as reformers than moderates, and the highly adaptable Sullivan quite readily took on a liberal coloration. And certainly the eastern half was virtually LaFontaine's. If not a one-party cabinet, then, it was a signal step in that direction: one more along the way from governor-directed "harmony" to responsible party rule in Canada.

More evident at the time, however, was the dramatic change in the state of the French Canadians. Their constitution suspended, their very allegiance in doubt, they had been brought into a union meant for their subordination.

Now their leaders sat in that union's government; their representatives supplied the government majority in the eastern section of parliament. There could scarcely have been a more impressive demonstration of the workings of LaFontaine's politics of co-operation, as compared to those of withdrawal; nor of the political strength of a cohesive minority, properly handled. The irony was that the union itself had made that strength so effective. It had stimulated, in reaction, the defensive unity of French Canada. It had placed a firm French garrison amid the contending, shifting divisions of the English majority. Stable government would henceforth need French backing, as Bagot in his realism had learned to recognize. And so, within eighteen months of the establishment of the union, the French Canadians, by very reason of their distinctive character, had come to share decisively in its direction. Social fact had confounded constitutional intent. Long before the full realization of responsible government the Canadian union had actually revealed itself to be anything but an instrument of assimilation, although English Canadians might still look to that end, and French fear it, for years to come. The union meant for assimilation would entrench duality instead.

Of course, the long-run implications were by no means clear in the autumn of 1842, though French Canadians might well rejoice over the reversal in their fortunes. Morin happily forecast "un avenir de repos, de confiance et de justice."[46] Parent, in a farewell message in his paper, lauded "l'heureuse révolution qui a succédé à nos malheurs," and no less praised Bagot, who had set government on "la base large et solide de l'opinion-générale."[47] And a younger supporter of LaFontaine, George-Etienne Cartier —who had already served him well as a party agent in Montreal—sent enthusiastic congratulations to his chief in a characteristic scrawl, adding a sentence that later historians could well appreciate, "J'ai écrit cette lettre lentement pour que vous puissiez la lire."[48]

Among English Canadians, convinced Baldwinites were similarly jubilant, moderates more uncertain, though not unfavourable; but tories were hotly indignant at the selling-out of British interests to disaffected French. The Montreal *Transcript* declared Bagot's action "infatuated imbecility."[49] The Orange Toronto *Herald* fulminated that, in circumstances "where the traitor has to be bribed" as a means of maintaining union, Canada would surely be separated from Britain within the generation.[50] Yet Bagot was not greatly concerned by tory anger, because his parliamentary position was now wholly secure. He was much more concerned over possible repercussions in England, since the action he had taken on his own initiative in reorganizing his council appeared so plainly to run counter to previous lines of policy under both whig and tory administrations.

And there were reverberations when his dispatches reached London in mid October. "What a fool the man must have been," exploded the Duke of Wellington, archetype of toryism—and Bagot's own uncle.[51] More crucial were the reactions of Peel and Stanley. The conservative prime minister, perturbed by the outcries on his tory wing, thought Bagot could have manoeuvred better, so as not to be dictated to. A severely troubled Stanley, much concerned by the wholesale admission of the French, not to mention Baldwin, regretted that the necessity for change had not, at least, been more clearly demonstrated, "to avoid the appearance of the Governor General *inviting* the co-operation of men tainted with violent suspicion of treasonable practices."[52] Yet both the Prime Minister and Colonial Secretary were ready to agree that Canada could not be governed against its will, and they felt compelled to support the judgement of the imperial representative there that his act had been wholly inescapable. Hence, early in November, the British cabinet gave official if rather constrained approval to Bagot's "great experiment" of conciliation and reconstruction.[53] There was little else to do with a *fait accompli*. But one might contemplate a rather different outcome, if the Atlantic cable had been in operation in the 1840's instead of the 60's, so that Bagot had faced his crisis with the benefit of London's views.

IV

The excitement over, the session that followed was short and workmanlike. The government had no trouble in keeping a majority. It rested essentially on LaFontaine's French liberals and the Upper Canadian reformers, reunited as a party behind Baldwin.[54] Yet some of the Lower Canadian British tories and some western conservatives still gave the administration their support, in what they regarded as their loyal duty to the Queen's governor rather than any expression of allegiance to the new leaders of his ministry. For the present, however, it was enough that the government was strong again, and able to get on with parliamentary business. The newly appointed executive councillors were actually out of the house at first, since in accord with British practice the law now required them to face by-elections on joining the ministry, and be returned to parliament anew. But there was no danger that the government would be beaten in their absence.

One of the major measures of the session was a law to punish election violence, bribery and intimidation—all three of which were blatantly illustrated by events in Hastings county early in October, where Robert Baldwin lost an initial by-election attempt. To a large extent, however, the act was inspired by hard memories of the elections of 1841; and there were other measures that were similarly a reaction against the recent past: the restoration of the old boundaries of Quebec and Montreal, for instance, or the repeal of ordinances by Sydenham and the Special Council that had particularly rankled with French Canadians—such as the unproclaimed ordinance against French civil law. But financial questions were also of importance. One significant act brought in by Hincks established a measure of agricultural protection in Canada, imposing a duty of three shillings a quarter on American grain brought into the province. This was meant both to please Canadian agricultural interests, long hostile to competition from American imports, and to suit Canadian mercantile interests, who normally wanted the free entry of American cereals to add to their shipments to the British market, but who now had cause to hope for lower duties on Canadian wheat imported into Britain, if the flow of American wheat via the St Lawrence should be restricted by a Canadian tariff.[55]

Quite as important was the matter of the promised imperial guaranteed loan of £1,500,000. The terms had been worked out for it in the year since Sydenham's announcement, and the British parliament had passed a Canadian loan act in the summer of 1842 making the funds available. In October, therefore, Hincks introduced another measure into the provincial house, to provide for the money to be used directly for public works and not to reduce the Canadian debt first. Canada's improved financial position in the prosperous times seemed to make her debt burden far less unmanageable. Hence the loan could go immediately into canal and road building, both of which were pushed forward by Bagot under the efficient supervision of Killaly at the Board of Works. And Hincks as Inspector General applied his talents to secure the effective management of finances: improving the system of keeping the accounts, reforming the customs service, and increasing the revenues by such means as his pioneering step toward tariff protection.[56]

Parliament rose in mid October with the expectation that it would soon be called again when the reconstructed ministry had had time to produce a fuller program. By now the work on the St Lawrence canals was in full swing once more. Gangs of labourers with pick and shovel, teams of horses and oxen, were at work to complete the Cornwall Canal, to dig the great eleven-mile trough of the Beauharnois. In the latter connection, the ubiquitous Edward Gibbon Wakefield had turned up in Canada, as agent for the splendidly named North American Colonial Association of Ireland, which had bought the seigneury of Beauharnois and was certainly strongly interested in a canal being built where it held lands for settlement. Wakefield, one of Durham's principal aides on his Canadian mission, had closely concerned himself with the fortunes of the Canadian union and its government —partly because he was an ardent advocate of colonial reform and development; partly because he had to know everything and set everyone right; and partly because the colonial world, from Australia to America, seemed admirably designed for the land schemes and general enhancement of E. G.

Wakefield. Now in Canada he ran for parliament. He was returned at a by-election in Beauharnois in November, as a candidate for LaFontaine's party and an admirer of Bagot's "great measure" of reconciliation. He would add a piquant note to the Canadian house when it assembled again.

But that meeting was delayed by the Governor's illness, and was put off through November and December, by which time it was clear that Bagot was gravely ill, his strength overtaxed by the long preceding months of strain. He asked for his recall; it was granted in mid January of 1843. By then, however, it was much too late to move an elderly invalid in the iron-hard Canadian winter. A successor was named for him, an experienced civil servant and colonial governor, Sir Charles Metcalfe. Yet until Metcalfe could arrive in Canada, Bagot continued with his duties, ever weaker but still urbanely cheerful and uncomplaining, supported by the sympathy and affection of the peoples of both Canadas, especially the French Canadians. He had long since lost any sense of disapproval or distrust of his reform ministers. He worked freely and in full confidence with them, and they repaid him with their warm esteem. Robert Baldwin, who had been Bagot's *bête noire*, but who could always forgive a man if not a principle, wrote sensitively of him, ". . . we owe a deep debt of gratitude to poor Sir Charles Bagot. He had many early prejudices to overcome before he could bring himself to make the great stand he did make. We must not estimate his course by what *we* know of ease and safety, but by what he may, nay *must*, have imagined of its difficulty and danger."[57] And Viger, the old *patriote* radical, declared for his part, "L'administration de Sir Charles Bagot a déjà refermé les plaies et parlé au cœur du peuple. . . ."[58]

It had certainly not been Bagot's work alone. Baldwin had shaped the doctrine; LaFontaine had faithfully applied it, to make Bagot accept a government reconstructed by the will of parliament, not his own. And by no means least was William Draper, who from the other side of politics had all but forced Bagot's hand, by his clear-sighted recognition that the ministry had to be remade on the French Canadians' terms, and by his own insistence on resigning to open the way.[59] Yet none of this removes Bagot's own responsibility for his action; nor did it, in the eyes of the British government or the Canadian people at the time.

The Governor himself saw things as plainly as always. "I leave this world," he told Stanley, "not satisfied that my measures will be successful, but that I had no choice in regard to them if the Union was to be maintained."[60] Yet he equally recognized that "whether the doctrine of responsible government is openly acknowledged or is only tacitly acquiesced in, virtually it exists."[61] Dying, he carried on as best as he could, because he felt "my own personal honour and reputation are involved—deeply and everlastingly involved in my remaining in this Country."[62] At last in March 1843, his successor, Metcalfe, reached Kingston, and Bagot sent a final message to his ministers: "My reputation is in your hands, I know that you will all protect it. I am too exhausted to say more. . . ."[63] He died a few weeks later. So passed not a great governor, but a man of honour and of calm good sense, whose diplomatic realism made him the instrument of changes he had never anticipated when he entered on his brief and critical period of office in Canada.

CHAPTER 5

Metcalfe and Check

1843-1844

The inhabitants of the lower St Lawrence county of Rimouski must have felt doubt as well as satisfaction on January 30, 1843. Ninety-nine per cent French-speaking, they had just elected an alien English-speaking Upper Canadian who had never yet been in the county—Robert Baldwin. Of course there was the precedent of LaFontaine's own election for an Upper Canadian seat; but he at least had visited Fourth York to present himself, while Baldwin, as Attorney General, would not find time to go down to Rimouski for several months to come. The whole episode demonstrated LaFontaine's hold on the French *réformistes*, and the power of the party alliance he and Baldwin had forged. Even before the western liberal leader had lost his by-election in Hastings the previous October, LaFontaine had offered to find him a Lower Canadian seat in case of failure, since Hastings was a difficult constituency with a large tory vote. And Baldwin had gladly agreed, recognizing the value of this reciprocal gesture from his French-Canadian allies.[1]

As a matter of fact, twenty-five French members—including Viger—offered to retire in favour of Baldwin, but it was finally decided that Borne of Rimouski should resign his seat.[2] LaFontaine told his western confrère that he had arranged to "do the needful" in the county.[3] In due course, in January 1843, the electors of Rimouski sent Baldwin a cordial invitation to stand as their member. He accepted as warmly, answering that the honour done him "seul réfute mieux que tous les arguments les fausses imputations si souvent portées contre les réformistes du Bas-Canada, que leur lutte était une lutte de races, qu'ils étaient des hommes intraitables, guidés par leur seule haine contre le gouvernement sous lequel ils vivaient."[4] He was elected by acclamation, to ready cheers for Baldwin, LaFontaine, and responsible government. However much they may have wondered, the men of Rimouski were obviously proud of the role they had been given to play in the now dominant political alliance.

Indeed, by the time the new governor-general, Sir Charles Metcalfe, arrived, there was virtually a reform ministry governing Canada. Because of Bagot's long illness, much of the conduct of affairs had fallen to the councillors themselves, led by LaFontaine and Baldwin almost as co-premiers of a cabinet. The government was functioning harmoniously under their direction, but by now it plainly had a strong party tinge. After all, only Daly and Killaly could not be considered as reformers of one shade or other, and they were officials rather than conservatives. Moreover, reformers in office were making the best use of their position to improve their party's lot. Patronage, the right to appoint to public posts, properly belonged to the governor himself, but much of it could be exercised through his ministers and the departments they controlled. And a reform associate of Baldwin, James Hervey Price, succinctly reminded him, "Patronage is power."[5] Bagot had shown a not unreasonable disposition still to make some appointments on his own. They were not always consonant with the party interests of Baldwin and LaFontaine; but after some heart-burning, protests were withheld in view of Bagot's failing health.[6] Aside from this, however, Hincks and Small in Upper Canada, LaFontaine in Lower, had been busy strengthening the popular basis of the reform alliance through the careful distribution of posts. LaFontaine had evinced particular care to give his people concrete proof of the benefits of union and his policies, by making strings of appointments from magistrates to postal clerks, and asking French-Canadian members of parliament to submit favoured party candidates of their own.[7] In brief, the reform alliance could scarcely have looked more fully in control of the situation.

Yet reformers were not so securely in the saddle. The bond between Baldwin and LaFontaine was personal and strong, but there were few ties lower down between their dual parties. Moreover, in the French party the Neilson-Viger-Papineau elements had not wholly succumbed to LaFontaine's authoritative direction; and as for the English-speaking liberals, it was really only within the ministry that their advanced and moderate wings were effectively joined. There was still a good deal of mutual suspicion and distrust between them, left from the time of their division under Sydenham. New issues might yet produce new combinations to shatter the apparent reform unity.

Then there were older issues, but temporarily set aside. There was the university question in Canada West. The very opening of King's College in 1843 stimulated forces hostile to Anglican control of the university endowment. Methodists and Presbyterians, struggling to develop their colleges, wanted shares of their own in the public funds for university support, while Baldwin and the advanced reformers generally thought in terms of a measure to create a wholly secularized provincial university. There was also the problem of the Orange Order, and the persistent power it wielded. Many western reformers, again recalling the elections of 1841, wanted to see Orangism curbed, while tories, already bitter over the reform invasion of their old realm of patronage, were determined to resist any further partisan attempt—as they saw it—to undermine their political strength. And there was the problem of the seat of government. Kingston in most eyes had proved too small and inconvenient. Bagot had thought so himself, preferring Montreal or Quebec;[8] the parliament of 1842 had passed a resolution declaring Kingston unsuitable. French Canadians particularly wanted the capital moved, preferably to Montreal, a central location where they would feel less alien. Yet the regional jealousies roused by this issue alone could shake the seeming reform dominance over the union.

Furthermore, trade had taken a down-turn since the boom of 1841, also rousing misgivings. The English market had slackened, and shipping had declined on the St Lawrence during the 1842 season, as both the timber and grain trades went through disturbances. That year, Britain had effectively cut the colonial timber preference by reducing the duty on foreign timber from fifty-five to thirty shillings, and there were other changes in Sir Robert Peel's broadly reforming budget of 1842 that could have serious consequences for Canada. The changes were obviously moving in the direction of free trade. Peel was not yet a convert to the pure doctrine: he was a pragmatic reformer in fiscal affairs, seeking to increase economic activity, and thus revenues, through lowering import duties on raw materials. He still accepted the need to protect British agriculture and to maintain some preference for staple colonial products. Yet the grand reduction of customs duties in his budget of 1842, and the establishment of an income tax to replace them, accorded well with the ideas of British free-traders. Conversely, Canadian merchants tied to a pattern of imperial trade protection might feel a sharp twinge of alarm. They also saw British North America's old privileges in the West Indies provisions trade lost, as the mother country threw open commerce with her island colonies. And when the new Corn Law of 1842, as part of the trend, lowered the scale of duties on grain entering Great Britain, the improvement for Canadian exporters was not large enough to make an important difference in the costs of the transatlantic trade. On balance, then, the imperial commercial changes of 1842 had been anything but helpful.

There was still one significant hope: that the process of tariff reduction might be carried onward in at least one instance to provide for the free, or all but free, entry of colonial grain into the United Kingdom. This would effectively combine the trend to freer trade with preferential treatment for colonies. It would not seriously threaten British agriculture, yet it would realize a long-sought goal for Canada. Peel and Stanley were by no means averse to such a concession to colonial interest, as long as Canada would act to limit the importation of bread-stuffs from the United States into the province, so that the British market could not be flooded with American wheat and flour coming via the St Lawrence in the guise of colonial produce at a much lower rate of duty.[9] Thus it was that the Canadian parliament had levied its three-shilling tariff on American cereals in the autumn session of 1842. And thus it was that the imperial parliament proceeded to pass the Canada Corn Act in its session of 1843, which admitted Canadian wheat at the almost nominal charge of one shilling a quarter, and flour milled in Canada at a rate proportionate.

This notable success for the Canadian commercial system offset the other losses, and seemed a victory extracted from the very threat of free trade. Yet the truth was that the Canada Corn Act was only a favourable tack in an imperial course set towards a free-trade destination, and hence to the elimination in the long run of the whole colonial preferential structure. In the short run, Canada's grain trade might thrive because of the enactment, and its milling industry expand rapidly, since it was still profitable to import American wheat under the provincial tariff and grind it into flour for export under the highly favourable preference.[10] But too great investment in a measure that to Britain was a minor concession in a broad sweep of change might only make the long-run results that much more drastic for the province. For the present, however, commercial conditions improved in Canada, in anticipation of the enlarged grain preference (which would not go into effect until October, 1843), while the merchants of the timber trade soon recovered, finding after their initial fright that they could still prosper even under the reduced differential rates set by the Peel government in 1842.

That government might be adopting changed economic views, but in appointing a new governor-general for Canada its political thinking had remained essentially unaltered. Sir Charles Theophilus Metcalfe was to continue the system of harmony instituted under Sydenham and challenged under Bagot. There was no thought of renouncing the developments of Bagot's régime, the admission of the French Canadians as a group to power, the demonstration of the ministers' responsibility to parliament. Yet, though even the term "responsible government" was itself now admitted and quite respectable, it was not to develop any further—to become fully party government, as Baldwin and his friends assumed.[11] The governor was still to play a decisive role in choosing and mediating between parties. The rights of the Crown's representative were to be upheld, and any diminution of them, as had occurred through Bagot's exigencies, was to be checked forthwith. Accordingly, the British authorities had chosen a highly competent and experienced colonial administrator in Metcalfe, to govern Canada. He was not to go back; but he was to stand firm. He was to maintain the imperial system of harmony—which, in reality, was steadily being transmuted into colonial party rule.

Metcalfe, indeed, seemed an excellent choice, both for firm and fair government. He had an admirable record as an efficient, liberal-minded governor in Jamaica and India; in England he favoured a wider franchise, and vote by ballot; he thought himself almost too radical to be a whig.[12] Certainly there was reason for Wakefield (always first) to pass the news exultantly to LaFontaine that Canada now had "the *perfect* Governor General."[13] Moreover, Metcalfe and Stanley both believed that the governor had to rule in Canada with public support, through ministers backed by parliament. But his own sphere of action, the Crown's prerogative he exercised, was to be preserved from over-mighty councillors, lest they make him a mere puppet and instrument of selfish party designs. Hence Stanley would instruct him to make clear to his council that, "although you consult with them, and are willing to pay due deference to their advice, you are yourself the head of your administration . . . not even bound to adopt their advice, although always bound to receive it."[14]

This concept of the governor's impartial leadership above partisan interests was not an unworthy one. The question, still, was whether it could be maintained in the face of Canadian party politics that grew naturally out of a popular representative system. And there was a further question raised by Metcalfe's own personality. He had unflinching courage, wise generosity, and the best of intentions to rule in justice and tolerance. He was a living embodiment of what the English, at least, would hold to be the native John Bull: kindly, sturdily reliable, unassuming and good-tempered. But there was an underlying rigidity of mind, a tendency to go by fixed conceptions, a doggedness that was not always a virtue. Perhaps, at fifty-eight, he came to Canada too late in his career to adapt. At any rate, there was little in his long experience as a benevolent despot in India or as overlord of a plantocracy in Jamaica to equip him for a Canadian democratic society fast consolidating out of the pioneer stage. In such an environment, determined directness was not necessarily a good substitute for the verve of Sydenham, the tactful prudence of Bagot. Too often Metcalfe tended to deal in black and white stereotypes of loyalty and disaffection, patriotism and self-seeking; not the kaleidoscopic greys of Canadian political facts. He would execute Stanley's policies efficiently, and carry out his instructions devotedly. But he would prove a gallant failure in his own cause.

II

Metcalfe arrived in Kingston at the end of March, 1843, a portly, jovial-looking figure, not unhandsome, though with the ominous swelling of a cancerous tumour on one cheek that had already failed to yield to surgery. He took over from the dying Bagot without difficulty. For the opening weeks of the new régime there was apparent tranquillity as the Governor General worked with ministers who were, after all, his legitimate councillors, deserving of his confidence until proved otherwise. But both sides were swiftly forming their impressions. By mid April the Solicitor General West, Small, was already relaying a report to Baldwin of the likelihood of a clash with this new and different Sir Charles,[15] and the Governor had written home deploring the violent party spirit he found in Canada. "My chief object," he said, "will be to bring all into harmony"—and added significantly—"but I do not expect success."[16] An air of pessimism, no good augury for concord, was there from the start. So were his all-too-sharp assumptions. He concluded that "republicans" and anti-British French held power, and that he was condemned to govern "to the utter exclusion of those on whom the mother country might consistently rely in the hour of need."[17] He could not, he declared, ". . . surrender the Queen's government into the hands of rebels. . . . I know not what the end will be. The only thing certain is that I cannot yield."[18]

To Stanley he sent a fuller judgement of the situation, reporting that the events under Bagot had led all parties in Canada to assume that responsible government had been fully established. The result was that "The Council are now spoken of by themselves and others generally as 'the Ministers', 'the Administration', 'the Cabinet', 'the Government', and so forth. Their pretensions are according to this new nomenclature. They regard themselves as a responsible ministry and expect that the policy and conduct of the governor shall be subservient to their views and party purposes."[19] Bagot had not lived long enough to face these consequences of his forced concessions; but, to Metcalfe, the one question now was "whether the Governor shall be solely and completely a tool in the hands of the Council, or whether he shall have any exercise of his own judgement in the administration of the government."[20]

It grew increasingly apparent in May that the testing of that question could come on the matter of patronage. Stanley specifically instructed the Governor to keep firm control of "the patronage of the Crown . . . as long as you keep it in your hands and refuse to apply it exclusively to party purposes, it will be felt that you have really substantial power."[21] Metcalfe himself was determined not to lend it. What, indeed, would be left for "his own judgement in the administration" if he merely filled up the offices through which the government exercised its authority at the behest of a faction that was temporarily dominant in his council? The answer was even plainer when it appeared that (in Metcalfe's terms) "the loyal portion of the people" could not obtain a fair share of places from "a rebel government."[22] Certainly any attempt on his part to spread favours to tories and conservatives would only rouse hostility in reform ranks.

As for the reformers in the council, it was quite true that they sought to use the Crown's patronage for party purposes. This was the vulgar, venal, yet inevitable corollary of the grand triumph of the people in government. Those who had won wanted the rewards of office that had once gone to a tory clientele. There was a hard practicality about politicians like LaFontaine and Hincks (Baldwin would prefer to deal in theory) which clearly recognized that patronage was the tie that binds, a powerful means of holding imperfect human beings together to make a party strong for gaining and keeping power. The dispensing of posts which they and their associates accordingly sought to effect might be viewed either as the entrenching and cementing of a reform party organization, or as the due admission to public appointments of elements long excluded in both Canadas by the old office-holding monopoly. It was both, no doubt. Yet the control of patronage was also vital to any government's authority. And in the absence of a well-developed non-partisan civil service, no reform administration could operate effectively through subordinates who might be active supporters of its party foes. Of course, to Metcalfe the government was not, and should not be, a reform administration. But once more he faced the inexorable growth of party rule within a popular representative system. It followed logically that if a reform alliance could dominate assembly and ministry, it would insist on controlling patronage as a basic attribute of the power it had achieved. Nor would tory-conservatives really want things otherwise for themselves.

Minor clashes arose over patronage matters during the late spring and summer. Captain Higginson, Metcalfe's civil secretary, interviewed LaFontaine on the subject, and both sides made clear their position and its relation to their view of responsible rule.[23] Yet governor and councillors avoided bringing the issue to a head in a mutual effort to show that they were being as co-operative and fair-minded as possible. Still, Metcalfe did begin probing approaches eastward to Viger and the still powerful Papineau family connection, who might bring him French-Canadian support alternative to LaFontaine. He already hoped to get rid of his "dictatorial Councillor," and rightly perceived that within the apparent unity of the French party Viger was prominent among ex-*patriotes* and particularists who had by no means fully accepted LaFontaine's peremptory control.[24] In another direction, also seeking to strengthen his position as arbiter between parties, and not their servant, the Governor opened a significant line of communication to western conservatives. In July he held a cordial interview with Ogle Gowan, Grand Master of the Orange Order, an able, clear-sighted politician, not personally an extremist, and particularly clear on the interests of Ogle Gowan. Metcalfe conferred also with other leading conservatives; again inviting resentment from his reform councillors, who believed not in the Governor's impartiality but in his obligation to rely solely on his official advisers. Indeed, by now he was on close terms only with Dominick Daly in the council: a veteran civil servant like himself, and not a party man.

Parliament met in late September. At first everything seemed to go well for the LaFontaine-Baldwin ministers. They passed a basic Common Schools Act for Upper Canada, replacing the rudimentary law of 1841. They reformed the judicial system of Canada East, and successfully carried a measure to move the seat of government to Montreal. But the last brought Harrison's resignation as a councillor, honour-bound to oppose it as member for Kingston. It also brought a growing Upper Canadian reaction, encouraged by the tories and based on the feeling that the ministers were sacrificing western interests to their French-Canadian allies. Then came Baldwin's bill to reduce political disorders by making all secret societies but the freemasons illegal. This was patently aimed at the Orange Order, and its members hotly denounced it as the outright persecution of loyal subjects by vindictive political foes. In Toronto, a mob gathered to burn effigies of Baldwin and Hincks outside the former's home. Little Eliza Baldwin wrote to her father in Kingston that Mr Hincks blazed nicely—"but they could not get you to burn at all."[25]

The Secret Societies Bill still passed easily; indeed, with a Protestant majority behind it.[26] But Metcalfe, regarding it as highly partisan legislation, though introduced by his own minister, unexpectedly reserved it for the authorities in London. There it was subsequently disallowed. The Governor's action scarcely improved relations with his councillors, although it assured him an enthusiastic Orange following. It also made this point: that Metcalfe's attempts to hold a judicious balance between parties was more likely instead to commit him to one side against the other, in the eyes of the public; and the commitment would surely be on the side of loyalty, as he saw it. Meanwhile parliament had moved on to another contentious measure, Baldwin's University Bill. Introduced early in November, it would transform King's College from an Anglican institution into a non-sectarian arts college in a "University of Toronto," with which other denominational colleges might affiliate, but as little more than divinity halls with small grants from the public funds. It expressed the Anglican Baldwin's own strong belief in state higher education; yet it invited the attack of John Strachan and the Church of England, and of other denominational interests as well.

Before the University Bill of 1843 could be put to the test, however, the long-brewing ministerial crisis had burst on the question of patronage. Metcalfe's selection of a conservative Clerk of the Peace for the Dalhousie district—ignoring and not even informing Baldwin—and his offering of the post of Speaker of the Legislative Council to leading opponents of his liberal ministers, supplied occasion rather than cause for the outburst.[27] They were only the latest of several examples of his exercise of patronage without consultation, much less agreement, and they came when the strains of the session had sharply aggravated friction between governor and reform ministers. Determined now to make a stand, Baldwin and LaFontaine saw Metcalfe on November 24, flatly demanding that he make no appointment without first receiving the executive council's advice, and after receiving it, make none prejudicial to their "influence."[28] Of course the Governor as flatly refused. And he rejected a further approach by the full council as implying "the virtual surrender into the hands of the Council of the prerogative of the Crown."[29] Nor was it any use to argue that the ministers only sought to carry out the principle of responsible government. In the sense that this meant party government, Metcalfe, obeying his own instructions, stood adamantly opposed.

On November 26, therefore, all the members of the executive council but Daly resigned. A grimly resolute governor informed Stanley, "Whatever may happen, I do not mean at any time to take back Mr Lafontaine or Mr Baldwin. Both are intolerable."[30] Explanations followed in an excited parliament, as both sides appealed to the vaguely worded Harrison-Baldwin Resolutions of 1841 for their justification. Baldwin strongly contended that the Governor's use of patronage against or without the council's advice was a denial of responsible government as acknowledged in those resolutions. Through Daly, Metcalfe readily endorsed the same resolutions, and a system of government "which recognizes the responsibility to the people and to the responsible assembly." But, he declared incisively, no principle was in question: only whether "the patronage of the Crown should be surrendered to the assembly for the purchase of parliamentary support."[31]

The assembly itself favoured the views of the ex-ministers, as might be expected, seeing that they had originally been brought into power by the alliance of French-Canadian and western reformers in the assembly. The grand debate that followed on the constitutional question made that basic fact plain, however forceful the oratory of Viger, MacNab and Wakefield on the one side against that of LaFontaine, Price and Baldwin on the other. Yet the Governor's position had won supporters other than the conservative members of the opposition. Wakefield's change of sides was at least partly influenced by his falling-out with the former liberal ministers over his Beauharnois schemes.[32] But men like Viger and Neilson would essentially prefer to deal with a forthright colonial governor, whose role of authority they could better understand than the new-fangled doctrines of responsible government upheld by LaFontaine and his dubious alliance with Upper Canadians. Furthermore, Metcalfe's claim to stand for patriotism above parties appealed to a man like William Draper, now a member of the legislative council, and no vehement partisan himself. As the debate went on in parliament in early December, the Governor thus was busily conferring with Draper, Wakefield, and Viger, as well as with regular tory chieftains like MacNab. But nothing could overcome the numbers which the indignant reform ex-ministers had behind them in the house. Consequently, nothing could prevent the passage of Price's motion, 46 to 23, deeply regretting the retirement of the former councillors, who, it was asserted, still had the confidence of parliament.[33] Faced with this bluntly hostile declaration, and needing time to reconstitute his council, Metcalfe reluctantly prorogued the legislature on December 9.

The government crisis still continued as 1843 drew to a close. Indeed, it would be a long time before Metcalfe's reaction to the power of partyism had fully worked itself out. Yet, in the truest sense, it was not so much a reaction as a check. It remained less an attempt to reverse change than to arrest its continued advance. And the development of the full implications of responsible rule in Canada had been only temporarily halted; nothing more. Nor had Metcalfe attempted to oppose responsible government head-on. He continued, quite sincerely, to admit much of it; he sought merely to hold back some of the Crown's prerogative, some of its scope for decision. The attempt would still not succeed; but because of its limited character, angry feelings would not give rise to wholly dangerous disorders. Political issues in the months ahead could still be handled within constitutional frames, especially since the future looked far from desperate for the reform forces now in opposition.

Upon the chessboard of Canadian politics, challenge to the ruling system had been followed by check to its opponents; but the game had been advanced, nevertheless. Through challenge under Bagot, the French Canadians and the Baldwin reformers had achieved governing power; dual participation had replaced assimilation as the essence of the union, and an all-but-party ministry had emerged. Through check under Metcalfe, the governor and tory-conservative elements would now be given an opportunity to show what they could do to rule Canada without yielding to party government. Yet notably enough, they would end virtually where the reformers would have done themselves.

III

The snows of a bitter January, 1844, flew scarcely thicker than rumours about the reconstruction of the Canadian government. It was said that Morin among others would defect from LaFontaine to join the Governor's council. The mighty Louis-Joseph Papineau, some averred, would soon be recalled from exile into office. And others claimed that the real governor now was Edward Gibbon Wakefield, who warmly defended Metcalfe as upholding the true principles of responsible rule.[34] The ingenious, enter-prising Wakefield, "in and out of the public offices all day," was certainly not one to disclaim high influence behind the scenes.[35] It would seem, however, that his prime concern still remained the promoting of his interest in Beauharnois lands and the new Beauharnois Canal.[36] In any case, he was shortly to leave Canada for ventures elsewhere. And there was very little in the other wildly spinning rumours either.

Yet they spread inevitably, as Metcalfe governed with only three councillors, postponing parliament until he could construct a ministry to face it anew. His provisional government consisted of faithful Dominick Daly (popularly termed Perpetual Secretary), together with Draper and Viger, both of whom had accepted places as executive councillors without precise ministerial offices on December 12, 1843. Draper's return to the Governor's side, with the essential task ahead of him of re-making the western half of the ministry, spurred the Toronto *Examiner* to cordial comments on Met-calfe's "infatuation" and "imbecility," comments similar to those that the tory press had so freely applied to Bagot's naming of liberal ministers.[37] Still, the moderate conservative Draper plainly shared Metcalfe's opinions on responsible government. The appointment of Denis-Benjamin Viger looked more startling—the French-Canadian nationalist elder statesman, cousin of Papineau, and hero of decades of parliamentary struggle against former British governors.

But Viger, without departing from any ultimate hope of a separate, self-governing French-Canadian nation, could see justice in the Governor Gen-eral's position under the existing provincial constitution. Indeed, as an expert on constitutional practice, he had felt called upon to defend Metcalfe against the high-handed, unseemly mode of resignation taken by his late advisers. More important, *le Vénérable* had grown convinced that more could presently be gained for French Canadians through their working as a distinct national bloc under a governor who desperately needed their aid, than by holding to a mongrel French-English alliance in the assembly. On his part, Metcalfe had every desire to maintain and develop the French-Cana-dian goodwill inherited from Bagot, and hoped to do so through Viger's high prestige. Hence he sought a general amnesty for the rebels of 1837 still prisoners in Van Diemen's Land, and even forwarded a remarkable request to London for the payment of arrears of salary to that proscribed exile, Papineau, as the former Speaker of the Lower Canadian assembly.[38] In any case, he wanted to maintain the French Canadians' participation as a group in government. His superiors in England were in agreement: so thin had the policy of assimilation worn by now. Metcalfe himself stood ready virtually to abandon it.[39]

In gaining Viger and Neilson, however, and some valuable press support, the Governor had not yet broken the hold which LaFontaine had acquired over his people. And there were problems in English Canada, too. Metcalfe's unchanging ideal, and his answer to party government, was a ministry of all the talents: the best men, drawn from every quarter; men whose patriotism would rise above narrow partisanship. It was a noble principle—but it had seldom worked, either in the high imperial politics of Britain or in the low colonial strife of Canada. Draper himself, earnestly trusting that "public consideration" would "prevail over party feeling," sought a broad liberal-conservative coalition of moderate men.[40] But he could not persuade the canny Harrison to re-enter office and bring with him some moderate Upper Canadian reform colleagues, nor could he even attract the conciliatory William Hamilton Merritt, the prominent western business man who had been a conservative and then a moderate before adopting Baldwin's version of responsible government. Draper's one real acquisition was Egerton Ryerson, now principal of Victoria College—an opponent, in turn, of tory and radical extremes in Upper Canada before 1837, and well worth having as a noted publicist and leading figure in the powerful Methodist community. But Ryerson, soon to be named superintendent of education for Canada West, would still not be of ministerial rank, despite the influence he might exert on public opinion.

Great as were the government's difficulties in the West, its difficulties in the East continued to be greater. There Viger enjoyed profound personal respect; he had his close connection with the still-powerful Papineau clan; and he stood in the strong French-Canadian tradition of acting as a separate national group, aloof from entanglement with *les Anglais*. Yet he faced one of the ablest party leaders in Canada's history, who represented an alternative tradition of political co-operation as a means to French national survival and who could point to the practical success of his policies under the once-dreaded union. Despite his best efforts and general air of confidence, Viger, the suave old aristocrat, could not detach men of ministerial calibre from the cold, brusque, expertly calculating LaFontaine. The latter had vigorous agents to run the party machinery in the key Lower Canadian centres: Thomas Cushing Aylwin in Quebec, Lewis Thomas Drummond in Montreal —both of English-speaking origin, but bilingual, and firmly identified with the French-Canadian interest. And keen, resourceful younger men were associated with the local LaFontaine *cadres*: Cartier in Montreal, Cauchon in Quebec. LaFontaine had also acquired the most powerful press support. He and his friends had secured the revival of *La Minerve* of Montreal in 1842, under Ludger Duvernay, its old editor, and founder of the Saint-Jean-

Baptiste Society. At the same time, Cauchon produced the new *Journal de Québec*, whose brilliant if ruthless invective made up for the falling-off of *Le Canadien* now that Parent had left politics. And this press pounded home the essentially simple argument that French Canadians had only to stay united under LaFontaine to compel the Governor to a full recognition of the responsible system and ensure *survivance*. It was no wonder that a worried Dominick Daly wrote to Viger hoping he was "in better spirits than I *own I am* at the moment. . . . *Mais le Bon Dieu est Canadien*. Espérons!"[41]

The LaFontaine party also made good use of their alliance with the western reformers. Francis Hincks moved to Montreal to apply his uncommon and unsparing skills to the cause in Lower Canada. In early March, 1844, he launched the *Pilot*, as a new, much-needed English liberal organ in Canada's capital-to-be. And he joined with relish in the Montreal by-election, brought on there as a test of strength by the LaFontaine forces through persuading one of the city members, Benjamin Holmes, to resign his seat. In his stead they put up Drummond, a handsome, popular Irish Catholic lawyer eloquent in both languages. Viger and the Montreal English conservatives finally agreed on the tory, William Molson, as government candidate; but he was no match for Drummond's flooding oratory and the efficient campaign of press propaganda and mass meetings run by Cartier and Hincks. The last-named also organized the Irish canal labourers into rowdy shock-troops for the polls. When they closed in mid April, after bloody violence on both sides, the LaFontaine interests had decisively defeated the Viger-Metcalfe forces and made a telling demonstration of unbroken party unity.

But in Canada West the situation was improving for the Governor. Metcalfe had steadily insisted that the only issue was control of patronage and that his administration had always followed the responsible principle—"in the reasonable construction of that undefined Theory," as he said to Stanley.[42] "I have avowed my adherence to Responsible Government views to the fullest extent which it can be avowed in a Colony, and it must be either Blindness or Disaffection that can desire to get further."[43] And while he stood for impartiality and British principle, the Baldwin reformers could be accused of throwing the country into crisis in a selfish grab for party power, in a blatant attempt to introduce the spoils system of American republican democracy. Even as the crisis dragged on, and as reform denunciations of the provisional council rose in vehement impatience, Metcalfe benefited from a growing apprehension in Upper Canada that the Baldwinites were indeed imperilling British institutions through simple greed for the fruits of office. Robert Baldwin Sullivan (who had now fully committed himself both to temperance and to reform) forecast the Governor's line of policy with gloomy insight: ". . . no dissolution of Parliament until the public are wearied with contention, no formation of a new ministry until corrupt men are wearied with a forced show of Patriotism, or until weak ones are frightened—no decisive step taken to close the door upon the tories until they are fully made use of ... for my part I shall not be surprised if the contest should turn out very doubtful."[44]

Isaac Buchanan, the wealthy Toronto business liberal who had backed the former ministers at their resignation, now came out for Metcalfe in the name of true, and moderate, reform. The middle-ground *British Colonist* of Toronto took up the cause of "Loyal Hearts and Liberal Measures."[45] In short, Baldwin and his adherents faced a serious danger that "moderate" sentiment for non-partisan rule would split western reform ranks anew and actually throw the balance to tory and conservative opponents. With due concern, they founded a Reform Association to organize party support throughout the West, and fostered a new reform paper in Toronto, the *Globe*, to preach the pure doctrine of responsible government to Upper Canada. It was launched in March, on the same day as Hincks's Montreal *Pilot*, by a forceful twenty-five-year-old Scots immigrant, George Brown. He had lately come from New York with his father to publish a weekly on behalf of the Free Church movement within Canadian Presbyterianism, which was breaking away from the main body of the Kirk—a reflection of the disruption of the church that had occurred in Scotland the year before. But Brown's real forte was zealous political journalism. As the *Examiner* had lost some of its power since Hincks had left it, Baldwin and company were glad to avail themselves of the young editor's new enterprise. "I am rather prepossessed in favour of the man, as far as manner goes," the cautious Baldwin wrote to LaFontaine, as a potent new force in Canadian affairs was born.[46]

Through the spring and into the summer, argument and recrimination raged across Canada West, as Metcalfe's defenders charged reformers with seeking to subvert the constitution, while the latter replied that the Governor himself had subverted it, having tossed away the Resolutions of 1841. Above all, Egerton Ryerson sailed full into battle thundering broadsides. He filled papers like the *British Colonist* with enormous disquisitions on the historical, constitutional, and moral rectitude of Metcalfe's stand. Neither the *Globe*'s lusty scorn nor Sullivan's witty articles in reply could offset Ryerson's appeal to those who felt that the Baldwinites had pressed too far and too hard.[47] Furthermore, the Governor's own appeals to loyal sentiments, in response to the host of addresses he received in praise or protest from public bodies, did not fail to make an impression in an Upper Canada sensitive to such a call from the time of original loyalist settlement, the War of 1812, or the Rebellion of 1837. Still further, in May, Metcalfe had undergone another agonizing operation on the malign tumour on his cheek. It did little to stop the cancerous growth; the sight of one eye was soon affected.[48] But there was sympathy for the governor who bore his private, unrelenting pain with quiet dignity; and the harsh outpourings of some of the western reformers did their cause more harm than good.

Marking, perhaps, the changing mood in Canada West, Draper's patient efforts to rebuild the ministry at last achieved a measure of success. William Morris consented to join as Receiver General: an influential moderate, who had long been the chief lay leader of the Church of Scotland element. Henry Sherwood also agreed to come in again as Solicitor General West, thus bringing the no-party administration significant tory support. In fact, matters were looking considerably better for the Metcalfe régime in the West. But in the eastern section they had scarcely improved at all. There, Viger for months had been promising with bland assurance that he would soon secure a substantial French-Canadian following; but the truth was, he had still been unable to break LaFontaine's grip. Draper had spent much of July in Montreal, studying the situation for himself, and finding what little headway Viger had made. It had not been for want of trying. The elderly ex-radical had written and published political tracts condemning the "ci-devant" ministers; worked his press organ, L'Aurore, to the full; tried to detach Morin and other prominent French Canadians—even sought unavailingly to persuade his cousin Louis-Joseph Papineau to return from exile and back Metcalfe.[49] About all he had managed to do was acquire Denis-Benjamin Papineau, the great man's brother, and now member for Ottawa county. Yet D.-B. Papineau, though he had the aura of the family name, had little political experience and was hampered by partial deafness besides.

Hence Draper could see no cause for further delay: the eastern offices would have to be filled up somehow; the ministry would have to look essentially to western backing. Late in August, Viger grandly announced the council to be completed. He would serve as President of the Council, Denis Papineau as Commissioner of Crown Lands, and James Smith, a little-known Montreal lawyer, as Attorney General East. The new ministers for Canada West were also sworn in early in September, while Draper now became officially Attorney General West. Metcalfe's government was still short of members, after ten months of protracted crisis and provisional rule. But at least it was complete enough to face the people and let the Governor try his case with them. For there seemed little use in meeting the old unfriendly parliament again, which through all these months had been repeatedly postponed by proclamation. On September 23, the legislature was formally dissolved, and a call for elections issued. As Metcalfe himself told Stanley, it was done not "with any great confidence, but as the least of all evils."[50]

IV

In Canada West, the autumn election campaigns poured out the passions that had built up for a year. Baldwinites, under the banner of the Reform Association, charged into action with the fierce righteousness of crusaders enabled at last to crush the infidels. Tories and conservatives rushed no less fiercely at the foes of British rule and the would-be assassins of empire. Calmer minds of course recognized that Baldwin and company were not out to impose Yankee republicanism or inspire revolt. Yet still they feared, with Ryerson, that the reformers' insistence on party rule, at the cost of destroying the governor's prerogative, would lead to "a practical declaration of independence."[51] And Stewart Derbishire, moderate reform member for Bytown, wrote to Baldwin, "Whatever the 'tendency' of your doctrines, which can but be matter of conjecture, the tendency of these denunciations against a large party in the Country to operate as invitations to another to attack them in the name of the Crown, and so lead to a civil War, cannot be doubted—*is not doubted* by any one with whom I speak."[52]

Metcalfe himself completely dismissed the reformers' own assertions, from Baldwin down, that they sought not to uproot the British system of government but to realize it. He regarded ". . . their faint profession of a desire to perpetuate the connexion of this Colony with the Mother Country as utterly worthless, although I do not imagine that generally they have separation as their immediate object. Their present views being to establish the power of their party, and to be sustained at the expense of the British Nation, but with perfect independence of its supremacy in the Government of the Province."[53] Holding these beliefs, Metcalfe inevitably thrust himself into the campaign in sheer duty to his office, in spite of agony as cancer ate across his face. He sought to be a Sydenham, guiding opinion as the people's leader above party. Instead, as tories, conservatives and Orangemen rallied to "the brave old Square-toed gentleman, he of the stainless name," he only became more fully committed as a partisan symbol himself.[54] Rather than a Sydenham, in fact, he became a Bond Head, intensifying the bitter party spirit on both sides.

Epithets flew freely. The Governor was not only Old Square-toes to ranting reformers; he was also a Hindu despot, the Old Squaw, and Charles the Simple.[55] In return, Baldwin, the qualifying, cautious Baldwin, was a raving republican, and Hincks, according to the tory Toronto *Patriot*, "transcendentally and undeniably the Arch-fiend of Canadian Agitators—the Satan among the fallen angels of Radicalism."[56] Charges of bribery, corruption, profligacy, religious and racial bias, filled press editorials and hustings oratory. The *Examiner*, in horror, denounced a tory candidate in Toronto as ". . . a gambler and horse-racer! The frequenter and encourager of the

Theatre and its Concomitants!"[57] The conservative candidate in Middlesex publicly characterized the local Reform Association supporters as a *"pack of lousy Scotch!"*[58]

Given this mood, it is not surprising that there should once more have been rioting and bloodshed at the polls in October, and troops called out in several places. What is surprising, rather, is that violence did not greatly exceed that of the elections of 1841, or even threaten the broad approach to civil war that Stewart Derbishire had feared. There were several reasons. One was that the penalties of the election act of 1842 did tend to restrain manipulation and intimidation.[59] Another was that, despite the common press furore, elections were still fairly localized affairs, often turning less on grand and fiery general principles than on particular local figures and practical concerns.[60] But the third and most important consideration was the absence of any serious social or economic unrest across the country, which could have made the political passions far more ugly. Agriculture, lumbering and commerce were all prosperous. The downturn of 1842 was well past; there were great expectations for the St Lawrence canals, still being steadily pushed forward; the Canada Corn Act of 1843 was in full operation. Moreover, the timber trade, for all the reduction in the preference, was thriving on the spread of the new railways in Britain, thanks to the booming demand for railway ties or sleepers. In fact, 1844 was a good year, with every hope of a still better one ahead. Crops were good and employment was plentiful. Immigration, at about 24,000, was satisfactory in both quantity and quality, producing problems neither of unmanageable numbers nor of destitution and disease.[61] Hence it was fortunate indeed that the political explosions of the elections came at a time when in other respects Canada had seldom been more tranquil.

Yet by any other standard than what might have been, the Canada West contests provided deplorably harsh and vehement expressions of partisan rancour. In Baldwin's own riding of Fourth York (he was running again for an Upper Canadian seat, while LaFontaine contested his old constituency of Terrebonne) feelings were notably high. After one wild meeting, the candidate reported, "Capt. Irving and myself were pursued by the mob of orangemen armed with clubs for a considerable distance and I have no doubt would have been severely beaten to say the least of it, had we been overtaken."[62] He was successfully returned, however, with a strong majority. Elsewhere, his party did not do so well. As the results began piling up early in November, it grew apparent that the cause of "The Governor-General—Responsible Government and British Connection" (a conservative version)[63] was winning throughout the West. Hincks himself had been beaten in Oxford, and Dunn badly defeated in Toronto, where two tory candidates were elected, one of them Sherwood. Baldwin and the Reform Association had carried only about twelve Upper Canadian seats, to nearly thirty for their tory-conservative and moderate foes.[64]

It was quite different in Canada East. The LaFontaine party grasp still held firm, and most of the elections were less closely contested and less violent. The appeal for "Metcalfe and Loyalty" did carry eight English tory seats in the Eastern Townships. Elsewhere, among French Canadians, the issue was, rather, responsible government and *survivance* according to LaFontaine or to Viger—though *La Minerve* argued boldly that "la loyauté inébranlable des Canadiens," not the tories, had saved Lower Canada for Britain in 1837; and that, under LaFontaine, the loyal French would again be "le boulevard contre la race Yankee et les idées républicaines," thus saving themselves and England's power in America.[65] *Le Canadien* spoke rather for solidarity: "Le peuple a généralement confiance dans ses représentants actuels, et nous croyons qu'il ne pourrait mieux faire que de les réélire, en leur laissant la liberté de prendre un parti d'après ce qui sera passé dans le Haut-Canada."[66] But French solidarity by now meant, above all, supporting LaFontaine's policies, the success of which had been so clearly demonstrated within the union.

Again his party campaign was skilfully managed, although he himself was tragically distracted by the sudden death, in its midst, of his thirteen-year-old niece and adopted daughter, Corinne. "You have children," he told Baldwin simply; "we have not."[67] The campaign arrangements went forward efficiently under Aylwin and Cauchon for the Quebec area, and Drummond and Cartier for Montreal. The former team not only secured their own elections and those of other party associates, but even managed to pull down the once invincible John Neilson in Quebec county, replacing him with Pierre-Joseph-Olivier Chauveau—talented and promising, if only twenty-four. As for the Montreal district, here Cartier made it his special charge to beat Viger in Richelieu. To do so, the LaFontaine men had a candidate no less illustrious as an erstwhile *patriote* champion: Dr Wolfred Nelson, once leader in battle in the rebellion of '37, but now returned from exile under amnesty, moderated, and practising medicine again. Nelson and Cartier virtually hounded poor Viger to defeat.[68] He was beaten again when he tried another constituency, Montreal county; nor would *le Vénérable* finally find a new parliamentary place until a by-election was held in the following year.

Aside from Montreal itself, where the Viger forces and the English tories did manage to defeat Drummond and elect George Moffatt and Sabrevois de Bleury, the LaFontaine side enjoyed an almost complete triumph. Drummond was found another seat. LaFontaine easily took Terrebonne. In sum, all Viger's efforts against his powerful rival elected only two French Canadians to back Metcalfe: Bleury, and D.-B. Papineau in Ottawa county.

By mid November, the LaFontaine party could count on having some twenty-eight members in parliament, including several English-speaking liberals.[69] The few remaining eastern representatives—tories, Viger men, and independents—indicated how sweeping had been the *réformiste* success in Lower Canada. Thanks to the reform disaster in Upper Canada, Metcalfe's government would still have a small over-all majority in the new assembly. Nevertheless, LaFontaine's victory in the East had at least saved the reform alliance to fight again.

When the returns were in, the eastern liberal leader was sharply dismayed by the failure in the West that had offset his own achievement, although he would still hold to the party alliance and carry on the fight in parliament.[70] The western liberal leader himself was characteristically restrained about the results in his own section.[71] Baldwin's election agent, however, burst out in exasperation, "I am sick of reformers, the infernal fools, they are so very independent, the tories would and do vote for any one their party puts up but we won't do so."[72] Still, there was more to the Upper Canadian reform defeat than this. The Baldwin liberals had gone into the elections of 1844 carrying the incubus of measures unpleasing in the West, put forward while their leaders were in the government; measures such as the removal of the capital to Lower Canada, the Secret Societies Bill, which had so outraged Orangemen and appeared to others as political proscription, and the Upper Canada Assessment Bill, brought in by Hincks, which had projected a much higher degree of local taxation, needed to make the new system of municipal government effective.

This last, "Hincks's Algerian Act" or "income tax bill," was widely attacked in western constituencies, where opponents rang the classic changes on the former ministry's combination of "waste"—high salaries, high costs—and higher taxes.[73] Charges of this sort were far more in evidence than any concerning Baldwin's presumably unpopular University Bill. Wakefield, indeed, had alleged that the reform ministers had really resigned in 1843 to avoid being defeated on the latter measure; but an examination of the weight of evidence refutes this not unbiased claim.[74] It has been well demonstrated that Baldwin's bill, far from being unpopular when before parliament in 1843, would probably have passed there, if, reversing Wakefield's assertion, the resignation of the ministers over patronage had not forced its abandonment: "The Governor, the late ministers, Reformers of all hues and even a number of moderate Tories—in short, the majority of the populace—favoured the abortive scheme of University reform. The only dissenters were High Churchmen."[75] Denominational opposition might later arise (at the time, even Ryerson favoured Baldwin's bill);[76] but it did not do so significantly even during the election of 1844, in which the university issue played no great part.[77]

In fact, a view that would ascribe the defeat of the Upper Canada reformers in 1844 pre-eminently to their failings in office rather than to the
question of patronage and loyalty does not appear to be borne out, when the
western elections are investigated constituency by constituency. Undoubtedly some measures like the Assessment Bill had an important effect; but
even the removal of the capital had manifestly lost much of its impact by
election time, and was accepted as decided fact.[78] Indeed, one comes to the
conclusion that whatever attacks there were on the reformers' past record
in office, the emotional issue of loyalty still played a critical part in deciding
the outcome in Canada West. Once again, as in 1836-38, Upper Canadians
had heard the cry that British institutions and the British tie that guaranteed their very existence were in danger. Taken up so widely, it must have
had its bearing on the results—whatever the weight of practical and local
issues—and particularly through the splitting of the reform party vote by
the loyally "moderate" movement. Actually the Metcalfe candidates, who
obtained just fifty-seven per cent of the total Upper Canada vote, seldom
won in erstwhile reform constituencies by any wide margin.[79] It seems
reasonable to assume that the "minor host called moderates," as the Toronto
Globe termed them, swung many of these seats over to the government
side.[80] Hence, Baldwin's election agent was probably not wholly wrong in
attributing the party debacle to the division of reform support.

In any case, the western reformers would need time to restore their
party's unity, so successfully maintained by LaFontaine in the East. They
would need time to convince Upper Canadians, who in the main approved
the basic idea of responsible government, that Metcalfe's interpretation of
it was inadequate; that ministerial control of patronage was not disloyalty;
that Ryerson's dire warnings of a return to the dangers of 1837 had had
little justification. And here the shortcomings of the Metcalfe system in the
next two years would do as much as anything to change public opinion
about the republican perils and party tyranny allegedly involved in the
Baldwin-LaFontaine stand. The check to the continued evolution of responsible party government would prove temporary indeed.

And yet that check perhaps had a positive function. Reformers had
evidently been pushing the pace too fast for the minds of many Upper
Canadians; and certainly for the mind of the British government, whose
policy, faithfully pursued by Metcalfe, was diametrically opposed to the
presumptions of the reform ministers of 1843. But a headlong collision
between imperial authority and Canadian popular claims had been avoided.
Despite months of crisis, Metcalfe had worked through the constitutional
process of reconstructing his ministry and holding elections. And his
government had won them, had gained a parliamentary majority, although
at considerable cost in heat and anger. Furthermore, without intending it,

the Governor had actually helped an incipient conservative party to take shape, as supporters rallied about him: one that was no longer the old tory Compact in essence, based on oligarchy; but which was based instead on the acceptance of at least a qualified form of responsible parliamentary government. Hence, out of check, would come continued development, as tory-conservatives themselves took up the business of evolving party rule.

CHAPTER 6

Crossing the Watershed

1844-1846

Montreal was now the capital of the union. The Governor General was in residence at Monklands, the handsome eighteenth-century estate once owned by Sir James Monk, which looked down on the city from the slopes of Mount Royal and far out beyond to the distant blue line of the Adirondacks. The legislature would be housed in town, in the long, plain, but capacious St Ann's Market building at the present Place Youville, well-equipped with offices and chambers for the council and assembly. Here on November 29, 1844, Sir Charles Metcalfe opened the second parliament of the union, stumbling resolutely through the Speech from the Throne. Spreading cancer made it painfully difficult for him to open his mouth; his right eye was totally blind, and the sight of the other was suffering. Nevertheless, he was satisfied with his work of shaping the new parliament—confident, as he told Stanley, of having some forty-six votes behind his government there, to only about thirty-eight for the LaFontaine-Baldwin alliance.[1]

Among those who assembled to hear the Governor deliver the Throne Speech from beneath a great red velvet canopy were many of the leaders and prominent members who had sat in the former parliament: Draper and Daly, Baldwin and LaFontaine, Morin and Taché, Merritt and Price. There were significant additions as well. Some were returning veterans such as Ogle Gowan or, on the other hand, Wolfred Nelson. Others were able new recruits like Cauchon (who would be as biting in debate as he was in journalism) or the new conservative member for Kingston, a twenty-nine-year-old Scots lawyer, John Alexander Macdonald—cheerfully unpretentious, but one day to become the most outstanding political figure of the union. In his own election campaign Macdonald had advocated the developing of Canada's resources and physical advantages, instead of wasting time and money "in fruitless discussions on abstract and theoretical questions of government."[2] It was still a far from unpopular "moderate" attitude, and would have a long future before it.

Not so theoretical, though, was the question of the existing government's strength in the new parliament. The opening trials in the assembly plainly revealed the limits of Metcalfe's would-be non-partisan administration. Its candidate for Speaker, tory Sir Allan MacNab, was elected by only three votes over the opposition's, Morin; it defeated Baldwin's want-of-confidence test on the Address by six alone.[3] Indeed, the basic problem of the Draper-Viger ministerial coalition was that it lacked a sufficiently strong and coherent party backing. Not only was it severely in the minority among the eastern members, where Viger could scarcely be said to have a party following at all, but also it was doubtful how far Draper could command the western ministerial adherents. True, they had rallied to the Governor, as in a common conservatism, to save British institutions yet operate a qualified kind of responsible government. But the Upper Canada tories who formed the core of the government majority distrusted Draper as a leader, and he returned the sentiment. They felt he had moved altogether too far from the Compact tory school where he had started, while he himself aimed at an adaptable and moderate conservative party, not one of hidebound toryism.[4] Removing the fiery, formidable MacNab to the Speaker's chair might assist him in that aim. Yet Draper's own conservative supporters were really still a minor faction within his Upper Canadian following.

Draper, then, strove to organize an effective conservative leadership, while Baldwin, supported by the *Globe*, the *Examiner* and other reform papers, tried to restore Upper Canadian confidence in liberal policy. At the same time Viger, backed by Metcalfe, went on trying to woo French Canada away from LaFontaine, while the latter sought to justify his own victory by proving that he could still advance French-Canadian interests, despite the defeat of the reform alliance in the province as a whole. Such were the party actualities beneath seeming no-party rule. Manoeuvre and counter-manoeuvre ceaselessly went on. Viger tried to capitalize on the pardoning of individual French-Canadian exiles under the Metcalfe régime. He gained a sizable advantage when in February, 1845, the Governor was able to transmit to the assembly Stanley's final agreement to a general amnesty, strongly urged by Metcalfe to win French support.[5] LaFontaine, on his part, pressed for the recognition of French as an official language of record, just as it had been in the old province of Lower Canada; only to be outplayed when D.-B. Papineau, with the Governor's concurrence, moved and carried an address requesting the removal of restrictions on the use of French. Yet this further retreat from assimilation did not stop LaFontaine's counter play of depicting the French-Canadian members of the government as *vendus*; and his powerful press spread the impression, still persisting, that he was the one great champion of French language rights.[6]

Similarly, in Canada West, Draper tried to make capital for sound, constructive conservatism, bringing in measures for retrenchment which reformers could scarcely oppose, and also for improving the administration of justice. At the same time the addition of the Compact tory, William Benjamin Robinson, to the council as Inspector General helped to strengthen Draper with the tory wing. Meanwhile the reform forces hit steadily at the government's inability to bring forward any really controversial measures. Thus headlines in the Toronto *Examiner* read: THE GREAT GOVERNMENT MEASURE OF THE SESSION, THE DOG BILL, CARRIED—THE MUSKRAT BILL LOST.[7] Nevertheless, one significant piece of legislation did go through. Papineau carried a School Act for Canada East (drafted by Morin the year before) which consolidated a distinctive educational system, basing the French majority's schools on the Catholic parish under local commissioners guided by the *curé*, with similar religiously-grounded schools for the English Protestant minority. It set the pattern for subsequent Lower Canadian measures in the same way that the Schools Act of 1843 had done for Upper Canada. But another educational measure nearly brought the government's collapse, and in any case made its weakness clear beyond dispute: Draper's own Upper Canadian University Bill.

The Anglican Attorney-General West wanted to settle the question of King's College, an institution which he had notably helped both to found and to defend. He sought a conservative compromise between the Anglican vested interest in the provincial university and the demands of its numerous opponents, above all avoiding the almost complete secularism of the Baldwin scheme of 1843.[8] Early in March, 1845, he introduced a bill to establish a University of Upper Canada, endowed with the public funds, within which Anglican King's, Presbyterian Queen's and Methodist Victoria would function as residential colleges supported from the endowment, yet maintaining their own religious instruction. There were the seeds here of a future concept of university federation; but in the Canada of 1845 the project was attacked from either end. Baldwin liberals condemned it as a device to pay public money for sectarian purposes. Draper's own tory associates saw it as the spoliation of King's College. His Inspector General, Robinson, was forced to resign on the issue. When Sherwood threatened to lead a tory revolt, Draper reluctantly agreed to drop the bill to which he had pledged himself. The leader had practically been defeated by his own followers.

Parliament adjourned a few days later, at the end of March. Draper continued on in office, not through any love of power ("I *hate* politics," he had written sincerely),[9] but from a strong sense of obligation to the Governor General. Desperately ill and exhausted, Metcalfe did not believe that he could form another ministry: all his effort had been spent with the elections.[10] Now, as spring came on, his government's credit had already worn thin, and he was slowly, cruelly, dying. The imperial government, which had warmly approved his effecting of their policies, had granted him a peer-age after the elections. It was an empty honour for Baron Metcalfe, sitting in darkened rooms at Monklands to shield his failing eyesight, stoically cheerful still—but sensing also that Canada was slipping from his grasp. He deeply relied on Draper, yet did not delude himself. He told Stanley that, although his chief minister's talents were "universally admitted . . . I do not know that, strictly speaking, he can be said to have a single follower. The same may be remarked of every other member of the Executive Council."[11]

Nevertheless, the Draper ministry, as it now might well be called, sur-vived in the absence of any viable alternative. Its leader turned to strengthen it in the one way that seemed possible, through effecting a combination with the mass of the French Canadians. Since Viger and Denis Papineau had repeatedly failed, Draper took up the effort for himself. By this time, however, he might hope to benefit from the idea of the double majority, an idea which was all but sweeping French Canada in the spring of 1845. Emerging in the French-speaking press the previous winter, and well elaborated by Viger in L'Aurore, this proposal called for the government of Canada to be based on a majority within each of its two sections.[12] As Le Canadien put it concisely, "L'administration du Haut et du Bas Canada doit être laissée aux conseillers de chaque province respectivement et la majorité du Bas Canada doit . . . s'allier à la majorité du Haut Canada sans égard à sa couleur politique."[13] It was a concept of Canada as almost a dual federation, of rule through two national blocks, not by party government. But above all, it would now require the French to ally with the tory-conservatives domi-nant in Upper Canada instead of with the western reform minority.

The double-majority principle naturally appealed to the French Can-adians' frustrated awareness that, although their representatives controlled the eastern half of the assembly, they were still excluded from power. And this was merely for the sake of a bond with feeble western liberals, main-tained, some said, only through LaFontaine's obduracy and excessive concern for Robert Baldwin.[14] Yet the eastern leader's attitude really involved two major practical considerations. First, there was the fact that double majority was not by itself responsible government, since it did not necessarily imply that the governor would have to follow the advice of his bi-sectional council: indeed, he might well seek to choose between two contending views there. Second, in order to achieve truly responsible rule, it was necessary that French Canadians take office on their own and not on the governor's terms. Accordingly, LaFontaine would prefer to wait, prefer to keep to western allies who supported the full responsible principle, and not be led into a dubious new combination for the sake of some transitory advantage. He approved the general concept of a double majority, without doubt. It had the highly attractive ring of national recognition, for him as for other French

Canadians. And the failure of the Upper Canadian voters to support reform and responsible government, when his own had been so faithful at the elections, led him to warn Baldwin that "They cannot expect that Lower Canadians will continue to injure their own interests by fighting for their cause which they have so shamefully abandoned."[15] But he held on to the liberal alliance, none the less. For joining with the western ministerialists would mean accepting the Metcalfe system and all that he had fought against in the crisis over the governor's prerogative.

At the moment, whatever LaFontaine might decide for himself, the reaction growing in French Canada appeared to favour Draper's efforts to create a new alliance. In July, Viger at last obtained a place in parliament by winning a by-election in Three Rivers, a conservative urban seat. More important, in early September, Viger forces carried the by-election in Dorchester county, which had formerly been held by a LaFontaine adherent. Meanwhile, Draper had opened careful negotiations through René-Edouard Caron, Speaker of the Legislative Council since 1843 and mayor of Quebec. Caron reflected a feeling in this important centre that Montreal interests had been all too dominant under LaFontaine. An exchange of confidential correspondence showed that Caron was certainly interested in Draper's proposal for joining the majorities, to be signalized by replacing Viger and Papineau in the government with Morin and probably Caron—along with shunting off LaFontaine to the honours of the judicial bench.[16]

Still, LaFontaine was the recognized party leader. With Draper's permission, therefore, an eager Caron informed him of the intent of the negotiations. After consulting with Francis Hincks (who thought rule by double majority impracticable, and that Metcalfe himself would never sanction it), LaFontaine sent a stiffly effective reply.[17] If the double-majority principle was to be recognized, then why, he asked, were only two French replacements to join the ministry—just two more *vendus*? Why not the complete reconstruction of the eastern half of the government?[18] He spoke for French party solidarity, which Draper was manifestly trying to divide. The eastern opposition should enter office as a body, by right of popular victory, which was bound to come—not by ministerial favour to a few purchased individuals. It was a sharp plea for party unity; but more particularly, it called Draper's hand. Caron replied to Draper, setting forth the double-majority principle explicitly, and the consequent requirement that all the Lower Canadian ministers should be replaced.[19] It was too high a price, one that Draper in his weakness could not readily afford. The negotiations dragged on through October and into November; indeed, they would be taken up anew the following year. But LaFontaine, without at all denying the double-majority doctrine or the duality that it embodied, had contained the French-Canadian reaction and maintained his own party leadership and policy.

In any case, another event now seized public attention: the retirement of Lord Metcalfe. Stanley had long since offered to relieve him because of his health, but he remained indomitably loyal to those who had loyally supported him. He would not leave them abandoned and disheartened, "so long as I can manage that I were of any utility."[20] The Governor was full of praise and kindness for all who had tried to help him. But in October he had to admit to the Colonial Secretary, "My disorder has recently made a serious advance."[21] Almost completely blind, he now could scarcely talk or eat, and there was a gaping hole in his cheek. Any further persistence was hopeless; will, stark courage and devotion could do no more. Late in November, 1845, Metcalfe drove from Monklands, through silent crowds that lined the way, to sail for home to die. Only the most hardened reformer could watch his passing unmoved. And only the most determined tory could believe that his labours, so unremitting, so well-intentioned, had achieved their essential aim.

II

The final irony of the Metcalfe régime was that, by its end, government was operating on much the same basis that Metcalfe had originally set out to oppose. The executive council was functioning practically as a responsible cabinet, the governor accepting its advice. If anything, its development had gone further. Draper's role now was that of a veritable prime minister, while the council allocated patronage in its own interest—after so much contention and bitterness![22] No doubt this was the joint result of Metcalfe's incapacity and his deserved trust in Draper. Nevertheless, a governor had once more let the ministry wield his authority, and to withdraw it anew would be doubly difficult. Nor was it unimportant that this ministry was based essentially on tory-conservative support. It would be equally difficult, hereafter, to charge reform ministers with disloyalty if they sought the same exercise of power that Draper and his associates had at their disposal. The sting had been drawn; the patronage question had settled itself. That check to responsible rule was virtually gone.

Canada, in fact, was crossing the watershed to self-government. Paradoxically, the Metcalfe era had advanced the process, by putting the responsible principle sharply to the issue, and failing to produce a real alternative. While imperial policy remained unaltered at Metcalfe's retirement, implicit in the situation that he left behind him were the loss of the governor's initiative in domestic affairs, the selection of ministries for the Crown by assembly majorities, and the final triumph of party over harmony.

For the time being, however, no major new developments occurred within Canada itself. The existing administration continued to hold its slight majority in parliament, and raised no fresh problems for imperial authority. Moreover, a serious boundary dispute had emerged in Anglo-American relations, the Oregon question of 1845-46. As it grew, and seemed to threaten Canada with the dangers of war with the United States, imperial protection looked of more consequence than any internal questions of government. As it ebbed, sweeping changes taking place in Britain commanded Canadian attention. Hence, as far as provincial affairs were concerned, the régime that followed Metcalfe seemed something of a breathing-space, even an intermission. Yet it would also constitute a time of notable transition between two different eras.

It was normal practice when the commander of the forces, Earl Cathcart, became administrator of Canada on Metcalfe's departure in November, 1845. But Cathcart's appointment as governor-general in his own right in April, 1846, was a mark of the Oregon crisis, and of the British government's belief that Canada should be fully in the hands of a professional soldier during a period of strained relations with the United States. Stanley had left the Colonial Office the December preceding. It was a new Colonial Secretary in Peel's cabinet, William Ewart Gladstone, who noted in his instructions to Governor Cathcart that Metcalfe's administration might "justly be regarded as a model for his successor"—indicating the approval still felt for Metcalfe's work.[23] Yet Cathcart, a Peninsular veteran, a no-nonsense military man concerned with military problems, left political affairs very much to Draper and his colleagues. He directed his own energies to matters of defence, made urgent by the dispute over the far western boundary of British America in the Oregon country, on the distant continental slopes to the Pacific.

Britain and the United States had long had conflicting claims in the Oregon territory, where spreading American settlement was contesting against the once-dominant power of the Hudson's Bay fur traders. The rival claims approached an open clash in 1845, when the new administration of President Polk, elected to a chant of "Fifty-four forty or fight," took up the American contentions with Great Britain—while congressional orators swellingly predicted, "The American eagle will stick his claws into the nose of the lion and make his blood spout like a whale."[24] Mere bombast might be dismissed; but there was a strong show of resolution on both sides, too much not to be treated seriously. Orders went to Canada from England for the building of vessels on the Great Lakes which might be used as gunboats.[25] The fortifications of Kingston, the main British naval base on the Lakes, were to be substantially strengthened.[26] During the winter of 1845-46 construction began on massive stone martello towers, mounting cannon, to protect Kingston harbour; and the Kingston Argus thundered, "The blood of the yeomanry of Canada which may be spilled in defence of their homes will attest their abhorrence of the tyranny of Democracy."[27] In January the Toronto *Globe*, contemplating a fight over Oregon, at least saw in it the chance to wipe out American slavery by British arms, thus ennobling the conflict as "a world's war for a world's jubilee."[28]

Yet behind the loud public excitement both the British and American governments were ready to settle their differences over Oregon. Britain had no wish for another American war; the United States was sufficiently committed already to an expansionist campaign against Mexico. Hence the negotiations that followed issued in an agreement to extend the existing boundary of the forty-ninth parallel across the plains westward beyond the Rockies to the Pacific. In June of 1846, the Oregon Treaty was signed. The Kingston fortifications would still go forward; but the heat and sense of danger over Oregon had been subsiding in Canada for some months.

By the time parliament met in March, in fact, the Oregon question had lost much of its urgency. It was a cautious, not too exciting session, as the Draper ministry steered a careful course, still with only its slim majority, often losing votes that were not tests of confidence. Nevertheless, some solid work was done, and several significant measures passed—as that, for example, providing for the transfer of the permanent civil list to Canadian hands.[29] This had been a matter at issue ever since the imperial Act of Union had included fixed provisions for the payment of the salaries of the chief provincial officers of state, thus effectively leaving the civil list outside full Canadian keeping. But now the British authorities had agreed to yield to, and trust, the Canadians' desire to maintain it for themselves. While the list of official salaries was not to be much changed, the colonial legislature would vote it hereafter, the British parliament repealing the requisite clause of the Act of 1840 in order to complete Canada's control over its own revenues.

Also worthy of note was a new school law for Canada West, the first in a long series to be drafted by Egerton Ryerson. A central Board of Education was established to assist Ryerson as Chief Superintendent, prescribing teacher-training, textbooks and common standards for separate as well as ordinary public schools. The superintendent's power to enforce these standards rested largely on the control he was given over the distribution of the provincial grant. There would still be local taxes levied through the districts for the additional support of the schools, of course; though a rate-bill requiring all the local property-holders and not only parents to contribute to public education was rejected by parliament. Draper tried, but had to give up that provision. None the less, the Common School Act of 1846 was of major importance in further shaping the enduring character of state schooling within the Upper Canadian community.

This, however, was nearly the limit of parliament's achievement. An attempt to revive the University Bill of 1845 as a private member's measure was defeated. Tory ministers like Sherwood and William Cayley (who had now been brought in as Inspector General) voted outright against Draper and his mere eighteen supporters. On the other hand, LaFontaine's all too clever disclosure to the assembly of Draper's confidential negotiations with Caron on the double majority in 1845 produced some light, much heat, and little result. For whatever the Lower Canadian leader may have gained by revealing the minister's strained manoeuvrings, he lost by the resentment of Caron and his Quebec friends at what they regarded as a flagrantly unjustified breach of trust, even though LaFontaine argued that he had been empowered as leader to publicize the Draper-Caron correspondence.[30]

Accordingly, after parliament rose in June, Draper began another newly hopeful approach to the French to join a ministerial alliance. It was facilitated by Denis Viger's dignified retirement from office that month, and by a resurgent Quebec reaction against LaFontaine and the power of Montreal interests. Through Caron, in fact, Draper even reached to Augustin Morin, a Quebec man himself.[31] For a moment the political balance seemed to tremble. Hincks reported to Baldwin anxiously, "A split between Morin and Lafontaine is to be made. I am very apprehensive of it. At this moment I am convinced that each is dissatisfied with the other."[32] The susceptible if indecisive Morin was very much swayed by Draper's bold new offer of three ministerial posts for his filling: in an anxious colloquy, Etienne Taché thought the French party could scarcely refuse to take office.[33] But, guided by Hincks's fluent persuasion at the critical moment, Morin rejected the bid.[34] By autumn, Draper had failed in Canada East again.

Meanwhile, in the West, the troubled prime minister had to force a malcontent Sherwood out of office and replace him as Solicitor General with a capable young Toronto lawyer, John Hillyard Cameron. He had no less trouble with Sir Allan MacNab, who, disappointed in one of his typical quests for fatter official preferment, angrily broke away, and even started boldly treating for a post under a future Baldwin reform government.[35] Yet, since MacNab was also feuding with Henry Sherwood, Draper did not have to fear a concerted right-wing movement against him. The tory knight was calmed; the reformers were unable to make capital out of him. And so the weak conservative administration survived, although Canadian politics by the closing months of 1846 had acquired all the monotony of futility. Still, political futility seemed of less moment when, as now, questions of economic well-being were beginning to loom so large before the Canadian union.

III

In general, the good times of 1844 had continued in Canada, as the staple trades flourished and economic growth went forward. Lumbering had been briskly busy, thanks to the high prices produced by the British railway boom. Some 27,000,000 feet of timber had come down the river to the Quebec market in 1845, and over 37,000,000 the next year.[36] The quantity actually exported was about 24,200,000 feet in 1845 and 24,240,000 in 1846, which meant a sizable winter carry-over and a fall in prices brought on by overcutting that had swamped the still continuing demand.[37] As yet, however, these results were not fully realized. Vigorous cutting would continue during the winter of 1846-47. As for grain sales, whether the colonial preference under the Canada Corn Act was particularly responsible, or generally favourable prices in the British market, the fact was that wheat and flour exports via the St Lawrence increased from about 1,194,000 bushels in 1843 to 2,350,000 in 1844, and from 2,500,000 in 1845 to 3,312,-000 in 1846.[38] The curve was still rising. The scale of flour-milling in Canada was also rapidly expanding. Its capacity would more than double between 1842 and 1848.[39]

The expansion of the milling industry along the province's main waterways again perhaps reflected the Canada Corn Act preference; or perhaps still more, the confident expectation of advantages to come from the great Canadian canal system, designed to channel the bulk of produce from the continental interior into the St Lawrence route. And certainly there seemed every reason to expect the improved St Lawrence "line of navigation" to triumph over American rivals like the Erie Canal, since the Canadian system would carry large cargo vessels under their own power by natural waters to the heart of the West, as compared with small horse-drawn barges and consequent trans-shipment required by way of the slackwater Erie route. The St Lawrence canals by 1846 were well advanced. Their construction as well as the anticipations and investments they inspired contributed to the general state of Canadian prosperity.

The Beauharnois Canal was finished in 1845, with nine locks 200 feet long and nine feet in depth, at a cost of $1,331,000.[40] The Cornwall Canal had been open since 1843. The Lachine to the east and the Welland in the west were both being enlarged and deepened to the nine-foot level. And already the new type of steamer, propellor-driven, was running between Kingston and Montreal, being able to pass through the old, narrow Lachine Canal where fat paddle-wheelers with outspread paddle-boxes could not.[41] The canals near Morrisburg were also building, to overcome the restrictive though not impassable rapids in that area. Although the imperial guaranteed loan was now about exhausted, everything seemed to point to grand success for the St Lawrence navigation within a year or two, when the whole series of works would finally be complete.

While the union's water transport was thus being improved (and navigational aids provided from the Gulf of St Lawrence to the Upper Lakes), land communications were also exhibiting development. The improvement of the main routes and the spreading system of stage-coaches were reflected in the establishment of regular mail service by coach in the early 1840's. Mail, passengers, and light freight could travel by daily stages across the length of Upper Canada from 1842 onward; and in the next ten years, the peak of the stage-coach era, the basic line of stages was extended from Quebec to the Detroit River, with multiple branches spreading from it.⁴² The main through roads, like the Temiscouata and the Matapedia in Canada East, that provided land access to the province of New Brunswick, or the Hamilton - Port Dover in Canada West, completed in 1846 to link the head of Lake Ontario overland to a Lake Erie port, were under the jurisdiction of the provincial Board of Works. "Productive" ones, however, were then leased to private turnpike trusts, who maintained them in return for collecting tolls.⁴³ The local roads, joining the countryside to town markets, mills, and forwarding services, were under the care of the district councils in both sections of Canada, and these councils were authorized to appoint road commissioners within the townships.

Considerable stretches of the main roads, at least near towns, were now macadamized and in the keeping of road companies. In 1841, the first plank road in Lower Canada had joined Longueuil and Chambly near Montreal; now the Montreal area was well served by roads laid down by the turnpike trusts.⁴⁴ The Toronto-Hamilton plank road was open by 1845, and the Toronto Roads generally formed another valuable network of communications, leased to private hands.⁴⁵ The plank roads, cheap and popular, seemed at first to have solved the problem of land transportation. Formed of rough planks nailed crosswise to long baulks embedded in the ground, they could be built by unskilled labour from material abundantly to hand; and they offered a flat surface on which wagons, coaches, the *calèche* of the East, the buggy of the West, could bowl easily along. The trouble was, however, their all too constant and costly need of upkeep. Winter frosts and spring thaws would heave their poorly prepared road-beds badly out of line. They rapidly decayed; and broken or rotted planks could make them a considerable menace. The truth was that the problem of Canadian inland, all-weather transportation was far from being solved, despite the glowing hopes of the mid forties.

At that period, in fact, even the major routes still had ungraded, broken or swampy stretches where coaches swayed sickeningly, jolted bruisingly, or simply mired hopelessly down. Wherever possible, passengers moved by the far more comfortable steamboats, or by cutter and *carriole* on hard-packed winter snows. In Canada East, the St Lawrence remained the main highway, consequently retarding the improvement of through land routes. And as for local roads, they still might be mere bush trails or ox-cart paths, where the old corduroy of unevenly-sized logs laid transversely, with or without earth piled between them, virtually prohibited movement faster than a walking pace. Lack of both capital and labour for drainage, bridges and general maintenance still kept much of Canada's land communications close to the pioneer stage.

But the real point was the relative improvement. It was going on steadily. The forties were a notable era of road-building; and year by year traffic, mails, and newspapers would thus enlarge their circulation, to increase the sense of community in Canada. All this was well under way before the coming of the railway. But by the mid forties, also, the railway era was already being projected for the province. The new mode of transport that had had such revolutionary effect in England and now was rapidly spreading in the United States offered an obvious answer to Canadian problems of inland, all-weather communication. What yet prevented its successful application was the same lack of adequate supplies of capital and labour, together with the evident need to develop the primary line of water transport first.

Nevertheless, hopeful railway schemes were increasingly being launched in Canada. Ten lines, for example, were given charters during the parliamentary session of 1846, some of which would ultimately end in functioning railways.[46] Most significant of them was the St Lawrence and Atlantic, chartered in 1845. It embodied Montreal's desire for a line of its own to the ice-free Atlantic; it was to run to Portland in Maine, thus providing a winter outlet for St Lawrence commerce. Only some forty miles of track would actually be laid by the St Lawrence and Atlantic before the end of the decade, but the plan and the beginnings had been made in the years before.

In the mid forties, moreover, economic growth also displayed itself in the increasing development and diversification of manufacturing enterprises in Canada. Once more the significance was relative. This was not the vast industrial revolution that had transformed England, was now at work in the United States, and would later arrive in Canada. But there was a notable expansion of water-powered industry (with some beginnings of steam) in various Canadian centres during the eighteen-forties; and this again represented a considerable change from the primitive simplicities of the pioneer era. Besides the ever-multiplying saw and grist mills, breweries, distilleries and tanneries, there were by 1846 three paper mills in Canada East, five in Canada West, cordage manufactories in Montreal, glass works at St Johns, boiler and engine works at Montreal and Toronto, and stove foundries, nail factories, and cabinet-making shops across the whole province.[47] Iron was produced on a sizable scale at the St Maurice forges near Three Rivers, in operation since French times, and at the Normandale furnaces in Upper Canada. A cotton factory had been established at Sherbrooke in 1845, another at Chambly in the same year; while in 1846 a woollen mill had opened at Cobourg in Canada West, "calculated to work off near 5000 yards of cloth a week."[48] Nor was this the complete list, which would include coach works at Toronto, steamboat yards at Kingston, knitting mills at Sherbrooke, and a good deal more as well.

It was another mark of economic growth and prosperity that Kingston and Hamilton were incorporated in 1846 as Canada West's second and third cities. Yet ultimately, this whole era of affluence and activity in the province depended on the farmer and lumberman, on the basic Canadian staples of grain and timber, and on the St Lawrence trading system that organized their export. And here, in the very height of good times, the Canadian staple trades and the St Lawrence commerce were already encountering significant threats to their future. In part, the threat came from the United States. In 1845 and 1846 Congress passed Drawback Laws which remitted duties on goods destined for Canada that were imported through the United States, and on Canadian exports sent overseas the same way. These acts expressed the concern of American interests themselves that the new Canadian St Lawrence canals might capture more of the trade of the continental interior, if the American transit routes to and from the west were not opened as freely as possible. The effects on the St Lawrence route grew increasingly plain. While Upper Canadians might enjoy now being able to use the Erie Canal route to the sea as readily as the St Lawrence, Montreal merchants saw imports like tea and sugar for the inland country decline in 1845 and 1846, and watched more and more western wheat go out by the Erie.[49]

Canada tried to counter by repealing in 1846 the duty on American wheat imported into the province for re-export, and Montreal in particular by launching the St Lawrence and Atlantic railway project in order to improve its own means of access to the ocean. But the St Lawrence commercial system was now fully exposed to American competition by this unwelcome way of removing tariff barriers. The completion of the St Lawrence canals to realize their promised advantages seemed more urgent than ever. And yet, while the existing Canadian commercial system was thus being seriously challenged within America, its whole established pattern of trade overseas with the imperial market was also facing prospects of disruption.

This was the other part of the threat, one which bulked still larger in Canadian minds in 1846. The trend to free trade had now reached critical proportions in Great Britain: that country indeed was entering on a wholesale transformation of its commercial and imperial policy. In a year that marked a high point in Canada's prosperity and a state of doldrums in its domestic politics, the most crucial events for the province were taking place on the other side of the Atlantic. They would reverberate in Canadian economic and political life with growing vehemence and force.

IV

It was the impact of disastrous famine in Ireland that had brought the government of Sir Robert Peel to the decisive step. The rapid spread of potato blight in 1845 had destroyed the basic Irish crop. Quantities of cheap grain were needed to meet the threat of mass starvation. "The remedy," wrote Peel, "is the removal of all impediments to the import of all kinds of human food—that is, the total and absolute repeal for ever of all duties on all articles of subsistence."[50] It meant the end of the Corn Laws, the traditional safeguard of the powerful British landed interest. And when the conservative prime minister, who had already moved far towards free trade, resolved on the removal of the very keystone of the British protective system, then the rest of the old mercantilistic structure—the remaining colonial preferential duties and the imperial Navigation Acts—must surely come down. All must follow from the repealing of the Corn Laws.

Peel's resolve, however, had split his own party. Thus Stanley, a landed tory and Corn Law protectionist, had left the Colonial Office and the cabinet in December 1845. Yet despite the loss of the protectionist tories, the Peelite conservatives backed by the whig-liberal opposition had gone on to repeal the Corn Laws in the spring of 1846. And while, in June, the abandoned tory landed interest had its revenge in pulling down Peel's government, the whigs who now took office under Lord John Russell had wholly adopted free-trade doctrines. They continued with fervour the work of dismantling protectionism and installing the full dispensation of free trade throughout the British Empire. In the forefront was their new Colonial Secretary, Earl Grey, not only a convinced free-trade liberal, but, as brother-in-law and associate of the late Lord Durham, for years an ardent believer in colonial reform. In August, Grey informed Lord Cathcart that he was being superseded as governor-general of Canada. In September, he named a new governor, the Earl of Elgin, although Elgin, home on leave from office in Jamaica, would not take up his new post for several months to come.

In the meantime, Canadians watched the transformation taking place in Britain with sharp concern. Their whole economy, their political existence, had taken shape within the old colonial system. The change to an empire dominated by free trade and laissez-faire liberalism could affect nearly every aspect of Canadian life. The repeal of the Corn Laws was supposed to take effect by stages; hence the preferences under the Canada Corn Act were not wholly to disappear until 1849. The timber preference was also to be reduced in two stages, in 1847 and 1848, thus again providing a little time for adjustment. But would the period be sufficient for a satisfactory transition—and could it be satisfactory at all? These were the deeply worrying questions that faced Canada. Above all, the trading interests of the St Lawrence, already feeling the competition unleashed by the American Drawback Acts, were now threatened with the loss of the advantages in the British market that would enable them to meet that competition.[51]

Many looked to the natural advantages of the St Lawrence route, the cheap transport it could provide in contrast to the "artificial" Erie route to New York. Thus the Montreal Gazette declared, perhaps whistling in the dark a little, ". . . when the internal communications of this colony are complete and the trade in western produce put on a regular footing, the artificial superiority [of New York] will rapidly disappear."[52] And the Free Trade Association in Montreal, presided over by the prominent merchant John Young, welcomed the removal of all encumbering duties and restrictions on commerce, confident that low costs, free trade and no favour, would let the St Lawrence meet all rivals.[53] The equally prominent western merchant, William Merritt, sounded a similar note in parliament in June, 1846, laying the stress on tariff autonomy for Canada—for if free trade was right for the mother country, it was no less proper for the province: "If the productions of Canada are to receive no advantage over the productions of foreign countries when admitted into Britain, the manufactures of Britain are not entitled to any advantage over the manufactures of foreign countries when admitted into Canada."[54]

This dictum, indeed, would be followed at parliament's next session, when in 1847 the Canadian legislature lowered the average duties on American manufactures from twelve to seven and a half per cent, while raising those on British to seven and a half from five per cent. The result was a tariff for revenue purposes only, which also invited reciprocal free trade with the Maritime Provinces.[55] Canada was doing its best to try the free-trade gospel for itself. But in Montreal more hope was placed in the St Lawrence canals or the projected St Lawrence and Atlantic railway; and in general, the mood in this centre of Canadian commercial life stayed full of dark foreboding, as forwarders, millers and financiers watched the progress of the abhorrent gospel across the Atlantic. It was all too plain. While the American drawbacks had broken open the Canadian system at one end, the British destruction of protection was ruining it at the other.

And yet, if the economic implications of the establishment of a free-trade empire looked so gravely ominous, the political implications for Canada were equally profound, though in quite a different way. The essence was this: free trade would make colonial responsible government acceptable to the rulers of the British Empire. For years, indeed, leaders in the free-trade movement had tended to associate themselves with "freeing" the colonies, just as British colonial reformers had expressed the views of economic liberalism in their attacks on the old imperial system. In actuality, leading free-traders like Richard Cobden were chiefly concerned to loose the burdens of unneeded, wasteful and warlike empire—mere outdoor relief for the aristocracy, as it seemed to them—while colonial reformers saw a positive value in a self-governing, freely associated community of British settlement. Yet both brands of liberal idealists, with varied blends between, could agree on the need to let colonies manage their own affairs.

Aside from liberal doctrinaires, there was a growing lack of interest in imperial concerns in Britain which could also serve the cause of colonial self-government. The very triumph of free trade expressed the unparalleled ascendancy of British industry in the mid nineteenth century. When the whole world was its domain for markets and supplies, what reason was there to guide and husband overseas possessions that cost much more to maintain than they could ever return? Colonies had to be maintained, perhaps, as commitments to be honoured. But their growth to self-support and eventual independence must also be encouraged: for that, surely, was their end. Such a view was Grey's at the Colonial Office, a sort of benevolent imperial pessimism. Indeed, one might almost say of the whig cabinet in general that they had assuredly become the Queen's ministers in order to preside over the liquidation of the British Empire. Among tories, on the other hand, turning away from empire might well be caused by heartfelt disillusion, as they surveyed the wreck of the protective system they had defended. So it largely was with Stanley, now the Earl of Derby.

Nevertheless, a concern for prestige, the underlying strength of old imperial feelings, and perhaps the very size of the task, did prevent any forthright British revolution against the empire. Talk of imperial change soon gave way to imperial habit, and to the effects of declining interest itself. Yet two changes did decisively occur. First, the old opposition in Britain to the granting of colonial responsible government lost influence and even meaning. Second, Lord Grey formulated a definite policy of recognizing executive responsibility to the assemblies in advanced colonies like Canada and Nova Scotia. As to the first, the logical dilemma that Russell had posed as colonial secretary in 1839 had not really been answered. How could a colonial executive be responsible both to imperial instructions and to local representatives? It no longer mattered: if a colony was not to be fitted into a general structure of imperial trade regulation, it was of little importance to control its local political activities. And as for the second, if colonies were to be led to self-reliance and ultimate independence, then the sooner they were enabled to govern their domestic affairs, the better. Liberal idealism, free-trade arguments, even lack of interest, pointed towards the same answer: responsible government.

Thus it was that the coming of British free trade brought a final ingredient to the development of responsible government in the Canadian union: the approval, even the backing, of the imperial power itself. It could be argued, of course, that the establishment of the responsible system had been implicit ever since Metcalfe's retirement; that the system of harmony had plainly proved bankrupt and left no alternative but the continued evolution of responsible rule. Moreover, it was true—and bears repeated emphasizing—that British policy had sought honestly and wholeheartedly to rule through Canadian accord. It was altogether unlikely that a British governor would seek to coerce Canadian opinion or now repudiate a responsible ministry. But in any case, the issue did not arise. The triumph of free trade removed it. The events of 1846 in Great Britain, and the changed imperial patterns that resulted, placed Canada beyond question across the watershed to self-government. Under Grey's policy at the Colonial Office, as administered by his new governor-general, Lord Elgin, it would essentially be up to Canadians to carry the political process through to completion for themselves. Yet this they would have to do while meeting the hard economic consequences of free trade as well.

CHAPTER 7

The Achievement of Responsible Rule

1847-1849

In 1847 the full horror of the Irish famine was brought home to Canada. That year destitute, despairing emigrants poured out of Ireland, to reach the St Lawrence crammed in rotting "coffin ships" or in sounder craft that nevertheless were racked with scurvy, dysentery, cholera, and the deadly typhus. The overladen vessels anchored off Grosse Isle, the quarantine station below Quebec, in a dread line miles long, all overhung with an intolerable stench of filth, disease and death. Even if the pitiable swarm they brought had been healthy, it would have posed a massive problem for the colony. Hitherto in the 1840's there had been a fairly steady and balanced emigration to Canada from England, Scotland and Ireland. The largest influx had been 44,000 in 1842, and though numbers had fallen thereafter, they had contained a notably high element with means and skills, while shipboard conditions had been good.[1] But in 1847 over ninety thousand immigrants came, chiefly Irish, under appalling conditions; starved, pauperized and demoralized, as well as being riddled with disease.[2]

The brutal fact was that a fifth of them would die before the year was out; some five thousand in the teeming camps and hospitals on Grosse Isle, nearly fifteen thousand in Quebec, Montreal, Kingston and Toronto, in hastily built "emigrant sheds" or wandering sick and helpless in roadways and back lanes.[3] Government, churches and private charity struggled desperately but could not cope with the sheer weight of disaster suddenly thrown on Canada. Doctors and clergy died with the sick in the plague pit of Grosse Isle. Mayor John Mills of Montreal and the Roman Catholic Bishop of Toronto, Dr. Michael Power, succumbed to fever caught in their efforts among the emigrant sheds. Hastily formed Boards of Health could do little to check the spread of typhus in the towns, until the onset of winter took away the worst of the infection, and the infected. In its report for 1847, the Montreal Emigrant Society provided this epitaph: "From Grosse Isle, the great charnel pit of victimized humanity, up to Port Sarnia and all along the borders of our magnificent river; upon the shores of Lake Ontario and Lake Erie—wherever the tide of emigration has extended, are to be found the final resting places of the sons and daughters of Erin; one unbroken chain of graves where repose fathers and mothers, sisters and brothers, in one commingled heap without a tear bedewing the soil or a stone marking the spot."[4]

Of those emigrants who survived, many moved on to the United States; but many stayed, markedly adding to the Irish community in Canada. The next year, and for several more, the movement from Ireland would resume as that country, devastated by continued potato blight and the wholesale eviction of impoverished tenants, went on sending forth its sufferers. But the numbers of emigrants to Canada diminished after the flood tide of 1847, while stricter regulations increasingly improved the ocean passage and reduced the influx of the infirm and hopelessly unsuited. Moreover, in 1848 the immigration service was transferred from imperial to Canadian responsibility, enabling the colony to control its own intake of settlers thereafter. By the close of the decade, immigration from Great Britain generally was back to a moderated and manageable level of under forty thousand a year.[5]

Yet the Irish famine migration of 1847 sent reverberations throughout Canada that did not quickly disappear, bringing social turmoil and financial burdens along with misery and disease. Apart from lavish expenditure by private charity and municipal councils on food, shelter and hospital care for the sufferers, the provincial government's own outlay was far in excess of the revenue from the head-tax that normally met the costs of settling immigrants in Canada. Within the next two years the imperial government undertook to pay the bill for the immigration crisis, but in the meantime the province faced an alarming deficit, when its resources had already been strained to the limit by the canal-building program. And at this point came the worst slump in a decade. In the spring of 1847 prices in England had broken and tumbled. Before winter both the Canadian timber and grain trades were caught in a steadily worsening world depression. The timber market had been glutted by overcutting: in 1847, forty-five million feet of square timber came to Quebec, to meet a demand for nineteen million.[6] The imperial government, regardless of the projected gradual reduction of colonial grain preference, had now completely suspended the Corn Laws because of the Irish emergency—though at the same time it was freely dumping Ireland's woes on Canada's shores. In consequence, famine migration and failing commerce combined to make the impact of laissez-faire imperial policies very much harder to bear, as Canada approached the achievement of responsible rule.

Fortunately, the governor-general who was to admit and foster the responsible system was as level-headed as he was discerning. The selection of the Earl of Elgin for Canada was one of the best imperial appointments made by the new whig-liberal régime in England. Only thirty-five, fine-featured, though tending to stoutness and a touch of grey, he was vigorous, quick, and resilient. Yet his firm convictions were tempered by cool common sense and a keen awareness of the currents of popular opinion. Qualities such as these —together with a sense of humour—equipped him well for governing a turbulent colonial democracy. In politics he had been a Peelite conservative; but the Peelites were generally in transition to mid-Victorian liberalism, and Elgin's views fitted in with Grey's at the Colonial Office. A family tie also made for close personal relations between the new governor and his superior, since Elgin's wife was Lord Grey's niece.

She was also the daughter of the late Lord Durham; and Elgin came to Canada with a strong desire to vindicate his father-in-law's proposal for responsible government. In fact he shared more of the positive hopes of Durham and the colonial reformers than the negative laissez-faire outlook of the rather doctrinaire Grey and the whig cabinet under Lord John Russell. To Elgin, responsible government was the prerequisite for keeping valued possessions within the empire, not a step towards ultimate separation. He thought Canada could, and should, be retained; and he would remonstrate with Grey over statements of colonial policy that seemed too flatly to anticipate the ending of the colonial tie.

The two were in full agreement, however, on the immediate need to grant responsible government. When Elgin reached Canada late in January, 1847, he carried with him a copy of a dispatch already sent by Grey to the lieutenant-governor of Nova Scotia the previous November, outlining the policy of recognizing the executive's responsibility to the colonial legislature, and declaring that "it is neither possible or desirable to carry on the government of any of the British provinces in North America in opposition to the opinion of the inhabitants."[7] No longer was a governor to contrive to harmonize colonial views with imperial requirements: the former were to decide. And the dispatch went further, virtually to concede party government as basic to the operation of responsible rule. The governor was now charged with "making it apparent that any transfer which may take place of political power from the hands of one party in the province to those of another is the result not of an act of yours but of the wishes of the people themselves." For that very reason, the governor was also "to abstain from changing your Executive Council until it shall be perfectly clear that they are unable, with such fair support from yourself as they have a right to expect, to carry on the government of the province satisfactorily, and to command the confidence of the Legislature."[8] In short, government was to rest on whatever party controlled parliament, and change only when that control itself had changed.

This meant that Elgin would properly sustain the Draper ministry which he found in office on his arrival, since it did have its slight parliamentary majority. Hence nothing altered immediately—though, in truth, the rules of play had been changed while the same team was still at bat. Elgin himself was well aware of the fact. He wrote to Grey in March, 1847, "I am determined to do nothing which will put it out of my power to act with the opposite party, if it is forced on me by the representatives of the people."[9] As for his own position in the new system, his aim was "to establish a moral influence in the province which will go far to compensate for the loss of power consequent on the surrender of patronage to an executive responsible to the local parliament."[10] This was to be the new power of the Crown: it was to rise above politics as an impartial arbiter, and not be pulled dangerously down into partisanship as had happened during Metcalfe's struggle over patronage.

To carry out Grey's instructions and his own intentions, Elgin gave full co-operation to the government that was his at present. But at the same time he sought to establish the new position of the governor, so that opposition forces, and the French especially, would have no cause to believe that they would be welcomed any less cordially into power. Accordingly, he supported one last effort to bring the French Canadians into the Draper ministry. Elgin himself saw Morin and Taché, while Caron, with revived hopes of the double majority, discussed terms with Inspector-General Cayley. Hincks, indeed, reported to Baldwin from Montreal that the French were "panting for office."[11] But Morin and Taché could not be moved; and Caron found that Draper and company would still not go as far as a fully double-majority administration. By mid April the LaFontaine party front was firm again, while Lewis Drummond averred that double majority was dead—"ce monstre à deux figures dont l'un regarde le passé et l'autre l'avenir."[12] The ministry had met its final failure in Canada East. Elgin, however, had shown his own perfect readiness to admit the French Canadians, and only gained goodwill from the negotiations.

With little left to do, Draper at least tried to improve his position in English Canada. He thought to increase the conservative element in his council, which might bring it more middle-ground support now withheld, as he said, "by mistaking ultra Toryism for Conservatism (i.e., selfishness for patriotism)."[13] Hence young John A. Macdonald was named Receiver General. Yet an effort to add Ogle Gowan, who was a fairly moderate conservative despite his prominence in the Orange Order, ran into jealous personal antipathy from the still powerful Sir Allan MacNab.[14] Sherwood, moreover, was rallying tory followers to push the government back towards the right. William Draper had had enough. Clear-sighted as always, he knew that all his patience, persuasion and ingenuity could not keep a tottering administration functioning much longer. In May of 1847 he gladly retired to the judicial bench, to let a tory-dominated government take over. He had not succeeded in building the strong, adaptable conservative party he had hoped for; but for three years he had been an invaluable buffer between die-hard tories and importunate reformers in a province undergoing the crucial transformation of its governing system.

The new Sherwood government expressed an emphatically resurgent toryism. Yet it was the resurgence of the last stand, before final collapse. The ministry by no means gained strength through being infused with Compact tories like Henry Sherwood himself, now Attorney General West, and members of the old Lower Canadian British party such as William Badgley, the Attorney General East, or Peter McGill, still president of the Bank of Montreal. When parliament met in early June, its majority was scarcely more than two. Consequently the government brought little forward, and another dull session ensued. The reform opposition was little disposed to fight, however, in a parliament that was obviously moribund. It was better to await the elections that could not be far away, and fight there for the new era foreshadowed by the whig régime in England and by Elgin's presence in Canada. In any case, the summer was fiercely hot, with "emigrant fever" raging. Parliament was prorogued at the end of July, and members thankfully escaped from the heat and disease in Montreal. It did not meet again. Throughout the autumn the tory ministers anxiously considered an election that seemed all too likely to defeat them. At last they decided that further postponements were useless. Parliament was dissolved. And early in November, 1847, the campaigning opened for the most decisive election since the union had begun.

II

The mid-winter elections of 1847-48 produced an overwhelming reform victory in both East and West. In Canada East, of course, the result was almost a foregone conclusion, since LaFontaine's hold was more complete than ever. Old foes like Viger and Denis Papineau had retired; temporary dissenters like Caron had been swung back into line; newly emerging radical critics had not yet made a significant mark. The well-knit LaFontaine forces returned some thirty-three eastern members, including a sizable number of English-speaking adherents.[15] Plainly, the old French party had developed a character more in keeping with the concept of reform alliance, as a politically liberal, not a narrowly ethnic grouping. At the same time, the former British party of old Lower Canadian "racial" politics largely disintegrated between conservatives and liberals. Thus Montreal itself went wholly liberal, with LaFontaine taking one of its two seats. So did the constituencies of Shefford and Drummond in the Eastern Townships.

The major shift, however, came in Canada West, where the Baldwin reformers won a smaller but no less decisive majority, twenty-four to eighteen.[16] The contests here were arduous enough, what with early December rains that melted the back roads into almost impassable bogs, and a spell of bitter cold in late December and early January—although this did harden the roads for vigorous campaigning by sleigh. The election mood was fairly orderly, in spite of a fervid tory-Orange cry of "French domination" raised against reformers. Baldwin in Fourth York, for example, had to face the maledictions of tory William Boulton, who horribly warned electors that their interests would be sacrificed to "Tobacco-smoking, Dram Drinking, Garlick Eating Frenchmen . . . foreign in blood, foreign in race and as ignorant as the ground they stand upon."[17] But such appeals had little effect. The swing of Upper Canadian opinion to reform could not be diverted.

It was not essentially a question of responsible government. The elections hardly turned on that issue, since by now it, too, seemed a foregone conclusion to both sides; they were decided mainly by the state of the times and dissatisfaction with the existing government, together with thoroughly effective reform organization. Undoubtedly, stagnant commerce, deepening depression, and fears of British free trade had stimulated a desire for change —a desire illustrated by the fact that fifteen of thirty-four sitting western members lost in their attempts at re-election.[18] But it was not only bad times that, as usual, worked against the side of the government. Its own obvious weakness and internal quarrels, its inadequacy in meeting the crisis of Irish immigration, its failure, still, to settle the throbbing university question, all redounded against tory-conservative supporters of the ministry.[19]

In contrast, there was the strong reform unity that Baldwin and his colleagues had by now built up. The loyalty issue, the patronage question, were dead; there was nothing of moment to divide moderate from advanced reformers. And Robert Baldwin in particular had worked tirelessly to consolidate the party organization. He wrote a solicitous stream of letters to constituency organizations ("Let unanimity mark your proceedings"), and made himself an effective link between local agents and the central party interests. Nor was the fast-growing Toronto *Globe* without its effect across the West. For months it had been preaching liberal unity and the true values of party government: "It is through party that public principle is defined and purified," it argued. "Party combinations give stability and permanence to public measures."[20] In apparent response, reform moderates and ultras worked in close accord for party victory, leaving any differences of their own till later. The results were manifest when the last polls closed in mid January, 1848: in all of Canada, a reform majority of well over fifty, to less than twenty-five tory-conservatives.

The new parliament assembled in Montreal towards the end of February.

The Sherwood government still held on, to the very last, awaiting the verdict of the representatives. This it could quite properly do, however, and the Governor General, carrying out the precepts of responsible rule, made no attempt to interfere. Indeed, he had scrupulously abstained from any connection with elections, which no doubt helped also to maintain their orderly mood, so different from that of 1844. In the assembly the inevitable was not long delayed. Soon after Morin was easily elected speaker, a want-of-confidence motion passed, 54 to 20.[21] On March 4, the old ministry resigned— including that hardy perennial, Dominick Daly. Elgin at once called on LaFontaine and Baldwin as leaders of the reform majority to form a new executive council.

It was done within a week. LaFontaine became Attorney General East, with primacy in the government since he led the larger reform group. In constitutional fact he was the prime minister; and Baldwin, writing to him, consistently referred to "your" cabinet and ministers.[22] But in political function they would be co-premiers, expressing the reform alliance and the duality it embodied. The other eastern ministers were James Leslie, a tested reformer and substantial Montreal merchant, as President of the Executive Council; Taché,[23] now Commissioner of Public Works; and Louis-Michel Viger, the wealthy president of the Banque du Peuple, as Receiver General. Drummond was shortly to be named Solicitor General East in addition, but the solicitors-general would no longer be of cabinet rank.

As Attorney General West, Baldwin of course led the western half of the new government, which consisted of Sullivan as Provincial Secretary, Hincks as Inspector General, Price, the Commissioner of Crown Lands, and Malcolm Cameron, a radical-minded, powerful lumber merchant, as Assistant Commissioner of Public Works. Sullivan would move to the judiciary within a few months, however, and William Hamilton Merritt would join the ministry. Similarly, the legal ability of William Hume Blake as Solicitor General West would in a year be replaced in that office by the lesser legal talent but sharp political acumen of John Sandfield Macdonald, the member for Glengarry, who was already building himself a minor reform empire in the eastern, Upper St Lawrence area of Canada West.

Patently, the new government was wholly reform, a true one-party cabinet, the first in the Province of Canada. It could be argued that the previous Sherwood tory administration had also really been a party government; but the presence in it still of Dominick Daly, who had always regarded himself as a non-partisan official, would qualify that argument; and, further, some on the tory side at least could still have viewed the members of the executive council as the governor's loyal servants, not as a party combination in their own right. But there was no possible doubt about the new La-Fontaine-Baldwin ministry. It had clearly taken office in direct consequence of its party majority in parliament. It had plainly come in as a unit, a cabinet constructed by the party leaders. And the fact that Elgin so readily accepted a body of reformers as his advisers effectively denied any lingering contention that only tried tory champions of the Crown had a prescriptive right to rule.

Accordingly, the events of March, 1848, demonstrated and confirmed the responsible government which had been accepted imperial policy since 1846. They did not, therefore, establish it; and it was still to be tested in the future. But in a real sense the entrance of the LaFontaine-Baldwin reformers to office was the culmination of a long and gradual process, through which internal self-government was worked out for Canada. Moreover, it did indisputably recognize party cabinet rule; it did substantiate the governor-general's own withdrawal from domestic politics. And so, while too often the accession of the "Great Reform Ministry" of 1848 is viewed in oversimplified or over-emphatic terms as a transforming victory in the "fight" for responsible rule, it does remain a major bench-mark in the evolution of Canadian and British colonial self-government.

The new liberal cabinet only briefly met the parliament it so thoroughly controlled, and then had it prorogued on March 23—the Governor cordially carrying out the advice of his fully responsible ministers—in order to have time to develop a broad program of reforms for the 1849 session. Indeed, there was much to work upon throughout the rest of 1848. There was the university question, inevitably, and another old issue involving church-and-state relations, the Upper Canada clergy reserves, now looming once again. Then there were Lower Canadian issues, like the reform of the antiquated seigneurial system of landholding or the question of compensation for damages incurred in the rebellion of 1837-38. Furthermore, there was the urgent need of adjustment to the loss of imperial trade protection; the demand particularly pressed by William Merritt for reciprocal free trade with the United States instead. And over all hung the cloud of depression, a miasma of unrest and fear fostered also by the prospect of renewed Irish migration, with more poverty, disease and death.

Still further, 1848 was the shattering year of revolutions in Europe. The upheavals in France, Germany, Italy, the Chartist agitation in England, had only limited influence on far-off Canada. But the shock-waves did reach there, to be reflected in revived and newly hopeful radicalism among elements in both the English and French-speaking communities. While Canadian tories grew increasingly bitter over the commercial collapse that they ascribed to Britain's desertion of old imperial interests, Canadian liberals felt a mounting anxiety over the rise of impatient radicals on their left; ultras who might well endanger reform unity anew. Just after the election, even before taking office, Baldwin had expressed concern to Sandfield Macdonald about "the extravagant expectations of oversanguine friends."[24] But while old radical reformers and young democratic enthusiasts were stirring restlessly in western ranks, a rising radical movement was still more in evidence in Canada East. And there it largely centred on the august figure of Louis-Joseph Papineau, who had returned amnestied to Canada in 1845.

Thereafter, the once-mighty *patriote* leader had stayed in retirement, living in Olympian retreat at his seigneury of La Petite Nation on the Ottawa and refusing repeated appeals to re-enter politics. But his views and feelings had not changed; his refusals grew less decided—until the election of 1847 brought Zeus sweeping down from Olympus to unleash his thunderbolts again. Returned for St Maurice by acclamation, Papineau made an open breach with the LaFontaine forces in mid March, 1848, as soon as the new reform ministry announced to parliament its intention to cut short the session in order to mature its program. In a majestic rolling speech, that showed he had lost none of his old oratorical power or glowing intransigence, he denounced the ministers for failing to bring long-overdue justice to French Canada and declared that he would lead the fight for freedom which they would not, to win the repeal of the iniquitous union. From April to June, through a series of grand manifestos and public meetings, he recited old and current British misdeeds, condemned responsible government—"un mot jeté au hasard, une vaine théorie"—and called for a separate Lower Canada under American elective institutions, "les plus parfaites dont on a jusqu'à présent doué l'humanité."[25]

The proud, still-potent name of Papineau was a rallying point for a group of remarkably young, remarkably talented French-Canadian idealists, who had already organized themselves about a cultural and debating society, the Institut Canadien, and in July 1847 had begun to publish a small Montreal paper, well-named L'Avenir. Under little Jean-Baptiste Eric Dorion, just over twenty-one, it now came out strongly for Papineau's cause of repeal, above all, on grounds of democracy and nationalism. Starting in April, 1848, L'Avenir launched a series of eloquent, finely drafted articles on "L'Union et la Nationalité"—the alternatives it saw for French Canadians—and referred with zealous hope to the liberal-democratic ferment sweeping Europe. "La révolution française doit bouleverser le monde. . . . Il faut que le peuple du Bas Canada puisse être prêt quand son heure arrivera."[26] With passionate conviction it inveighed against tyrannical British domination and urged republican democratic liberty on French Canadians. The bold impact of the journal, coupled with Papineau's own vibrant manifestos, spread a new agitation for repeal of the union across French Canada during the later months of 1848, as old followers of Neilson (now dead) turned to his campaign anew, in company with veteran *patriotes* and the eager young radical democrats.

While other papers took up the cause of Papineau and *L'Avenir*, LaFontaine's own powerful press replied, warmly defending the gains won within union by the responsible system, and ruthlessly but effectively attacking Papineau's own dubious record as the people's guide and leader. Cauchon's *Journal de Québec*, Duvernay's *La Minerve* and Langevin's *Mélanges Religieux* in Montreal made steady headway. By the end of 1848 it appeared likely that this threat, too, would be contained by the LaFontaine forces. Besides, their policies had the obvious seal of success: government power. Nevertheless, in December, Hector Langevin privately confessed his own worries for the future. It all depended on the workings of the new reform ministry: ". . . s'il réussit, nous sommes pour longtemps encore sous la protection de l'Angleterre; s'il ne réussit pas, nous sommes Américains avant cinq ans."[27] In any case, what with serious radical unrest in French Canada and its beginnings in English Canada, what with deepening tory frustration and the all-pervading depression, the year ahead seemed bound to be an angry one.

<h2 style="text-align:center">III</h2>

The warehouses of Montreal were crammed with goods for which there were no markets; the vessels frozen at the wharves looked as if they might never sail again. Wheat and flour exports had fallen from 3,883,000 bushels in 1847 to 2,248,000 the next year.[28] And though the full St Lawrence system of canals had become available at last in 1848 with the opening of the enlarged Lachine Canal, after all the costs and hopes, the traffic in the bad times had not come to fill them. Their revenue for 1848 was less than half that of 1847.[29] Merchants, forwarders and millers who had invested heavily in improvements, counting on the new canals and the vanished Canada Corn Act preference, were all in deep distress. The unprecedented need for winter poor-relief was straining charity to the breaking point. And while the Montreal business community bitterly faced the final ruin of the old protected St Lawrence commercial empire, there was sharp cause for concern over the effects on French and Irish unemployed labourers of red republican revolution and socialism in France, and the Young Ireland revolt in the Irish homeland. Elgin himself wrote apprehensively to Grey of "the generally uneasy and diseased condition of the public mind."[30] So opened the year intended as the *annus mirabilis* of reform—the angry year of 1849.

Certainly, reform was the epitome of the ministerial program announced as parliament met in Montreal in January: the lifting of the restriction on the official use of French (signalized by Elgin's reading the Speech from the Throne in French as well as English),[31] the prospective transfer of postal services from imperial to Canadian control, a new Upper Canada university bill, and a whole set of measures to reform the province's judicial, municipal, and educational systems. Much of the legislation proposed went through without serious difficulty. Hincks carried a Guarantee Act to back the railway projects increasingly being put forward in Canada in spite of depression. Baldwin sponsored a notable Municipal Corporations Act for Canada West (which still remains at the basis of Ontario's municipal structure) to do away with the old partly-appointed, partly-representative district councils and set up a complete, integrated system of elected local self-governing bodies, from county and city councils to those for townships and police villages. He also succeeded at last with his bill to abolish King's College and establish a state, non-sectarian University of Toronto enjoying full control of the provincial endowment. It represented an entire victory for the forces of secularization and centralism in Upper Canadian higher education; and it went even further than Baldwin's abortive university bill of 1843, in that the denominational colleges might affiliate with the university only as divinity halls, without even small grants from the public funds.

But one projected piece of legislation, this in LaFontaine's keeping, ran headlong into trouble and threatened to arouse all the explosive forces latent in Montreal. It was the measure he introduced in the form of resolutions on February 13, to meet claims for losses suffered in Lower Canada during the rebellion of 1837. And the resultant Rebellion Losses Bill was of vital concern to LaFontaine and his followers, ever conscious of the looming shadow of Papineau. In the house, LaFontaine skilfully handled Papineau as a respected figure from the past wholly out of place in present politics. But if the Rebellion Losses Bill failed to satisfy French Canada, sentiment there might yet turn to the old champion of the people's rights. The issue was far larger than any mere financial claims.

Compensation for property destroyed in the Upper Canada rebellion of 1837 had been approved early in the union, although the £40,000 required was not paid until 1845, when an indemnity for similar Lower Canadian damages had also been approved in principle.[32] Under Draper, a commission had reported in 1846 on the substantially larger claims in Lower Canada, estimated at £100,000; but no action had been taken during the political confusion of the time. In any event, old, rankling Anglo-French antipathies were deeply involved. Damages in the east had largely arisen from the suppressing of revolt in a French countryside by English forces. It was uncertain, moreover, how many of the claimants had actually supported the rebel cause—though there was not much doubt about Wolfred Nelson's own unabashed claim for £12,000.[33] Yet now in 1849 there was a large French majority sharing government power and determined to secure equal justice, too long deferred, for the Lower Canadian community. Tory charges that the real aim was to indemnify rebels, and the urgings of worried Upper

Canadian reformers, did bring LaFontaine at least to exclude the relatively few Lower Canadians who had been exiled or convicted in the courts from obtaining compensation under an amended bill. Further than this he would not go. Indeed, there could be no sure way of determining the past loyalty of those in the indefinite realm beyond actual court decisions. And the plain fact was that French Canadians were far less concerned to discriminate between the loyal and disloyal than to obtain a broad unstinted measure of indemnity that would finally allay their bitter memories of the rebellion period, and close the raw wound of what they regarded as racial persecution.

The Rebellion Losses Bill was a symbol: an emotional, communal symbol. It would prove to the French Canadians that the union had truly been recast to bring them equality and power; it would test the validity of the arguments for responsible government; it would substantiate LaFontaine's whole course of politics—or else swing French Canada towards Papineau and the separatist radical republicans. For English tory-conservatives the bill was no less a symbol. English-speaking liberals themselves might be dubious about the sweep of the measure; but they shared in the new power balance achieved by the dual alliance, and were ready to meet its conditions. For tories, however, it was a stark sign of their dispossession in a black new era, since if it passed, their world had indeed been turned upside-down.

The traditional defenders of English ascendancy and British loyalty still saw the bill as a flagrant device to compensate for treason, the sheer repudiation of every patriotic effort made to put down rebellion in Lower Canada in 1837-38. Yet it was the tory commercial class of Montreal who reacted most acutely to the symbol of Rebellion Losses. As an enclave in a Lower Canada now thoroughly under French control, their past political authority lost, their economic future in jeopardy, they viewed the bill as a fearful demonstration of what newly triumphant French power might do to dictate to the British minority. Their response was passionate. It grew the more so, as the battle over Rebellion Losses developed in full force in the assembly. There were violent scenes there as the bill went through its stages. Allan MacNab, almost beside himself, vehemently denounced the entire French-Canadian people as rebels and aliens; William Blake hotly retorted that MacNab and the tories were "the rebels to their constitution and country."[34] A fight was just averted on the floor, and the galleries had to be cleared when a brawl burst out there. But the government majority held firm through February and March, keeping within it an Upper Canadian majority also, as Baldwin and his followers upheld their alliance and endorsed the amended measure for Lower Canada. Conclusively beaten in the legislature, the tories had still one final hope. They looked to the governor-general to refuse assent to a bill rewarding treason, and dissolve parliament; to uphold the true guardians of British interests as governors had done before. They did not yet comprehend the full meaning of responsible government.

Elgin did. The Rebellion Losses Bill was the policy of his ministers, who were responsible to parliament and unquestionably had its confidence. There was no reason to withhold his sanction or to dissolve a parliament only a year old and with a strong majority in control. The governor-general was out of politics; he was no longer a tory party patron. With no illusions as to the repercussions that might follow, Elgin concluded that the established fact of responsible rule required him to give his assent. It was a judgement of clearsighted courage. "If I pass the bill," he soberly told Grey, "whatever mischief may ensue may probably be repaired if the worse comes to worst by the sacrifice of me—Whereas, if the case be referred to England, it is not impossible that Her Majesty may only have before her the alternative of provoking a rebellion in Lower Canada by refusing her assent to a measure deeply affecting the interests of the Habitans and thus throwing the whole population into Papineau's hands, or of wounding the susceptibilities of some of the best subjects she has in the Province."[35]

Meanwhile, as tories eagerly awaited the Governor's action, their press breathed ominous warnings. Assent to the bill, declared the *Montreal Gazette*, "would raise all the Anglo-Saxon blood between Port Sarnia and Gaspé to 'the boiling point.' "[36] The Toronto *Patriot* fulminated, ". . . we will dare anything rather than submit to the wicked, irreligious principle that the innocent should be taxed to reward the guilty."[37] The Montreal *Courier* direly added: ". . . let the Governor sanction it if he pleases, *but while there is an axe and rifle on the frontier and Saxon hands to wield them these claims will not be paid.*"[38] The answer came on April 25. On that day Elgin drove down to the legislature and accepted the Rebellion Losses Bill. Tories, incredulous, felt shock, a sense of betrayal, then surging anger. As the Governor left the building he was booed by the crowd that had quickly collected outside. And stones and rotten eggs came pelting down on his carriage as it bounced away at full gallop back to Monklands.

That night, a tory mass meeting gathered in the Champ-de-Mars. Under flaming torches a crowd of fifteen hundred were lashed to vengeful fury by wild speeches on French domination and the ruin of British interests: but unleashed as well were the pent-up frustrations of poverty, unemployment, disease and despair. All the fever and fury in Montreal exploded. A blindly savage mob marched on the parliament building, seat of French power. The house was still sitting as they burst in, smashing gas lights, breaking up furniture, ripping down hangings. Fire broke out. But Morin sat tight-lipped and unheeding in the Speaker's chair until a motion to adjourn was properly passed. The members filed out of the parliament house in ordered dignity behind their Speaker, ignoring flames and chaos.[39] If the governor-general would maintain the role of constituted authority despite the mob, so would the Canadian parliament.

The blaze roared in the keen April night until the building was entirely gutted. The next day, though soldiers were called from the garrison to patrol the streets, riots and tory outcries against the French and their English reform dupes continued. Hincks's lodgings, Nelson's and Drummond's all were assaulted, and LaFontaine's fine new house, still empty, was left a ravaged hulk. It was a week, in fact, before rage and rioting finally ran their course in Montreal; during which time Elgin was again fiercely attacked, when he felt duty-bound to come into town again to receive an address of loyal support from parliament, now housed in Bonsecours Market. A howling crowd battered the viceregal carriage with rocks and brickbats, tried to block its escape, then chased it and its cavalry escort half way back to Monklands, the Governor refusing to allow any reprisals. He wrote privately to Grey: "We were for a time I believe in great danger. . . . Excesses correct themselves, and I have no doubt that the violence of the disaffected will elicit a great counter-demonstration—At the same time I confess I did not before know how thin is the crust of order which covers the anarchical elements that boil and toss beneath our feet."[40]

Lesser disturbances also took place in other towns, from Quebec to Bytown, Toronto and Hamilton; but outside of Montreal, tories and conservatives generally showed far less vehemence and quickly returned to constitutional loyalty, if they ever forsook it. Meanwhile counter-demonstrations, and a flood of petitions and addresses from both sections of Canada, proved the correctness of Elgin's underlying assumption: that the weight of public feeling, whether eager French or merely acquiescent English, lay with his ministers and his acceptance of their policies under responsible government.

The harsh emotions raised by the Rebellion Losses Bill would not quickly disappear; but, as the crisis itself passed, Elgin's cool statesmanship had left notable consequences. In near-desperate circumstances he had demonstrated the deepest meaning of responsible rule: that Canadians would, and had to, take the responsibility henceforth for running their own affairs. And his calm restraint in not reacting to the mindless violence of tory mobs had helped prevent the English populace from committing themselves enduringly against him—even while he had consolidated the French Canadians behind his régime and behind LaFontaine, not Papineau. In fact, by upholding strict constitutional process in face of serious personal danger, Lord Elgin had brought Canada safely through the racial storm inherent in the Rebellion Losses question.

IV

Though violence departed, except for fitful outbursts after parliament rose in late May, sullen discontent remained. Above all, world depression weighed remorselessly on Canadian trade. The magnificent St Lawrence canals, that now provided an open seaway nine feet in depth to the interior and cut freight charges by fifty per cent from Lake Ontario to Montreal, still remained half empty.[41] Because of them, the public debt by 1846 was already more than double what it had been in 1843; the situation was much worse by 1848, when through falling revenues the province faced a large current deficit and credit so poor that it could not borrow.[42] The American Drawback Acts and the advantages of the much bigger port of New York over Montreal as an Atlantic outlet had greatly contributed to the failure of the grand commercial design of the Canadian canal system. But the drying-up of world trade did still more to harm the river and canal route, though the loss of protected British markets got most of the blame.

At the same time, efforts to improve the flow of trade brought little result. The anxiously awaited repeal of the imperial Navigation Acts in June, 1849, which ended the exclusion of foreign vessels from the St Lawrence, would not bring any significant increase in shipping. And the policy so ardently preached by Merritt, and now taken up by the reform administration, of finding new markets in the United States through the joint removal of tariff barriers, also proved abortive. A Canadian act of 1849 offering reciprocal free trade in a variety of products failed to produce the necessary concurrent legislation in the United States, insufficiently interested in its northern neighbours. Bankruptcies spread in Montreal. Lord Elgin calculated that "Property in most Canadian towns, and more especially in the Capital, has fallen 50 p[er] c[ent] in value within the past three years."[43] For the business men of the St Lawrence, at least, Canada in the third year of depression was a country almost without hope.

The cause seemed clear enough to them: Britain's abandoning of the old preferential colonial system. The faithful upholders of the St Lawrence empire had been thrust aside politically by the cold new precept of responsible rule, so harshly exemplified in the French-dictated Rebellion Losses Act, and sacrificed economically to British indifference and the rigid dogmas of free trade. It was natural that they should thus view the loss of their privileged position and its consequences, even though stagnant trade was actually a world condition. And the wound as well as the loss drove many Montreal commercial tories to espouse a perennial drastic remedy for Canadian troubles—guaranteed to end them by ending Canada itself—the annexation of the country to the United States. This would provide desperately needed access to the American market, would swamp French power, and be no more than Britain had deserved.

Elgin had earlier written to Grey of the rise of annexationist sentiment in the depressed times, and noted both its superficial and significant qualities: "Whether it be alleged that the French are oppressing the British, or the British the French—that Upper Canada Debt presses on Lower Canada, or Lower Canada claims on Upper—whether merchants be bankrupt, stocks depreciated, roads bad, or seasons unfavourable—annexation is invoked as the remedy for all ills imaginary or real. —A great deal of this talk is however bravado, and a great deal the mere product of thoughtlessness—Undoubtedly it is in some quarters the utterance of very sincere convictions —And if England will not make the sacrifices which are absolutely necessary to put the Colonists here in as good a position commercially as the citizens of the States—in order to which *free navigation* and *reciprocal trade with the States are indispensable* . . . the end may be nearer at hand than we wot of."[44]

Annexationism undoubtedly appealed to others besides disheartened and embittered tories. It attracted the young French radicals of *L'Avenir* (soon to be termed *rouges* by analogy with the advanced *républicains rouges* of France) who dreamed rosily of a French democratic nation within the republican sisterhood of the American states. And it seemed likely that resurgent English radicals, impatient with the traditional and ceremonial trappings of British ministerial government and parliamentary rule, might take up annexation in a similar desire for republican simplicity and equality. Nevertheless, the essential question by the summer of 1849 was whether tory-conservatism, defeated, dispossessed, but still widely powerful, would accept annexation as party policy. The developing British American League, presided over by George Moffatt, provided a forum for debating and determining the answer.

The League had been formed to consider the problems caused by the change in imperial policies. Some reformers joined, concerned themselves about the effects of British free trade; but the branches that sprang up in towns across the province were chiefly composed of tories and conservatives, who talked variously of annexation, adopting tariff protection for Canada itself, and especially of counteracting French domination. All these views and others were expressed at a grand conference of the League, held at Kingston in July 1849, which was virtually conservatism in convention. Out of the steam and gloom of complaint it grew apparent that the annexationists there were still very much in a minority. Upper Canadian delegates, above all, upheld the British tie. The convention brought forth three resolutions: for retrenchment, a Canadian protective tariff, and an investigation of the possibility of federal union among the British North American colonies. These were little more than insubstantial wishes at the time; but the latter two would have considerable future. In any case, the vital point demonstrated was that annexation had by no means captured the main forces of tory-conservatism.

Nevertheless, there were still annexationists; among Lower Canadian tories, *rouge* French Canadians, and a scattering of both radical and tory extremists in Upper Canada. As autumn made clear the failure of still another season on the St Lawrence, annexationism rose to vociferous new heights. In Montreal, the *Gazette* and three other leading English papers had come out for it, while the Annexation Association in the city was busily enrolling members, making strange comrades of the devoted enemies of '37, Papineau supporters and tory partisans.[45] In Toronto the small but ardent *Canadian Independent* urged annexation (in the odd but not infrequent Canadian belief that annexation and independence were the same thing). And Baldwin and Hincks worried over the fact that the party's candidate in a by-election to be held in nearby Third York, an old reformer, Peter Perry, cannily refused to commit himself to oppose the severing of the tie with Britain. Baldwin, indeed, felt it necessary to publish a letter he had sent to Perry, declaring pointedly, "I can look upon those only who are for the continuance of that connexion as political friends"—while Elgin commented that Baldwin himself was "of more importance to the connexion than three regiments."[46]

The peak come in October, when in Montreal the Annexation Association issued a jolting manifesto. Pointing darkly to "ruin and decay" throughout Canada, the barren hope of the canals, the vital need for new markets and capital, the document called for "friendly and peaceful" separation from Britain and union with the United States.[47] Its three hundred and twenty-five signatories included a future father of Confederation, Alexander Tilloch Galt, a later conservative prime minister, J. J. C. Abbott, and two subsequent leading liberals, Antoine-Aimé Dorion and Luther Holton; but the list read chiefly like a roster of Montreal's business élite. Response was rapid. There was a clamour of anti-annexation meetings and addresses, drowning minor echoes elsewhere of the Montreal declaration. Indignant argument and agitation went on through the winter. Yet well before the year's end it was evident that the Annexation Manifesto had been scarcely more than a final bout of Montreal fever, not the herald of a new popular upheaval.

It had shown, in fact, that the mass of Canadians were essentially satisfied with their political state, whatever the burdens of depression. In French Canada, the very success of responsible government, of LaFontaine's leadership, of the Rebellion Losses Act, had left small margin for Papineau and the *rouges'* annexationism. A largely cautious, conservative-minded people were in the mass but little stirred by visions of democratic and republican perfection; and they saw joining the United States as the virtual extinction, not the realization, of the national identity which they had so resolutely defended. *Survivance* within the Canadian union looked far more feasible and desirable than the radicals' dream of *nationalité* within the American union. Furthermore, the fact that *rouges* revived the old anti-clericalism of the *patriotes*, and warmly hailed the liberal, anti-papal revolution of 1848 in Rome, turned the potent influence of the church with increasing effect against them.[48]

In Upper Canada among all parties, the strength of British allegiance, the ingrained resistance to the United States, and the feeling also for a separate identity in America, had brought the emphatic rejection of annexationism. Besides, now that responsible rule had so clearly been established, any former association of annexation with self-government had lost much of its meaning. Joining the republic meant, instead, associating with slavery and sectional conflict, and (as the Toronto *Globe* energetically informed the West) abandoning the free, efficient system of British cabinet and parliamentary rule for a rigid, unwieldly, even old-fashioned, American written constitution.[49] Moreover, Upper Canada was still growing and expanding, despite depression, and felt a good deal of confidence about the future. One western anti-annexation writer even proved to his own satisfaction that "*The British Canadian people are winning the race of improvement hollow —from the American!*"[50]

Still further, Lower Canadian tories who had adopted annexation had done so with the claim that an indifferent mother country would not oppose it. On Elgin's urging, however, the Colonial Secretary emphatically made clear that Britain had no intention of abandoning her North American empire: a fact that cut the very ground from under tory annexationism.[51] There was also economic fact. The depression affecting Canada had centred in St Lawrence commerce and in the towns; yet the population of the union was overwhelmingly agrarian and rural. There had been no such protracted series of bad harvests as in the thirties, and a good deal of grain had still gone out to market through the American drawback system. Nor was the public debt of the province really beyond its capacity to bear; by the end of 1849 Hincks had new hopes of selling Canadian debentures in England with Grey's backing.[52] Finally, towards the close of 1849 world trade was at last reviving. With improving conditions and in the absence of any heavy load of farm debt, Canadian recovery would advance rapidly in 1850. Indeed, a whole new phase of boom development was about to begin.

Thus, with 1849, an era ended. While annexationist currents continued into the next year, and Elgin and Grey remained acutely aware of them, they were really the dwindling traces of a time that had passed. Different prospects and problems lay ahead. The decade whose largest theme for the Canadian union had been the evolution of self-government had closed with its firm achievement—for all the storm over Rebellion Losses, and the sharp annexationist spasm that had followed.

CHAPTER 8

Prosperity, Reciprocity and Railways

1850–1857

In the new decade of the 1850's Canada moved with gathering speed from recovery to boom. The world had entered another trade cycle, marked by rising prices, gold pouring forth from California and Australia, and the spread of railway networks in both Europe and America. For the province it meant restored exports to Britain, as well as fast-rising new markets in the United States: markets which grew the faster when reciprocal free trade between British North America and the republic was achieved by treaty in 1854. Buoyant times also brought outside capital to invest in Canadian railway and commercial development. And thriving exports, capital influx and railway-building together ministered to rapid growth and social change, before the boom years ended in 1857. This was an era of glowing economic success for the Canadian union, whatever the political strains that also might emerge.

Well before reciprocity or the coming of railways could have their effect on the colony, the business revival under way in 1850 proved that the removal of the old imperial protective duties had not ruined the Canadian commercial system, after all. The St Lawrence transport artery filled again. Cheaper inland charges, thanks to the canals, lower ocean rates because of larger, faster, iron ships, the excellent harvest of 1849, traffic with the Maritime Provinces stimulated by a reciprocal trade agreement in 1850—all these played some part. But the most obvious factor was the newly vigorous demand for Canada's staples of wood and grain.

As for the wood staple, it had been overcutting more than the reduction in preferential duties that had jammed the Quebec booms with unsalable timber in the later forties. But Canadian squared pine was a good and competitive product, and reviving needs in industrial Britain from 1850 onward gave it a strong market there. An enlarged Canadian deal trade also managed to cope with Baltic competition overseas. More significant in the long run, however, was the emergence of alternative markets for Canada's wood within North America. The prime cause was the swelling growth of population, industry and towns in the neighbouring United States. There in the east, factory centres ate up the resources of building timber in their own immediate regions, while in the midwest, American settlement spread out across prairies with little tree-cover of their own. From the late forties Canadian forest resources were linked with an ever-mounting continental demand. Traffic in sawn lumber flowed southward across the Great Lakes, or moved by the Richelieu and the newly improved Chambly Canal to New York and New England. American capital increasingly invested in Ottawa lumbering; the great pine stands of Simcoe county, the Grand Valley and Georgian Bay were cut into for the export mills. And at the same time Canada's own growing population and urban development created a rising home market for the products of local saw and planing mills, sash and shingle factories, and even cabinet works.

What has been well entitled "the North American assault on the Canadian forest" actually had beginnings before the union of the Canadas.[1] Despite the American tariff barriers and the old colonial commercial system directed to the British market, lumber had been exported to the United States via St Johns on the Richelieu, Kingston on the Rideau Canal route, or through the Welland to the Erie Canal. By the mid thirties, lumbermen in favourably located areas were already turning from the more wasteful production of prime square timber and deals for the far-off British market to the milling of cheaper boards and planks for American sale, while American lumber interests were starting to seek Canadian timber-limits. The rebellions of 1837 and the depression thereafter had, however, checked the development of these tentative American alignments; and in the earlier forties the generally prosperous state of the square timber market and the British railway boom had tended to direct lumbering enterprise to production for overseas. But the dismantling of the imperial preferential system in the later forties inevitably influenced producers to look to American outlets anew.

At the same time, American needs for Canadian sawn lumber were growing in the populous, industrial east. Half unheeded, the trade across the border mounted in the last years of the forties, in spite of the depression. Even in 1849, of a total Canadian export of forest products worth some £1,327,000, £314,000 came from American sales; and by 1853, out of a total of over £2,350,000, more than £652,000 was similarly derived.[2] Oswego, on the Erie Canal feeder, had imported less than two million feet from the Canadian forests above Lake Ontario in 1840. In 1850 it took over sixty million feet.[3] Hand in hand with this rising trade went American business penetration of Canadian lumber regions. To supplement water routes, railroads were promoted to bring down wood from Canada, such as the line from Boston to Ogdensburg on the upper St Lawrence, completed in 1850. By 1854, the Bytown and Prescott, backed with Boston money, carried it on to the Ottawa. And the fifties were to see also the rise of powerful American lumber firms and large sawmill owners in the Ottawa region. There, centred on Bytown, they would come to overshadow the older, British-oriented square-timber makers of the district. The whole process thus initiated in Canada's forest industry, the exploitation of one of the country's basic resources by American capital, has had a long and ever-complicating history, bringing growth, wealth, waste, and new problems of external domination all in heaping measure.

As for the other great Canadian staple, grain, it similarly overcame the dislocations caused by loss of the imperial preference, once the bad times of the later forties ebbed away. Higher bread-stuff prices, improved Atlantic shipping facilities, and fertile Upper Canadian fields, all enabled the province to compete effectively in an open British market. In fact, a veritable wheat boom developed for Canada when the Crimean War of 1854-56 excluded Russian grain from Britain's supply. Exports of wheat and flour by the St Lawrence, which in 1849 had stood at 3,645,000 bushels, rose to 4,547,000 in 1850, and 6,597,000 in 1853.[4] In 1856 it reached 9,391,531 bushels, a figure not surpassed until the next decade.[5] Meanwhile, advancing industrialism and urbanism in the United States produced alternative markets for Canadian cereals in that country, no less than for Canadian lumber. Indeed, the increase that resulted over-all in the province's agricultural exports was even greater than that in forest products. Thus the wood staple actually lost its old primacy in Canadian trade during this era. It declined to forty-two per cent of the total of Canada's exports in the years from 1849 to 1858, and would become thirty-two per cent in the next decade.[6]

To a considerable extent this was because of the expansion of the Canada West granary in the mid-century years—the Manitoba of its day. It grew twelve million bushels of wheat in 1851; twenty-five million a decade later.[7] This crop not only went to Britain via the St Lawrence or out by the Erie in bond for re-export; it helped as well to feed the populous adjacent American states. Canada East also gained new markets in New York and New England for its coarse grains, livestock and dairy produce. It was still hampered by agricultural methods inferior to those of Canada West; but at least the long-term decline in Lower Canadian farm prices came to an end in 1850, as eastern farmers also benefited from generally high demand.

While the growth of American sales for Canadian staples was a notable feature of this new era of the fifties, the north-south movement of commerce did not inhibit an ample east-west flow along the St Lawrence system. In spite of the development of trade with the United States, the larger markets for Canadian staples continued to lie in the industrial metropolis of Britain.

Even in forest exports, for example, British sales were worth four million dollars to something over one million for American in 1850; eight million to about three and a half million in the peak boom year of 1857.[8] The Canadian commercial pattern had not been transformed but had been broadened and strengthened through ending its sole dependence on a protected imperial market. In this respect, free trade had not proved a disaster at all.

The St Lawrence canals played a major part in the vigorous flow of east-west commerce. While the bulk of Upper Canada's wheat exports continued to travel via the Erie out to Britain, grain, lumber and other produce assuredly moved in quantity to Montreal; and there was sizable return traffic up the waterway in manufactures and consumer goods imported for the prosperous farming West. Hence Montreal, the master of the St Law-rence, was thriving again. It was aided also by the deepening of the river channel below the city, completed in 1852. This enabled larger transatlantic vessels that had made Quebec their terminus to sail direct to the up-river port. The increasing use of steam by ocean craft (better able to navigate the river passage than sailing-ships), and the new growth of the sawn lumber market in relation to the square timber trade, also tended to profit Montreal rather than the older Canadian port. Above all, the steady advance in the inland country, and the flourishing state of its trade, could not fail to benefit the city that commanded the St Lawrence canal route to the West.

Nevertheless, the St Lawrence trading system had not succeeded in the greatest purpose that lay behind the building of the canal route. It had not made the vast mid-continent interior its own; it had not brought Montreal any victory over New York. Even after the depression of the forties had departed, the loss of preferential access to the British market and the drain through the American drawbacks had prevented the provincial chain of canals from capturing the whole sweep of commerce for which they had been designed. Furthermore, they had come too late, for the Americans now had railroads to the West, offering year-round, through transport to their ocean harbours. Still further, in view of the higher Atlantic freight rates to the St Lawrence, and its winter closing, together with the much wider cargo facilities at New York, it seems unlikely that the grand hopes of St Lawrence empire could have been realized in any case.[9] Yet that empire and its water-way had failed only in degree. Its Montreal capital, busy enough with traffic, was now looking to land transport to supplement the water system; to the railway as its instrument of Canadian commercial strategy in the effort still to achieve the St Lawrence dream.

II

Because a prosperous Canada was finding new or restored markets despite the end of the old colonial system, the demand for reciprocal free trade with the United States lost much of its urgency in the early fifties. William Merritt, the apostle of reciprocity since 1846, had emphatically presented it as the alternative to annexation—the free-trade policy suited to Canada's own needs—while annexationists of 1849 had certainly looked to political union with the United States because of the failure to obtain commercial access to that country through a reciprocal trade agreement. Lord Elgin himself had told Grey after the appearance of the Montreal Manifesto that if reciprocity were not achieved "there is nothing before us but violent agitation ending in convulsion or annexation." "Give us Reciprocity with the States," he had declared, "and I am ready to answer for the tranquillity of Canada."[10] And Grey in the emergency had urged the Foreign Office to do all possible to aid Canadian negotiations in Washington through the British minister there.[11]

Yet the attempts to obtain concurrent legislation from Congress on the tariff failed again in 1850, as in '48 and '49, in spite of the best efforts of Merritt and Hincks at Washington. Now, however, Elgin wrote to Grey, "The Yankees have given the go by to the reciprocity Bill. Fortunately the desire for the measure has very much abated on this side."[12] Indeed, from 1850 onward the colony was clearly flourishing without reciprocity, while annexationism was a spent rocket. Besides, United States markets were developing in any case because of the needs that Americans had for Canadian resources: a fact particularly evinced by the mounting lumber traffic.[13] The truth was that any reciprocity agreement now would be as much a result as a cause of Canadian-American trade.

Nevertheless, it was obvious that this growing trade could grow still larger if United States tariff barriers were removed. The emerging economic pattern of the early fifties, one might say, indicated that if Canada could do without reciprocity, she could do much better with it. And if Canadian interest, while real enough, was now less acute, the movement for a trade agreement had been put on a broader, more promising basis. The other British North American colonies had voiced their own desires for reciprocal free trade with the United States. Great Britain had taken up the cause of obtaining by treaty for her North American domains what had failed of achievement by joint Canadian-American legislation alone: the free exchange of natural products between the British provinces and the republic.

Grey's own interest in this move largely embodied the belief that through strengthening the colonies economically they would be enabled to assume more burdens on their own, particularly the costs of defence. Here Elgin had astutely played on the whig secretary's laissez-faire predilections and his concern for imperial retrenchment. These, accordingly, overrode Grey's other concern, that colonies should not make special tariff arrangements that might infringe the general fiscal freedom of the empire. In fact, in

Grey's desire to push the colonies to self-reliance, Elgin's desire to hold a self-governing Canada happily within the empire, they were actually clearing the way for the principle of colonial fiscal autonomy, which before the end of the decade would be invoked by Canada to defend the imposition of protectionist duties against the mother country herself.

Prolonged negotiations failed again in Washington by the end of 1851, although there Sir Henry Bulwer had been empowered to offer the Americans free navigation of the St Lawrence canals and privileges in the colonies' Atlantic fisheries in addition to reciprocity in trade. The mass of American political opinion was still indifferent to the value of trade across the northern border, and in any event engrossed in the sectional struggle in Congress between the interests of North and South. Besides, the administration under Millard Fillmore was in the hands of the protectionist Whigs, scarcely the party to reduce the tariff. The next year, furthermore, the Russell cabinet fell in England, and the conservative Derby government that replaced it took a stiffer line towards the United States. They were far less willing than Grey to offer concessions, above all in the matter of the fisheries. Yet here, in consequence, although unwittingly, they brought a new factor to bear on the question of obtaining reciprocity with the republic.

The rich fishing grounds off the Atlantic shores of British America had long been a source of disagreements between Britain and the United States. Disputes had especially arisen over the definition of territorial waters from which American fishermen were excluded under the existing Convention of 1818; from time to time American fishing vessels had been arrested by the Royal Navy for transgressing the British claims. In May 1852, the new Colonial Secretary, Sir John Pakington, urged on by the colonies, announced a firm policy of protecting the British American coastal fisheries. The situation grew tense in 1852-53, as both British and American warships were dispatched to back up their nationals in the fisheries dispute. Neither side, however, wanted an armed conflict; and it grew apparent that a settlement might be reached, essentially by trading American free access to the colonial fisheries for colonial free access to the American market. Moreover, the threat of war over the fisheries brought both the American government and public at last to focus their attention on commercial relations with the British colonies. The British minister in Washington reported: "The notion that a collision and rupture with England might grow out of the matter has presented it in a very different light."[14]

Negotiations were renewed; but lapsed again through most of 1853, while the Democrats took over the administration under Franklin Pierce. Renewed once more, it was not until the spring of 1854 that they finally came near success. By this time booming Canada felt the need of reciprocity even less. Still, her farming and lumbering interests obviously stood to gain from the bargaining of the maritime colonies' fisheries for free trade with the United States, her own chief contribution to the bargain being the use of the St Lawrence canals by American shipping. And now the scales of United States opinion had swung to favour reciprocity.

Protectionism was at a low point under a Democratic administration, traditionally the party of lower tariffs. Atlantic fishing interests, Great Lakes traders, lumber buyers, all vigorously backed a reciprocity agreement. Israel D. Andrews, American consular official and confirmed free-trader, waged an expensive and skilful campaign for it, both by building press support and by lobbying among prominent politicians and business men.[15] Furthermore, the deep sectional division in the United States worked with remarkable effect to promote a reciprocity treaty. Northern forces espoused it in Congress, in the belief that it would lead to annexation of the British provinces, and thus to a clear preponderance of free states in the union. Southern defenders of slavery approved it for the precisely opposite reason —that it would render annexation unnecessary for the provinces, and so preserve the sectional balance. Finally there was the suave, convivial diplomacy of Lord Elgin, who came down to Washington in May, 1854, accompanied by Hincks, to take charge of the British side of the negotiations. After ten days he announced that a Senate majority for a treaty was assured.[16] On June 6 it was signed.

The Reciprocity Treaty, duly approved by Congress in August, was to run for a ten-year period from the beginning of 1855, and to be terminated or renewed thereafter on one year's notice. Ratified by the colonial legislatures (a notable enhancement of their powers), it provided for the reciprocal free admission of major natural products of the United States and British America, including grain, lumber, coal, livestock, meat and fish; and joint access to all coastal fisheries north of the thirty-sixth parallel. American use of the St Lawrence and Canadian navigation of Lake Michigan were also included in the terms. For Canada, however, the abolition of United States duties on lumber, grain and flour were undoubtedly the greatest benefits. Yet the reception of the treaty in the province was certainly not what it might have been a few years before. While William Hamilton Merritt might exult at the realization of his long endeavours, the Montreal Gazette thought the measure of little interest "to the people of Canada East," however beneficial to the interests of their western fellow-subjects; and even the Toronto Globe, by now the leading western journal, considered the treaty of qualified benefit in the existing state of prosperity.[17]

Whatever the reaction in Canada, trade with the United States grew markedly in the first years of the Reciprocity Treaty, and through its lifetime generally would go on expanding. It is, of course, impossible to estimate how much that trade might have grown without the treaty, during prosperous times of high demand, and so to calculate how much the agreement itself was responsible for the advance. Still, certain points are apparent. Exports to the United States from Canada, chiefly grain, flour and lumber, which were valued at some eight millions of dollars in both 1853 and 1854, jumped to sixteen million in the first year of the treaty and reached nearly eighteen million in 1856; though they fell to thirteen in 1857, during which year the Canadian boom broke.[18] Moreover, the increased flow moved in either direction: imports from the United States grew almost as notably.[19] The evident effect in the two countries was a considerably increased consumption of each other's products.

Another evident consequence was growing joint use of each other's transportation systems to re-export natural products to outside markets. Since these cargoes could move freely under reciprocity, one result of the Treaty of 1854 was to integrate Canadian and American lines of water and rail transport more closely together on a continental basis. Thus, for example, wheat gathered beyond Chicago might move through Canada West and, supplemented by Canadian wheat, go on out the Erie to the ocean. Or flour shipped by Boston to the Maritimes might have been produced by mills at Montreal. In this way the treaty developed a "commerce of convenience," as goods moved readily both ways across the borders to the most immediate markets, especially in the broad Great Lakes basin, which to a large extent had become a continental free-trade unit.[20] Still further, American manufactures, though not included under the Reciprocity Treaty, found a growing market in prosperous Canada, their use encouraged by trading contacts and buying patterns set through the commerce of convenience.

At any rate, the final and obvious summation is that Canada thrived heartily under reciprocity—a fact which would make the era of the treaty, when it ended in 1866, look in future like a golden age in Canadian-American relations. Yet the orienting of more of Canada's exports to the American market, which reciprocity fostered, by no means reduced the continuing trade with Britain. And the new orientation itself took its origins less from the treaty than from increasing American demands for Canadian raw materials and food-stuffs that had emerged in the years before. Finally, the flush times under reciprocity had another source as well: the resounding Canadian railway boom that had accompanied the whole period of negotiating and inaugurating the Treaty of 1854.

III

Although the age of railway-building really began for Canada with the 1850's, railways had been projected for years past, ever since the early thirties had demonstrated their success in England and brought their beginnings in the United States. The London and Gore, for example, had been chartered in Upper Canada in 1834. The Champlain and St Lawrence had actually been built in Lower Canada in 1836, running fourteen and a half miles to by-pass the Richelieu Rapids on the Montreal - Lake Champlain water route. And in 1839 a similar short "portage road" had been opened in Upper Canada around Niagara Falls, but had taken to horse traction when the grades proved too steep for early steam locomotives. A number of other lines had also been chartered by the union legislature during the forties; yet very little more actual construction had occurred. By 1850 all British North America had only sixty-six miles of track, to nine thousand in the United States.[21]

In the 1840's, however, the Province of Canada had been concentrating its hopes and public funds on St Lawrence canal-building, although in the more advanced United States the canal era was then fast giving way to the railroad. Moreover, there was no great amount of private capital being produced in a community just passing out of the pioneer stage, while the world depression of the later forties effectively prevented the importation of capital from outside. Yet conditions changed greatly with the 1850's. In the renewed good times there was British and American capital looking for investments; a rapidly expanding Canadian economy was also accumulating wealth on its own. The mounting trade to the United States, even before reciprocity, called for better means of north-south transport; and railways seemed increasingly required to supplement the completed east-west St Lawrence system of waterways. Public policy, private promotion, and popular enthusiasm all came eagerly together to launch an era of strenuous railway-building that produced eighteen hundred miles of track in the Canadian union by 1859.

The first major new line, the St Lawrence and Atlantic, was opened between Montreal and Portland, Maine, in 1853, having been chiefly built since 1850. It had been planned, of course, well back in the forties, in Montreal's response to the challenge of the American drawbacks and the coming of British free trade. Although the city had still pinned its faith to the canals, these threats seemed to require that the inland water system be supplemented by an all-year land line to the open sea. Hence, to enable the St Lawrence route to meet the free competition of the American Atlantic ports, it was proposed to give the city its own through railway access to the Atlantic. This would overcome the winter closing of the river route, make Montreal a year-round trans-shipment centre, and lower freight charges there in consequence.

Alternative projects to link the St Lawrence by an Intercolonial Railway to ice-free ports in the British Maritimes had broken down in the late forties over disagreements concerning routes, forbidding costs, and the lack of an essential financial guarantee from the British government. The depression of those years had also held back Montreal's railway plans. But the scheme that nevertheless emerged was to join Montreal with Boston or Portland by a line backed by New England capital interests. Portland, some 280 miles away, became the outlet, largely through the persuasive powers of John A. Poor, a zealous Maine railway promoter. The organizing drive of Alexander Galt, commissioner of the British American Land Company in the Eastern Townships, was also well applied in his role as president of the St Lawrence and Atlantic after 1849. In 1852 the railway reached Sherbrooke, and the next year crossed into Vermont to meet the track building from the coast.

The triumphant completion of this direct rail link between Canada and the ocean was also the result of financial aid secured under the railway promotion measure which that bold financier, Francis Hincks, had carried through parliament in 1849, in spite of hard times and shortage of funds. By this act the government guaranteed payment of six-per-cent interest on half the bonds of any railway over seventy-five miles in length, once half the line had been built. Fortunately, before the St Lawrence and Atlantic or any other line was sufficiently advanced to qualify for the guarantee, public revenues had revived; and Hincks had also been able to float a £500,000 loan through the great London house of Baring in 1850. As for his Guarantee Act, it gave effective public support to private Canadian railway development, by assuring investors a return on their capital even before the lines were finished. But in time it also invited overbuilding, and the floating of railway projects more for quick profits on their promotion than for their actual completion and operation.

Stimulated by the Guarantee Act and the return of good times, other considerable lines were constructed. The Great Western Railway took up the old London and Gore charter. It built across Canada West from the Niagara River to the Detroit, thus directly connecting the New York network of railroads with the Michigan Central, with the aim of exploiting Upper Canada's position between the populous seaboard and the fast-filling midwest. Presided over by Sir Allan MacNab (whose lusty toryism by no means clashed with his ardent railway politics) and backed by British and American capital, the Great Western was completed in 1855, to run for 360 miles from Niagara Falls via Hamilton and London to Windsor opposite Detroit. An immediate success, it was soon extended from Hamilton to Toronto. Toronto interests meanwhile enthusiastically launched the Ontario, Simcoe and Huron, later the Northern Railway, a steam and iron version of the old Toronto portage route between Lake Ontario and the Upper Lakes at Georgian Bay. The line, a hundred miles long, reached to Collingwood on the Bay by 1855. It not only tied fertile new farming districts to the city, but also opened the rich forest resources of Simcoe,

Georgian Bay, and ultimately Muskoka, to rapid exploitation for the American market. It played a significant role in the expanding north-south trade under reciprocity, and helped to make Toronto a major lumber port.[22]

Other lines were similarly thrust northward to feed Canadian trade down to American connections: railways like the Bytown and Prescott, or Brockville and Ottawa, the Port Hope and Lindsay, the Buffalo, Brantford and Goderich—all of which underwent various changes of name. And a further measure of government aid, the Municipal Loan Act of 1852 (which was followed by a similar act for Lower Canada) brought on an eager flurry of still more railway projects, since it essentially made provincial credit available to municipalities to back local lines of their own. Conceived as a measure to make railway progress available througout the countryside, contrived by the ingenious Hincks as a sort of boot-strap raising, the Act nevertheless greatly ministered to growing railway inflation. It made the boom a bubble, which, when it burst in 1857, carried many a municipality into financial disaster, with only short miles of rusting track to show.

But while the golden railway boom expanded, it grew clear that Canada, Canada West particularly, was being tied in to the American railroad network by "feeder" lines directed to the south. This posed a major challenge to the St Lawrence east-west transport system. Even though the canals were busy in boom times, the water route would have to be reinforced by a through line of railways to defend the St Lawrence commercial domain, and especially to equip it to compete on an equal basis with American routes for the trade of the continental interior. This had increasingly become Montreal's concern, as it watched not only the Erie but also the American railroads take western traffic from the St Lawrence. Out of such considerations grew the Grand Trunk Railway scheme, the greatest of them all.

The concept of a main or trunk line traversing Canada was also related to the project for a railway to the Maritimes. In 1851, hopes for an Intercolonial had revived, for it now appeared that the British government would guarantee a joint provincial loan to build a line from Halifax to Quebec. Under the anticipated guarantee, Canada confidently planned not only to share with Nova Scotia and New Brunswick in the Halifax-to-Quebec scheme, but also to build on its own from Quebec to the western tip of the province, thus linking the whole American midwest by direct rail through Canada to Maritime ports that were closest to Europe. An act for this "Main Trunk Railway" passed the Canadian legislature in 1851, and Hincks went to England to negotiate with the imperial authorities and the delegates of the other provinces on the whole vast design. But negotiations on the Intercolonial portion collapsed there in 1852, when limits set to the imperial guarantee by the somewhat cool Derby government proved unacceptable. Hincks came home to proceed with Canada's main line in any case—in fact, committed to do so by a contract with the powerful British railway-building firm, Peto, Brassey, Jackson and Betts.[23]

The Brassey interests, looking for new fields of activity, had offered to finance and build the Canadian trunk under guarantee of their bonds by the provincial government. In 1853, accordingly, the Grand Trunk Railway of Canada was buoyantly chartered by parliament, with a capital set at £9,500,000 and an imposing list of directors, including the London bankers, Thomas Baring and George Glyn, the province's financial agents in London, and six members of the Canadian cabinet. The inevitably close connection between the great British-financed project and provincial political interests was accordingly clear at the start. But Canadian railway and financial interests no less inevitably became involved.

The St Lawrence and Atlantic, taken over on a 999-year lease, was now to provide the Grand Trunk's outlet to the sea. Its owners and bondholders had to be provided for, as did the promoters who held charters for lines as yet unbuilt between Montreal, Kingston and Toronto and eastward in Lower Canada to Quebec. It was originally intended, also, to absorb the Great Western as the westernmost link in the trans-provincial system; but when agreement could not be reached, the Grand Trunk optimistically decided to build a new competing line west from Toronto to Sarnia on Lake Huron, contracting for it with Alexander Galt and other financiers formerly concerned with the St Lawrence and Atlantic. Hence, before construction had begun, the Grand Trunk's capital was already spreading thin; and it was enmeshed in complex deals in bonds that might pay promoters but would surely not pay either the investors or the government that stood behind the Company.

Quite aside from this heavy initial load of bonded indebtedness, the engineering difficulties the Brassey firm met in building the railway in unfamiliar North American terrain, the competition from existing water routes and American lines, and the runaway inflation of costs caused by the boom itself (prices doubled or even tripled between 1852 and 1854), together pressed the Grand Trunk deep in financial trouble long before its completion. The provincial government repeatedly had to advance aid to prevent utter collapse, so increasing it own involvement that the railway and the ministry were brought into mutual political dependence. Each felt a compelling need to maintain the other, while opposition forces increasingly denounced Grand Trunk influence, waste, and corruption. None the less, the line hopefully went forward. By 1854 the rails from Montreal extended to Levis opposite Quebec. In 1856 the Montreal-Toronto section was opened with hearty celebration. Work on the westernmost part of the line was briefly suspended when the roaring boom broke at last in 1857. But the track reached Sarnia in 1859, the same year that the great tubular, wrought-iron Victoria Bridge, a world masterpiece of nineteenth-century iron engineering, was completed for the railway across the St Lawrence at Montreal. In spite of all disorders, delays, and costly fumblings, a main-line Canadian rail system over a thousand miles long had been constructed, and most of it by 1857.

The Grand Trunk, however, failed to turn much American western traffic into the St Lawrence route after 1857; the lines already built below the border had set the patterns for the trade. It had trouble even meeting its operating expenses when completed, much less its debt charges.[24] Running expenses had been optimistically calculated at forty per cent of gross revenue, but they turned out to be eighty—the result, in part, of hard curves and grades, poor ballasting, and a track gauge of 5 ft. 6 ins. which impeded connection with standard-gauge lines of 4 ft. 8½ ins. The Canadian union was left with a public debt that had risen from eighteen million dollars in 1850 to fifty-four million in 1858, thanks chiefly to railways, and pre-eminently to the Grand Trunk.[25] The burden of debt and insolvent lines would remain for Canada, as the heritage of reckless years of speculation, over-confidence and over-building. Yet there were still more significant aspects of the railway boom.

It quickened the very tempo of Canadian life. No longer need it move at the pace of the lumbering ox-cart, or even the thrashing steamboat, when the broad-stacked locomotive, belching wood smoke, clattered the cars at speeds up to forty miles an hour across the province, and its whistle screeched "down brakes" at once-isolated inland hamlets. The railway, besides, lifted the old, retarding barrier of the winter freeze-up. For the first time there were facilities for year-round bulk transport. Farmers and shippers saw goods flow regularly and speedily to distant markets; lumber mills sent huge cuts out by rail. Furthermore, towns strategically located on the railway system grew rapidly when the new communications enabled them to dominate much larger hinterlands. Steam industry expanded with them, to feed the markets they could now command. Hamilton rose as an industrial centre with the railway, displacing its older water-power rival, Dundas. London's population jumped from 5,000 to 15,000 between 1850 and 1856; Toronto's property values more than doubled in that time.[26] And Toronto, in particular, advanced towards the stature of a dominant metropolis in western Canada, thanks largely to its excellent rail facilities radiating to west, north and east.

In a real sense, the age of industrialism and urbanism opened for Canada with the coming of the railway. Its technology of steam and steel demanded locomotive works, car shops and rolling mills, all rudiments of heavy industry. In decreasing rural isolation, it expanded urban influence. Newspapers printed in the cities circulated ever more widely; social and cultural activities increased; and railway progress brought a new degree of opulence that was vaunted in "elegant" public and private buildings, still scattered through the towns of Ontario and Quebec. In short, the first Canadian railway boom was no mere passing phase, a few dazzling years of feverish inflation. It left a permanent mark instead on the work and well-being of the country.

IV

Another consequence of railway-building was the link it tended to develop between government fiscal policy and the Canadian transportation system. Railways required large expenditures of public funds, funds derived from provincial revenue, of which the only major source lay in the customs and excise duties levied through the tariff. Almost inevitably, the rising debt produced by railways would have to be met by raising the tariff: perhaps to the level where duties would in effect become protectionist, by making imported goods significantly more expensive than comparable domestic products. In 1856, the tariff on most imported manufactures was advanced from twelve and a half per cent to fifteen. It did not reach levels of twenty and twenty-five per cent, high enough to give "incidental" protection to Canadian manufactured products, until 1858 and '59. But the beginnings of the protective tariff at that time were essentially related to the coming of the railway in the years before, and hence to the demand of the Canadian people for an efficient transport system of their own.

Of course, the canals had already been closely linked to public policy. Indeed, they had been built by the province, since they were much too costly for private capital at the time to undertake. Railways, on the other hand, were deemed to be private concerns, in an age that regarded state enterprise as uneconomic unless unavoidable. Yet because of the extent and difficulties of Canadian terrain and the relatively limited sources, still, of private capital, public aid had played an ever-growing role in railway-building, from the Guarantee Act onward to the Grand Trunk. And in some respects it had resulted in the worst of both worlds, in private waste and public venality, as well as in associating government with capital projects on a far wider scale than the canal era had done.

Nevertheless, the first railway era shaped an enduring Canadian pattern that tied investment in national transportation to tariff revenues within public fiscal policy. The process began under Francis Hincks. It was carried further in the later fifties by another vigorous finance minister, Alexander Galt. Meanwhile Canadians of both parties had come in theory to subscribe to the doctrines of British free trade, except for a high-tory remnant that looked back to old outright imperial protectionism. But in practice the need for a revenue tariff was accepted, along with the heavy public spending on transport that meant higher duties and could even bring an edging-in to protection. Accordingly, the Province of Canada really laid foundations for the National Policy of the Canadian federal union after 1867, the policy which sought to build a transcontinental economy based on a protective tariff and a through east-west rail system. For the united province developed the tariff as a fiscal instrument in its own hands, created a railway system of its own, and then of necessity linked the two together.

Other developments in fiscal policy concerned banking and currency. A Free Banking Act of 1850 provided for "free" banks issuing government notes based on their holdings of government securities. It was an attempt to reduce the power of the relatively few big chartered banks that issued their own notes, by providing new alternatives and new sources of credit. As such, it largely failed: the dominant chartered banks with spreading branches remained a distinctive Canadian feature, in contrast to the multiplicity of small banks in the United States. Yet the act did constitute the first general law applying to all the banks of the province, and it did carry forward a process of public regulation that already limited a bank's note circulation to the amount of its paid-up capital. Furthermore, it looked forward to the government issue of paper currency, to be accomplished in the Provincial Note Act of 1866. Meanwhile the province had taken other significant steps. In 1851 Hincks had proposed that a Canadian decimal currency be established and that the public accounts be kept in dollars and cents. These measures were given force in the Currency Acts of 1853 and 1857, and the first shipment of Canadian silver and copper coins arrived from the Royal Mint in 1858.

Banking itself grew with the prosperous fifties. The Molson's Bank and two others came into existence as a result of the Free Banking Act of 1850; the Bank of Toronto was chartered in 1855; and, in all, twelve banks were incorporated between 1855 and 1857[27] Other financial institutions multiplied: loan and savings societies, fire and life insurance companies. The Canada Life was organized in Hamilton in 1847, the Canada Permanent in Toronto in 1855. The Toronto Stock Exchange made its own appearance in 1852. Not all the financial growth was healthy, in a period of increasing over-expansion, but a good deal would survive the hard shaking-down of the later 1850's.

Under the impetus of flourishing staple trades, high employment, and railway spending, Canadian manufacturing also made a marked advance in the good years of the fifties. One aspect was the application of steam power, particularly to flour milling. The great increase in wheat production and the growth of towns brought larger "steam mills" concentrated there: the number of small local mills declined, as the size of the major ones grew.[28]

Textile manufacturing also expanded with a larger population and prosperous consumers. In 1855 it was reported: "In cotton fabrics Canada has made but little progress, but in woollen goods and mixed fabrics she is a large producer."[29] The Canadian manufacturer obviously did better when he did not rely on imported raw material, a fact exhibited also in the boot and shoe industry, which developed notably in Montreal.

A partial exception was the rising iron industry that used considerable quantities of British iron, made cheaper by the improved St Lawrence navigation system. Yet as a result, Canada after 1851 stopped importing English wrought nails, and brought in sheet iron to make cut nails at Montreal instead; while by 1857 puddling and rolling mills there reduced the importation of sheet iron, as raw pig-iron entered in its place.[30] There was some reliance on Canadian iron ore and furnaces, of course, and deposits were worked in both sections of the province. But coal for iron-making and for steam industry had to be imported. It came readily and cheaply from the United States under the Reciprocity Treaty. Toronto and Hamilton industries especially benefited from their access by lake transport to American coal fields below the Great Lakes.

Significant development also took place in the manufacture of agricultural implements—a natural concern for an agrarian country like Canada. At Newcastle in Canada West, Daniel and Hart Massey produced the first mowing machine in the province in 1852 and a combined rake, reaper and mower three years later, thus founding an increasingly complex agricultural machinery enterprise to be closely associated with the subsequent growth of Canadian farming.[31] Meanwhile, wood-working was carried on throughout the province, wooden ship-building at lake and river ports and especially, still, at Quebec; while locomotive, steamboat and stationary engine works were busy at Montreal, Toronto, Kingston and Hamilton. Stove, pottery and glass-making in the West, organ-building and piano-manufacturing in the East, were among other specialized industrial activities that developed considerable craftsmanship and character of their own. With such a varied growth of industry, it was indeed not too surprising that within a year of the signing of the Reciprocity Treaty a movement had begun among Canadian manufacturers for tariff protection of their growing enterprises. This issued in the Association for the Promotion of Canadian Industry, established in Toronto in 1858 but also backed in Hamilton, Montreal and Kingston. It could find satisfaction, though not all it wanted, in the tariff of that year.

Industry, however, still remained a relatively minor factor in a province overwhelmingly concerned with staple grain and wood production. Thus any labour movement that grew with industry was very limited, and it would be many years yet before the labouring elements, or the "mechanics," as the age preferred to call them, exercised significant economic or political influence. Nevertheless, in the towns and in certain skilled trades labour was already organizing in unions. This was so among metal workers, railway machinists, the building trades, and particularly printers. A typographical union, still in being, was founded in Toronto in 1844. The fifties, moreover, saw a number of small, sharp strikes by unions in the leading towns, as among the Toronto printers who went out in 1853 and '54, chiefly because of the steep rise of prices that pressed on wages. And the journeymen tailors organized successfully in 1852 to stave off the introduction of the Singer Sewing Machine.[32]

Unions were local and often only temporary organizations. But they did maintain continuity in the printing trade, at least, and found useful purposes as benevolent societies. As bargaining instruments they were in actual fact still under prohibition of old English common law, as combinations in restraint of trade. The prohibition would not finally be lifted until the 1870's, though in the small strikes of the fifties it did not act as an effective deterrent. Wages in any case rose markedly, in some instances more than doubling in the one year, 1854.[33] At the same time, prices were being similarly inflated; yet it does seem evident that, over the years of the union, labour generally benefited from the growth in the province's wealth. Thus, for example, stone-masons who had earned 7s. 6d. a day in Toronto in the earlier boom year of 1841 were getting as much as 12s. 6d. in 1855, while unskilled labourers who had received 2s. 6d. daily in Montreal could expect about 6s. by the later date.[34]

One industry that employed wage-earners on a large scale, lumbering, showed scant signs of an organized labour movement. There was undoubted militancy, and veritable outbreaks of gang warfare over wages on the turbulent Ottawa. But the clashes occurred between lumbermen themselves competing for the wages that the masters offered, often on the basis of the ethnic rivalry between the French-Canadian shantymen and Irish "shiners." The forest proletariat was too rootless and reckless a labour force to furnish a basis for effective organization. It was of the frontier world, with its expectation always of ready opportunity and reward for individual strength and effort, although at the same time lumbering was a giant commercial operation dominated by large capital interests.

This was the pattern of the commercial as distinct from the agrarian frontier. The commercial frontier revealed itself also in the first tentative extensions of mining into the northern wilderness of the Province of Canada during the 1850's. Hopeful enterprises like the Montreal Mining Company probed the resources of the Shield along its edges on the north shores of lakes Huron and Superior. Copper had thus been found at Bruce Mines on Lake Huron in 1847, and was being actively exploited by the mid fifties.[35]

Yet markets were still limited for minerals so far away, and the mining investors and steamboat operators made scant profit from the attempt to tap even that part of the Shield most accessible to water transport. Mining, indeed, was little developed throughout the province. Bog-iron production, clay for bricks, stone-quarrying—these were the limited kinds of mineral exploitation of the time. The opening of rich petroleum fields in south-western Upper Canada was only to begin in the later fifties. A good deal of work on potential mineral resources was already being done by the Geo-logical Survey of Canada, instituted in 1843 under the masterly direction of William Logan. Its reports through the next twenty years would prove invaluable for subsequent mine development. But the Mining North lay far in the future.

The northern interior of the province, beyond the limits of farming and the outreaching lumber frontier, remained the preserve of that old initial Canadian industry, fur trapping and trading. Furs still came down the streams and rivers from the unchanging wilderness, to the "King's posts" on the lower St Lawrence that dated back to the French régime, to posts on the upper Ottawa or in the Lake Nipigon region, to Pic and Fort William on Lake Superior. The mighty Hudson's Bay Company did not enjoy the same fur-trade monopoly within Canadian boundaries that it held in its own chartered domain of Rupert's Land, west and north beyond the heights of land where the rivers ran to Hudson and James bays. It was dominant, nevertheless, where its "southern" posts in the Ottawa and Lake Superior regions freely bought up furs to discourage competitors, and so shield the monopoly in the wide areas above Canada East and West.[36]

In physical terms, more than half the Canadian union was northern wilderness still, in the 1850's, and hence had known little change. But as for the human community dwelling in the southern sectors, it had known almost constant change, through railways, reciprocity, and seven fat years of prosperity. And the social and cultural developments that were under way projected still another dimension to the changes of the surging fifties in Canada.

CHAPTER 9

Social and Cultural Development

Under the Union

A process of social change was already evident in Canada in the 1840's, well before the boom years of the next decade. Essentially, this was the integrating and consolidating of Canadian society as frontiers of settlement were filled in, pioneer conditions passed away, and the organizing role of towns and the business community expanded. The railway era speeded up the process, so that by the late fifties the Central Canada of today may be said to have been moulded in its basic outlines.

In large part, social change was simply the result of steadily rising numbers, the growing density of population. The census of 1851-52 indicated that the population of the union had increased by some 692,000 in its first decade, and was nearing the two-million mark.[1] Montreal had advanced from 40,000 to 57,000 in the period, Toronto from 14,000 to 30,000; Canada West, with about 952,000 inhabitants to 890,000 for Canada East, had doubled its numbers in the ten years. Birth rates were high in both sections: one in twenty-five of the western population was under one year of age; one in twenty-two of the eastern.[2] Infant mortality was also high, especially in the East. But the greater net growth in the West was obviously the result of immigration; since it contained the chief settlement frontiers, most of the immigrants from Britain regularly went on to Upper Canada, in good years and in bad. The numbers arriving in Canada annually during the forties and on into the fifties varied on the whole between 25,000 and 40,000, except for the 90,000 in the Irish famine year of 1847 and over 54,000, the largest element English, in 1853.[3] Thanks to this continuing flow of immigrants, more than forty per cent of the Upper Canadian population in 1851 were still British-born.[4]

Yet the yearly figures for arriving immigrants by no means told the full story. Some of the newcomers proceeding to Upper Canada were merely in transit to the American midwest. There was also a movement of native-born out of both sections of the province to seek greater opportunities in the

United States. In evidence since the rebellion of 1837 in English Canada, and even earlier in French Canada, the outflow appeared sufficiently grave in the dark years of the later forties to bring a committee of the legislature to investigate it in 1849. They reported that experienced farmers left for richer lands in the midwestern prairies, while labourers—chiefly French Canadians—went to work in New England factories, or on American railroads.[5] This very movement, however, was a sign that Canada was filling up, or at least that prime agricultural land was no longer so readily available. The exodus, moreover, was to some degree offset by a continual influx of Americans and returning Canadians. In the earlier forties the two movements were roughly in balance; it was only in the late forties that there was a sizable net outflow over the border (15,000 in 1849)[6] and the prosperous fifties brought a better balance again. Furthermore, concern in French Canada over the drain to the United States had led to colonizing ventures to open new lands within Canada East, such as that of the Association des Etablissements Canadiens des Townships, founded in 1848, which helped to carry increasing French settlement into a region that had been so predominantly English.

In any case, despite emigration to the United States, the substantial numbers of British immigrants who did stay in Canada and the high rate of natural increase in both French and English-speaking communities produced a notable rise in the provincial population. This was particularly evident in former frontier farming areas. Megantic county in the Eastern Townships, for example, grew by 115 per cent in the 1840's; Huron and Perth counties, in the Canada Company's great western tract, by 571 per cent.[7] Indeed, the Toronto Globe blithely declared in 1848: "The backwoods can now scarcely be said to exist in Upper Canada."[8] Whatever the exaggeration, the fact was that by the fifties there was no considerable area still undergoing frontier agrarian settlement in the western half of the United Province, except in the Bruce Peninsula that thrust up into Lake Huron. Consequently, in the mid fifties the provincial government even launched a program of building colonization roads northward from occupied regions in both Canadas, in an attempt to open new settlement frontiers by offering free land grants along roads like the Muskoka or the Ottawa and Opeongo, in partial use by 1854.[9] But these forays into the thin soil of the Shield would have scant success, except in opening more areas to lumbering. Some farming might develop along their course, largely to feed the lumber camps; a government free homestead policy might encourage a trickle of settlers on to marginal lands. But in general, the relative failure of attempts to keep the farm frontier moving merely demonstrated further that natural limits of soil and climate had turned Canada to intensifying rather than extending her basic pattern of settlement.

Accordingly, a well-knit commercial-agricultural community had developed, particularly in Canada West, dominated by prosperous farmers and country merchants. Even before the railway arrived, the clearing of land and the steady improvement of roads were tying this rural community effectively to the rising towns and villages. There, doctors and lawyers, as well as millers and merchants, joined with wealthy local farmers to provide leadership for a substantial agrarian society. And the spreading significance of thriving country centres was well illustrated by the number of western towns and villages incorporated under the Municipal Corporations Act during the earlier fifties. Another indication was the much greater use made of the Municipal Loan Fund in Canada West than in Canada East—which also meant a heavier load of debt for abortive local railway projects, and greater anti-government feeling among resentful western farmers, as time went on.

The farming community of Canada West depended, of course, on wheat-raising. Continued immigration, broader acreage under cultivation, and the introduction of machinery (by 1843 binders and threshers were in use on the farms of the "front"), all served to bring much higher productivity.[10] The use of stumping machines also helped clear the land of the rotting remnants of the old hardwood forest, while improvements in horse-drawn ploughs and cultivators made for more efficient tillage. Significant, too, was the development of a hardy, rust-resistant spring wheat, Red Fife, near Peterborough in the mid forties, which spread through Upper Canada in the next decade.[11] But though the Upper Canada farmers prospered on raising a grain surplus for export, they were often exhausting their soil with unrestrained "wheat-mining." Fortunately there were other markets in lumber camps, the towns, or across the border under reciprocity, which called for forage crops, dairy produce, and livestock, and so provided alternatives to wheat-raising. Agricultural societies and the annual provincial fair in Canada West encouraged better breeds of livestock: short-horn cattle and Leicester sheep were being largely imported by the mid fifties.[12] The Niagara Peninsula was acquiring its reputation for fruit-growing, and wine was being produced there before the end of the decade.[13]

More diversified farming, considerable rural investment in improvements and machinery, better local communications with denser settlement and more effective municipal government—these were all aspects of the intensive developments taking place in the Upper Canadian community, quite apart from the effects of railways or reciprocity. Yet the latter obviously pressed the changes forward, thanks to the money they brought in, the markets they spread out, and the closer ties they established between the country community and the business life of the towns. A coherent, relatively mature regional society had replaced the old disjoined settlements and frontiers of Canada West in the 1850's; and the greater regional organization and awareness would be expressed in growing western sectionalism in politics.

The society that had thus developed was bound to believe in progress. It was bound to believe in the triumphant virtues of thrift and hard work among a sturdy "British yeomanry": the proof seemed so tangible in yellow grain fields, broad barns and trim clapboard or brick farmhouses. Frustration or failure appeared the product of waste, corruption or external intervention to such a society, confident of its own self-sustaining powers and not a little convinced of its superiority to reckless Yankees on one side, indolent French on the other. And this attitude also would minister to sectionalism and sectional politics in Canada West during the mid-century years.

II

One Canadian community had undergone little change: the several thousand Indians who dwelled on reserves in the south or ranged in bands in the north, hunting and trapping in the life of the forests and the fur trade. True, on the Indian reserves scattered through both the Canadas agriculture was being widely practised, while mission schools, French and Catholic or English and Protestant, were labouring to spread the uncertain benefits of white civilization. But agriculture was scarcely a European innovation for the Six Nations Indians of the big Grand River Reserve, corn-growers through their Iroquoian past; and Indians such as the Caughnawaga Mohawks on the St Lawrence near Lachine had been settled in rural Catholicism since the days of New France. In general, Indian life even on the reserves was not sharing greatly in the steady development going on about it, though it could feel that growth to its own detriment. For example, smaller Indian reserves might be relocated to suit the demands of spreading settlement; the moving of "improvident" Indians to back townships scarcely ever bettered the quality of their holdings. The relatively powerful and well-organized Grand River Indians themselves faced repeated attempts of white speculators to nibble away their lands, and lengthy litigation in the courts ensued.

The chief problem, however, was that the Indians lived in a cultural backwater; one which even their well-wishers could only assume would ultimately dry up and disappear. They no longer had the military value they had had as scouts and allies in the War of 1812. While in the north they still played an important role in the fur trade, the trade itself was in continual retreat and decline as a part of the Canadian economy. The best, the inevitable, solution for the Indians seemed to be their absorption in white civilization. Yet there was a logical inconsistency in a policy that looked to their assimilation but placed them on reserves, even if this was meant in all sincerity to guard them from the perils of too close contact with civilized white men: disease, debauchery and social degeneration. At the best, native inhabitants were to be educated and saved in moral separation; at the worst, they were to dwindle and die away where few would notice them. But on the whole, the ideals of Protestant progress in English Canada or of Catholic salvation in French Canada accomplished little that was positive and constructive for the Indian.

The most that might be said is that the record in Canada was a good deal better than in the neighbouring United States. The Canadian Indian had been moved gradually and peaceably to reserves; an honest if uninspired Indian Department, under imperial control until 1860, at least maintained the observance of treaty terms and restrained would-be exploiters. Still, Lord Grey could write to Lord Elgin in 1850, "It seems to me that less has been accomplished towards the civilization and improvement of the Indians in Canada in proportion to the expense incurred than has been done for the native Tribes in any of our other Colonies."[14] It is worth noting Grey's reference to the "expense incurred," however. In large part, the concern of the retrenchment-minded Colonial Secretary was over the cost of the Indian presents annually distributed from the imperial treasury, now that the natives constituted neither a military advantage nor a danger. Elgin's response, moreover, largely expressed his own concern that throwing the cost of long-assumed imperial expenditures on the provincial exchequer would add to "the taunts of annexationists."[15] At any rate, the imperial government declared in 1851 that it would pay for no more Indian presents after 1858, which gave time for a reluctant Canadian legislature to prepare to take them over. It is obvious how much attention both sides paid to the interests of the Indians themselves throughout the whole dispute.

It would nevertheless be wrong to fail to mark the diligent efforts of Indian Department officials and missionaries, Anglicans, Methodists and Roman Catholics, among the tribes and bands of Indians. The farmers of the populous Grand River Reserve were competing effectively with their white neighbours. The major venture on Manitoulin Island in Lake Huron, which shortly before the union had set apart the world's largest freshwater island as an Indian reserve, seemed to be succeeding in bringing varied tribal groups together in agricultural settlement. And in the summer of 1850 the reserves system was extended to the northern reaches of Canada above lakes Huron and Superior, to the heights of land that formed the boundary with the Hudson's Bay Territory. In September, at Sault Ste Marie, two treaties were signed with the Ojibwa chiefs of the Lake Superior and Lake Huron regions respectively, ceding their lands from Batchawana Bay to the Pigeon

River, and from Batchawana to Penetanguishene, in return for reserves, annual payments, and the Indians' right to hunt and fish freely in all areas that remained unoccupied.

Most of this northern realm would remain unoccupied; but the treaties signed by W. B. Robinson as provincial commissioner were the culmination of a long process in the Canadas of clearing Indian title for the advance of settlement. In a sense, it was another indication of the filling up of the old Canadian frontiers, since lands for pioneering would now have to be opened in the difficult north—or in the prairie territories of the Hudson's Bay Company beyond the western limits of Canada.

It might appear that there were still eastern land frontiers. Certainly settlement in Canada East continued to expand outward from its St Lawrence base during the union period, though not on the same scale as in Canada West. Farming frontiers moved eastward down the south shore towards the fishing ports of Gaspé, above Quebec into the Lake St John region, and westward up the Ottawa into the Laurentian plateau. But it was a movement into colder, harder areas, largely pushed by French-Canadian colonization societies and the zeal of the Church.[16] The habitant in general preferred to remain on the traditional lands of seigneurial farming, while the immigrant, of course, went on to the West. Still, on these older settled lands the Lower Canadian farmers were generally doing better after 1850 than during the long period of declining agricultural prices that had preceded. Lacking the West's wheat riches, they raised their coarse grains, livestock and dairy produce for the urban markets of Quebec and Montreal, for the lumber districts, or for shipment across the American borders. Although their farming techniques still lagged behind those of the West, they were nevertheless engaged in a relatively flourishing commercial agriculture. And that, indeed, had some connection with the ending of the old French seigneurial landholding system during the 1850's.

In the era before the union, French Canadians in Lower Canada had widely regarded seigneurial tenure as intrinsic to their society; in part perhaps because English opinion opposed it as an anomalous feudal survival. Though imperial statutes of the 1820's had set provisions for the voluntary commutation of seigneurial tenure into English freehold, they had remained virtually unused. Instead, Papineau radicalism in the 1830's had made a grievance of British attempts to interfere with French Canada's own land law.[17] But the forties manifestly brought a change. Bagot, acting on a request of the union legislature, appointed commissioners to investigate seigneurial tenure in Lower Canada. Their exhaustive report of 1843 recommended its outright abolition, with compensation to the seigneurs for the loss of their ancient rights.[18] It had become recognized, in short, that seigneurialism was only a shell of a once viable social system; and that its traditional rural structure of dues and services, mutual obligations and hierarchical relations had lost meaning in an era of spreading urban and commercial influences, to which agrarian French Canada itself was not immune.

In fact, one of the most notable aspects of social transformation was the growing demand among French Canadians themselves for the lifting of seigneurial obligations. But the vested rights were centuries old, and a tangle of costly claims was involved. An act of 1845, in response to the commission's report, merely sought "the better to facilitate optional Commutation," while another of 1849 simply amended it.[19] By then, however, the opinion was rising that commutation could only be effectively achieved on a general compulsory basis. In the next few years new schemes were weighed in parliament, while outside, French-Canadian sentiment for abolition became decisive. At length, in 1854, an "Act for the Abolition of Feudal Rights and Duties in Lower Canada" was passed. Commissioners under the act were to assess the value of dues and rights in every seigneury, and on this basis fix a charge on land which could be paid to the seigneur by the habitant as an annual rent or else paid off in a lump sum. The seigneur was also to be indemnified for the loss of his feudal privileges by decision of a special court. Hence he would become simply a landlord; the habitant merely a tenant farmer or farm owner. The time-honoured, distinctive French land-holding system that had helped protect and maintain French-Canadian society was discarded by a community that no longer feared its loss.

Also significant of social change was the French Canadians' rising interest in business undertakings. Still pre-eminently a people of the land, they could not be unaffected by the forces of development at work about them, especially among their own political and professional leaders in the towns. And they did not recoil or refuse to participate. Indeed, as early as 1845 the influential French Catholic organ, *Mélanges Religieux*, deprecated "la préoccupation générale du moment, l'industrie, les chemins de fer, canaux, steamboats, télégraphes électriques, etc. etc." as showing far more concern with personal fortunes than with those of the community at large.[20] Yet the church itself came to terms with economic development; Bishop Bourget of Montreal readily served as patron of a new Canadian savings bank in 1846 (with Morin and Drummond among its directors), and the powerful Sulpician order invested substantially in Montreal's St Lawrence and Atlantic Railway.[21] Furthermore, the influential voice of Etienne Parent was raised to urge French Canadians to develop their economic as well as their political strength. In a forceful series of lectures from 1846 to 1848 he criticized the French classical educational system, the emphasis on the professions, politics, or the religious life, and sought to direct his compatriots to the world of business and progress, "l'empire du monde moderne."[22]

In 1846, moreover, *La Minerve* could note ". . . il n'y a encore que peu d'années il n'existait que deux ou trois marchands canadiens qui se livrassent au commerce d'importation, maintenant il s'en trouve un grand nombre qui font d'excellentes affaires."[23] In fact, one of the wealthiest Montreal merchants was the French Canadian, Joseph Masson. French Canadians launched a new steamboat line, the Compagnie du Richelieu, which eventually became part of the Canada Steamship Company. Leading French liberals like G.-E. Cartier and C.-S. Cherrier joined with an old tory foe like George Moffatt to acquire large holdings in the St Lawrence and Atlantic—while Cherrier went on to the presidency of the Banque du Peuple, in which Moffatt had also invested.[24] As for Cartier (who entered parliament in 1848), he became solicitor for the St Lawrence and Atlantic, then rose to greater heights with the broader scheme that embraced that company, when he was made solicitor for the Grand Trunk Railway itself.

It still was true that control of grand commerce and high finance remained decisively in English hands. Yet if Cartier and others like him were French exceptions, they were not so completely exceptional. Road and shipping companies, wholesaling, milling, banking, railways—all these had invited significant French-Canadian participation by the 1850's. Above all, the old economic and social breach between French agrarianism and English commercialism had to some degree been spanned. While, in the old days before the union, major French and English interests had opposed each other over canals and public works, they would not do so in the railway age. The way had been cleared for effective political collaboration between the two peoples to sustain the expensive cause of economic development. In the 1840's the two had worked in party alliance under Baldwin and La-Fontaine to achieve responsible government. They were to do so again under new leaders in the 1850's, to underwrite railway expansion, maintain the Grand Trunk, and take the first steps towards the policy of tariff protection for fostering Canadian industry.

If, however, French concern with business interests was increasingly significant, it was only a part of the broad commercial and financial expansion that produced the powerful capitalists and entrepreneurs who came to dominate the mid-century Canadian business community. In the square-timber trade there was William Price, outstanding among the wealthy timber merchants of Quebec and known as "the father of the Saguenay" from the business operations he carried into that area. And there was Allan Gilmour, a big Quebec shipbuilder as well as timber dealer. On the Ottawa, the rising sawn-lumber industry brought F. H. Bronson and E. B. Eddy from the United States in the early fifties to build their empires, while the Canadian, John R. Booth, founded an even greater lumber domain. In the Montreal realm of trade and finance, the Molsons, Moffatts, Torrances and

McGills were joined by men like Alexander Galt, John Young, Luther Holton, and Hugh Allan, founder of a major line of transatlantic steamships. And in Canada West, railways made prominent figures of promoters and builders such as Samuel Zimmerman and David Macpherson, the English architect Frederick Cumberland, and the expatriate Polish engineer, Casimir Gzowski.

Montreal and Toronto most fully displayed the enterprise and affluence of this expanding business élite; but Quebec, Hamilton, and Ottawa (Bytown's new name, on being incorporated as a city in 1855) showed similar manifestations. In the chief cities, business power grew more complex in its activities. Montreal enlarged its banking operations, chartered fire-insurance companies, and built telegraph lines to Toronto and Quebec in the 1840's. Toronto founded its stock exchange in the 1850's, increased its wholesale trade facilities, and established branch agencies across the West. The dominance of Montreal and Toronto over their hinterlands would increase with the building of railways. Expansion would also bring rivalry between them, reflected in politics, as the older and the newer metropolitan communities competed for mastery over a wide area of Canada. And in them centred quite considerable cultural developments, which were further indications of their enlarging social role.

III

Newspapers, agents of popular culture and instruments of urban dominance, grew notably in the later forties and earlier fifties. Daily editions were introduced, together with the rotary, steam-powered press that could produce the daily paper in quantity for a city audience and a weekly for more distant rural readers. The Toronto *Globe*, which became a daily in 1853, built up the greatest influence in English Canada, though the new moderate Toronto *Leader* and the conservative *Montreal Gazette* also held large followings. In French Canada, *Le Canadien* had never really regained its pre-eminence after Parent's departure in 1842. But *La Minerve* of Montreal flourished along with the *Journal de Québec* as leading organs of LaFontaine reform, while since 1847 *L'Avenir* had represented the incisive French-Canadian tradition of intellectual, radical journalism. Also after 1847, able editing by young Hector Langevin made the Montreal diocesan paper, *Mélanges Religieux*, a widely popular mouthpiece for pro-clerical opinion.

Through the newspapers, novels by Charles Dickens or Victor Hugo reached the countryside in instalments, together with essays on literature, science and travel taken from British, American or French periodicals, and lengthy reports or editorials on Canadian political affairs. In the absence of other mass media, the journals served a cultural need and wielded a public influence beyond the press of today. Men like Brown of the *Globe* or Cauchon of the *Journal de Québec* were made by their power over opinion, not the size of their advertising receipts. And there was more than flourishing journalism in the towns. Increasingly, drama, art and music developed there.

The drama often amounted to indiscriminate offerings of wild farce and crude melodrama by threadbare touring groups; the art might be limited to florid French church ornamentation or stiff portraiture of English merchant worthies; the music to evenings of song by dubious tenors and wavering sopranos—Scots ballads, perhaps, or "The Rat-Catcher's Daughter," a hit of 1852. Yet permanent theatre was established, and grew; at the Royal Lyceum in Toronto, for example, or Montreal's Theatre Royal. Painters such as Paul Kane and Cornelius Krieghoff were making their vivid records of western Indian or French habitant life; A. S. Plamondon in Quebec, G. T. Berthon in Toronto, both European-trained, were reaching significantly higher standards in portrait art. And Montreal was producing orchestras, choirs and music festivals, while international artists like Jenny Lind or Ole Bull performed in St Lawrence Hall, Toronto's handsome new civic auditorium, opened in 1851. Important also was the foundation of the Canadian Institute (now the Royal Canadian Institute) at Toronto in 1849, to furnish lectures, discussions, and a library on science and the arts.

Somewhat similar were the Instituts Canadiens of Quebec and Montreal established in the mid forties, where debates, reading rooms and libraries provided gathering-points for French-Canadian intellectuals and littérateurs.[25] François-Xavier Garneau, for example, whose profoundly influential four volumes on the national history of French Canada were published between 1845 and 1852, was a central figure in the Quebec institute. Another influential moulder of French-Canadian literary tradition, Antoine Gérin-Lajoie—sometime editor of *La Minerve*, novelist, and author of a noted patriotic song, "Un Canadien errant"—was a founder of the Montreal institute in 1844 and president in its formative years. Here, of course, the young radical enthusiasts who launched the *rouge* movement foregathered: men like the Dorions, Joseph Doutre, and Papineau's nephew, Louis- Antoine Dessaulles. They made the institute the glowing heart of intellectual ferment, aggressive *patriotisme* and zeal for democratic progress. But they also made it a forum for free-thinking and the questioning of church power in French-Canadian education and society, which roused ecclesiastical alarm about the importation of French rationalist ideas and the resurgence of anticlericalism.

In any event, the Instituts Canadiens both expressed and stimulated a French-Canadian national feeling. The *rouge* movement, indeed, was a full expression of political nationalism, seeking as it did to carve out a specifically

French-Canadian democratic state. Yet the LaFontaine forces no less sought national ends, through policies of collaboration. And generally the years since the union had produced a heightened national awareness among French Canadians: in politics, through the defeat of assimilation and the gaining of government power; in literature, through the defining of the national historical epic by Garneau and the celebration of the virtues of rural French-Canadian society by rising romantic authors; in ordinary life, through the prosperity and self-confidence that had replaced the bleak discouragement with which union had begun.

The growing confidence and self-awareness, the freshening spirit of romanticism largely derived from France, deepened and broadened the literary culture, carrying it beyond its earlier utilitarian emphasis on political writing and journalism to a burgeoning of works of fiction, folk tales and poems of lasting significance.[26] A richer national era in French-Canadian literature was emerging by the 1850's. Pierre Chauveau, who was to have a notable career in public life, brought out his *Charles Guérin* anonymously in *La Revue Canadienne* in 1846 and as a book under his name in 1853. Influenced by Chateaubriand in style, it was nevertheless a warmly indigenous product. It set a classic model for the French-Canadian novel in contrasting the charm, vitality and security of rural life with the urban world of overcrowded professions and alien commercial dominance. Gérin-Lajoie no less fostered the agrarian theme and the idealization of the habitant, simple, vigorous and devout, as the national folk hero analogous to English America's pioneer settler, pushing back the wilderness to raise new communities —though the key adjective applied to the habitant was "Christian" rather than "freedom-loving."

Quite as significant in the growth of the new literary movement was the work of Octave Crémazie. From the late forties his Quebec bookshop, stocked with the writings of French romantics like Lamartine and Hugo, became the centre of a lively circle of authors and intellectuals; and his own poems published in the Quebec press during the fifties won eager acclaim. The first major French-Canadian poet, his work was patriotic and historical in content, romantic in form, and it set the mode for years to come. Indeed, by the 1860's, L'Ecole patriotique de Québec had taken shape to dominate French-Canadian writing, thanks largely to Crémazie himself and those who gathered at his bookshop in the Rue de la Fabrique.[26]

Crémazie's first published verses appeared in 1854 to hail the Anglo-French partnership in the Crimean War as a noble example for both Canadas. The war that made allies of traditional antagonists, England and France, also produced an event that had a marked effect on the French-Canadian mind. In 1855, taking the opportunity of war-time fellowship, the French government of Emperor Napoleon III sent the warship *La Capricieuse* on a goodwill mission to Canada, carrying the French flag there for the first time since the Conquest.[27] Inevitably the visit stirred ancestral memories, and strengthened emotional ties with France that long years of separation had worn thin. Yet all the fervour and eloquence expended over the occasion did not indicate any desire among French Canadians to return to French political allegiance. Their allegiance had belonged to the vanished France of Louis XIV, and now belonged to their North American homeland. The voyage of *La Capricieuse* stimulated the *Canadien's* sense of his distinctive origin and place in a proud world culture: his Frenchness—but his Frenchness in Canada.

The sense of history and of culture to be cherished, instilled by Garneau, Crémazie and a host of others, fed the power of national sentiment in French Canada. This in one direction was associated with *rouge* idealists and anti-clericals. But in another, it was strongly—ever more strongly—linked with a pro-clerical conservatism. Romantic concern with history and reverence for the past were attributes which inevitably had conservative affiliations. And these conservative tendencies could be closely associated as well with the great traditional defender of the French-Canadian way of life, the Roman Catholic Church. In the later 1840's and on into the fifties, a renewed alliance of the church with strong popular interests was taking form in French Canada. Catholic political action was evolving to meet the changed conditions of responsible government, which required ecclesiastical leaders to deal with party politicians instead of conducting diplomacy in the old manner with chief officials of the British governing oligarchy. The ultimate result would be the Catholic conservative grouping that emerged in Lower Canadian politics during the 1850's, called *bleu* in contradistinction to the anti-clerical radicalism of the *rouges*. Yet this was a development that ran well back into the preceding decade.

The French-Canadian Catholic Church of course had never abandoned its traditionally strong concern with secular affairs. But in the earlier forties its influence had been rather uncertainly exercised. Church authorities had been disposed to distrust LaFontaine as a former radical and as a supporter of the "anglicizing" union, though they also had reason to doubt the Viger-Papineau clan, which had been still more closely identified with the old *patriote* strain of anti-clericalism. The issue began to resolve itself in 1846. At that time, while still in the government, Viger had dismayed the hierarchy by defending the ministry's decision to apply the income from the once extensive Jesuit estates in Lower Canada (vested in the Crown since the 1770's) to the purposes of both Protestant and Catholic education, and not to Catholic alone.[28] On the other hand, LaFontaine and his followers espoused the church's claims to control the Jesuit inheritance. They failed in their effort, but the press controversy that followed marked out the LaFontaine group as the manifest defenders of the corporate rights of Roman Catholicism as against Viger-Papineau advocates of individualist liberalism.[29]

The LaFontaine party also worked to carry an education bill in 1846 which enlarged church rights of supervision over Lower Canadian schools; and men like Morin and Cauchon formed close connections with the episcopate at Montreal and Quebec respectively. Church leaders came to recognize the basic moderation of the LaFontaine reformers, and to appreciate their aim of using the union to preserve French-Canadian rights. The growing entente between priests and party politicians was further signalized by Langevin's effective combination of ecclesiastical interests with LaFontaine politics in the *Mélanges Religieux*. Still further, the vigorous renewal of anti-clerical criticism after 1847 by the radicals of *L'Avenir*, and Louis-Joseph Papineau himself, brought the church in reaction even closer to the LaFontaine party.[30] Indeed, priests and clerical papers soon became involved in combating *rouge* demands for the repeal of the union, annexation, and democracy.[31] The most popular preacher in French Canada, Father Charles Chiniquy, leader of a fervent mass movement as the "Apostle of Temperance," was specially valuable to the LaFontaine ministers in 1849 for his denunciation of irreligious republican annexationists and his appearance at anti-annexation meetings.[32]

Hence by the 1850's there was a swelling current of Catholic conservatism evident in French-Canadian affairs, even though its political exponents would still keep the label of LaFontaine reformers. It was, moreover, a reaction not only to the free-thinking of the *rouges* but also to that rationalist liberalism in Europe which had attacked the church in the revolutions of 1848 and even fought against the Pope at Rome. Its strength continued to grow in the fifties, while *rouge* support did not. In fact, a freshly zealous Catholicism, mingling with that other potent French-Canadian current, historically-minded nationalism, spread through Canada East, to produce a powerful *bleu* conservative predominance in politics there by the middle of the decade. But these forces were to face almost totally opposite currents arising at the same time within the English half of the union.

IV

In English Canada, there could be no such strong alliance of church and politicians. The old connection between toryism and the Church of England suggested it; but not all tories were Anglicans, by any means, and the religious divisions in Upper Canada made identification of the tory-conservative party with Anglican privilege increasingly precarious, as the conditions of responsible rule developed. By the 1850's in the West, unlike the

East, the stress was increasingly on the secularization of public affairs, not on the emergence of stronger clerical influence. Moreover, an ardent left-wing or evangelical Protestant movement which gained force in Canada West after 1848 demanded the complete separation of church and state. This, the "voluntary movement," aspired to make churches truly voluntary organizations dependent on their members' free consciences for support, not on state aid or privilege, while the state was to guarantee religious equality to all but be tied to none.[33] Liberal voluntaryism was as natural a manifestation of Protestant diversity in English Canada as clerical conservatism was of Catholic uniformity in French Canada. But much of the union's politics in the fifties came to involve the clash of these opposing expressions of two very different societies and points of view.

The Orange Order, still vigorously active, had assuredly tended to take a similar stand in regard to "Protestant freedom" and the temporal dangers inherent in French-Canadian Catholicism. But at least in theory Protestant voluntaryism abjured the racial and religious prejudices of Orangism, claiming to stand for religious freedom for all and not for Protestant factionalism or Orange violence. In practice, at any rate, the left-wing, liberal associations of the voluntaryists largely kept them apart from Orangemen, long identified with the tory cause and even with the defence of the old state privileges of the Church of England. Nevertheless, voluntaryist and Orange forces could operate as co-belligerents against presumed aggressions by French Catholic power. Besides, voluntaryism expressed the strength of increasingly well-organized evangelical Protestant denominations, grown in wealth with the material progress of western society, and advanced in organization with the knitting-together of the Upper Canadian community, focused on the towns.[34] The towns, particularly Toronto, were the centres of an emerging intellectual element, no less than a business élite, for here were the rising university and church colleges along with the various church headquarters. The voluntaryist movement found backing in urban educational circles and newspapers, as well as in evangelical pulpits. In fact, it was imbued with much of the energy and assurance of fast-growing English Canada, confident that its course was that of progress and enlightenment—whatever misguided French Canadians might believe.

If Protestant voluntaryism conflicted with one major cultural current in French Canada, Catholic conservatism, what of the other powerful strain, nationalism? In English Canada any national feeling was undoubtedly much weaker, confused as it was with a sense of a wider British nationality embracing the whole empire. The great mass of English Canadians still expressed a fervent British loyalty; it is worth noting that the custom of celebrating May 24, Queen Victoria's birthday, as a major public occasion began in Toronto in the troubled year of 1849.[35] Some might term this sentiment mere colonialism; yet the fact was that a sense of particular British American identity within the empire as a whole was growing, as English Canada matured beyond the frontier stage. Developments in English-Canadian literature in the period indicated an increasing self-awareness; although attainments here were less distinctive than in the still more self-conscious French-Canadian society.

The older generation of emigré writers continued active in Canada West: Bonnycastle and Dr. William Dunlop during the forties, Mrs Traill and Mrs Moodie on through the fifties. The *Literary Garland* of Montreal remained a principal outlet for authors such as these, until the competition from American periodicals killed it in 1851.[36] But new names and new vehicles—like the *Canadian Journal* of Toronto—were emerging. William Kirby of Niagara wrote his long poem, *The U.E.*, in 1846 (though it was not published until 1859), which in twelve heavy cantos sought to make a historical epic of the Niagara Loyalist migration. His ambition was more significant than his achievement; he would do much better as a novelist later on. But at least he pointed to new beginnings in poetry, notably in relation to a major theme in English Canada's past. Charles Heavysege ventured into another poetic field with his *Sonnets*, published in Montreal in 1855. And when Charles Sangster at Kingston the next year issued a collection of his verse, *The St. Lawrence and the Saguenay*, he touched on the sweep of the Canadian natural scene, and at once was hailed as "Canada's National Poet."[37]

English-Canadian drama made an initial appearance with Heavysege's grandiose *Saul* in 1857. Novels, however, were little in evidence, apart from one or two late, inferior works of John Richardson. But history had a better showing in Richardson's *War of 1812*, a lucid, extensive study published in 1842; and in Robert Christie's massive *History of the Late Province of Lower Canada*, which came out in six volumes between 1848 and 1855: dull, but thorough and enduring. In 1855, moreover, John McMullen produced the first creditable general account of Canada's past in English, *The History of Canada from its First Discovery to the Present Times*. It was certainly not Garneau, in scale, research, or literary eloquence; nor was its impact on its own Canada comparable. Yet McMullen had his special aim, also: "To infuse a spirit of Canadian nationality into the people generally—to mould the native born citizen, the Scotch, the English and the Irish emigrant into a compact whole."[38] And he felt little doubt about the future of Canada, where the slothful Indians and the unprogressive French had been "succeeded by an orderly, industrious and enterprising people, whose genius and resources embody all the germs of a mighty nation."[39]

It was evident that thoughts of nationality were in the English-Canadian mind by the mid-century. The press repeatedly raised it as an ideal, the goal for the future. "We have a national character to win," proclaimed the Toronto *Globe* in 1847; and again, "Oh for a Canadian nationality which would ameliorate the unmitigated personal selfishness which pervades the land!"[40] In the 1850's a fast-growing and aggressive society, aglow with prosperity and railway hopes, was conceiving a belief in its own transcontinental national destiny, as a second version of American national expansion. "The dark sluggish period, always incident on the first settlement of the forests of America has been accomplished," declared the *Globe* in 1852. "We awake to the importance of our position, and grasp with a manly hand the blessings with which Providence has so amply endowed our Province."[41]

And yet the dream of British American destiny, still firmly British, based on a sure belief in superior gifts of progress, left small room for the separate aspirations of French Canada's own idealized nationalism. The very enthusiasm for two manifest destinies, each blessed by Providence, could bring the two Canadas into conflict. So could the contradictory impulses of voluntaryism and Catholic clericalism. And so could the radical spirit that emerged anew in Canada West after 1850, when Canada East was increasingly displaying conservative tendencies. In short, this was the irony of the union in the 1850's: that while railways, commercial prosperity and rapid economic growth were binding its two Canadian communities ever more closely together, powerful cultural and social forces were rising to drive them angrily apart.

CHAPTER 10

New Forces of Disruption

1850–1853

"It seems to me that this is much the most dangerous party in Canada."[1] So Lord Grey wrote apprehensively to Elgin of the Clear Grits, the new radical faction that was taking shape in Upper Canada at the outset of the 1850's. The Colonial Secretary and the Governor both felt cause for concern over the "extremism" of the radical movement spreading in the West. It had obvious affinities with *rougisme* in the East in its link with annexationism, its belief in democracy and elective institutions, and its hostility to connections between church and state. Both throbbed with enthusiasm and impatience to change the political structure of Canada. Yet each movement had its own distinctive character as well, derived from the differing communities in which they emerged. Their subsequent careers would differ also. While the *rouges* would remain a minor power in Canada East, the Clear Grits—though much modified—would eventually rise to ascendancy in Canada West. In fact, they would come to represent the growing disruptive force of western sectionalism in the union.

Like *rougisme*, Clear Grittism stemmed from the political ferment of the late forties in the province, when the reform sweep of 1847-48 and Europe's Year of Revolution gave new encouragement to radicalism, eclipsed in Canada since the rebellion era. But the LaFontaine-Baldwin program of 1849 had looked tame to left-wing elements in Upper Canada who had viewed responsible government as a means of attaining power to effect basic constitutional changes, and not as a constitutional end in itself. Moreover, some of the "old reformers," pre-1837 stalwarts who had been identified with the cause in the rough, bold days of William Lyon Mackenzie, felt that they had been cast aside by a newer and all too blandly moderate group of leaders, while ardent young Upper Canadian progressives, like the *rouge* idealists of *L'Avenir*, dreamed of a purged party organization that would "roll the country down to a common-sense democracy."[2] Then the annexation issue exposed the differences between the Baldwin ministerial liberals and the left-wing dissentients. Western radicals did not necessarily espouse annexation but they did admire the American political system in itself. "Must we abjure a republican simplicity and assume the paraphernalia . . . of an aristocratical government?" asked the "old reform" Toronto *Examiner*, warmly championing advanced views.[3] In any event, radicals wanted full consideration of the merits of the American model. They reacted sharply to attempts by ministerial leaders and their chief organ, the Toronto *Globe*, to exorcise annexationism from the Upper Canada party, bell, book and candle.

The by-election held in Third York late in 1849 brought matters to a head. The reform candidate, tough old Peter Perry, who had sat in the Upper Canada assembly from 1824 to '36, refused to deny at least the future possibility of annexation, despite every pressure from Baldwin, Hincks, and George Brown's strident *Globe*. Perry became the embattled hero of left-wing protest against ministerial dictation. Locally popular also, he was elected by acclamation in December, 1849, when his tory opponent withdrew. The *Examiner* joyously hailed the emergence of the true "Reform and Progress Party" from government domination.[4] And a group of radicals, old and young, now met in Toronto to organize and direct its growth.

They gathered in the King Street office of William McDougall, a tall young lawyer turned journalist who had already published a little agricultural weekly for the countryside. Aged twenty-seven, clever, aggressive, bubbling with enthusiasm, he was at the heart of the group. Its other younger members included Charles Lindsey, the English "little prodigy" who wrote volubly for the *Examiner*, and David Christie, an earnest, prosperous Scots farmer.[5] Among Old Reformers who joined in the meetings were Peter Perry himself and another veteran parliamentary representative, Malcolm Cameron of Sarnia, the shrewd and wealthy lumber merchant with the hearty backwoods manner. As Assistant Commissioner of Public Works in the Baldwin cabinet, Cameron had fallen out with his fellow ministers. With a sharp eye on the main chance, he had resigned on the day of Perry's triumph, proclaiming his adherence to radical reform, retrenchment, and party regeneration. And David Christie, looking to righteous regeneration, scorned all effete, self-seeking ministerialists. "We want," he said emphatically, "only men who are *Clear Grit*."[6]

The name would cling. The Toronto *Globe* applied it to these party rebels as 1850 began; though "clear grit" was a term already in political parlance, implying an out-and-out purist, and so a thorough-going radical. The Clear Grit movement grew rapidly in Canada West in the next few months. Several reform journals rallied to it. William Lyon Mackenzie, the radicals' old hero-martyr of '37, returned amnestied from exile to take up the cause in the press, and William McDougall shortly announced a new radical organ to be published in Toronto, the *North American*. In March, left-wing elements carried a by-election in nearby Halton, where with Cameron's vigorous assistance another radical, Caleb Hopkins, defeated the government's candidate. Thereafter, vociferous popular meetings were held at Markham and Brooklin in Perry's riding to frame a specifically radical program. These drafting conventions, deplored by conservatives as Yankee democratic devices, and disliked by Baldwin liberals as threatening the control of the party leadership, produced wholesale demands for change. They called for universal suffrage and for election of the governor, the upper house, and "all our public functionaries of every grade," not to mention various legal reforms to ensure "a poor man's law," and the appropriation of the Upper Canada clergy reserves income—that old bone of contention—for purposes of public education.[7]

McDougall's new *North American* discussed and embellished these proposals until a definite Clear Grit platform had been set forth. Another young Clear Grit, Charles Clarke, produced an able series of articles for the journal, "Planks of our Platform," expounding and explaining them with glowing liberal faith.[8] Among the planks, and "subjects for immediate legislation," were a completely elective constitution, fixed biennial parliaments, the ballot, no property qualifications for members, and representation by population. There were also free trade and direct taxation, the abolition of the Courts of Chancery and Common Pleas, the secularization of the reserves, and even Canadian control of external policy. When fully braced and built in the ensuing months, the Clear Grit platform of the *North American* emerged as a remarkably comprehensive structure, incorporating the unfinished business of the Upper Canada reform movement, the chief current doctrines of advanced British liberalism, and the plans to emulate the great working example of popular democracy in American states so close at hand.

The appeal to the American example was patent. Not so directly evident, but quite discernible, were those influences on Clear Grit thinking derived from contemporary British liberal and democratic movements. The points of the People's Charter and the ideals of Cobdenism could be found within this major manifesto of English-Canadian radicalism: leading Clear Grits like Lindsey, Christie, and notably Charles Clarke, had been raised in a British background of parliamentary reform, Chartism, and the free-trade movement. But at the same time Clear Grittism was in close accord with a restless rural democracy in Canada West, most fully manifested in the fast-advancing districts of the western peninsula beyond Toronto and Hamilton. Here older American settlers and newer British immigrants alike looked for the march of progress to wipe out privilege in both church and state; to bring a frugal, limited government under close control of the people, and establish cheap and simple legal processes readily accessible to ordinary landholders.

Yet other elements in Canada West looked with total disapproval on these agrarian democratic aspirations. While Lord Elgin, like Lord Grey, still saw an annexationist threat in the designs of Grit radicals, Upper Canada conservatives condemned their rustic crudity, their Yankee-worship, their Jacobin levelling delusions. And the reform establishment, represented by the *Globe*, flatly rejected the Clear Grit program. Part, it recognized, dealt with practical problems on which reformers were generally agreed, and for which no party break-away was needed. But as for the bulk of the Grits' proposals, "The adoption of their platform would amount to an entire revolution in our constitutional system, and we oppose it, because we vastly prefer British constitutional to American republican government."[9] Consequently the *Globe*, echoed by other liberal ministerial papers, waged a vigorous press war against the Clear Grit journals, upholding the superiority of British cabinet and parliamentary government as the freest and most flexible in the world; decrying the American elective system as clumsy and corrupt, and stained as well with lynch law and the shame of slavery.

By the late spring of 1850, as another legislative session neared, it was clear that the ministerial forces were far more concerned about Clear Grit insurgents on their left than with tory-conservative opponents on their right. The latter, under the blustering leadership of Sir Allan MacNab, were still demoralized by the collapse of old colonialism and by the Montreal tory excesses of 1849. But it was also evident that French-Canadian government supporters were likely to show little enthusiasm for further proposals for reform, as they recoiled from the utopian zeal of *rougisme* in their own section and grew fearful of Clear Grit ardour in the West. Drummond, Solicitor-General East, observed to LaFontaine, "Je dois vous avouer que je regarde ce parti extrême dans le Haut Canada comme fortement entaché de socialism [sic] et presque aussi ingouvernable que notre jeune Canada."[10] Cauchon's *Journal de Québec*, moreover, warned the western radicals that an "all or nothing policy" could bring division and ruin to the united reform party front.[11] With his usual percipience, Lord Elgin saw what might occur: "If clear Gritism absorbs all the hues of Upper Canadian liberalism the French, unless some interference from without checks the natural course of events, will fall off from them and form an alliance with the Upper Canadian Tories."[12]

It was no longer really a question of any radical associations with annexationism. Though *rouges* and a scattered handful in the West would still pursue that cause, it plainly by now had no significant popular support. It was rather the possibility, or threat, that radical zeal for sweeping change might once more divide the dominant reform party between moderates and ultras, and so disrupt its rule in Canada. In short, the rise of the Clear Grit movement of western sectional democracy threatened the very power balance in the Canadian union.

II

In May, 1850, parliament opened in Toronto, the capital having been moved there after the destruction and disorder in Montreal in the violent year of 1849. The union's seat of government was now to alternate between the two former provincial capitals, Quebec and Toronto, settling first in Upper Canada's old, plain, red-brick parliament buildings on Front Street by sparkling Toronto Bay. Tests of voting strength soon proved that the Clear Grits were not as yet a major danger to the government. Their little band of outright adherents made scant inroads with their proposals for basic constitutional or "organic" changes. Yet they did begin collaborating with Lower Canadian radicals, in attacking government waste and tepid moderation. And they did make a significant mark on the question of the Upper Canada clergy reserves, which had once again emerged as an active issue, pressed by the western left wing and promised consideration by the government.

James Price, Commissioner of Crown Lands, put a long series of resolutions through parliament that recited the shortcomings of the existing reserves settlement in dividing the clergy lands endowment among the churches, and requested imperial authorization for the Canadian legislature to enact a new one. It was a not unreasonable way to proceed, considering the old vexed nature of the problem. But Malcolm Cameron, deeming the Price Resolutions to be mere temporizing, moved for a bill to sweep away the reserves provisions at once and seek imperial sanction for the move thereafter. Though his attempt was defeated, he managed to draw the support of nearly half the Upper Canada liberals in the house: so strong was western sectional sentiment becoming for the abolition of all religious endowment from public lands.

After parliament rose in August, the Clear Grits continued to advance. They had effectively identified themselves with the rising agitation in the West for the secularization of the reserves, and with the voluntaryist opinion spreading there that no church should be privileged or supported by the state. Indeed, by the end of 1850 the Grits were no less concerned to demand secularization and "perfect religious equality" than to urge elective democratic institutions.[18] Moreover, they had come to believe, and say, that French-Canadian power in government was holding back secularization and other reforms, thus appealing to an inbred Upper Canadian presumption that the French were inherently opposed to change. They were growing stronger —by invoking sectional feelings. Nevertheless it was unquestionably true that the French Canadians had their own essentially sectional outlook; and they were increasingly displaying conservative caution in a natural desire to guard what they had won. This, indeed, was a truly influential position at the strategic core of government, since under responsible rule any enduring ministry had to look to the substantial support of the main French block of votes, the latter held together by the defensive solidarity of a national minority while the English-speaking majority remained split by its political and religious differences.

Then, early in 1851, an aging but still highly belligerent William Lyon Mackenzie stamped back into active politics. He was too irascibly independent to work in harness long with anyone, even with close friends like the leading Grits. But he was soon a vengeful enemy of the existing party leaders; he found "The Assembly here and the system worthy of each other—behind the age."[14] And the aura of his name roused strong response among radical-minded farmers of the West. He was hailed as "a terror to tyrants," the scourge of faithless moderates like "Mr Reformer Tory Baldwin" and of all the old hateful forces of tory loyalism: "the spawn of the puke of the American Revolution," as one of Mackenzie's correspondents elegantly phrased it.[15] In April he was returned at a by-election in Haldimand over the government candidate, no less than George Brown of the weighty *Globe*.

When parliament met again in May, the Clear Grit drive was at a peak, and Mackenzie led in blistering criticism of ministerial policies. Late in June, he and Caleb Hopkins moved for the abolition of the Court of Chancery. The motion was defeated, but only by Lower Canadian votes: a majority of Upper Canada reformers sided with Mackenzie.[16] Robert Baldwin was deeply affected. As a lawyer he had carried through a careful and expert reform of Chancery but two years before, only to see it condemned by a protest within by his own party. Acutely sensitive, ill besides, and deeply disturbed by the discords in western liberalism, Baldwin took the temporary defection as a personal blow. Though he was not required to resign, on June 30 he left the ministry. He had achieved the one great end for which he had entered politics, responsible government. He had remained a British constitutional liberal, and socially a conservative. At forty-seven, he was wholly out of sympathy with the new surge of radicalism and its democratic egalitarian trend.

The "Great Ministry" of Baldwin and LaFontaine was at its close. While Francis Hincks took over from Baldwin as western leader and began protracted negotiations for cabinet reconstruction, LaFontaine announced his own intention to retire. He too was worn and out of sympathy with new radical trends in politics: "L'école des clear-grits est une école que je n'aime point," he asserted shortly.[17] As a believer in vested rights he disliked both the movement for the secularization of the clergy reserves and that for the abolition of the seigneurial system. The grave, imperious eastern premier was still the unrivalled leader of his people; but equally with Baldwin he had achieved his main purpose in politics, by ensuring French Canada its identity under responsible government. Though he would remain in office until after parliament had risen in the autumn, the resignation of his deeply-trusted friend and partner impelled Louis LaFontaine, not yet forty-four, to make the same decision.

Meanwhile, Hincks faced the double task of coping with the Clear Grits and remaking the western half of the liberal government. Price also planned to retire; Merritt had left the year before: only James Morris, Postmaster General, and Sandfield Macdonald, Solicitor General West, were not withdrawing. With this room for manoeuvre, Hincks by August reached a confidential agreement with William McDougall and David Christie that was ratified by the other Clear Grit leaders. The *North American* was to become a ministerial organ, and two Grit representatives would be taken into the cabinet, Malcolm Cameron as President of the Council and Dr John Rolph as Commissioner of Crown Lands. The latter, another noted old reformer, Mackenzie's chief associate before the rebellion, was intelligent and smoothly affable—though not a little devious. In return for these concessions to the Grits, the more sweeping designs of the radical platform were to be set aside; above all, the demand for a wholly elective constitution. McDougall himself buoyantly affirmed that the reconstituted ministry would proceed with "all reasonable progressive measures," and believed that the Grits' entrance to office would open the way for the ultimate triumph of their principles.[18] Yet a far more experienced and astute Hincks had his own intentions of absorbing the troublesome radicals, whose two representatives could be easily outweighed within the executive council.

The eastern half of the government also faced reconstruction by September. Here, Morin was the unquestioned successor to LaFontaine, and so would be co-premier as well as Provincial Secretary. Morally and intellectually his stature was high: "Je ne connais qu'un défaut à Morin," wrote Cauchon a bit unkindly; "c'est la faiblesse."[19] Drummond was to become Attorney General East, Caron and Taché to remain in their existing posts. John Young, the prominent Montreal business liberal and free-trader, was named Commissioner of Public Works, while the literary Pierre Chauveau, an erstwhile *rouge* associate, came in as Solicitor General East. Since the *rouges*' annexationism had plainly failed to make any headway in French Canada during 1850, and their anti-clericalism was facing increasing opposition there, they no longer constituted a serious threat to Morin's rather conservative-minded liberals. "Les républicains et socialistes" did not have to be taken too much into account in reconstructing the eastern half of the cabinet, but it was with some qualms that the French ministers accepted Clear Grit radical colleagues from the West. And Cauchon, powerful in the party though not a cabinet member, was particularly distressed to see Grit foes of vested interests brought into the administration. Still, he could tell LaFontaine, "Le socialisme dans le gouvernement a desuite rangé tout le clergé de mon côté."[20]

A final ministerial problem arose in the West. Because Hincks was to keep his financial post in the cabinet, as a thoroughly adept Inspector General, a new Attorney General West was needed to take Baldwin's ministerial office. The western leader chose a reliable supporter of his own, W. B. Richards, for the position, but this pricked the considerable pride of Sandfield Macdonald, who had looked to be moved up from his own post of Solicitor General West. Sandfield dourly refused to be mollified.[21] Hincks had made a far from insignificant enemy in the leading reformer from the upper St Lawrence district, and also had to bring in John Ross, Baldwin's son-in-law, to take over the solicitor-generalship in Sandfield Macdonald's stead. At all events, after a summer of travail the new Hincks-Morin administration was in full being by the autumn of 1851. The liberal régime had successfully weathered the closing session of the Third Parliament of the union, elected in such different times back in 1847.

The last weeks of the dying parliament were indeed far quieter, since the Clear Grits had been successfully brought into government alliance; and rising excitement over railways was tending to blur party divisions in any case. Thus Hincks put through his bill for the "Main Trunk" line across the province amid general enthusiasm, and railway fever mounted still higher as ground was broken for new tracks. When writs were issued in November for another general election, one might even have anticipated that an era of railway-building harmony under continued liberal rule would follow, since radicalism, after failing to grow substantially in the East, had now been harnessed in its more powerful western manifestation.

III

In actuality, still more disruptive forces than sectional radicalism had been developing in the same period and had already made their presence felt by the autumn of 1851. They concerned the emotion-filled relations of church and state. While pro-clerical Catholic influence was spreading in French Canada, the spirit of voluntaryism was advancing in Canada West. Rooted in the very conscience of evangelical Protestantism, which sought to free the church from worldly interests and the state from religious privilege, voluntaryism had already been displayed in the 1840's during the struggle for a non-sectarian provincial university in Upper Canada. It had indeed appeared well before the union, in the demand to secularize the Upper Canada clergy reserves. And it was particularly exemplified among the Free Kirk Presbyterians, the substantial element who had left the main Presbyterian body in 1843, after the Great Disruption in Scotland had split the national church there on the issue of state "intrusion" into church affairs. Yet it was only in the early fifties that the voluntary movement rose to its peak in Canada.

To some extent this reflected a new moral fervour in the West, also expressed in the temperance (soon "teetotal") movement, which by 1850 was multiplying Good Templar lodges throughout the region. It was seen as well in the campaign that developed for sabbath observance laws. The former failed to achieve legal prohibition on the then popular model of the State of Maine, but it did obtain a form of local option by 1853. The latter inspired many restrictive local by-laws, and some enactments against Sunday labour in the public services. These efforts, described by one critic as a quest for a "moral Eldorado,"[22] undoubtedly represented an evangelical ardour for the moral reform of society that was evident in both the contemporary United States and Victorian Britain. But the upsurge of voluntaryism in Upper Canada after 1850 also reflected the very success of the reform movement there in the previous decade, which had opened the way to further endeavours.

Above all, the Upper Canadian clergy reserves, those dire embodiments of church privilege and the state endowment of religion, could now be dealt with. The reserves question had been relatively quiescent during the forties, overshadowed by the primary problem of responsible government. But once responsible rule had been achieved, the way seemed open for the final disposition of the incubus. So it appeared to voluntaryist Protestants no less than to Clear Grit farmers. Often, indeed, they were the same thing: though it was probably a more materially-minded Grit agrarian who bluntly remarked to William Lyon Mackenzie in 1851, "For my part I do not see why God should hold land and not pay taxes."[23]

The existing reserves settlement rested on an imperial Act of 1840, which had revised and replaced the compromise division of the income from clergy lands steered by Sydenham through the last session of the old Upper Canada legislature. Since the reserves system had initially been erected under the Constitutional Act of 1791, the final authority to alter it had remained with the British parliament which had passed that law. Accordingly, the imperial measure of 1840 had changed Sydenham's settlement to favour the Church of England more. It had divided the reserves endowment between "old sales" —lands already sold by that time—the proceeds of which would be shared by the Churches of England and Scotland in the proportion of two to one, and "new sales," of which half the proceeds would go to these same churches in the same ratio, leaving the rest for distribution among other denominations that applied for them. The net result was a disproportionate endowment for both Anglican and Presbyterian Churches (especially after the

Free Kirk split in the latter), which allocated not much more than a third of future reserves income for denominations that comprised close to half of the Upper Canadian population.[24]

Hence the settlement of 1840 had left considerable dissatisfaction among the churches not favoured, but particularly among voluntaryist elements who objected to the very principle of state-church endowment: many Methodists, especially in the minor sects, with Baptists, Congregationalists, Free Kirk, and others. The issue had come to a head when the Clear Grit dissentients took it up strongly in 1850. At the same time, Baldwin and other Anglican or Presbyterian reformers had recognized that action would have to be taken on the reserves, although their own aim was rather a more equitable division than the denial of state support to religion.

Moreover, their Lower Canadian colleagues saw cause to fear that an assault on religious endowments might be turned against the wide Catholic holdings in Canada East. Drummond, for instance, discerned the threat in Upper Canada that "les spoliateurs se revêtent du manteau [du] puritanisme. . . . Et puis l'appétit vient en mangeant; ces sectaires affamés après avoir partagé les biens du clergé n'hésiteraient peut-être pas porter une main sacrilège sur les propriétés de nos communautés religieuses."[25] LaFontaine himself, speaking in parliament in 1850, had made a strong defence of state recognition of vested religious interests. Accordingly, in view of the doubts and difficulties in government ranks, the Price Resolutions of that session had only considered the initial, though requisite, step for any Canadian settlement of the reserves question, the transfer of final control over them from the imperial to the provincial legislature.

Spurred by hope of the coming abolition of the reserves, yet fearful as well that dark forces meant to delay or prevent it, voluntaryists and radicals formed the Anti-Clergy-Reserves Association in Toronto in the summer of 1850. It led to a more broadly named Anti-State-Church Association. For the reserves issue really focused, then radiated, all the anti-state-church sentiments of voluntaryism in Canada West. These feelings were stimulated also by reactions among evangelical Protestants to the ritualistic Oxford Movement in Anglicanism in England, and to the newly assertive papal power displayed in Catholic Europe after the revolutions of 1848. The forces of "state churchism" were clearly on the march: they had to be countered. That resolve helped to widen the anti-state-church movement in Canada, for which the state endowments represented by the reserves became only the first and most immediate battleground. Furthermore, the surge of voluntaryism affected the strongest reform organ in the West, since George Brown of the *Globe* was a staunch adherent of the Free Kirk. He had at first defended the Baldwin ministry's cautious approach to the reserves (especially as he thoroughly opposed the Clear Grits who were pushing the agitation), arguing that it was indeed first necessary for Canada to obtain full power to legislate a new reserves settlement. But later he wondered whether the Price Resolutions of 1850 had been merely a delaying tactic, and whether there was not something in Clear Grit charges that French and Catholic influence on the government was preventing it from taking a decisive stand.[26] Concerns of this sort, spreading among voluntaryists, drew some of their attention from Anglican defenders of the reserves towards the Roman Catholics, no less convinced upholders of the ties of church and state. And at this juncture, another church-and-state issue made its appearance: the question of separate schools.

In June 1850, a new Common School Bill for Upper Canada was introduced in parliament. In many respects this was an unexceptionable measure, carefully drafted by the Chief Superintendent of Schools, Egerton Ryerson, to improve and consolidate the entire western public-school system. It would remain the basic Upper Canadian education act for the next twenty years. But its nineteenth clause, dealing with separate schools, raised particular problems. Of course, the education acts of both sections of the union already contained provisions for these schools for religious minorities, separate from the respective majority systems though sharing in the public education grants. Yet in Upper Canada, at least, the number of state-aided separate schools (Roman Catholic, Anglican and some negro) had been few, since most children attended the ordinary "mixed" common schools. In Ryerson's view, separate schools had existed simply as "protection from insult," for exceptional cases where a minority's beliefs might otherwise be threatened.[27] Their numbers were actually tending to decline—before the Bill of 1850.

This measure, however, brought demands from both Catholic reformers and High Anglican tories for broader separate-school provisions; and to forestall a possibly threatening political combination, Hincks, who was piloting the bill, took up the Roman Catholic requests only. He carried a revised clause nineteen, which declared that the erecting of separate schools was not to rest henceforth with the discretion of municipal authorities, but would be their "duty" whenever twelve resident Catholic heads of families applied for one in any area where the common-school teacher was a Protestant.[28] This effectively widened the basis of western separate schools, by making them requisite under a general rule. It also emphasized a Catholic-Protestant division in the western school system, not so evident before. Still further, the change in the school law responded to a growing demand for distinctive educational rights among Upper Canadian Roman Catholics, whose numbers had been notably increased by the heavy Irish immigration. And finally, the change spread alarm among the voluntaryists, who saw state-church forces cutting into the non-sectarian public school system, and even threatening its existence, if other denominations besides the Roman Catholics similarly pressed for their own structure of state-supported schools. With anxiety, the *Globe* viewed the new School Act as "the entering wedge."[29]

While voluntaryism was thus being led to turn its anti-state-church zeal against Catholic influences on public policy, Roman Catholicism was evincing its own rising mood of ardour. The emerging campaign for Catholic separate schools in Canada West was part of it, as was the advance of French clerical conservatism in Canada East. But both also reflected the ultramontane spirit of resolute, energetic leaders of the hierarchy like Bishop Ignace Bourget of Montreal or Armand de Charbonnel, the austere French aristocrat who became Bishop of Toronto in 1850. It was Bourget who had brought about the return of the powerful Jesuit order to Lower Canada in 1842. It was Charbonnel, recalling the indifferentism and irreligion in his native France, who launched a strong effort to tighten the bonds of Catholic faith in Upper Canada. And these forceful clerical statesmen in turn reflected the militant enthusiasm of the papacy of Pius IX, now shaping a great Catholic revival after the excesses of European liberalism in 1848.

It was, indeed, the papal mood of reform and renewal which produced the so-called "Papal Aggression" question in England late in 1850, and so inspired an angry clash of fervent Protestant and Catholic opinion in Canada. When the Vatican proclaimed a full Catholic hierarchy with territorial titles for England (for the first time since the Reformation), there were loud outcries in that officially Protestant state. They were soon echoed by the press in the Protestant English-speaking world beyond. In Canada, the *Globe* especially took up "papal aggression"—after Etienne Taché had jocularly challenged George Brown to do so.[30] Its militant articles on papal pretensions and Roman Catholic propensities to interfere in state affairs brought hot answers from Catholic journals like the Irish Toronto *Mirror*. The sectarian wrangle spread into the spring of 1851, and undoubtedly entered into Brown's own defeat in the Haldimand by-election in April, when a vigorous propaganda campaign in the constituency carried a substantial Catholic Irish vote against him. As well as radicalism, therefore, antipathies between Catholic and Protestant reformers were threatening to divide the liberal party ranks.

Furthermore, Brown's own growing estrangement from the party leadership was confirmed by the ministry's failure to help his cause in Haldimand. The French-Canadian members of the cabinet obviously had no liking for his course of "fanatisme extravagant" (to quote *La Minerve*), and there was rooted distrust and rivalry between Hincks and Brown, Baldwin's two most able party lieutenants for some years past.[31] Consequently, when Baldwin resigned as Upper Canadian leader at the end of June, 1851, Brown, the man of righteous principle, was quick to dissociate himself from a government led by an opportunist like Hincks. He condemned it utterly for its continued failure to settle the reserves, check state-church inroads into the schools, or espouse the true voluntaryist liberalism that sought religious equality within a neutral state. The entrance of the Clear Grits into the Hincks ministry only hardened the opposition of the *Globe* and its powerful master, who had gone on warring against Grit advocacy of American elective institutions and expected no good from Grits in office, with their "constitution-tinkering trumpery."[32] Of course, they readily returned the favour, the *North American* scorning the mean hostility of "the discarded toady of the Baldwin-Lafontaine cabinet."[33]

Accordingly, in the fall of 1851, the *Globe* editor shaped a concentrated attack on the Hincksite leadership. He called anew for party regeneration: not for radical regeneration in Grit terms—his own political tenets were essentially those of a moderate, mid-Victorian British liberalism—but for a voluntaryist reform party to deal boldly with the reserves, sectarian schools, and state-church influence in Upper Canada. And when the general election campaign began in mid November, Brown stood as an independent reformer in the far-western riding of Kent. Tall, imposing, full of tireless energy and torrential speech, the massive red-haired Scot made an incisive impact this time. Thanks to the power of his *Globe*, moreover, and the strength of Upper Canadian voluntaryism, "Big George" might yet lead a western party revolt to unseat the Hincks régime. But whatever the outcome of the elections, the rise of sectarian controversy seemed henceforth bound to embitter relations between Catholic French and Protestant English Canada.

IV

Despite all the stir of the previous months, the elections of December 1851 were relatively quiet. The *Montreal Gazette* even remarked that not in twenty years had a general election caused "so little excitement. . . . In Lower Canada, indeed, it may be said that it has been regarded with total indifference."[34] As regards Upper Canada, this might somewhat overstate the case. Still, the elections had brought few apparent changes. The Hincks-Morin government was returned to office by the opening of 1852 with about the same strength it had had before the dissolution: some eighteen firm supporters in the West and about thirty in the East.[35] For the time being, at least, railway prosperity, harmony and material projects had prevailed in most areas over more explosive political and religious issues. Yet a closer look would show some considerable portents of change. In the first place, George Brown and William Lyon Mackenzie had both been elected as independent reformers opposing the Hincksite cabinet, largely on the grounds of voluntaryism. In other matters they were almost equally opposed to one another; but both would exert great influence because of their own forceful personalities and standing in the West, and because the voluntaryist sentiment was far wider than the two constituencies they represented.

In the second place, half the western ministerial contingent was now composed of Clear Grit supporters. The moderate or truly Hincksite element had actually lost ground to radicals, who had particularly campaigned for secularization of the reserves. Third, the tory-conservatives had shown signs of recovery in Canada West, increasing their seats there from sixteen to twenty, though still having only a corporal's guard in the eastern section. More notably, very few old tories had been returned, apart from a much-mellowed and railway-minded MacNab; and while he remained ostensibly the party leader, more liberal conservatives had come to the fore; men like John A. Macdonald, virtually William Draper's heir, who were pulling the party away from right-wing dominance and adjusting it to the new dispensation of responsible government. Fourth, and finally, the *rouges* had elected only three or four members in Lower Canada, along with a few English radical allies. In the East, the trend had clearly continued towards conservatism among the main French block of Morin liberals and their own English-speaking associates. Significantly, *L'Avenir* suspended publication in January, 1852, with an eloquent farewell to "Amis de la cause démocratique," and the more circumspect, less doctrinaire *Le Pays* became the *rouge* Montreal organ.[36]

There was, in short, every sign of a new era emerging in politics. In Canada West, there had been a shift away from the old opponents of the contest over responsible government, Compact tories and Baldwinite (now Hincksite) liberals, towards a confrontation of middle-ground conservatives and more radical reformers. In Canada East, French-Canadian liberalism was plainly more concerned to preserve its gains than go on further: in fact, the inherent conservatism of a people on the defensive was inevitably altering the old "reform" alliance. There was reason to look with Lord Elgin for the emergence of new political combinations. In reality, the Hincks-Morin régime was only a stop-gap, in a movement from, not a return to, the days of LaFontaine-Baldwin reform dominance.

The new parliament that would prove these points did not assemble for some months after the elections. The seat of government was being moved again, this time to Quebec, while Premier Hincks was away in the Maritimes and England throughout the winter and spring. He was negotiating with the other colonial governments and the imperial authorities on financing the Halifax-to-Quebec railway, which was meant to connect with the projected provincial trunk line across Canada. Though the Intercolonial Railway scheme broke down, Hincks, of course, returned from England that summer with a contract with the Brassey firm instead: the contract to build the Grand Trunk of Canada as a government-assisted private venture.

With a great rail enterprise like this in the offing, and other lines in the province actually building, the railway era of hopeful, though largely superficial, good feelings continued on through 1852. But the clashing aspirations of voluntaryist and ultramontane Catholic interests remained very much in being: Bishop de Charbonnel denounced the existing western school system as "a regular disguised persecution"; the *Globe* proclaimed, "There is no safety for Canada but the entire separation of church and state."[37] And the clergy-reserves question entered a new phase after February, 1852, when the Russell whig administration in England was replaced by the tories under Lord Derby, the former Lord Stanley, who were decidedly opposed to interfering with the existing Canadian settlement. This led secularizationists in Upper Canada to demand a bill abolishing the reserves, with a clause suspending its operation until Britain had agreed. Their aim was to test the Hincksite ministry's good faith, and keep up pressure on the British government at the same time.

In consequence, good feelings soon ebbed away, once parliament met in August in the old grey stone legislative buildings of Lower Canada, high above the St Lawrence in Quebec's Upper Town. At the start, on August 19, the government managed easily enough to dispose of the speakership, giving it to Sandfield Macdonald as something of a consolation prize. But Papineau, leading the little group now described as *le parti rouge*, Brown and his few "tadpoles," Mackenzie the one-man host, MacNab and Macdonald and their followers, attacked the ministerial forces from every direction. Hincks's new resolutions on the reserves, reiterating the request for their transfer to Canadian control, were denounced by Brown and Mackenzie as sheer pretence, since they still did not commit the government to secularization. For quite different reasons the Upper Canada conservatives lined up strongly, though fruitlessly, against the resolutions, voicing Anglican and Presbyterian support for the principle of church endowments, and in general defending vested interests. As for Hincks's Grand Trunk Railway Bill, it too was strenuously opposed by George Brown, and by conservatives like John A. Macdonald, who, droll and devastating by turns, was clearly becoming his party's ablest spokesman. This extravagant design, it was charged, would benefit only the contractors and English investors, at the heavy expense of the Canadian people. The bill did not pass until November, when parliament adjourned because of the frightening spread of cholera at Quebec.

It did not meet again till February, 1853. And now a whole series of measures came up, which brought sectarian controversy harshly to the fore. These were bills to charter ecclesiastical corporations in Canada East, where Roman Catholic zeal combined with growing affluence was proliferating new religious foundations, colleges, hospitals and charitable institutions, all under clerical auspices. A homogeneous French Catholic community looked to the church to play a leading role in providing its social institutions. But in the Protestant heterogeneity of the West, secular authority and private philanthropy were expected to furnish hospitals and educational or welfare agencies. Two different cultures clashed in misunderstanding—the "priest-ridden" and the "godless." And western voluntaryists were perfectly outraged by the state so freely authorizing these sectarian institutions; especially when the government, itself concerned, put through a blanket Ecclesiastical Corporations Bill that was meant to cover the whole multiplicity of religious bodies seeking charters.

Brown fought the measure hotly; Macdonald coolly, to harass the government's western followers, not for any reason of voluntaryism. And certainly the Clear Grits chafed painfully at the kind of ministerial policies they were being called on to support. One of their two cabinet representatives, John Rolph, indeed developed such facility at plunging for the lobby when embarrassing votes came up that he won the name of "Old Dissolving Views."[38] His colleague, Malcolm Cameron, tried a bold front and fast talk instead. "When a dirty dive is to be taken, Cameron always goes down deepest," observed the *Globe* succinctly.[39] Then, early in March, George Brown introduced another measure of sharp significance, which indicated how far the sectarian clash was merging into outright sectional struggle, engaging Upper Canadian interests directly against Lower Canadian—a proposal for representation by population.

This idea was by no means new. Durham had originally intended to base the Canadian union upon it, not on the equal representation of the two sections in parliament. French-Canadian objections to the Union Act as passed had partly derived from the fact that its equal division of seats had effectively under-represented their own section. The *rouges* had taken up the cause of "Réforme électorale basée sur le chiffre des populations";[40] Papineau had brought in a motion for it in 1849. And in Upper Canada, Clear Grits espoused representation by population from 1850 onward, both because it expressed the democratic principle of "one man, one vote" and because they wanted a redistribution of seats to take account of fast-expanding population in newer western farming areas, which would quite likely vote radical. Even some western tories and conservatives had supported "Rep-by-Pop" in 1850 and '51, hopeful that an increased number of Upper Canadian seats might enable them to overcome the persistent reform majority that was largely based on the firm French block behind the government. For by that time it was becoming altogether probable that the rapid growth of settlement in Canada West would give it a preponderance of representatives, if Rep-by-Pop should be applied.

The findings of the decennial census for 1851-52 confirmed that expectation. Canada West now had a population of 952,000, to 890,000 for Canada East, and all the indications were that through immigration the West's faster rate of growth would continue. The census, therefore, greatly sharpened the sectional implications of representation by population. Western interests saw it as the means of overcoming "French domination." French Canadians feared it as threatening English domination instead. Equal sectional representation, which once they had endured as an injustice, now seemed an essential protection for their rights and very identity. As a result, when Brown in March, 1853, brought in the first motion for representation by population since the revelations of the census, it was resoundingly defeated—57 to 15—by French-Canadian members and their western ministerial allies.[41]

He had moved it in amendment to Morin's Representation Bill, which did propose to increase the seats in parliament in response to Canada's growth in population, but to do so equally within the two sections, thus preserving the existing balance and division of the union. Brown's amendment called for a redistribution based on population "without regard to a separating line between Upper Canada and Lower."[42] In one sense, he was trying to make the union of the Canadas what it was supposed to be, truly a legislative union. In another, as a voluntaryist, he was trying to reduce the influence of the French state-church adherents, who showed no hesitation in voting on Upper Canadian questions like clergy reserves and Catholic separate schools. "Can anyone fail to see," he argued, "that so long as Lower Canada has one-half of the representatives, and four-fifths of the Lower Canada members vote as one man—that by political divisions of Upper Canada the views of a compact body will control the progressive opinions of the majority of the legislature?"[43] Yet his very arguments fanned sectional controversy, and aroused old fears of assimilation in French-Canadian minds. In any event, Brown's motion brought the basic problem of the union—a unitary state, but divided in two—squarely into the open. "Some gentlemen," he told parliament, "seem to think this is an ordinary question—but it is the question of questions—it lies at the foundation of all reforms."[44] It was indeed only the beginning of a series of Rep-by-Pop motions by Brown and his associates in years ahead, which would attract mounting western support as sectional differences grew and Upper Canadians increasingly demanded "justice" for their larger population.

But now another church-and-state question appeared, a Supplementary School Bill for Upper Canada. It made much broader provisions for western separate schools, sought by Bishop Charbonnel and the Catholic hierarchy in both sections, and by many petitions to parliament, all of them, significantly, from Lower Canada.[45] Moreover, Morin had pledged to Archbishop Turgeon of Quebec "to give the Catholics of Upper Canada the same advantages which the Protestants in our part of the Province enjoy."[46] One might argue that the two cases were different. Because the majority schools in the East were confessional and Catholic, the minority schools were religiously-based and Protestant; whereas the public schools in the West were non-denominational and without religious connection. But Catholics, believing in an integral tie between religion and education, would consider this lack of religious connection in the western public system a crucial fault in itself. Two very different approaches could find no meeting place.

Accordingly, Roman Catholic pressure on the western system had continued, while voluntaryists like Brown and Mackenzie, armed with their own mass of opposing petitions from the West, counter-attacked by demanding the complete abolition of separate schools. "The State shall have nothing whatever to do with religious teachings in any shape," insisted Brown; and the *Globe* demanded, "Let our School system be destroyed, and what remains to us of hope for the country?"[47] But after intense debate the School Bill of 1853 was finally passed in June by virtue of a government majority dependent on Canada East.[48] The act divided public and separate school finances, incorporated separate school boards to collect and disburse funds, and freed Roman Catholic supporters of separate schools from public school taxes. It went much further than previous enactments to establish a dual school system in Canada West, and to strengthen sectional feeling there against the interfering power of eastern Catholic votes.

The long, embittering session finally drew to a close in June 1853, while tempers flared in parliament and tension climbed outside. It was at this critical moment that the fiery figure of Alessandro Gavazzi swept down on Lower Canada. He was an Italian patriot, a former monk who had broken with Rome over its reaction to the Italian revolution of 1848. Now he was touring North America to raise funds for the patriot cause and denouncing the sins of popery with fierce evangelism. His towering, black-robed presence, impassioned and melodramatic, swayed enthusiastic Protestant audiences in Canada West. Then, rashly, dangerously, he moved on to lecture in the East—to Quebec, already roused as it was by the vehement Protestant-Catholic disputes so long resounding in the legislature. The consequence came quickly. At Quebec on the night of June 6, a roaring mob broke into the Free Presbyterian Church as Gavazzi was speaking. A wild brawl followed, until soldiers hastily arrived to restore order. When the incendiary preacher left for Montreal the next day, guards were posted through the streets, and sixty armed men went aboard the steamboat with him.[49]

Worse still occurred in Montreal. Gavazzi's meeting at Zion Church on June 9 inspired another violent outbreak, as Irish Roman Catholics attacked the building and shots cracked out on both sides. In the swirling confusion, the troops that had been called out fired a wild volley and struck the

Protestant congregation that was struggling into the street to make for home. Ten were killed and more wounded; but the tragedy did not immediately shock the city into order. Instead, other though less violent outbursts followed in the next few days of June, when crowds gathered to stone evangelical Protestant churches in Montreal, and provincial and civil authorities seemed powerless at first to check them.[50] So the chief community of Canada East gave vent to stormy anti-Protestant passions, while in Canada West there were no less passionate outcries against Catholic violence, and excited calls for "Protestant union" to meet it and retaliate.

But order was soon restored, and explosive fury passed. The deeper clash it symbolized remained. When parliament, exhausted and somewhat chastened by the recent events, rose at last on June 14, 1853, it seemed evident that the growth of sectarian and sectional issues between the two Canadian communities was straining the very fabric of union. Nor was there any sign of a solution to this cultural conflict, for all the political autonomy and economic prosperity that had been achieved under the union of the Canadas.

CHAPTER 11

The Impact of Sectionalism

1853-1856

In the aftermath of the Gavazzi riots and the rancorous session of 1853, there was growing recognition that the existing pattern of politics in the Canadian union was breaking down. Talk of new party alignments went on persistently through the latter months of the year. Some speculated on an alliance between Upper Canada tories, defenders of church endowments, and French-Canadian supporters of similar state-church views. Others looked for Protestant Union, to combine Orangemen, Lower Canadian tories and western voluntaryist reformers against "Catholic aggression." Still others hoped for a conjunction of English-speaking conservatives with both French and English moderate liberals in a broad new centre coalition: a coalition which would defeat both eastern *rouge* extremists and western "pharisaical brawlers"—Taché's phrase.[1] In any case it was evident that, thanks to cultural and sectional discord, the once invincible reform party front was disintegrating into a loose, unhappy collection of jarring elements.

In Canada West, the continued failure to achieve the secularization of the reserves, and the recent separate school and ecclesiastical corporation measures, had swung the Clear Grits away again from the Hincksite moderate liberals. The radicals brimmed with resentful suspicions that the moderates had indeed sold out to French power in order to keep themselves in office and to indulge in a costly, and lucrative, series of railway deals. And suspicions of waste and corruption seemed all too plainly confirmed when, in September 1853, it was revealed that Premier Hincks himself had used his position to make a fat personal profit from railway debentures. He and Mayor John Bowes of Toronto had carried out a scheme to replace old depreciated bonds granted by the city to the Northern Railway with a new, more valuable issue—and had quietly bought up the old bonds themselves for £40,000, which they then exchanged for new ones worth £50,000 under the very act that Hincks put through: thus clearing a neat £10,000 in the transaction.[2]

This "Ten Thousand Pound Job" was only the first of a number of dubious deals unearthed in the next few months which effectively blackened Hincks's political reputation. He had proved entirely too clever a financier, and the chances offered in an era of frantic railway promotion all too inviting. The aura of scandal spread to the whole lavish Grand Trunk scheme, to the Hincksite "railway men" who backed it, to members of the cabinet who sat both as ministers and as directors of the line. A sense of public morality had been little developed as yet, in a society just emerging from pioneer rawness into an era of heavy capital investment, but the easy mixing of public policy with private speculation alarmed even popular opinion of the time. Grit probity was shocked. "What in the name of heaven are we coming to as a party?" cried William McDougall, at the £10,000 revelation of September.[3] Starkly disillusioned, he took his *North American* into opposition. The two Clear Grit cabinet members, Rolph and Cameron, were left in increasing isolation as some sort of Upper Canadian *vendus*, distrusted by their former followers. "I am ashamed to have been connected with a movement that has come to such an impotent conclusion," wrote McDougall bitterly.[4]

Meanwhile George Brown and his supporters continued to oppose both Clear Grits and Hincksites, seeking their own projected party combination: an alignment of western voluntaryist reformers with advanced conservatives and "truly liberal" French Canadians, to exclude both radical and tory extremes and secure "a liberal progressive government."[5] Within its limits, the *Globe* even made overtures for French-Canadian support. "It is a great mistake," it said in July of 1853, "to fancy there is no truly liberal party in Lower Canada. There is a large and increasing section who bemoan the slavery in which their country is enthralled by priestcraft. . . . Not that they wish to leave the Communion of the Papal Church—but they . . . long to see it shorn of its perilous power."[6] Brown praised the Institut Canadien for defending free discussion, and was pleased to note that the *Moniteur Canadien*, a *rouge* organ, had declared him "the best friend of the Canadiens" for his anti-state-church stand.[7]

Reform division and confusion were more apparent in Canada West, but were far from absent in Canada East. There, while the main group of ministerial liberals under Morin was larger and more solid than its western counterpart, it still faced powerful critics on the left. For *le parti rouge*, if limited in numbers, had stayed strong in intellectual vigour, reflected still in the lively Institut Canadien, despite a growing threat of clerical censorship and censure by the diocese of Montreal.[8] Papineau, it is true, was about to retire, sick of unending frustration. He had never really found his *métier* under responsible government. But younger men were rising who would do so: Louis-Victor Sicotte, for instance, who had joined parliament in 1852.

Sicotte himself was less a *rouge* radical than an emphatic anti-government liberal; yet in this he represented a growing group of French critics of the ministry. There was a good deal of impatience at its failure thus far to settle the seigneurial question, and *rouges* who had muted their earlier unsuccessful appeals to republicanism and annexation could now reap the benefit of their strong attacks on seigneurial tenure. Moreover, in reaction to western sectional pressure, French Canadians might well conclude that the existing Anglo-French ministerial combination was not sufficiently alive to their national interests. Hence the *rouges*, self-proclaimed heirs of the old *patriote* tradition, could look to gain support within their own community, as the impact of sectionalism weakened the whole concept of reform alliance in the union.

Anti-ministerial critics had emerged on the right in French Canada as well. They were expressive of the strong pro-clerical Catholic current; indeed, they marked the furthest political reach of ultramontane enthusiasm. Yet they could join quite readily with democratic radicals in condemning the weak-kneed, inactive Morin moderates. Cauchon in particular had identified himself with right-wing unrest, and in 1852 had broken with the ministry as a French conservative insurgent. His zeal, as opposed to his ambition, might be doubted. His vigour and vituperative skill could not. He would invite equally abusive returns, as in a rudely obvious broadsheet caricature, *Mores Porci:*

> When Cauchon is meek
> He is weak, weak, weak . . .
> When he tries to look big
> He is pig, pig, pig.
> When he thinks he can shine
> He is swine, swine, swine.[9]

Harried from right and left, the moderate centre group of French liberals still held together behind the eastern ministers. To a large degree their continued cohesion reflected the LaFontaine tradition that French Canadians to be effective in politics must maintain a united party that could work with western allies. It also reflected the very practical patronage system built up under LaFontaine, and perhaps also the growing practical influence of his real future successor as leader of the main French forces, George-Etienne Cartier. A pugnacious but keenly perceptive politician, stocky, high-spirited, and with a jaunty sense of humour, Cartier was playing a critically important role in politics as a bridge between French interests and the English business community. As a prominent Montreal lawyer and solicitor for the St Lawrence and Atlantic, he had taken a leading role in promoting both that line and the Grand Trunk Railway. He had enthusiastically pressed for material development ever since entering the assembly in 1848, and now held a strategic position for guiding necessary transactions as chairman of its powerful Railway Committee.[10]

For all his lobbying expediency, however, Cartier remained a devoted champion of French Canada, a moderate nationalist who would co-operate with English interests but none the less hold the preservation of French-Canadian identity as an essential term of the bargain. Morin, perhaps, better portrayed another dominant aspect of the chief French party grouping, their strong association with Catholic clericalism. Without going as far as right-wing ultramontanes, the French moderate or conservative liberals—to be dubbed *bleus* as opposed to *rouges*—readily accepted close ties with church interests. The devout Morin particularly exemplified the link with the hierarchy and the bond between priests and politicians that had developed since the mid forties. But, scholarly and sensitive, he was not well suited to lead in the new era of mounting passions in politics. He could not give his embattled followers the confident direction that the brusque Cartier could provide, nor readily supply the *bleus* with that faculty which the *rouge* Letellier chaffingly described as "l'art d'être anglais en dessus et canadien-français en dedans."[11]

So much for the problems of reform party elements. The opposing tory-conservative ranks had problems of their own. In Canada East, the English tories, descendants of the old British party, had never really recovered from their last desperate outbursts in 1849: they were a scant rearguard now in towns and Townships. Most eastern English-speaking representatives were associated with the Morin moderates, and some even with the *rouges*. Certainly, Montreal commercial toryism had had to face the fact of assured French political predominance in Lower Canada. Nevertheless, in a renewed mood of angry desperation after the Gavazzi riots, the eminent *Montreal Gazette* had gone as far as declaring that the conservative party was impotent and doomed; that a new combination must arise to secure equality for all denominations, the fusion of the Canadas, free schools for all, and Rep-by-Pop—a remarkable echoing of George Brown's own voluntaryist liberal program.[12]

Tories and conservatives in Upper Canada were almost as troubled. Their titular leader, Sir Allan MacNab, now aging and gouty, gave little effective direction. The Orange Order, with some sixty thousand members now, had divided between the followers of Ogle Gowan, Grand Master, who advocated a common conservative front with French moderates, and those of George Benjamin who sought a common Protestant front with Grit radicals.[13] The Gowanites loomed larger than the Benjaminites; Orange anti-reform animus was more deeply rooted than Orange fears of French Catholics; but the dilemma for the Order was real. Then there was growing conservative

disarray over the clergy reserves, some party adherents being ready to yield
to secularization as inevitable, others still determined to fight it to the end.
Upper Canadian tories toyed with the proposal of joining with French-
Canadian Catholics to resist anti-state-church onslaughts, or else responded
as before to anti-French outcries. All seemed flux and disorder within the
party. But one leading western conservative, at least, had a clear and calm
appreciation of what the future might be.

John A. Macdonald, no less pragmatic and perceptive than Cartier, but
genially easy rather than ebullient, had himself established good relations
with French Canadians in parliament on a basis of mutual respect for
cultural and national differences. "Treat them as a nation," he wrote later,
"and they will act as a free people generally do—generously."[14] He looked
for an inevitable change of ministry after the next general election, and
for the new governing combination to include both conservatives and
French. Not for him the delusive appeal to form a western sectional coalition
of conservatives and voluntaryist reformers: "No man in his senses can
suppose that this country can for a century to come be governed by a totally
unfrenchified government."[15] And for the present, as he recorded in February, 1854, "Our aim should be to enlarge the bounds of our party so as
to embrace every person desirous of being counted as a progressive Conservative."[16] It was an aim that projected a rallying at the political centre,
one without sectarian or sectional overtones. It was an aim put forward also
by Ogle Gowan in his Toronto *Patriot*, which urged western tories and
conservatives to join with both the Hincksite liberals and the Morin moderates in the cause of Canadian harmony and progress.[17]

The political uncertainty, the conflicting speculations on the future,
continued well on into 1854, for the meeting of parliament that would
almost surely bring about a crisis had twice to be postponed. In February
the old Lower Canada legislative buildings at Quebec were destroyed in a
disastrous fire. In May the convent of the Sisters of Charity, which was
being remodelled there to house the legislature, was also burned out. Work
was hastily begun to adapt Quebec's Music Hall for the ill-omened session,
but it could not be finished until June. Meanwhile Canadian attention was
somewhat distracted from domestic affairs by the opening rounds of the
Anglo-French war with Russia, and by the signing of the Reciprocity Treaty
on June 6 in Washington, where Hincks had gone with Elgin for the final
successful negotiations. A week later, parliament opened at last—to unleash
the forces of turmoil that had been gathering for a year.

II

The house as it met was bristling, looking for trouble. It soon found it, when
the Speech from the Throne revealed a sketchy government program not

touching major issues like the seigneuries or the clergy reserves. There was really no barrier left to settling the latter question. At the end of 1852, the short-lived Derby tory régime in England had been replaced by a whig and Peelite coalition under Lord Aberdeen; and this had brought in a measure, transferring final control of the reserves to Canada, that had carried even before the last Canadian session had ended. But the Hincks-Morin ministry was now contending that, since the provincial Representation Act, passed in 1853 to increase the parliamentary membership in each section from 42 to 65, was to go into effect with the next election, matters of such basic importance as reserves and seigneuries should properly be left to the new enlarged assembly to decide. It looked like a sheer evasion. The house angrily greeted it as such.

Certainly the weakened ministry might want to put off all that it possibly could to the future. Yet it was also true that Elgin himself was insistent on delaying action on the clergy reserves until after the next election. He held to the belief that an immediate measure for secularization would have "enabled the friends of the endowment to say that the opinion of the Province had not fairly been taken on the question, and this allegation would certainly have been believed in England. In the new Parliament, the fate of the endowment will be the same, but at any rate it will be impossible to say that the country was taken by surprise; and the divisions in the Provincial Parliament will probably show that its preservation was impossible."[18] However well-intentioned, Lord Elgin's stand revealed the limitations that still might operate on internal responsible government, at least when the governor deemed a matter to be of imperial concern. Above all, it did not help his ministers in their shaky position.

Attacks rose rapidly from all sides in parliament, on the government's waste and railway corruption no less than on its delay. Macdonald and Brown, MacNab and Mackenzie, Cauchon and Sicotte, each battered at the ministry from their different quarters. Hincks, "the Hyena," fighting back with all his years of skill, was elusive, sharp, indignant and savage in turn; but nothing could avail against the torrent of charges that swept the assembly. Cauchon and Sicotte produced amendments to the Address in Reply to the throne speech, deploring the failure to settle the seigneurial and reserves questions. Erstwhile government adherents joined the opposition in supporting them—impatient Morin moderates and wholly-frustrated Clear Grits. The motions of censure passed, 42 to 29.[19] From the whole western section the defeated ministers drew only five votes beyond their own. The crisis had arrived.

The government had crumbled under combined sectional onslaughts. Everyone expected it to resign. Hincks and Morin, however, had determined to take their chance at an election, and they forthwith advised the Governor

General to dissolve parliament. It was a properly constitutional option;[20] but Elgin's sudden descent on the Music Hall to prorogue the house took it completely by surprise. Uproar burst forth again as opposition leaders howled in outrage to see their prize slipping away. Yet there was nothing to be done, and the assembly, reduced to steaming impotence, filed out to the legislative council chamber for the closing ceremonies. There the Speaker of the assembly, peppery Sandfield Macdonald, earned more than a little fame by reporting on the regrettably unfinished deliberations of the house in terms that were virtually a reprimand to the Governor General. None the less, it was all over on June 22, little more than a week after the opening. The province faced a general election, still in its angry, unresolved state of mind.

The elections of 1854 were fought vehemently through July and into August; temperatures ranged in the nineties and tempers were not far behind. Yet for all the vehemence of the campaigns, the final results were still indefinite and confused. In Canada East, it is true, the main group of Morin liberals came back to the fold, returning some thirty-five French and English members; but this was a smaller proportion than at the previous election, since the assembly had been enlarged. Morin himself was beaten in Terrebonne and had to find another seat in Chicoutimi-Tadoussac. Moreover, the *rouges* and anti-government liberals made decided gains. The largest element among nearly thirty eastern members likely to be in opposition were *rouges*, now including such capable reinforcements as Antoine and Eric Dorion and Luther Holton; and there were also Cauchon and his rightist friends. Generally then, while the ministry had won a small majority in the East, it had lost ground there in an anti-government swing away from the old reform alliance. Its position was by no means certain. Cauchon's judgement on the gains of the *rouges* was sound enough, however: ". . . ils peuvent aider à renverser une administration, ils sont littéralement impuissants à en former une."[21]

Affairs were still more uncertain in the West. Here about two dozen supporters of the Hincks ministry had been elected, to an equal number of conservatives. The rest were seceding Grits or reform voluntaryists like Brown, who had personally vanquished Malcolm Cameron in Lambton. Through valiant efforts by Francis Hincks, appeals to railway prosperity and assurances of secularization at last, the government had gained back some ground. Yet if the opposition forces held together, the ministry would be decidedly in the minority in the West. If they held together—that was the prime uncertainty. To add to the confusion, secularization had cut across conservative party lines, some candidates endorsing it, others still resisting. The *Globe* might well assert, "Never before were party bonds so relaxed."[22] It had even backed secularizationist conservatives against ministerial candidates itself, while the *North American* and Mackenzie's fire-and-brimstone *Message* made common cause with it against Hincks. About the only sizable ministerial paper was the well-written Toronto *Leader*, founded in the government cause two years before. If the weight of the press was proof, "Emperor Francis" was already beaten. But no one could foretell what the actual power balance would be when the new parliament assembled.

It opened in Quebec on September 5, 1854, whereupon the jockeying immediately began. The critical first test was the election of the speaker of the new legislative assembly. The ministry's candidate, Cartier, was defeated, 59 to 62—and the ministry's days at once were numbered.[23] Manifestly, it had not managed to redeem itself. Sicotte, put forward by the eastern opposition forces, was elected instead; but largely because Hincks swiftly threw his own contingent to him rather than see George Brown's candidate, Sandfield Macdonald, draw away the votes of western reform. Deft as ever, even in defeat, Hincks succeeded in beating a personal enemy and in blocking the plans of his strongest liberal rival at the same time; for Brown had hoped to rally the forces of discontent behind Sandfield as a prominent reform figure, and then go on to build his own projected voluntaryist liberal and conservative coalition.[24] The way was cleared instead for a different political design.

Francis Hincks resigned two days later. Yet he still controlled a sizable body of liberal votes; and if he would not turn them towards Brown, the man he declared "determined to destroy the government,"[25] he could look all the more readily in another direction, towards moderate conservatives like John A. Macdonald. And Morin, who still commanded a majority within the eastern section, might well prefer to deal, if he had to, with Upper Canadian state-church tories than with western voluntaryists and radicals. In any case, Lord Elgin duly called upon Sir Allan MacNab as opposition leader to rebuild the government. He and John A. Macdonald undertook negotiations to do so, while rumours bred and parliament waited. The answer came on September 11. There was to be a MacNab-Morin cabinet, pledged finally to settle both the reserves and the seigneuries, and backed by the ministerial block in Canada East, by the tories and conservatives, and by the Hincksite liberals of Canada West. The old reform party was dead, killed by sectional dissension; an Anglo-French liberal-conservative coalition had supplanted it in power. It would remain to be seen how far this new party formation could meet the blows of sectionalism and maintain the vital political alliance between the two Canadian communities in the union.

Yet this coalition of 1854 was more than a political converging on the centre, a middle-ground compromise between liberal, conservative and tory factions. It emphasized a widespread concern for economic development, something that transcended sectionalism and touched the union as a whole. Conservatives endorsed the Sydenham tradition of linking government and business interests to promote provincial growth. Hincksite reformers, the group most closely identified with the building of the Grand Trunk, wholeheartedly shared that view. Commercial tories were equally in sympathy, while MacNab's own familiar dictum was "my politics now are railroads."[26] Moreover, French Canadians had made their peace with Montreal business, and leading French politicians like Cartier were fully committed to the locomotive age. And for the rank and file of the main French party there was an essential entente, to be expressed in acts if not in words: in return for support of developmental policies, the coalition provided a renewed safeguard for French cultural and religious rights and the distinctive role which French Canadians had achieved within the union. The liberal-conservative alliance, therefore, was no mere fortuitous conjunction. It was a potent mingling of Montreal commercial interests and Hincksite railwaymen, French Catholic *bleus* and western conservatives, all with mutual reason to sustain the Canadian union.

Nevertheless, it should be noted, this liberal-conservative coalition could not simply be described as a combination of commercial interests and French numbers. It is a vast oversimplification to see the political party division of the Province of Canada as a clear-cut economic separation, with conservatism representing urban business power and liberalism the agrarian producers. After all, in point of population, Canada in both its sections was still overwhelmingly a rural, farming country and the franchise was chiefly in the hands of farmers.[27] If tories or conservatives had had to depend on the city vote alone, they could have won very few constituencies. And, on the other hand, from William Merritt and John Young to George Brown of Toronto and Luther Holton of Montreal, one could detail many influential business figures and urban constituents firmly identified with reform politics. The fact was that ethnic and religious appeals, traditional political loyalties, and sectional and regional attitudes could and did cut across a merely economic structuring of parties in terms of land and commerce. Nor was social class any clearer basis for party division, in a country where there were class distinctions to be noted, but a good deal of social mobility as well; together with a general assumption that everyone could be a property-holder and rise by diligence to affluence.

In the last analysis, only this much could be said: that tory-conservatism had generally a stronger base of power in the urban business community, while reform found particularly devoted adherents in the western countryside. But any enduringly strong political party had to comprehend both urban and rural elements. This the liberal-conservative coalition had now achieved, though it placed discernible emphasis on business interests. It would later be answered by another reform front, also combining agrarian and business elements, just as had been done in the earlier successful days of reform under Baldwin and LaFontaine.

The new liberal-conservative cabinet that was to function under MacNab and Morin was unchanged in its eastern half. The western section, led by MacNab as President of the Council and Minister of Agriculture, comprised the conservatives, John A. Macdonald and William Cayley, as Attorney General West and Inspector General respectively, and the Hincksite liberals, Robert Spence, Postmaster General, and John Ross, now Speaker of the Legislative Council—and President of the Grand Trunk, besides. Macdonald, in the important post of Attorney General, undoubtedly had the critical role in the Upper Canadian half of the ministry. "Sir Allan will not be in our way," he had written a few months earlier, though explaining also that MacNab wished only not to be cast off in his old age, a thing which he, Macdonald, would never assent to, "by reason of his past kindnesses."[28] The new government met the house, secured an overwhelming endorsement, 70 to 33, then carried an adjournment to prepare its program.[29] The anxious months of undecided crisis seemed over at last. The centrist coalition —shades of Sydenham—had a two-to-one ministerial majority; the reform fragments left in opposition were as yet demoralized and mutually divided. The union could surely look to more constructive work ahead.

III

The first results were the bills to abolish seigneurial tenure and secularize the reserves, introduced in October and passed by the house on the same day in mid November, 1854. One significant difference in the two settlements was that the Seigneurial Tenure Bill laid charges on the provincial revenue to compensate the seigneurs, while the Clergy Reserves Bill essentially added to the public income by allocating the reserves funds to municipalities. Nevertheless the latter bill, ably sponsored by John A. Macdonald, was attacked from both sides. A last-ditch group of tories struggled to preserve some part of the state endowment for religion. Grits and Brownites objected to the measure's commutation clause, which allowed stipends presently being paid to clerics to be commuted into permanent capital funds for their churches; for to thorough voluntaryists this provision to respect vested interests seemed precisely a device to perpetuate some of the religious endowment after all.[30] But there was a solid majority in favour of accepting the settlement, and at length the bill passed easily enough.

Meanwhile, as the debates went on, opposition forces began to recover and regroup after the sweeping change in party alignments. The liberal-con-

servative coalition had left only the remnants of reform and a few independents in opposition: some twenty-four Grits and Brownites from Canada
West, some fourteen *rouges* and anti-government liberals from Canada East
—where Cauchon and his right-wing associates had also swung over to the
MacNab-Morin ministry. These fragments at first had little more in common than righteous detestation of the "unprincipled" and overwhelming
coalition. But they necessarily began to co-ordinate efforts in criticizing the
seigneurial and reserves bills, George Brown, for example, co-operating with
Antoine-Aimé Dorion, whose polished intellect and eloquence were rapidly
making him a leading figure in the eastern opposition. And in the western
section, Brown and Clear Grits inevitably moved closer together, setting aside
past differences in their common struggle against the new ministerial combination of Lower Canadian Catholic power with the old conservative
enemy.

At the end of 1854, looking back on recent achievements, the government
organ, *La Minerve*, could congratulate Canada on "sa marche rapide vers le
progrès . . . la Réciprocité du commerce avec les Etats-Unis, la sécularisation
des Réserves du Clergé anglican, et la réforme de la Tenure territoriale . . .
ouvrent une ère nouvelle à notre pays."[31] Meanwhile Lord Elgin had left
the province in December, after seven judicious years of statesmanship
superintending Canada's transition to responsible rule. His successor, named
by the Duke of Newcastle, Colonial Secretary in the Aberdeen cabinet, had
already arrived in Quebec. This was Sir Edmund Walker Head, a one-time
Oxford don and an industrious, efficient administrator, who had already
earned a sound reputation as lieutenant-governor of New Brunswick; a man
of broad views and scholarly pursuits, though rather dry, didactic and withdrawn in manner. Head's assumption of office was followed by the reconstruction of the eastern half of the ministry in January, 1855. Morin, who
had been anxious to retire, now joined his old colleague LaFontaine on the
Lower Canadian judicial bench. Taché, the Receiver General, replaced him
as eastern government leader. In other changes, Cartier came in as Provincial Secretary, Cauchon as an energetic Crown Lands Commissioner, and
François Lemieux as Commissioner of Public Works. The resulting MacNab-
Taché administration laid the basis for a growing acquaintance and understanding between Macdonald and Cartier. Their increasing personal entente
would in time become as vital to the liberal-conservative coalition as that
of Baldwin and LaFontaine had been to the old reform alliance.

Another change evident in Lower Canada, which only tended to strength-
en the position of the dominant ministerial party there, was the increasing
"frenchification" of the parliamentary membership. English Lower-Cana-
dian toryism had finally disappeared as a parliamentary force in the elections of 1854, although its economic power and its presence behind the

political scene still had to be reckoned with. But to all intents, no tories of the old British party were left in the house.[32] Montreal had elected a French *rouge*, A.-A. Dorion, and an English liberal, John Young, in 1854; Quebec city's one English (Irish) member, its mayor, Charles Alleyn, was associated with the *bleu* group; in the Townships, the little band of English-speaking representatives were similarly linked with French *bleus* or *rouges*, and no longer formed a tory faction of their own. Indeed, one of the ablest of the "English *rouges*" at this time was the member for Sherbrooke town, the powerful Montreal railway financier, Alexander Galt. But he was soon in transition towards the ministerial side, where he would fit in readily with the developmental aims of the liberal-conservative coalition. And in general, the English politicians in Canada East had been chiefly brought into conjunction with the French-led sectional block behind the ministry, where Cartier in particular provided a congenial connection for them.

While these changes helped principally to consolidate the ministerial side, the re-unifying of reform had been going on in the opposition. George Brown and his journal wooed the Clear Grits; the latter responded by playing down their affection for American institutions and their old antagonism towards the *Globe* owner. Ingrained radicals in the western agrarian peninsula might still suspect the Toronto journalist's over-moderation, and distrust his plea to drop their demands for organic changes in face of the present emergency. But there was increasing sentiment in the West for agreement among reformers to meet the threats of eastern power, Grand Trunk jobbery, and "French Catholic domination." The Brownite cause only stood to gain from the sectionalism and voluntaryism inherent among the Clear Grit following. It gained further when, in February 1855, a prosperous Brown bought out the chief Grit organ, the *North American*, and William McDougall joined the staff of that powerful propaganda instrument, the *Globe*.[33] A Brownite-Grit reform party was clearly emerging in the West. It could, moreover, hope to win dissatisfied Hincksites back to the cause of reform-party unity. And if sectional feeling continued to grow in Upper Canada, it could surely cut further into the liberal-conservatives' support there, identified as they were with Lower Canadian allies.

In parliament, in the spring of 1855, the forceful, fiery Brown was rapidly coming to be the effective leader of the western opposition, as the discredited Rolphs and Camerons withdrew, and as Sandfield Macdonald proved too fractious and erratic to give any clear direction. Brown indeed failed to reverse the clergy reserves commutation agreement, or to block the Elective Legislative Council Bill. The latter, which he held unsuited to the British system of government responsibility to one elected body, was advocated by both French and English moderates on grounds very different from those put forward by democratic radicals—as a check on popular excess in the lower house supposedly more effective than the existing appointed upper chamber. Still, the latter body threw out the elective bill, so that it would have to be re-enacted the next year. And Brown also inserted a new Rep-by-Pop amendment which, though defeated, carried Grit support. Then in May there came another Upper Canada school measure, which strongly stirred sectional feeling anew, and gave added force to the advancing movement for the re-unification of western reform.

The School Bill of 1855 reflected the continued pressure of the Roman Catholic hierarchy for enlarged separate-school rights in Upper Canada, and the desires of French ministerialists to see their co-religionists there gain educational privileges equal to those accorded to Protestants in Lower Canada. The bill accordingly proposed to permit any ten freeholders to form a separate school and share in the public grants. Western Protestant supporters of the government viewed the measures, with some misgivings, as necessary to ensure religious tolerance and coalition harmony. But western reformers saw it as another deep cut into the public non-denominational school system. And still more than the actual contents of the bill—which were to be qualified by amendments—the manner of handling it, half clumsy, half conspiratorial, aroused their bitter protests. It was introduced in the legislative council by Taché, very late in the session at Quebec, and quite unknown to the western schools superintendent, Ryerson. It was then taken up by John A. Macdonald in the assembly, when many of the Upper Canadian members had already left for home. And it was pushed through by Lower Canadian votes, even though a majority of those Upper Canadians still present struggled and voted against it.[34] Here, it appeared, was stark evidence of eastern domination over the West, of French Catholic dictation within the liberal-conservative régime.

Parliament rose, but angry reaction spread through Upper Canada. It could scarcely help but benefit the growth of a sectional reform party under George Brown. "Are we slaves to Popish Prelates?" the old radical Toronto *Examiner* demanded fiercely.[35] Some exasperated Grits, indeed, urged a simple, drastic, response: a return to the separation of the Canadas, to free the West from French power. It was Upper Canadians now who sought repeal of the union. But Brown, if a sectionalist, was not a separatist. As a business man in the rising western metropolis of Toronto, he was well aware of the economic values of the union and the unified St Lawrence trading route it furnished. Meanwhile, John A. Macdonald, busy settling up the accounts of the clergy reserves, made his own assessment of the situation: "The milk is spilt—the money expended—and George Brown must get some new hobby to bestride. Representation by population is too abstract a question to be enthusiastic about and he has too much sense to go for Repeal."[36] Yet Brown's own remedy, of course, was representation by population, to maintain but remake the union of the Canadas. He and the *Globe* waged a strenuous campaign on its behalf that summer. By autumn they had gone a long way towards consolidating Clear Grittism behind it, and to securing the united Upper Canada reform party they had so earnestly preached. As a further sign of it, in September, the *Examiner* was also absorbed in the *Globe*. By the next month the hostile *Leader*, the government organ, itself was recognizing Brown as leader of the opposition.[37]

The seat of government returned to Toronto in October 1855 in that awkward, periodic shifting of the capital which the deep sectional division of the province compelled. The division was there, inherent in the very cultural and constitutional nature of the union; Brown and the Grits had not created it. Nor had the ruling liberal-conservatives demonstrated in the year past that they could offer any answer to the problem.

IV

There were new aggravations as 1856 began. Governor Head, on tour in Upper Canada, had allegedly made some unwise remarks at Hamilton on the "superiority" of the British race that had so successfully built up the West. French Canadians readily reacted. A newly revived *L'Avenir*, speaking for "les hommes inférieurs," declared, "Tous les Canadiens qui ont du coeur ont senti l'injure, et ils ne doivent pas oublier que ce n'est pas la première fois qu'ils ont été insultés par les gouverneurs."[38] Then the Corrigan murder case roused Upper Canadian opinion. The victim, a Protestant Irish convert, had been battered to death by a gang of Catholic Irishmen at St Sylvestre in Canada East, in what was really a transfer of old Irish religious hatreds to the province. But in spite of strong evidence, Corrigan's seven assailants were all acquitted by a French-Canadian judge and a Roman Catholic jury.[39] At once the cry went up in the West that there was one justice for Protestants and another for Catholics in Lower Canada—and a demand that Judge Duval's charge to his jury be investigated. Meanwhile Bishop Charbonnel had further sharpened religious antagonisms by issuing a pastoral in January asserting that Upper Canadian Catholics who did not use their votes to advance the cause of separate schools were guilty of mortal sin. Even the fairly moderate *News of the Week* replied, ". . . we raise our voice against a despotism that would crush freedom of conscience and liberty of thought," and saw in Corrigan's murder the results of bigotry instilled by sectarian education.[40] Parliament met in February in a renewed state of tension and sectional friction.

Almost at once the separate-school question came up. John Bowes (Hincks's associate in the £10,000 Job, now purged and re-accepted) produced a bill on behalf of the Upper Canadian Catholics that in effect would have lifted qualifications placed on the original Taché Act, and particularly have enabled Catholics in one school section to transfer their taxes to support a separate school in another. But the capital was now in Toronto, not Quebec; there was the resentment over the Corrigan case and Bishop Charbonnel's emphatic pastoral; and there were the piled-up western grievances over the mode of passing the School Act of 1855. Bowes' bill simply released a flood of anti-separate-schools protest in the West. Sixty-five long petitions came in demanding their abolition, to one in their defence.⁴¹ Bowes dropped his measure. Brown and the Grits, together with *rouges* such as Joseph Papin, moved instead for a uniform secular system of "National Schools" which would still protect religious conviction from insult. A strenuous debate followed over separate schools, which the coalition government only managed to adjourn by again using the strength of its Lower Canadian following. The *status quo* in the western school law was preserved. Still, it was clear that there would not likely be new separate-school measures for some time: not unless a ministry should be bold and strong enough to impose them on the West by eastern votes once more.

There was another kind of strain developing within the ministerial coalition itself. The Hincksite liberal element was growing increasingly restive over the "fossil toryism" of Sir Allan MacNab, his repeated absences from duty with gout, his hearty enjoyment of the powers of patronage, and the avid troop of clients to whom he dispensed it. Some of the Hincksites had already shifted in disgust to Brown's camp, and more might go if MacNab remained premier much longer. The two Hincksite leaders in the government, Ross and Spence (Francis Hincks himself had left the country to become imperial governor of Barbados), were insistent on stopping the drift. They sought to get rid of MacNab, and make Macdonald the western government leader. The wrangling within the council could scarcely be hidden. At the same time there was unrest and intriguing on the ministerial right wing. Here John Hillyard Cameron, a wealthy Toronto lawyer and able debater, solicitor-general in the old Draper government in 1847, was fast emerging as a younger, far stronger tory alternative to Sir Allan. Conceivably he might replace both MacNab and Macdonald in leading the western conservatives. If he did, Cameron would inevitably lead them in a tory direction—which by no means precluded their adopting Rep-by-Pop and a sectional stance of their own. In times past, after all, Upper Canada toryism had recurrently been anti-French, anti-Catholic, and anti-eastern in its views. In the current mood of western grievance it might well capture the conservative party anew: though to do so would surely be to disrupt the existing alliance with the French Canadians and to break up the governing coalition.

Major government measures of the session concerned the Grand Trunk, the tariff, and the upper house. The railway was granted £800,000 in cash and empowered to raise £2,000,000 more through new preferential bonds, to take prior claim over the government's own mortgage on the line. The Cayley tariff carried duties on manufactures generally as high as fifteen per cent in order to supply the needed additional revenue. And the Elective Legislative Council Act was passed at last, providing for the election of twenty-four councillors from each section for eight-year terms, six each to be elected biennially, the old appointed councillors to remain for the rest of their lives. Yet the discussion of these measures was really less significant than parliament's general state of irritable friction. That within the government ranks showed itself when, early in March, John Hillyard Cameron brought in a motion for the production of the judge's charge in the Corrigan case. He readily collected a strong Upper Canadian majority behind it, drawn from all quarters; and even carried his motion. But when the matter was made an outright test of confidence, Upper Canadian ministerial supporters came back into line, and Cameron's incipient tory revolt was checked. Accordingly, on the cabinet's advice, the Governor General refused the request to have the judge brought to account, as an interference with the independence of the judiciary.

The clash over the Corrigan case was serious, but it was only one of a series in an assembly spoiling for trouble. There were repeated explosions of bad temper, vehement exchanges of accusations, as members on all sides proceeded to rake up their opponents' old misdeeds. One of the hottest eruptions of all came when a sharply stung John A. Macdonald poured out violent charges against his hard-pressing opponent, George Brown, accusing him of perjury, falsifying evidence and suborning witnesses, when secretary of the royal commission that had investigated the provincial penitentiary at Kingston in 1849. Brown, controlling himself by desperate effort, demanded an inquiry. The issue went to a parliamentary committee, which conducted a lengthy and laborious investigation. The evidence it took effectively disproved the charges; but its vaguely-presented judgement gave Brown's jealous sense of honour little satisfaction.[42] A bitter, enduring personal rift opened between the two great Upper Canadian party rivals that went far deeper than their purely political antagonisms.

The Hincksite moderates, meanwhile, were still demanding that MacNab be ousted from the government leadership. In April, John Ross resigned over the question. It took John A. Macdonald's best charm and skill to persuade another Hincksite, Joseph Morrison, to replace him. A few weeks later, the jagged problem of a future capital for Canada brought the troubles within the coalition to a sudden climax. A resolution actually passed, in a free vote, to make Quebec the permanent seat of government after 1859. But it was not a ministerial measure, since the cabinet itself was divided on this most sectional of issues, and the decision on the capital could hardly rest on a purely haphazard collection of votes. Accordingly, Brown and two *rouges*, Papin and Holton, turned the seat-of-government issue into a question of the ministry's responsibility for settling it. After intense debate, the ministry won a vote of confidence, 70 to 47.[43] Yet it was left in a minority of six votes within Upper Canada itself. And that offered a crucial opportunity to remake the cabinet.

On May 21, all the western ministers but Sir Allan MacNab resigned, contending that the cabinet's loss of support in Upper Canada compelled its reconstruction in that section. This was not, they asserted, a recognition of the old doctrine of the double majority—which had never fully died out, particularly in French Canada. It was simply sound politics: a section could not long be ruled against its will; and the defections, if not met, would place the coalition ministry in a decided minority in Canada West.[44] In any case, poor old MacNab, left abandoned and isolated, had no choice but to submit his resignation to the governor, Sir Edmund Head. Thereupon the other ex-ministers promptly returned to office. On May 24 they were sworn in: John A. Macdonald, now western government leader, together with Cayley, Spence and Morrison, and an additional conservative, Philip Vankoughnet, in MacNab's stead. There was another change, this time in the eastern half of the cabinet. Drummond withdrew as Attorney General East and was succeeded by Cartier, while Timothy Terrill came in to replace the latter as Provincial Secretary.

The new Taché-Macdonald administration, the reconstructed coalition government, barely scraped through a first vote of confidence with an over-all majority of four.[45] The house was too dubious, too shaken by the whole proceedings; and the dramatic entrance of Sir Allan MacNab, arising from a bed of gouty pain, only strengthened sentiment against those who had so flatly deposed him. Wrapped in bandages, the ex-premier was carried in by two strong servants to his chair, from where, seated, he made a moving vale-dictory—creating the keen impression that nothing so became him in political life as the leaving of it. Yet the fact was that no one really doubted that his day was over. It was the new Macdonald régime that survived.

It did so, again, by Lower Canadian votes. Within Upper Canada the ministry was fifteen in the minority this time, nine worse than before the resignations.[46] Yet, though Taché apparently suggested it, the western ministers did not choose to resign again.[47] Their position, after all, was that having double-majority support was a matter of long-run, practical expedi-ence, not a constant and absolute requirement; and they argued that public business could not further be delayed. It all went to demonstrate that the essential purpose of the operation had been to remove MacNab. Governor Head himself was quite satisfied with his new ministers, and sympathetic to their treatment of the problem of double majority.[48] "You may judge," he wrote privately to a correspondent, "how the difficulty of my position has been complicated by this quasi-federal question, which I am bound to treat as theoretically absurd, though I know full well that in practice it must be looked to."[49]

In any case, if not admirable, the ministerial manoeuvre was legitimate, and it soon proved to have been effective. Temporarily-withdrawn support returned to the western half of the government, both among Hincksites and the disgruntled tories who had no better alternative left than the liberal-conservative coalition. The moderates had been appeased; Cameron and the right wing had been outplayed. Thereafter the reconstituted government held fairly safe majorities within the West (where it left separate schools severely alone), which indicated that its own interpretation of the double majority had indeed been validated.

Above all, the ministerial crisis of 1856 put the more liberal elements in the governing coalition, and John A. Macdonald especially, in an assured place of power. The "progressive conservatives" he had looked to in 1854 were now uppermost in the forces that he led. The designs of Sydenham, the hopes of Draper, were being fulfilled in a party of union and development, a party guided by one of Canada's most constructive, and indestructible, political masters. Still further, since Premier Taché sat in the legislative council, Macdonald's true counterpart in the assembly was Cartier, the war chief of the *bleus*, who the next year would replace Taché to become co-premier in his own right. In short, a liberal-conservative party was taking lasting form out of the older, looser, coalition of 1854, as the tories were reduced, the Hincksite elements were gradually assimilated, and Macdonald and Cartier began their long-lived political partnership at the head of dual parliamentary contingents.

As the wearing session concluded on July 1, the reorganization of the reform party was also advancing, no less than that of the liberal conservatives. The *Montreal Gazette* might aver that, "Whatever may be said of the government, the present opposition is the least respectable in numbers and in principle that the people of the province have witnessed since the union."[50] Nevertheless, respectable or not, the opposition forces were growing, both in numbers and coherence. The same redefining process was under way as on the government side, as Grit and *rouge* liberal parties took shape out of older radical factions and the reform remnants that would not absorb into a liberal-conservative party. Through sheer parliamentary ability, A.-A. Dorion had gained primacy in a *parti rouge* that could collaborate with Brownite Grits in supporting a secular public-school system and opposing clerical influence, government waste and Grand Trunk folly. George Brown similarly led forces turned from urging fundamental political change to seeking more pragmatic adjustments. Like Cartier and Macdonald, the two liberal champions were also to lead enduring party formations, through which the tensions and differences between the two Canadian societies might yet be resolved into continuous, working political relationships. In fact, if the last few years in the Province of Canada had witnessed the breakdown of its old party system amidst the spread of sectional strife, they had also seen the emergence of viable new political groupings. These groupings would go onward, to fight the increasing battles of disunion; but then go further still, to long careers in a much wider union—indeed, as national parties in the transcontinental Canada that was to come.

CHAPTER 12

The Pattern of Disunion

1856-1857

New questions began emerging for Canada in the second half of 1856; questions that marked a gradual transition for the union from one era to another. There was no sweeping change. The older internal, sectional and cultural issues assuredly remained. Yet external, imperial and continental concerns now were gaining ground, and from 1857 onward they would tie the Province of Canada ever more fully and directly into developments affecting all British North America. In this respect Canada was crossing another watershed, however imperceptible at first. The past course of events had largely derived from the pattern of union formed in 1841. The course ahead moved more and more decisively to the destruction of that pattern, and to the creation of the greater federal scheme of 1867. The old incorporation of French and English Canada in one political entity still had ten years of existence in 1857—years of dying and rebirth. But in a real sense, by that date, the era of the union of the Canadas was already giving way to the era of Confederation.

Broader questions that would confront Canada in the Confederation era were foreshadowed during the summer of 1856, when Governor-General Sir Edmund Head was visited in Toronto by Robert Lowe, Vice-President of the Board of Trade in the Palmerston whig ministry. The cabinet of Lord Palmerston that had taken office in England the year before was now faced with the costs of the just-concluded Crimean War; and it was full of whig-liberal dislike of colonial burdens, emphatically expressed in Lowe himself. Consequently, the imperial government was concerned to reduce its commitments in British North America. Furthermore, the recent "foreign enlistment crisis" in Anglo-American relations had given it additional cause for concern. Ill-advised British attempts to enlist recruits in the United States during the Crimean struggle had roused an angry uproar in the republic, and spread-eagle talk, besides, of annexing Canada. Five British regiments had been shipped out to the colony's defence in the spring of 1856, while the provincial parliament passed Militia Acts in 1855 and 1856 to organize an active volunteer force beyond the nominal "sedentary militia" in which all able-bodied male colonists were liable to serve.

The American war scare, the first to invite military preparations since the Oregon alarms of ten years earlier, evaporated in the summer of 1856 without the regulars or militia in Canada seeing action. But it emphasized for Great Britain what hazardous and vulnerable hostages to fortune her American possessions were. Accordingly, during his transatlantic visit, Lowe raised with Governor Head the possibility of the Canadian government taking the initiative on certain grand projects that were calculated to lessen the heavy imperial risk and burden in America.[1] They comprised, first, a new effort to build the Intercolonial Railway, to provide a defensive link between the ocean and the interior; second, the union of the British provinces, to strengthen their ability to look after themselves; and, third, the transfer to Canada of that huge northwestern expanse still ruled by the Hudson's Bay Company, to open and develop before the spread of American settlement pulled it from the tenuous hold of the fur trade. Sceptical and diffident, but interested nevertheless, Head wrote to the Colonial Secretary, Henry Labouchere, early in September offering to prepare opinions on these matters.[2] He was quickly asked to do so in detail. In December, Labouchere informed him that the imperial government meant to examine the whole problem of Hudson's Bay rule in the Northwest before a British parliamentary committee.[3] The new questions were rising with remarkable speed.

Meanwhile, the question of the Northwest had taken shape in Canada itself. Canadians had long felt they had claims to the British territories beyond the Great Lakes, derived from the days of New France and from the vanished era of the North West Company, whose fur trade had extended from Montreal to the Arctic and Pacific. But it was only in the mid 1850's that the few voices raised in Canada to urge the promise of the great Northwest, or to warn of the danger that it would be lost like Oregon to the Americans, merged in a swelling popular agitation that demanded the annexation of the Hudson's Bay Territory to the Canadian union. In 1855 the last block of wild land had been auctioned in the western peninsula of Upper Canada.[4] The same year, Toronto's Northern Railway was opened through to Georgian Bay. And in August, 1856, a group of city business men, including leading figures of the Northern Railway, founded the Northwestern Steamboat Company to establish communications from Collingwood to the head of the Lakes. The desires of Upper Canadian farmers for new frontiers of settlement, the ambitions of the rising Toronto metropolis for a new western trading empire, combined in a vigorous campaign to acquire the Northwest for Canada. The influential Toronto Board of Trade took it up before the end of the year, petitioning the legislature for an inquiry into the Hudson's Bay Company title to the West.

George Brown had particularly pressed the campaign in the *Globe* through the fall and winter of 1856. He had long advocated the acquisition of the Hudson's Bay lands by Canada; his brother Gordon who shared with him in directing the *Globe* shared also in founding the Northwestern steamboat enterprise. Some of Toronto's chief business men and members of the Board of Trade were "thorough-paced Brownites."[5] Accordingly, the columns of Brown's journal shone with glowing articles on the riches of the "Great North West," the wealth of trade Toronto could enjoy, the farms it promised for hardy Upper Canadian yeomen, the weakness of the Bay Company's charter of 1670, by which a mere fur monopoly held an enormous fertile empire out of productive development.[6] Furthermore, Brown used the Northwest agitation to complete the re-unification of Upper Canada's liberal party, merging Toronto urban and business leadership with Clear Grit agrarian strength in a dynamic party front that also attracted back more Hincksite moderates. In December, a circular went out from the *Globe* office inviting six prominent liberals from each Upper Canadian constituency to a party convention in Toronto.[7] On January 8, 1857, 150 leading reformers assembled there in the public hall on Temperance Street. Far more weighty than the local Grit conventions of 1850, the meeting adopted a platform that included free trade, no sectarian grants, representation by population: and the annexation of the Northwest. The "Reform Alliance" thus erected was a significant step in the evolution of party organization in Canada— hailed by the *Globe*, though scorned by the ministerial Toronto *Leader* as the "Temperance Street Conspiracy."[8] It was also significant of what railways had done to focus the western section effectively on Toronto, and to enable such a meeting to gather in mid-winter from the snow-bound reaches of Canada West.

The Northwest question was canvassed in the parliament that opened in Toronto in February, 1857; the Taché-Macdonald ministry announced that William Draper would be called from the judicial bench to represent Canada's interests in England at the forthcoming inquiry of the Select Committee of the House of Commons into the Hudson's Bay Territory. And another hot Canadian question, the divisive seat-of-government issue, also took on broader imperial overtones when the liberal-conservative cabinet, in a shrewdly loyal move, proposed to submit the choice of a permanent capital to Queen Victoria herself. The *Globe* condemned the decision taken in March as in reality voting "to destroy Responsible Government by sending to Downing Street for Mr. Labouchere to fix the seat of government."[9] But it at least postponed a dangerous subject for the present. It also allowed the Governor General to busy himself in preparing views for the Colonial Office on his own favoured choice for capital, the centrally-placed city of Ottawa that lay on the great river bordering the two Canadas.

That summer, indeed, Head went to England to submit carefully drafted memoranda to the Colonial Office on the seat of government, the Hudson's Bay Territory, and the confederation of the British North American provinces.[10] John A. Macdonald joined him in London to try as well to revive the Intercolonial railway project. Now, however, that the defence crisis in regard to the United States had lifted, Macdonald found the imperial authorities unwilling to consider financial aid for the building of a strategic Quebec-to-Halifax line. Moreover, the report of the Select Committee on the Hudson's Bay Territory, issued in July, also proved disappointing to those in Canada who had sought the wholesale incorporation of the Northwest. It merely recommended that southern districts suitable for settlement be transferred to Canada's charge to administer and develop, when the province was ready to do so. Furthermore, while Head's recommendation of Ottawa as the capital was to have its effect on the Queen's choice, announced at the end of the year, any project he might present at the moment for confederation would obviously have a long distance to go before the Canadian government and people—not to mention those of the other colonies—would be ready to bring it into the realm of practical politics.

In short, these newer, broader questions of 1856-57 were still far from any answers. To a large degree the old issues and pattern of the Canadian union still obtained. The assembly wrangled over, but passed, a new Grand Trunk relief bill: it would cost the province sixteen million dollars more. (Yet at least the line had been open from Montreal to Toronto since November 1856 —a journey that took fifteen hours.) Lengthy, acrimonious inquests were conducted into railway jobbery. And Brown moved a representation-by-population resolution which, though defeated, carried an Upper Canadian majority, 24 to 22.[11] Parliament rose in June, to be dissolved in November, just as the great Canadian boom was ending in another onset of world trade depression. That autumn, the liberal-conservative administration was reorganized as the Macdonald-Cartier cabinet to meet the general election. The Upper Canadian section remained unchanged this time; but in Cartier's section N.-F. Belleau, Charles Alleyn and T.-J.-J. Loranger replaced Taché, Lemieux and Terrill respectively. Notably, too, Cauchon had resigned the Crown Lands commissionership when it was agreed to aid the Grand Trunk again but not to support his own favoured North Shore railway project. Yet Sicotte was prevailed upon to enter in his stead, and it was a stronger government in Lower Canada that faced the polls in December.

At the elections, again, the old issues of union and disunion predominated: French domination, Grand Trunk influence, and Rep-by-Pop among the strongly aggressive reformers of the West; Brownite fanaticism, *rouge* infidelity, and the defence of French national interest among the preponderant Cartier *bleus* of the East. By the end of 1857, the election results indeed showed how far sectional cleavage had gone in the union of the Canadas, for the reform forces had gained a decisive majority in Upper Canada, the liberal-conservative in Lower.[12] Not since 1841 had the province been so clearly divided, so embattled in society and politics. And so, if 1857 marked a transition to a new era in the larger, constructive issues it raised, it also evinced a state of grave disunion that would compel Canadians to consider the constitutional problem of their country as never before.

II

"Où allons nous de ce train? En vérité un bon despotisme éclairé et paternel, comme celui du 1er Napoléon, vaut cent fois mieux que notre fantôme de représentation."[13] So the former premier, Etienne Taché, wrote of the disquieting results of the polls in December, 1857, marred as they were besides by election frauds in a number of Lower Canada ridings. Many others might have shared his disillusionment with the Canadian parliamentary constitution, or at least agreed that the matter of representation lay at the heart of the province's troubles. True, behind the problem lay the divergent aims and desires of the two cultural communities bound within one structure of government; and aside from shared interests in material development, they seemed to have found few common aims since their joint achievement of responsible home rule. But for all the underlying differences of the two Canadas, the crucial problem of their union in the later 1850's was still a political one.

That union was a political creation, and the essential, operative link between the two communities remained political. Socially and culturally they were almost wholly separate; they were closely bound together in the economic sphere, yet largely worked apart. Politics provided the chief meeting ground for French and English Canadians, the realm of their necessary, and often very effective, association through the party system. Above all, then, the common strand running through the history of the united Canadas had been a political one. What validity had it now? Could they indeed continue to function within one political frame?

There was this validity. The prime fact that the two Canadian communities still had in common was their general, even inherent, recognition that the best chance they each had to survive and grow in North America lay in their joint political action inside the provincial union. Hincks and Parent had taught it; Baldwin and LaFontaine had governed their careers by it, just as Macdonald and Cartier were doing now. Even Brown, vehement assailant of French power, stood for the maintenance of union, while Dorion, heir to *rouge* ultra-nationalism, suggested reconstruction not abandonment. It was old William Lyon Mackenzie who now talked vigorously of separation, just as Papineau had before him; and both had plainly showed themselves to be outside the mainstream of Canadian opinion.

Events had also demonstrated that the strongest sentiment in that opinion was for the maintenance and extension of two Canadian identities, whether against direction by Britain or absorption in the United States. Thus the two identities had worked together towards responsible government, and had both rejected annexation. It seemed that they could best be two by being one. And if they could provide for their duality, French and English Canada could still function within the framework of a single state; within one union, however much it might have to be altered from its existing pattern of discord and disunity.

Discord had arisen essentially because the union which expressed the fundamental fact of the Canadian duality had evolved only partially successful means of dealing with it: the containing party system and a quasi-federal division of spheres of authority, eastern and western, within the single legislative structure. By the later fifties, all the indications were that these means were no longer successful enough. Sectionalism, which had disrupted the old reform party alliance, now menaced the conservative front which had replaced it. And while an incipient federation had emerged within a legislative union, both from the Union Act itself and from the cultural separation of the Canadas, it was clumsy and inadequate in its operation. It was complicated, yet incomplete.

This quasi-federalism, of course, had found its basis in the very constitution of the union, in the principle of equal representation which had effectively divided the legislature into two provincial halves under one general government. The failure of the over-all English majority to hold together, the abandonment of the policy of assimilation, the successful cooperation of French and English reformers to win responsible rule, had all together led to the development of double-compartmented governments, each half of which had primary responsibility for its own section. But quasi-federalism went further. Many laws were passed for one or the other section alone. Not only had each developed its own educational, judicial and municipal systems, but also many supposedly unitary government departments had separate administrative staffs and regulations to deal with Upper or Lower Canadian affairs. Moreover, since Lower Canada had kept its structure of French civil law (codified under an act introduced by Cartier in 1857), legislation had to suit two different legal patterns regarding property and civil rights. This fact also necessitated the separate posts in the government for the attorneys and solicitors general East and West. Indeed, two provincial jurisdictions were still so much in evidence within United Canada that it was not just popular habit that kept the old names, Upper and Lower Canada, in use. They could be found in the official terminology of statutes that concerned one half of the union or the other.

Yet for all the quasi-federal structure in Canada, there was no effective separation of sectional from common concerns within the single legislature. The cumbersome expedient had frequently confused the two, and so made for angry friction. Certainly Upper or Lower Canadians tended to adopt the view that the province was one, or two, just as the occasion suited them. Thus, in the 1850's, Lower Canadians had voted on Upper Canada clergy reserves and Court of Chancery, and had helped erect a separate school system even against the will of an Upper Canadian majority. Thus, in the years 1842-46, LaFontaine had counted seventeen divisions on Lower Canadian matters decided by Upper Canadian votes.[14] If quasi-federalism was a response to duality, it aggravated rather than resolved inherent Canadian differences.

A closely-related response was the notion of double majority, of course requiring a government to have majority support for its measures within the section they particularly affected as well as in the union as a whole. This, in effect, meant maintaining majorities within both halves of the province, which governments had generally managed to do since the clear achievement of responsible rule in 1848. The LaFontaine-Baldwin cabinet then had plainly been organized on the basis of double-majority support, with dual premiers leading two groups of ministers and party adherents in the house. And in 1851 Hincks had reconstructed the western half of the cabinet to regain its majority in Upper Canada, even though the ministry had not been beaten in the union as a whole. On resigning in 1854, moreover, he had declared that he did so because "I could not command the confidence of the section of the province to which I belong."[15] Still further, when in 1856 John A. Macdonald and his colleagues resigned to force the reorganization of the MacNab administration, they once more gave as a reason that its western half had lost its Upper Canadian majority.

Unquestionably, therefore, double majority was acknowledged in practice as a necessary basis for a lasting provincial régime. As Macdonald said in explaining his course in 1856, "I felt . . . that no government could long continue governing one section with the assistance of the votes of the other; that a continuation of that system would destroy any government."[16] But accepting double majority as a political expedient for managing a union divided in representation and culture was a very different matter from elevating that expedient into a constitutional doctrine: as some had sought to do ever since Caron and his French-Canadian allies had first taken it up in negotiating for an alliance with Draper's tories during the mid 1840's.

Most of the English-speaking political leaders had always rejected double majority as a binding principle. Hincks had thought it "exceedingly desirable" in practical politics, but "quite absurd" as a constitutional requirement.[17] Baldwin had agreed "that in the practical work of legislation a certain deference should be paid to the majorities from the respective sections," and that a measure applicable to one should not be forced on it "against the decided opinion of a considerable majority of representatives from such a section."[18] Yet he had also held that if two halves of a government were deemed responsible to two separate sections, "it will perpetuate distinctions, invite animosities, sever the bonds of political sympathy and sap the foundations of political morality."[19] When he resigned in 1851 after his defeat in Upper Canada over Chancery, he made clear that this was a personal act, because of the defection of his own followers, and did not even bind the other western ministers, much less endorse the principle of double-majority rule. And when in 1856, Macdonald asserted the empirical truth that a section could not long be governed against its will, he equally declared the double-majority principle "in the abstract indefensible."[20]

Theoretically considered, one parliament could know but one constitutional majority, not two derived from quasi-federal devices adopted to keep the union going. And even in practice, double majority could surely not have worked as an obligatory basis of government. The pattern of Canadian disunion arose from the sharpening opposition of sectional forces within the province. For example, the election results of 1857 would, under double-majority doctrine, dictate the combining of opposites in one administration, the Brownite western majority with Cartier's *bleus*—rule by mixing fire and gunpowder. Apart from this particular implausibility, the plain fact of the double-majority principle was that it sought to solve the basic trouble of the union, sectionalism, by turning the very malady itself into a form of constitutional government.

Nevertheless, some in Canada still thought to make a working method (only really effective before sectionalism became too acute) into a categorical solution. LaFontaine had earlier played with the idea of double-majority rule as a kind of corollary of responsible government. Other French-Canadian politicians had often looked to the doctrine as a safeguard for their distinctive interests and national culture. But the rise of complaints in the 1850's that French influence was deciding Upper Canadian issues brought some western voices to urge the double majority in defence of their own sectional interests. The most notable was Sandfield Macdonald's. In a major debate on double majority following the ministerial crisis of 1856, he firmly identified himself with that principle as the means of maintaining union through preventing the domination of one section by the other. His motion of June 3, declaring in essence that western questions should be settled by western votes, and *vice versa*, had a certain specious appeal, though it ignored the difficulty of separating sectional from general questions within a single legislature that was the source of so much discord.[21] The *Globe*, of course, rejected the contention utterly, believing in "one union" and pointing out that the double-majority notion had "caused the political ruin of every Western man who has taken office for the last eight years."[22] But even *Le Canadien* agreed that the double majority could not be raised to a constitutional principle, since it would violate the very idea of one parliament legislating on matters of common interest.[23]

The principle that chiefly appealed to western sectional feelings and grievances instead was representation by population. It was virtually the antithesis of double majority. It sought to solve the constitutional problem not by enshrining quasi-federalism in Canada but by making it a truly legislative union: by obliterating divided representation and putting the province decisively under a single majority—western and English at that. The result would be to replace one presumed domination with another, and to revert effectively from duality to a policy of French assimilation. Rep-by-Pop had a seeming clarity lacking to double majority; but that scarcely gave it any greater promise of success. The fact that in the session of 1857 it carried for the first time a bare majority of Upper Canada votes simply invited alarmed French Canadians to stand the more resolutely against it. Its strength would go on rising in the West, as population growth there continued to outpace the East, as western resentment mounted against a government dependent on the votes of "over-represented" Lower Canada, and as the Brownite reform party kept up its powerful pressure. Yet, for French Canadians, Rep-by-Pop could only recall the sombre days of 1841, when a union then intended to absorb them had taken effect.

Sixteen years later, in 1857, the auspices for the union of the Canadas perhaps looked little brighter than they had at its grey beginnings. There were great differences, none the less. The mass of the French Canadians had committed themselves to the union; repeated agitations for repeal in Lower Canada had gathered only passing support. It was English elements who attacked the union now; and in the main they sought its emendation, not abolition. What was needed was a way between the opposing extremes of double majority and representation by population, to meet the former's aim of protecting distinctive cultural and sectional interests and the latter's purpose to secure coherent union under a single parliamentary majority. The answer was already suggested within the Canadian union itself: to build on quasi-federal practice, and establish a truly federal system.

It was Dorion who, in April 1856, first proposed in parliament a federal union of the Canadas as the answer to disunion.[24] The thought came naturally from *rouges*; as reformers, led to recognize the grievances protested by their Brownite partners in the opposition; as French Canadians, scarcely satisfied to accept Rep-by-Pop; as democratic idealists, admirers of the American federal model. Yet, however significant was Dorion's proposal of 1856 in injecting a new, though well-recognized constitutional principle into Canadian debates on union, it was the whole experience of the union of the Canadas which provided the most fertile ground for the growth of the federal idea.

Cabinets all but federalized into dual sets of departments and offices, structures of law for two sections which were almost provinces, local consideration of local matters (at least in aim) and joint handling of general problems—what else were these but the rudiments of a federal relationship? Give local issues, laws and departments to provincial governments and legislatures ruled by each sectional majority, give general affairs to a general parliament based on representation by population, and the bastard federation of united Canada would be legitimized. This was the ultimate solution to the divisive sectional issues, the one which Canadians were to work out for themselves in the decade ahead. Furthermore, the broader questions of the future of all British North America would be naturally related by Canadians to the federal idea. The British American League of 1849 had proposed a general colonial federation, as a tory-conservative answer to the crucial problems of that time. And the liberal *Globe* in 1856 plainly predicted, "If Upper and Lower Canada cannot be made to agree, a federal union of all the provinces will probably be the result."[25] Eleven years before Confederation, the very pattern of disunion in the Canadas was projecting a different sort of outline for the years to come.

III

The sixteen years' experience of the Canadian union had also produced other patterns of lasting significance: in education, in public administration, and in social policy. In these respects, the later Canadian confederation and provinces of Ontario and Quebec owed a sizable debt to the old province of Canada. Most notably, the union period virtually set the outlines of the school systems of Ontario and Quebec, almost as two alternative modes, with profound consequence both for the course of their cultural development and for educational issues that subsequently emerged in the federal Canadian union after 1867.

The educational system in Canada East, or Quebec, was above all religiously based and directed. It expressed the power which the eastern French majority had gained within the union under responsible government to determine its own cultural public policies. It also naturally expressed Roman Catholic belief in the integration of church and state, religion and education. And it marked the conclusive triumph of that powerful force in French-

Canadian society, ecclesiastical leadership, over various attempts made by both French and English in the period before the union to establish a secular school system in Lower Canada. For the union itself, that so intensified the French struggle for *survivance*, had increasingly allied the dominant LaFontaine politicians with the priests, the older guardians of French-Canadian interests. Even LaFontaine's rivals of the mid 1840's, Viger and Denis Papineau, had to some degree competed for public support with educational measures that the church hierarchy would favour.[26] Only the *rouges*, reviving anti-clericalism at the close of the decade, had again urged public education separate from the church; and the course of the fifties showed how limited their appeal was on this issue in French Canada.

The Lower Canada School Act of 1846, which amended and completed the religiously based system set up under the Act of 1845, virtually established the structure of Quebec education for more than a century thereafter.[27] Both acts decreed, as the French majority particularly desired, the union of religion and education. They provided two state-aided school systems, Catholic and Protestant, the latter being treated as synonymous with "non-Catholic." Difference in language also practically divided them, but the essential basis of separation was creed, not tongue. While elected local school commissioners managed the schools, the role of the clerical visitors, the resident clergy, was of decisive importance, especially since the Act of 1846 gave the curé or minister an effective veto over the selection of teachers and textbooks. The role of provincial authority itself was chiefly that of providing finances or establishing lists of textbooks for selection, although in 1859 an advisory Council of Public Instruction would be established to assist the Superintendent of Education in drafting general regulations and registering teachers.

The state still played a significant part in developing the eastern school system, thanks largely to able, energetic Superintendents like J.-B. Meilleur and Pierre Chauveau. The former shaped the essential foundations and spread public schools across Lower Canada between 1842 and 1855. The latter, in office from 1855 until he became first premier of the Province of Quebec at Confederation, established a bilingual journal of public instruction in 1857, founded normal schools for teacher training, and worked to develop higher education generally. Despite all this, the power of the church remained pervasive in French-Canadian education. Much of the teaching in the Catholic majority schools was done by members of religious teaching orders. They also maintained a number of residential schools and colleges outside the public system. Of these the *collèges classiques* were particularly important in providing secondary and even university education for the wealthier classes, preserving the distinctive French tradition of classical humanistic learning that went back to seventeenth-century New France and old France beyond.

But higher education was not limited to the *collèges classiques*. McGill University continued to grow in Montreal, attracting French Canadians as well as English for advanced training in law and medicine. And its role in scientific research would particularly develop under William Dawson, appointed principal of the university in 1855. A brilliant naturalist and geologist, the former superintendent of schools for Nova Scotia, he was to guide McGill for nearly forty years. Meanwhile, by royal charter in 1852, Laval University had emerged out of the ancient Séminaire de Québec founded in 1663. With faculties of theology, civil law, medicine and arts, it came to hold a place in Lower Canadian education analogous to McGill's— though the one was modelled on the universities of Catholic France, the other on the non-sectarian, privately-endowed universities of English America.

Non-sectarianism, of course, was a major premise in English Upper Canada as well. The educational system in Canada West, and in Ontario thereafter, above all remained secularly based and directed. This did not at all mean the full and formal separation of church and state, whatever thorough-going voluntaryists demanded. Not only were there the state-supported separate schools, but also some degree of state recognition and government grants for denominational colleges. Yet in general, the system of public education that concerned the large majority was under non-sectarian state authority at the centre and lay control in the localities. It was really the reverse of the Lower Canadian pattern, where the pre-eminent influence was the church, though the state was a necessary agent. In the Upper Canadian scheme, the state represented the predominant power, though the church remained an important adjunct. The difference embodied and sustained a vital cultural distinction between the two Canadas that had made their living together difficult and could do so in future.

The basic structure of public education in Canada West, or Ontario, had been set by the mid fifties. Indeed, it went back to the Common Schools Act of 1843, which had replaced the union's initial, embryonic, school law of 1841 for Upper Canada, just as the School Act of 1845 replaced that original measure for Lower Canada. The Act of 1843 effectively fitted non-sectarian elementary schools into the emerging Upper Canadian municipal system. Supervision over locally elected school trustees rested with the township and district councils. The provincial government paid education grants to each township, the property-holders in each an equivalent amount —or double, if the elected township councillors so decided. This sum constituted the School Fund, which was allocated among the local school sections, and their trustees raised a supplementary sum by a rate bill on the parents of the pupils.

The Act of 1843 continued a provision for denominational separate schools, loosely set forth in the original law of 1841, but in defining it, limited it to special circumstances. It was neither a broad permissive possibility, as before, nor a distinctively Roman Catholic right, as later. It enabled ten resident Protestant or Catholic freeholders to apply for a school of their own, if the teacher of the common school should "happen to be" not of their religious faith.[28] Such separate schools, if granted, would then be entitled to share in the government funds and be subject to the same conditions as the common schools. Indeed, they were treated virtually as special common schools, not as having a system of their own, and they did not become numerous.

The Upper Canada School Act of 1846 did not change these separate-school provisions. Its importance lay in shaping a lasting combination of local autonomy and central authority in Ontario education. Local democratic interest in schools was encouraged by the provision of annual school-district meetings, and by the election of school boards, which, then as now, might first launch citizens into public activities. General cohesion was promoted by the establishment of a provincial Board of Education (later, Council of Public Instruction) to advise the Chief Superintendent on maintaining common regulations and standards, and by the founding of a normal school to train teachers. The first Chairman of the new Board of Education was Dr Michael Power, Roman Catholic Bishop of Toronto, who, with Ryerson and an Anglican clergyman and four laymen as its other members, led it in a non-sectarian rather than a wholly secular direction. But after Bishop Power's tragic death while ministering to fever-ridden Irish immigrants late in 1847, his successor, Bishop Charbonnel, soon withdrew from contact with the public system, which he labelled "a regular school of pyrrhonism, of indifferentism, of infidelity, and consequently of all vices and crimes."[29]

The Act of 1846 really settled the outlines of public education in Upper Canada, although that of 1850 was of major significance in refining and codifying arrangements under Ryerson's skilled draftsmanship. It was no less significant, of course, in regard to separate schools, since it reversed a trend to curtail or even do away with them in recent western legislation, and instead consolidated the provisions of the old Act of 1843, now making them binding obligations to meet the Roman Catholic demands. The Acts of 1853 and 1855 then followed to erect a full-scale Catholic separate-school system. The former gave separate-school boards their own financial structure, exempting their supporters from common-school taxes. The latter— the Taché Act, the first completely separate-school measure—enabled ten resident Roman Catholic freeholders to set up a separate school simply by electing three trustees to inform the local authorities of that intention; and no longer was it necessary for the common-school teacher in the area to be a Protestant. One might say, in short, that if the forties produced the majority public-school system in Upper Canada, the fifties produced the Catholic minority system with all its repercussions on politics. Both would go forward into Confederation without any great change.

In higher education in Canada West, the establishment of the nonsectarian state university of Toronto in 1849 brought a determined response from indefatigable old Bishop Strachan. Obtaining a new royal charter, he opened Trinity College at Toronto in 1852 as an Anglican reply and reproach to the "godless University." Bishop Charbonnel also began St Michael's College there on a small scale the same year, while the Free Presbyterians organized Knox College in the city. Victoria at Cobourg and Queen's at Kingston had been producing arts graduates since the mid forties. But the University of Toronto, enjoying the state endowment, was the most affluent of all.

This led to new pressure from the western denominational colleges for state aid. The movement to secularism, which had gone so far in Baldwin's University Act of 1849, swung back part way towards denominationalism in Hincks's University Act of 1853. It established University College as the non-sectarian teaching institution of the University of Toronto, leaving the university as the examining and endowment-holding body, with which the religious colleges might affiliate—and earnestly hope for shares in the surplus income from its endowment. There was no surplus, however; especially when in 1856 the university resolved to weigh down its right to the capital funds with a grand new building in Queen's Park. The cornerstone of this University College was laid almost by stealth: "Secretly, as though it had been a deed of shame"—so Daniel Wilson, the professor of history and English, future principal of the college and president of the university, described it.[30] But when finished in 1859 the University of Toronto had a monumental stone edifice, to remain impressive through the years with its Norman arches, French château roofs, and Victorian sense of the picturesque that somehow made the total effect attractive rather than ungainly.

The complaints of the church colleges grew in indignation as the construction of expensive University College advanced. But again the western educational pattern would remain with little change until Confederation, a conjunction of one central state university with various denominational institutions partly acknowledged by the state. Still, in this distinctive Upper Canadian mixture there was the basis for a distinctive Ontario answer in the future to problems of higher education: university federation, that could combine the advantages of broader, central state facilities with the variety of smaller, church-based residential colleges.

Bases, too, were being laid for higher education in science, medicine and engineering. While McGill pioneered in medical teaching, the first professor of chemistry in Canada was appointed to King's College at Toronto in 1842, when Sir Charles Bagot named Henry Croft, a pupil of the great Michael Faraday, on Faraday's own recommendation. At Toronto also, John Rolph (as physician, not politician) opened a School of Medicine in 1843, later to be attached to Victoria. In similar fashion the Quebec School of Medicine begun in 1847 was incorporated in Laval University in 1852. As for engineering, McGill under William Dawson began to teach a course in 1855. But the chief contributions to engineering were made by men in practice, the canal and railway builders—sometimes turned architects as well, like Frederick Cumberland, builder of University College in Toronto. Most significant among them was Sandford Fleming, a Scottish civil engineer who served on the Northern Railway after 1845 and became its chief engineer in 1857. He was to construct the Intercolonial, survey the route for a Canadian Pacific Railway, and propose the world-wide system of Standard Time now basic to modern communications. Indeed, in the days of the union, men like Fleming or Croft or Dawson were harbingers of a coming era of rapidly developing technology.

IV

The basic governmental machinery of modern Canada developed during the union period, and much of it from the administrative reorganization carried through by Sydenham at the outset for the new province that he was charged with ruling. His well-planned work produced a unified executive council, with a President of Council to co-ordinate its business under the governor (or later the prime minister, when the council grew into a cabinet), and a set of major government departments that included Crown Lands, the Inspector General's and Receiver General's Offices, and the Board of Works. This last became the Department of Public Works in 1846; the Inspector General was retitled Minister of Finance in 1859. In between, the continued transfer of imperial authority consequent on the development of free trade and responsible government brought the Customs Branch and the Post Office under Canadian control by the early fifties. The Bureau of Agriculture was set up in 1853, and also took charge of immigration. The Crown Law Office, predecessor of the Department of Justice, was organized in 1855. Militia and Indian Affairs were added in the early sixties, the latter delayed by rather sorry Canadian attempts to avoid the cost and leave Britain saddled with that burden.

Hence much of the post-1867 administrative structure had been established in the Canadian union by the middle fifties. Further than that, a sizable body of trained public servants was being developed, which would mainly staff the new Dominion public service after Confederation. They numbered 437 in 1842, 880 in 1852, and 2,660 in 1867; showing that deplorable habits of bureaucratic multiplication also go back to this earlier Canada.[31] Moreover, the comprehensive Civil Service Act of 1857 set significant lines for subsequent administrative development, establishing a board of civil-service examiners as some check on patronage, and recognizing the need for a permanent, non-political head in each department, one with the first application of the title "deputy minister."[32]

Significant, too, was the establishment of the Audit Office under the executive council in 1855, when John Langton, able, dedicated, with a relieving sense of humour, became Auditor General, and practically laid the basis of the modern Canadian system of budgeting.[33] Langton, a former Upper Canadian conservative member, strove to promote financial reforms along with William Lyon Mackenzie, the chairman of parliament's new standing committee on Public Accounts in 1854-55. Here the old radical performed one of his least known and most constructive services in a stormy and decidedly public career. He and Langton worked to tighten control over the accounts in an era of recklessly free spending. The Act of Union had given the executive the power to initiate money bills, which under responsible government meant that the cabinet determined expenditure. But to be complete, responsible government required that ministers be truly responsible for expenditure—that parliament should know what they were doing. Parliamentary control of the purse properly extended not only over the raising of revenues but also over their use; and through the careful examination of public accounts, Mackenzie and Langton did much to provide that faculty.

The two biggest administrative departments of the union era were Crown Lands and Public Works. Crown Lands had the two traditionally large Canadian tasks of providing land for settlers and managing timber resources. As to the first of these, the main policy remained one of instalment purchase, both to provide revenue and to place bona fide settlers on the land; but free grants were provided along the colonization roads which the department developed in the 1850's. As for the second function, the chief aim again was revenue, by making easy the private exploitation of seemingly inexhaustible forests. And since A. J. Russell, Crown Timber Agent on the Ottawa, controlled concessions in an area half the size of Ireland, the potential wealth he managed was vast indeed. Fisheries also came under Crown Lands, as did mines; but the supervision of mining was not much developed in the period.

Public Works above all had charge of the basic water transport system of Canada, the expensive chain of canals. Harbours, navigation aids, timber slides, some major roads in both Canadas, and government buildings—these comprised its other main concerns. But it had little contact with the great new means of transport, railways, left under the union to private, government-aided, enterprise. Yet some of the ablest engineers of the railway era began with the Works Department, men like Casimir Gzowski and Samuel Keefer. Others, like the blithely unorthodox Hamilton Killaly— promenading the capital in battered hat, open shirt, satin breeches and dancing-pumps—long remained as first-rate public servants. In fact, the growing administrative institutions of the union were served by a number of outstandingly able and colourful individuals, such as Captain Doctor Pierre Fortin, J.P., M.P.P., who commanded the Crown Lands department's fishery protection vessel in the Gulf of St Lawrence, *La Canadienne* (owned by Public Works). He attracted some heavy-handed humour about the Canadian "navy" from the press, but efficiently dispensed justice and maintained order down the river and gulf with his smartly drilled and uniformed naval-style crew.

Administrative development under the union of the Canadas of course comprehended education. It also entered the realm of social policy, and both of these would fall generally to provincial authority in the federal structure after 1867. Social policy, as it first emerged in the union, particularly concerned penal institutions. Apart from the state maintaining a provincial asylum in Toronto and a marine hospital and quarantine hospital at Quebec, social welfare functions such as poor relief, correctional training and care of the sick and aged were essentially left to the municipalities and voluntary interdenominationl bodies in Upper Canada and to the Roman Catholic Church in Lower Canada; though with some aid from varied public grants. Prisons, however, were seen as a provincial responsibility; and on that inauspicious foundation, state action in the social sphere began to grow.

The Upper Canada penitentiary outside Kingston had been taken over as Provincial Penitentiary for long-term prisoners at the outset of the union. But a rising tide of rumours and charges of maltreatment and mismanagement there led to a major investigation by a Royal Commission appointed in 1848. George Brown was a leading member of that body, as its secretary; John A. Macdonald was a friend and champion of the warden of the penitentiary, Henry Smith. The report of the commission that devastatingly condemned Smith, the repeated efforts of Macdonald to redeem him, led finally to the violent, lasting rupture between Brown and Macdonald in 1856, when the latter, carried away, accused the former of an array of unsubstantiated misdeeds during the inquiry of 1848-49. But the Penitentiary Report of 1849 had an importance far beyond that. It offered humane, constructive recommendations for the improvement of the management of the penitentiary and prisons generally. In particular, it proposed the appointment of permanent, salaried government inspectors to replace the unpaid amateurs who had signally failed to supervise penal administration at Kingston. And this idea of an official inspectorate would prove the small but vital beginning of a long and extensive development of state social action.

Salaried inspectors were provided in the Penitentiary Act of 1851, which followed from the Report. In their own reports thereafter, these individuals advocated the co-ordination and "uniform direction" of all prisons, including local gaols.[34] This led by 1857 to the concept of a general provincial inspectorate with wide administrative authority, which was established by the Prison Inspection Act of that year. It was to inspect asylums and hospitals as well as prisons and gaols, and to examine and report on every benevolent institution supported by public money or "by money levied under the authority of Law."[35] Out of this critical statute of 1857 came a consolidating, more detailed measure in 1859. Under its authority, the highly important Board of Inspectors of Prisons, Asylums and Public Charities was founded: "for the first time in Canada an administrative body charged with the general direction of Public Institutions."[36]

It was this Board that expressed a growing awareness of public responsibility for social welfare. It formed the link between provincial authority and municipal, religious, or private philanthropic activity that enabled the state in time to enter with more and more effect into shaping institutions it now supervised as well as aided; it dealt with the indigent, the orphaned, the elderly, and the mentally and physically ill. In short, however limited were its initial functions, the growth of the activities of the provincial inspectorate both expressed and stimulated a similar growth of the Canadian social conscience.

At Confederation, since social welfare responsibilities went to the provinces, they followed separate courses of development thereafter under the jurisdictions of Quebec and Ontario. Yet unquestionably, the emergence of an experienced group of officials within this field during the 1850's was of major consequence for the future growth of provincial social services and welfare legislation. It eased the transition from pioneer self-reliance and family care to the colder world of urban industrialism, and reduced the application of stern doctrines of laissez-faire—always, however, more recited in theory than applied in practice. Indeed, the evolution of prison inspectors in the Canadian union as effective instruments of state social policy is analogous to the evolution of factory inspectors in contemporary Britain. That the one sprang out of colonial prison brutality and the other from British industrial prisons may be regarded as a tribute to the realistic humanity of those Canadian and British Victorians who put first things first.

V

An incipient federal system, from federalized cabinets to law and administration; an effective civil service, a structure of public education, the beginnings of the welfare state; these in themselves would make the heritage of a disunited Canadian union anything but negative. But there was much more than that. Constitutionally, it had achieved self-government and the cabinet system, founded the national political parties of the future, and evolved the vital working principle of Anglo-French majority alliance. Economically, it had provided a main line of uninterrupted water communications, opened the railway age, and constructed a flourishing and far more complex pattern of trade—across the border as well as over the ocean—one in which increasing specialization was easing the old colonial reliance on the primitive, extractive staples of square timber and grain. And this whole, many-sided process had so bound the two Canadas together that, if they could no longer live comfortably within a sectionally divided union, neither could they readily foresee living apart. Duality was the fact and problem. But few regarded separation as an answer.

The persistence of duality: that indeed had been the most profound experience of the union. Assimilation and an unqualified single majority were unreal, as Bagot had first been compelled to recognize. Equally unreal was an absolute double majority, pointing to paralysis and the politics of "race"—whereby minority racialism invited majority racialism, and a return to coercion and violence. There were English Canadians who would hold to the delusive simplicity of the one, recast as representation by population; there were French Canadians who would not abandon the superficial logic of the other. But the general attitude in both communities, expressed in conduct more than doctrine, was to accept an empirical duality in Canadian life. Nevertheless, this was restricted also by the plain necessity of majority rule, for, under free institutions, the only known mode of decision was still by counting votes. There might be two nations in society and culture, as Hincks had said, but they formed one politically self-governing state.[37]

The experience of duality in the united province was vitally important for the British North American federation that followed. In many respects this was less the joining together of four or five individual colonies than the adding of a third, Atlantic, community to the two communities of the Canadas. In the resultant federal state, the Maritimes, and the western provinces that came later, had never had the same experience of duality as the partners in the former province of Canada, Ontario and Quebec. The latter two might very well represent opposed forces in federal affairs; and yet each would tend to show an inherent recognition of dualism that was assuredly less evident in the western and eastern regions beyond. Furthermore, the very understanding of federalism in Canada at the time of Confederation was intimately related to the years of the old legislative union. Certainly the Canadian designers of federal union in 1864-67 often appeared to see the essence of the federal system in the provision of sectional equality in the upper chamber of the proposed new central legislature and representation by population in the lower.[38] Here, indeed, was the obvious lesson that seemed to emerge from the life of the Canadian union: that dualism had to be combined far more effectively with majority rule, thus demanding equal representation of distinct communities in the one house and representation on the basis of numbers in the other. The character of Canadian federation might owe much to American example, much to the experience of living in the British colonial system. But it owed a great deal as well to the old union of the Canadas.

That union, which by 1857 was well on its course to ultimate disunion and sectional deadlock, was succeeding even as it failed. It had tied the two Canadas inextricably together; inextricably, at least, in all the circumstances of that day. It would have to be changed, not abandoned; built on, not destroyed; and the wider horizons that were opening invited conceptions of a greater state. In the apparent pattern of disunion, the threads were already being woven for a design far more vast and enduring than this first union of the Canadas.

Its sixteenth anniversary caused little stir, however. In Toronto, the capital, on February 10, 1857, society might mark the occasion by attending Sir Edward Bulwer Lytton's play *Lady of Lyons*, at the Royal Lyceum.[39] Hamilton planned other pleasures. A dog fight had been arranged between a local animal and a challenger brought in from Buffalo. The prize was a hundred dollars; tickets had sold at fifty cents a head, and betting was heavy —until the mayor and twenty police dashed up in sleighs and stopped the whole amusement.[40] Montreal paid little attention, in any case, as it discussed the establishment of a new tradesman's bank. In Quebec, the news was of the founding of another daily paper, *Le Courier du Canada*, to which Hector Langevin, once of *Mélanges Religieux*, was to lend his journalistic talents: contemplating the uncertain political shade of the projected journal, the rouge *Le Pays* decided it was "violet."[41] As for the first capital of the union, Kingston, here something perhaps of more significance was going on. The garrison of the Royal Canadian Rifles were playing a game on the cleared river ice, using skates on boots, field hockey sticks and a lacrosse ball. Generations would know of it, when the old Canadian union had long since disappeared.

ABBREVIATIONS

A.P.Q.: Archives of the Province of Quebec.
B.R.H.: *Bulletin des Recherches Historiques*.
C.H.A.A.R.: *Canadian Historical Association, Annual Report*.
C.H.R.: *Canadian Historical Review*.
C.J.E.P.S.: *Canadian Journal of Economics and Political Science*.
C.O.: *Colonial Office*.
M.G.: Manuscript Group.
M.S.R.C.: *Mémoires de la Société Royale du Canada*.
O.H.: *Ontario History*.
O.H.S.P.R.: *Ontario Historical Society, Papers and Records*.
P.A.C.: Public Archives of Canada.
P.A.O.: Public Archives of Ontario.
R.G.: Record Group.
R.H.A.F.: *Revue d'Histoire de l'Amérique Française*.
T.P.L.: Toronto Public Library.

1. *Le Canadien* (Québec), 12 fév. 1841.
2. *Montreal Gazette*, 13 Feb. 1841.
3. *Quebec Gazette*, 15 Feb. 1841.
4. *Montreal Gazette*, 10 Feb. 1841.
5. *Le Fantasque* (Québec), 11 fév. 1841.
6. *Le Canadien*, 15 fév. 1841.
7. *Ibid.*, 22 fév. 1841.
8. C. P. Lucas, ed., *Lord Durham's Report on the Affairs of British North America* (3 vols., Oxford, 1912), II, 278.
9. See W. G. Ormsby, "Canadian Union, 1839-45. The Emergence of a Federal Concept," M. A. thesis for Carleton University, Ottawa, 1960, pp. 84 ff.
10. *Quebec Gazette*, 10 Feb. 1841.
11. V. Jensen, "Lafontaine and the Canadian Union," M. A. thesis, University of Toronto, 1942, pp. ii-iii.
12. *Quebec Gazette*, 10 Feb. 1841.
13. *Le Canadien*, 12 fév. 1841.
14. *Proceedings of the Toronto Tandem Club*, 1839-41 (Toronto, 1841), p. 27. By "Erin" (Lt.-Col. Wingfield).
15. *Patriot* (Toronto), 12 Feb. 1841. See also *ibid.*, 9 Feb. 1841.
16. C. R. Sanderson, ed., *The Arthur Papers* (3 vols., Toronto, 1957, 1959), III, 311, Arthur to Sydenham, 10 Feb. 1841. See also *ibid.*, 316, Arthur to Sydenham, 13 Feb. 1841.
17. *Chronicle and Gazette* (Kingston), 6 Feb. 1841.
18. G. Poulett Scrope, *Memoir of the Life of the Right Honourable Charles, Lord Sydenham* (London, 1844), p. 156, Poulett Thomson to a friend, 31 Dec. 1839.
19. P.A.C., Record Group 7, G5/27, Russell to Thomson, 14 Oct. 1839.
20. *Ibid.*, Russell to Thomson, 7 Sept. 1839. See also the dispatch cited immediately above.

21. Poulett Thomson to House of Assembly of Upper Canada, 14 Jan. 1840. Printed in *Journals of the Legislative Assembly of the United Province of Canada*, 1841, Appendix BB.
22. P.A.C., LaFontaine Papers (copies), Manuscript Group 24, B14, Hincks to LaFontaine, 12 Apr. 1839. Louis Hippolyte LaFontaine's surname is variously spelled LaFontaine, Lafontaine and La Fontaine. The first form has been preferred for the text of this volume, since it follows his own usage. (Indeed, he laid claim to aristocratic descent, thus exhibited, though his "pretensions" might be derided by opponents.) In titles or quotations cited in this book, however, his name has been spelled according to the usage of the authors.
23. *Ibid.*, 14 May 1839.
24. *Ibid.*, 17 June 1840.
25. P. M. Knaplund, ed., *Letters of Lord Sydenham to Lord John Russell* (London, 1931), p. 42. Thomson to Russell, 18 Jan. 1840.
26. For text of the Union Act of 1840 see W. P. M. Kennedy, ed., *Statutes, Treaties and Documents of the Canadian Constitution, 1713-1929* (Toronto, 1930), pp. 433-45. With regard to the right to vote, in the rural or county constituencies this was still based on the possesssion of land worth forty shillings annually—in origin, the mediaeval forty-shilling freehold franchise of the counties of England. In the eight urban or town constituencies the vote was given to owners of houses worth £5 a year or tenants paying £10 rent a year. The consequence was a broadly popular franchise, since in Canada–pre-eminently a country of

agricultural lands undergoing settlement –there was a wide distribution of farms worth forty shillings annually. In effect, therefore, the Canadian union had a democratic electorate. Nevertheless, the right to vote remained qualified in actual fact. Farm labourers and town shop-clerks, for example, could find themselves excluded, as would a growing urban proletariat. Indeed, under the union, despite modifying franchise acts of the 1850's, the electorate continued to be one of property-holders. This was in high degree a "farmers' franchise": a a fact which perhaps bore some relation to the rowdy, "irresponsible" (non-voting) urban mobs reported on at election times and often contrasted with the worthy, respectable "yeomen" of the countryside.

27. See Clause XLV, Union Act of 1840. Kennedy, op. cit., p. 442.

28. On the background and consequences of the financial arrangements in the Act of Union see in particular W. G. Ormsby, "The Civil List Question in the Province of Canada," C.H.R., XXXV, June 1954, 93-118.

29. C.O. 42, vol. 472 (microfilm), Sydenham to Russell, 16 Sept. 1840.

30. H. A. Innis and A. R. M. Lower, eds., Select Documents in Canadian Economic History, 1783-1885 (Toronto, 1933), p. 274.

31. H. Y. Hind et al., Eighty Years' Progress of British America (Toronto, 1863), p. 291.

32. D. G. Creighton, The Commercial Empire of the St. Lawrence (Toronto, 1937), p. 343.

33. C. P. Stacey, Canada and the British Army, 1846-1871 (revised edition, Toronto, 1963), pp. 13-17.

34. Ibid., pp. 34-46.

35. Quebec Gazette, 8 Feb. 1841.

36. St. Catharines Journal, 18 Feb. 1841. (Extract from the Springs Mercury, undated.)

NOTES TO CHAPTER TWO

1. "A Four Years' Resident," in Views of Canada and the Colonists (Edinburgh, 1844), p. 202.

2. Figures here and below on cultivation, population and related statistics for Canada East at the time of union have been calculated from the Lower Canadian census for 1844, as given in The Censuses of Canada, 1665 to 1871 (Ottawa, 1876), pp. 141-158. There is no Lower Canadian census for 1841; that for 1844 supplies the closest approximate figures. These have been adjusted backward for 1841 by applying a population growth factor of 2 per cent per annum, as estimated for the period 1841-1844 by A. R. M. Lower in "The Growth of the French Population of Canada," Canadian Political Science Association Papers and Proceedings for 1930 (Kingston, 1931), p. 38. The growth rate for the English-speaking minority in Lower Canada would not differ significantly enough to affect estimates based on the French majority in so short a time-span as the three years involved (ibid). There are census returns for Canada West in 1841, given in the Journals of the Legislative Assembly of the Province of Canada, 1842, Appendix MM. These have also been used below. It is believed that the quantitative data obtained by according the 1841 western figures with the adjusted 1844 eastern set are broadly valid enough to permit general comparisons.

3. Henry Taylor, Journal of a Tour from Montreal to the Eastern Townships (Quebec, 1840), pp. 59, 61.

4. R. B. Sneyd, "The Role of the Rideau Waterway 1826-1856," M. A. thesis, University of Toronto, 1965. Chapter 4.

5. Canada and the Colonists, p. 260.

6. Ibid., p. 203.

7. G. P. de T. Glazebrook, A History of Transportation in Canada (Toronto, 1938), p. 84.

8. *Canada and the Colonists*, p. 202.

9. See H. C. McLeod, *The Montreal Almanack for 1841* (Montreal, 1841) for contemporary Montreal business community.

10. Sir Richard Bonnycastle, *The Canadas in 1841* (2 vols., London, 1842), II, 76-77.

11. *Canada and the Colonists*, p. 259.

12. *Ibid.*, p. 213.

13. J. C. Dent, *The Last Forty Years: Canada Since the Union of 1841* (2 vols., Toronto, 1881), I, 56.

14. See note 2 above.

15. *Ibid.*

16. On the contemporary French-Canadian class pattern, see F. Ouellet, "Les Fondements historiques de l'option séparatiste dans le Québec," *C.H.R.*, XLIII, September 1962, 185-203.

17. F. Ouellet et J. Hamelin, "La Crise agricole dans le Bas-Canada (1802-1837)," *Etudes Rurales* (Québec), octobre-décembre 1962, pp. 50-52, 56.

18. Taylor, *op. cit.*, Preface, iii-iv and *passim*.

19. Ouellet et Hamelin, *loc. cit.*, pp. 39-57. W. H. Parker, "A New Look at Unrest in Lower Canada in the 1830's," *C.H.R.*, XL, September 1959, 208-18.

20. G. Langlois, *Histoire de la Population Canadienne-Française* (Montreal, 1935), pp. 163-174. A. R. M. Lower, *loc. cit.*, p. 38.

21. R. L. Jones, "French Canadian Agriculture in the St. Lawrence Valley, 1815-50," *Agricultural History*, XVI, July 1942, 139-41. Ouellet et Hamelin, *loc. cit.*, pp. 45-47.

22. F. Ouellet, "Le Nationalisme Canadien-Français: de ses Origines à l'Insurrection de 1837," *C.H.R.*, XLV, December 1964, 285.

23. See note 2 above.

24. *Canada and the Colonists*, p. 213.

25. See note 2 above.

26. *Canada and the Colonists*, p. 190.

27. Anna Jameson, *Winter Studies and Summer Rambles in Canada* (London, 1838), p. 1.

28. Bonnycastle, *op. cit.*, II, 156.

29. See F. Lewis, *The Toronto Directory and Street Guide for 1843-4* (Toronto, 1844), for contemporary Toronto business community.

30. S. D. Clark, *The Social Development of Canada* (Toronto, 1942), pp. 224, 228-31.

31. *Canada and the Colonists*, p. 190.

32. V. C. Fowke, "The Myth of the Self-Sufficient Pioneer," in *Transactions of the Royal Society of Canada*, Section II, 1962, 23-37.

33. R. L. Jones, *The History of Agriculture in Ontario, 1613-1880* (Toronto, 1946), pp. 51-54.

34. *Ibid.*

35. This judgement is based on the comparison of returns for the two Canadas in the census reports referred to above in note 2.

36. Jones, *op. cit.*, pp. 53-54.

37. See W. T. Easterbrook and H. G. J. Aitken, *Canadian Economic History* (Toronto, 1956), pp. 197-98; A. R. M. Lower, "The Trade in Square Timber," in *University of Toronto Studies, Contributions to Canadian Economics*, VI (Toronto, 1933), 40-61.

38. A. R. M. Lower, *Settlement and the Forest Frontier of Eastern Canada* (Toronto, 1936), pp. 45-46.

39. Jones, *op. cit.*, p. 111.

40. *Ibid.*

41. M. S. Cross, "The Lumber Community of Upper Canada," *O.H.*, LII, 1960, 228-30.

42. *Bathurst Courier and Ottawa General Advertiser*, 12 Feb. 1841.

43. Upper Canada Census for 1841. See note 2.

44. *Ibid.*

45. *Ibid.*

46. See J. S. Moir, *Church and State in Canada West* (Toronto, 1959), Appendix 1, for comparative growth of denominations.

47. Jacques Monet, s.j., "The Last Cannon Shot: A Study of French-Canadian Nationalism, 1837-1850," Ph.D. thesis, University of Toronto, 1964, pp. 48-53.

48. Cauchon's later public career was to be marred by political scandal, which may account for his being considerably underrated by historians as a force in politics before Confederation–as a party tactician, a parliamentarian, and a highly competent minister.

49. Monet, *op. cit.*, pp. 9-15. W. S. Wallace, "The Periodical Literature of Upper Canada," *C.H.R.*, XII, March 1931, 4-22.

50. See C. F. Klinck, ed., *The Literary History of Canada* (Toronto, 1965), pp. 143-44.

51. In actuality, at the time of union many of the schools in Lower Canada

had been closed since 1836. Nevertheless the pattern indicated had been present, and would be continued in the far more effective school system under the union.

52. See Chapter 9 below.

53. *Quebec Gazette*, 8 Feb. 1841.

54. T.P.L., "Memoranda upon the nature and value of Materials and also on Labour in Canada from information in the Office of the Commanding R. Engineer, 1841," p. 91.

55. F. H. Armstrong, "Toronto's First Railway Venture, 1834-1838," *O.H.*, LVIII, 1966, 28-34.

NOTES TO CHAPTER THREE

1. See J. R. M. Butler, "Note on the Origin of Lord John Russell's Dispatch of October 16, 1839 on the Tenure of Crown Office in the Colonies," *Cambridge Historical Journal*, II, 3 (1928), 248-51. On Russell's general aims and objectives see O. A. Kinchen, *Lord Russell's Canadian Policy* (Lubbock, Texas, 1945).

2. J. E. Hodgetts, *Pioneer Public Service* (Toronto, 1955), pp. 25-27.

3. *Ibid.*, pp. 30-31.

4. C.O. 42/480, Sydenham to Russell, 18 July 1841.

5. Scrope, *Lord Sydenham*, p. 143. Thomson to a friend, 12 Dec. 1839.

6. P.A.C., R.G. 7, G5/27, Russell to Thomson, 14 Oct. 1839.

7. *Ibid.*

8. P.A.C., LaFontaine Papers, Hincks to LaFontaine, 23 Aug. 1840, 6 Apr. 1841.

9. Scrope, *op. cit.*, p. 172. Thomson to —?. Undated.

10. Jensen, "Lafontaine and the Canadian Union," pp. 58-60.

11. T.P.L., Baldwin Papers, Baldwin to Sydenham, 18 Feb. 1841.

12. Sanderson, *Arthur Papers*, III, 372, Baldwin to Sydenham, 5 Mar. 1841.

13. *Ibid.*, 345, Sydenham to Arthur, 27 Feb. 1841.

14. Baldwin Papers, W. H. Draper to Baldwin, 22 Feb. 1841.

15. *Arthur Papers*, III, 371. Sydenham to Baldwin, 1 Mar. 1841.

16. LaFontaine Papers, Hincks to LaFontaine, 16 Feb. 1841. See also *ibid.*, 22 Feb. 1841.

17. P.A.C., R.G. 4, Civil Secretary Drafts Miscellaneous, A3, vol. 23, Murdoch to S. B. Harrison, 26 Feb. 1840.

18. *Ibid.*, vol. 29, Murdock to Harrison, 2 Aug. 1840.

19. LaFontaine Papers, Hincks to LaFontaine, 15 Aug. 1840.

20. *Arthur Papers*, III, 168, Sydenham to Arthur, 1 Nov. 1840.

21. *Quebec Gazette*, 14 Oct. 1840.

22. Text published in *Le Canadien*, 18 Oct. 1840.

23. *Ibid.*

24. P.A.C., Neilson Collection, M.G. 24, B1, vol. 12, Neilson to Bellingham, 23 Dec. 1840.

25. Knaplund, *Sydenham Letters*, p. 119, Sydenham to Russell, 24 Feb. 1841.

26. C.O. 42/477, Sydenham to Russell, 6 Mar. 1841.

27. Knaplund, *op. cit.*, p. 107, Sydenham to Russell, 20 Dec. 1840.

28. *Quebec Gazette*, 10 Mar. 1841; *Le Canadien*, 8 mars 1841.

29. *Quebec Mercury*, 28 Feb. 1841, quoted in *Quebec Gazette*, 2 Mar. 1841; *Montreal Gazette*, 23 Feb. 1841.

30. *L'Aurore* (Montréal), 13 oct. 1841.

31. P.A.C., R.G. 7, G19, Military Secretary's Records, Campbell to Murdoch, 18 Feb. 1841.

32. *Ibid.* See research paper by I. M. Abella, "The Sydenham Election of 1841," University of Toronto, 1964, since published in revised form under the same title in C.H.R., XLVII, December 1966, 326-343. Any references here are to the unabridged original version.

33. *Le Canadien*, 18 mars 1841.

34. *Montreal Gazette*, 25 Mar. 1841.

35. *Journals of the Assembly* (1841), p. 29.

36. *Ibid.*, p. 19.

37. *Montreal Herald*, 15 Mar. 1841, quoted in *Quebec Gazette*, 24 Mar. 1841.

38. LaFontaine Papers, Dumont to LaFontaine, 19 Mar. 1841; McAdam to LaFontaine, 22 Mar. 1841; Turgeon to LaFontaine, 23 Mar. 1841.

39. *Ibid.*, "A friend" to LaFontaine, 22 Mar. 1841.

40. *Le Canadien*, 2 avr. 1841.

41. *Quebec Gazette*, 9 Apr. 1841.

42. W. J. S. Mood, "The Orange Order in Canadian Politics," M. A. thesis, University of Toronto, 1950, p. 98.

43. *Patriot*, 3 Apr. 1841.

44. *Quebec Gazette*, 7 Apr. 1841.

45. P.A.C., Merritt Papers, M.G. 24, E1, William H. Merritt to H. Bliss, 18 Aug. 1840.

46. Abella, *op. cit.*, p. 51.

47. *Ibid.*, p. 79.

48. Arthur Papers, III, 346, Sydenham to Arthur, 27 Feb. 1841.

49. *Journals of the Assembly* (1841), Appendix Y, p. 53. Harrison to R. Berrie, 5 Mar. 1841.

50. *Ibid.*

51. P. G. Cornell, *The Alignment of Political Groups in Canada, 1841-1867* (Toronto, 1962), p. 7. In general, throughout the present study, statements on election returns and parliamentary party strengths have been based upon this scholarly examination of voting patterns during the union. Some modifications in Cornell's estimates may be made from time to time, on the basis of other information noted in the text. For, as indeed Professor Cornell makes clear himself, it is often difficult to categorize voting strengths and parliamentary alignments precisely for any given moment under the union, since party lines were looser then and groupings far more subject to shifts than in modern Canadian politics. There were normally some members undecided between parties; there were also independents decidedly outside them; and party lines in any case did not hold on all issues. Accordingly, in enumerating election results or parliamentary contingents below, it is virtually necessary always to speak in terms of "about", "close to", "broadly" and so on. Furthermore, the total figures for the party groups enumerated may still not add up to the total number of seats in the house. For, apart from the Speaker (necessarily subtracted), there could be double returns or seats left vacant through illness or death; and subsequent by-elections might affect the party strengths again. Nevertheless, these qualifications or cautions do not preclude broadly valid statements being made about election returns and political alignments. There were undoubtedly certain major "core" groupings in union politics. And party labels–regularly applied by the era itself–were significant enough *in toto*, even though they might prove misleading in various individual instances.

52. Knaplund, *op. cit.*, pp. 128, 137, Sydenham to Russell, 10 Apr., 25 May 1841.

53. *Chronicle and Gazette* (Kingston), 17, 27 Feb. *et seq.*, 1841.

54. Knaplund, *op. cit.*, p. 143, Sydenham to Russell, 12 June 1841.

55. *Quebec Gazette*, 2 June 1841.

56. *Ibid.*, 14 May 1841.

57. *Chronicle and Gazette*, 18 Aug. 1841.

58. Baldwin Papers, Baldwin to his father, 6 and 13 May, 1841.

59. *Ibid.*, 15 June 1841.

60. *Ibid.*, Baldwin to Sydenham, 12 June 1841.

61. P.A.C., Hincks Papers, M.G. 24, B68, Morin to Hincks, 8 May 1841.

62. C.O. 42/479, Sydenham to Russell, 23 June 1841.

63. *Ibid.*

64. *The Mirror of Parliament* (Kingston), 18 June 1841.

65. *Journals of the Assembly* (1841), pp. 65-67.

66. *Examiner* (Toronto), 27 June 1841.

67. *Journals of the Assembly* (1841), p. 65.

68. Knaplund, *op. cit.*, p. 145, Sydenham to Russell, 27 June 1841.

69. *Chronicle and Gazette*, 17 July 1841.

70. C.O. 42/494, Sydenham to Russell, 18 July 1841.

71. Knaplund, *op. cit.*, p. 146, Sydenham to Russell, 27 June 1841.

72. *Chronicle and Gazette*, 7 Aug. 1841; *Quebec Gazette*, 16 Aug. 1841.

73. Knaplund, *op. cit.*, p. 164, Sydenham to Russell, 11 Sept. 1841.

74. *Examiner*, 7 July 1841.

75. Baldwin Papers, Hincks to Dr Baldwin, 7 July 1841.

76. See J. H. Aitchison, "The Development of Local Government in Upper Canada, 1783-1850," Ph.D. thesis, University of Toronto, 1953.

77. Scrope, *op. cit.*, p. 555, Thomson to a friend, 1840 (?).

78. Knaplund, *op. cit.*, p. 162, Sydenham to Russell, 28 Aug. 1841.

79. Baldwin Papers, Baldwin to his father, 29 Aug. 1841.

80. Monet, "The Last Cannon Shot," p. 154.

81. *Ibid*, pp. 155-56.

82. LaFontaine Papers, B. W. Smith to Baldwin, 13 Aug. 1841, forwarded to LaFontaine by Baldwin, 15 Aug. 1841.

83. Baldwin Papers, LaFontaine to Baldwin, 19 Aug. 1841.

84. *Le Canadien*, 27 sept. 1841.

85. *Journals of the Assembly* (1841), pp. 480 ff.

86. Knaplund, *op. cit.*, p. 157, Sydenham to Russell, 4 Aug. 1841.

87. Scrope, *op. cit.*, Sydenham to —?, 5 June 1841.

88. See Sir Robert Peel's comment–admittedly with the wisdom of two years' hindsight: "Lord Sydenham's death, untimely as it might be in every other respect, was a very timely relief to him from Canadian embarrassments. It is evident that his policy was on the eve of exposure." P.A.C., Peel Papers (microfilm), Peel to Stanley, 31 Aug. 1843.

NOTES TO CHAPTER FOUR

1. *Montreal Gazette*, 9 Sept. 1841.

2. *Views of Canada and the Colonists*, pp. 218, 226.

3. Paul Knaplund, ed., "The Buller-Peel Correspondence regarding Canada, 1841," *C.H.R.*, VIII, March 1927, 41, Stanley to Peel, 19 July 1841.

4. *Ibid.*, 43, Buller to Peel, 9 Sept. 1841.

5. *Ibid.*, 46, Peel to Buller, 10 Sept. 1841.

6. *Chronicle and Gazette*, 3 Nov. 1841.

7. Dent, *Last Forty Years*, I, 183. *Montreal Gazette*, 12 Jan. 1842.

8. Knaplund, *loc. cit.*, 46, Peel to Buller, 10 Sept. 1841.

9. See Alastair Watt, "The Case of Alexander McLeod," *C.H.R.*, XII, June 1931,

145-46. See also A. B. Corey, *The Crisis of 1830-1842 in Canadian-American Relations* (New Haven, 1941).

10. See J. W. Pratt, *A History of United States Foreign Policy* (Englewood Cliffs, N.J., 1955), pp. 190-95.

11. P.A.C., R.G. 7, G1/111, Stanley to Bagot, 8 Oct. 1841.

12. P.A.C., Bagot Papers, M.G. 24, A13, Bagot to Stanley, 23 Feb. 1842.

13. *Ibid.*, Bagot to Stanley, 8 Feb. 1842.

14. *Ibid.*, Bagot to Grenville, 27 Mar. 1842.

15. Monet, "The Last Cannon Shot," pp. 179-81.

16. P.A.C., Bagot Papers, Bagot to Stanley, 8 Feb. 1842.

17. G. P. de T. Glazebrook, *Sir Charles Bagot in Canada* (London, 1929), 37-38.
18. Bagot Papers, Bagot to Stanley, 28 Apr. 1842.
19. *Examiner* (Toronto), 22 June 1842.
20. *British Whig* (Kingston), quoted in *Quebec Gazette*, 24 June 1842.
21. G. Metcalf, "The Political Career of William Henry Draper, 1836-1847," M.A. thesis, University of Toronto, 1959, pp. 103-7.
22. Bagot Papers, MacNab to Stanley, 2 Aug. 1842.
23. Cornell, *Political Groups*, p. 9.
24. Bagot Papers, Harrison to Bagot, 11 July 1842.
25. *Ibid.*, Stanley to Bagot, 1 Sept. 1842.
26. *Ibid.*, Bagot to Stanley, 12 June 1842.
27. *Ibid.*, Harrison to Bagot, 11 July 1842.
28. *Ibid.*, Draper to Bagot, 16 July 1842.
29. *Ibid.*, Bagot to Stanley, 10 July 1842.
30. *Ibid.*, 26 Sept. 1842, confidential.
31. *Ibid.*
32. *Ibid.*, 10 July 1842.
33. *Ibid.*, 28 July 1842.
34. *Ibid.*, Stanley to Peel, 27 Aug. 1842.
35. C.O. 537, vol. 140 (microfilm), Bagot to Stanley, 13 Sept. 1842.
36. P.A.C., LaFontaine Papers, Baldwin to LaFontaine, 1 Sept. 1842.
37. Bagot Papers, Bagot to Stanley, 13 Sept. 1842.
38. C.O. 42/495, Bagot to Stanley, 26 Sept. 1842.
39. LaFontaine Papers, Baldwin to LaFontaine, 28 June, 1842.
40. See G. Metcalf, "Draper Conservatism and Responsible Government in the Canadas," *C.H.R.*, XLII, December 1961, 305-17.
41. C.O. 537/140, Memorandum, 12 Sept. 1842.
42. Bagot Papers, Bagot to Stanley, 26

Sept. 1842, confidential; Bagot to LaFontaine, 13 Sept. 1832. See also C.O. 537/140, Bagot to Stanley, 26 Sept. 1842.
43. Bagot Papers, Bagot to Stanley, 26 Sept. 1842.
44. *Ibid.*
45. *Ibid.* The other two tories were Moffatt, "the sole representative of the old British party at Montreal," and Johnston of Carleton, "who always votes against the Government, because they refused him an appointment." *Ibid.*
46. LaFontaine Papers, vol. 3, Morin to LaFontaine, 27 Sept. 1842.
47. *Le Canadien*, 21 Oct. 1842.
48. LaFontaine Papers, 18 Sept. 1842.
49. *Transcript* (Montreal), 27 Sept. 1842. See also 5 Oct. 1842.
50. *Herald* (Toronto), 19 Sept. 1842.
51. P.A.C., Peel Papers, Arbuthnot to Peel, 18 Oct. 1842.
52. Bagot Papers, Stanley to Bagot, 3 Nov. 1842.
53. P.A.C., R.G. 7, G5/32, Stanley to Bagot, 2 Nov. 1842; Bagot Papers, Stanley to Bagot, 3 Dec. 1842.
54. On reform reconciliation see G. E. Wilson, *The Life of Robert Baldwin* (Toronto, 1933), pp. 160-61, and R. S. Longley, *Sir Francis Hincks* (Toronto, 1943), pp. 113-14.
55. Creighton, *Commercial Empire*, pp. 344-45.
56. Longley, *op. cit.*, pp. 115-26.
57. T.P.L., Baldwin Papers, Baldwin to his father, 19 May 1843.
58. *L'Aurore*, 6 déc. 1842.
59. Metcalf, *loc. cit.*
60. Bagot Papers, Bagot to Stanley, 11 Dec. 1842.
61. *Ibid.*, 28 Oct. 1842.
62. *Ibid.*, 27 Dec. 1842.
63. *Ibid.*, Bagot to Aylwin, 29 March 1843.

NOTES TO CHAPTER FIVE

1. P.A.C., LaFontaine Papers, Baldwin to LaFontaine, 1 Oct. 1842.
2. *Quebec Gazette*, 9 Oct. 1842.
3. T.P.L., Baldwin Papers, LaFontaine to

Baldwin, 23 Nov. 1842.
4. Quoted in A. Gérin-Lajoie, *Dix Ans au Canada, 1840-1850* (Quebec, 1888), p. 145.
5. Baldwin Papers, Price to Baldwin, 6

Feb. 1843.

6. *Ibid.*, LaFontaine to Baldwin, 26 Nov. 1842.

7. Monet, "The Last Cannon Shot," p. 220.

8. P.A.C., Bagot Papers, Bagot to Stanley, 19 Jan. 1842.

9. P.A.C., Derby Papers (microfilm), M. G. 24, A15, Cabinet memorandum by Stanley, 23 Jan. 1843.

10. W. T. Easterbrook and H. G. J. Aitken, *Canadian Economic History* (Toronto, 1956), p. 290. See also G. N. Tucker, *The Canadian Commercial Revolution, 1845-1851* (New Haven, 1936), pp. 90-94, for qualifications in regard to consequences of the Canada Corn Act.

11. C.O. 537/142, Metcalfe to Stanley, 29 Apr. 1843. See also *ibid.*, 5 Aug. 1843: a full and important statement of policy on responsible government.

12. J. W. Kaye, *Life and Correspondence of Charles, Lord Metcalfe* (2 vols., London, 1854), II, 313.

13. LaFontaine Papers, Wakefield to LaFontaine, 2 Feb. 1843. See also *ibid.*, 2 Jan. 1843.

14. C.O. 537/141, Stanley to Metcalfe, 29 May 1843.

15. T.P.L., Baldwin Papers, Small to Baldwin, 15 Apr. 1843.

16. Kaye (*op. cit.*, II, 471, Metcalfe to his sister, 9 Apr. 1843.

17. C.O. 537/142, Metcalfe to Stanley, 25 Apr. 1843.

18. Kaye, *op. cit.*, II, 528, Metcalfe to Col. Stokes, no date.

19. C.O. 537/142, Metcalfe to Stanley, 24 Apr. 1843, confidential.

20. *Ibid.*, Metcalfe to Stanley, 12 May 1843.

21. P.A.C., Derby Papers, Stanley to Metcalfe, 1 Nov. 1843; C.O. 537/141, *ibid.*, 29 May 1843.

22. C.O. 537/142, Metcalfe to Stanley, 24 Apr. 1843.

23. Sir Francis Hincks, *Reminiscences of his Public Life* (Montreal, 1884), pp. 92-102. See also W. G. Ormsby, "Sir Charles Metcalfe and the Canadian Union," C.H.A.A.R., 1961, 37-38, to note why

patronage rather than the civil list or amnesty for rebels became the critical issue.

24. C.O. 537/142, Metcalfe to Stanley, 10 and 17 May, 1843.

25. Baldwin Papers, Eliza Baldwin to R. Baldwin, postmarked 9 Nov. 1843.

26. *Examiner*, 8 Nov. 1843.

27. Metcalfe had dealt on his own with Peter McGill, John Neilson and René Caron over the Speakership, though the last, who accepted it, was a reputed LaFontaine supporter.

28. *Chronicle and Gazette*, 2 Dec. 1843.

29. C.O. 537/142, Metcalfe to Stanley, 26 Nov. 1843.

30. Derby Papers, Metcalfe to Stanley, 26 Nov. 1843, private.

31. *Chronicle and Gazette*, 2 Dec. 1843.

32. Hincks, *Reminiscences*, p. 109.

33. *Chronicle and Gazette*, 6 Dec. 1843.

34. LaFontaine Papers, Dunn to LaFontaine, 27 Dec. 1843. Baldwin Papers, LaFontaine to Baldwin, 28 Jan. 1844.

35. LaFontaine Papers, Dunn to LaFontaine, 22 Dec. 1843.

36. On his Beauharnois interests see H. T. Manning, "Edward Wakefield and the Beauharnois Canal," *C.H.R.*, XLVIII, March 1967, 1-25.

37. *Examiner*, 6 Dec. 1843.

38. C.O. 537/142, Metcalfe to Stanley, 3 May 1843; *ibid.*, 11 Nov. 1843; Stanley to Metcalfe, 1 Jan. 1844.

39. *Ibid.*, Metcalfe to Stanley, 27 June 1843; Stanley to Metcalfe, 3 July 1843, 18 Aug. 1843. On the fate of the policy of assimilation see Ormsby, "Canadian Union, 1839-1845," pp. 196-209. He concludes that by the end of Metcalfe's régime the "policy of enforced assimilation had been completely, albeit reluctantly, abandoned" by the imperial authorities (p.209).

40. P.A.O., Hodgins Papers, Draper to Ryerson, 26 Jan. 1844.

41. P.A.C., Viger Papers, M.G. 24, B6, Daly to Viger, 13 Feb. 1844.

42. C.O. 42/509, Metcalfe to Stanley, 11 Dec. 1843.

43. Derby Papers, Metcalfe to Stanley, 25 Feb. 1844.

44. Baldwin Papers, R. B. Sullivan to H. Sullivan, 20 Dec. 1843.

45. *British Colonist* (Toronto), 5, 19 Jan. 1844, *et seq.*

46. LaFontaine Papers, Baldwin to LaFontaine, 20 Jan. 1844.

47. *British Colonist*, 31 May 1844, *et seq.*; *Globe* (Toronto), 18 June 1844, *et seq.*

48. Derby Papers, Metcalfe to Stanley, 16 May, 27 June, 1844.

49. Viger Papers, Daly to Viger, 15, 17 Feb. 1844; Baldwin Papers, LaFontaine to Baldwin, 2 July 1844; Monet, *op. cit.*, pp. 277-79, 344-46.

50. C.O. 537/143, Metcalfe to Stanley, 17 Sept. 1844.

51. *British Colonist*, 31 May 1844.

52. Baldwin Papers, Derbishire to Baldwin, 6 May 1844.

53. C.O. 42/514, Metcalfe to Stanley, 30 Mar. 1844.

54. Quoted in Dent, *Last Forty Years*, I, 360.

55. *Ibid.* See also LaFontaine Papers, Dunn to LaFontaine, 22 Dec. 1843.

56. *Patriot*, 4 Oct. 1844.

57. *Examiner*, 23 Oct. 1844.

58. *British Colonist*, 1 Nov. 1844.

59. *St. Catharines Journal*, 31 Oct. 1844.

60. Study of these elections, constituency by constituency in the press of the day, makes this point very evident.

61. Frances Morehouse, "Canadian Migration in the Forties," *C.H.R.*, IX, December 1928, 312.

62. LaFontaine Papers, Baldwin to LaFontaine, 15 June, 1844.

63. P.A.O., Jessup Papers, 30 Sept. 1844. *Montreal Transcript*, 5 Oct. 1844.

64. Cornell, *Political Groups*, pp. 17, 98.

65. *La Minerve* (Montréal), 7 nov., 25 sept. 1844.

66. *Le Canadien*, 25 sept. 1844.

67. Baldwin Papers, LaFontaine to Baldwin, 12 Nov. 1844.

68. *La Minerve*, 3, 5 oct. 1844.

69. Cornell, *op. cit.*, pp. 17, 98.

70. Baldwin Papers, LaFontaine to Baldwin, 12 Nov. 1844.

71. LaFontaine Papers, Baldwin to LaFontaine, 7 Nov. 1844.

72. Baldwin Papers, Heyden to Baldwin, 17 Feb. 1845.

73. *Ibid.*, Grant to Baldwin, 8 Nov. 1843. Sister Mary Joyce Roberts, "The Elections of 1844," unpublished research paper, University of Toronto, 1964, pp. 10-11.

74. *Chronicle and Gazette*, 16 Dec. 1843.

75. Moir, *Church and State*, p. 90.

76. *Ibid.*, p. 89.

77. *Ibid.*, p. 91.

78. The move was actually carried out by Draper and Viger, and had little impact on the election campaigns outside of the Midland District (Kingston area). See Sister Mary Roberts, *loc. cit.*, p. 10.

79. *Ibid.*, p. 73.

80. *Ibid.*, p. 72. *Globe*, 14 Jan. 1845.

NOTES TO CHAPTER SIX

1. Kaye, *Metcalfe*, II, 390, Metcalfe to Stanley, 23 Nov. 1844; C.O. 537/142, Metcalfe to Stanley, 12. Nov. 1844.

2. P.A.C., Macdonald Papers, vol. 336, pt. 1. Copy of J. A. Macdonald's election address of 1844.

3. *Journals of the Assembly* (1844-45), p. 20.

4. D. G. Creighton, *John A. Macdonald, the Young Politician* (Toronto, 1952), p. 105.

5. *Journals of the Assembly* (1844-45), p.

301. Metcalfe of course had long been pressing for a general pardon for the Lower Canadian rebels of 1837-38 (see p. 85 above) and had gradually won Stanley's support for partial, then complete, amnesty. See particularly C.O. 537/142, Metcalfe to Stanley, 3 May 1843; Stanley to Metcalfe, 3 July 1843.

6. *La Minerve*, 16 déc. 1844, 6 fév. 1845.

7. *Examiner*, 5 Mar. 1845.

8. Moir, *Church and State*, pp. 91-92.

9. P.A.C., Merritt Papers, Draper to Merritt, 20 June 1844.

10. C.O. 537/143, Metcalfe to Stanley, 4 Apr. 1845.

11. Ibid., 13 May 1845.

12. L'Aurore, 17 déc. 1844 et seq.

13. Le Canadien, 5 sept. 1845.

14. Ibid., 25 avr., 5, 12 mars 1845.

15. T.P.L., Baldwin Papers, LaFontaine to Baldwin, 23 Sept. 1845.

16. Correspondence between the Hon. W. H. Draper and the Hon. R. E. Caron (Montreal, 1846), Caron to LaFontaine, 7 Sept. 1845. The French version of this important series of letters is Correspondence entre l'honorable R. E. Caron et les honorables L. H. Lafontaine et A. N. Morin (Montreal, 1846). Both versions, of course, contain translations into English or French. The letters read into the Assembly Journals by LaFontaine on 7 April 1846 are also given in Hincks, Reminiscences, pp. 147-63.

17. Baldwin Papers, Hincks to Baldwin, 23 Sept. 1845.

18. Draper-Caron Correspondence, LaFontaine to Caron, 10 Sept. 1845.

19. Ibid., Caron to Draper, 17 Sept. 1845.

20. P.A.C., Derby Papers, Metcalfe to Stanley, 26 Dec. 1844.

21. Ibid., 13 Oct. 1845.

22. Sir A. G. Doughty, ed., The Elgin-Grey Papers (4 vols., Ottawa, 1937), Vol. I, Elgin to Grey, March 14, 1849.

23. P.A.C., R.G. 7, G5/34, Gladstone to Cathcart, 3 Feb. 1846.

24. Dent, Last Forty Years, II, 60.

25. P.A.C., G5/33, Stanley to Metcalfe, 4 Apr. 1845.

26. G. F. G. Stanley and R. A. Preston, A Short History of Kingston as a Naval and Military Centre (Kingston, 1950), p. 25.

27. Ibid.

28. Globe, 6 Jan. 1846.

29. Ormsby, "The Civil List Question," C.H.R., XXXV, 1954, 113-15.

30. Draper-Caron Correspondence, Caron to LaFontaine, 6 Apr. 1846; Caron to LaFontaine, 7 Apr. 1846.

31. Baldwin Papers, Hincks to Baldwin, 16 Aug. 1846.

32. Ibid.

33. Ibid.

34. Ibid., LaFontaine to Baldwin, 20 Sept. 1846.

35. Ibid., Hincks to Baldwin, 16 Nov. 1846.

36. Journals of the Assembly (1849), Appendix PPPP.

37. Ibid.

38. Hind, Eighty Years' Progress, p. 291.

39. Tucker, Commercial Revolution, p. 94.

40. Glazebrook, Transportation in Canada, p. 84.

41. Ibid., p. 85.

42. J. E. Hodgetts, Pioneer Public Service, 1841-1867 (Toronto, 1955), p. 4.

43. Ibid., p. 181.

44. Glazebrook, op. cit., p. 120.

45. Hodgetts, op. cit., p. 181.

46. Journals of the Assembly (1846). See Index, pp. xxvii-xxviii, for lines chartered.

47. H. A. Innis and A. R. M. Lower, Select Documents in Canadian Economic History, 1783-1885 (Toronto, 1933), p. 303; Canadian Economist, 12 Sept. 1846.

48. Ibid.

49. Journals of the Assembly (1849), Appendix Z.

50. C. Woodham-Smith, The Great Hunger (New York, 1962), p. 50, Peel to Heytesbury, 15 Oct. 1845.

51. Creighton, Commercial Empire, p. 361.

52. Montreal Gazette, 6 Apr. 1846.

53. Ibid., 30 Mar. 1846.

54. Mirror of Parliament, 1846, p. 209.

55. Tucker, Commercial Revolution, pp. 105-6.

NOTES TO CHAPTER SEVEN

1. F. Morehouse, "Canadian Migration in the Forties," C.H.R., IX, December 1928, 309-18.

2. Ibid., 322.

3. Woodham-Smith, *Great Hunger*, p. 238.

4. Quoted in Norman Macdonald, *Canada, Immigration and Colonization, 1841-1903* (Toronto, 1966), p. 41.

5. Morehouse, *loc. cit.*, p. 322.

6. *Journals of the Assembly* (1849), Appendix PPPP.

7. Earl Grey, *The Colonial Administration of Lord John Russell* (London, 1853), I, 209-13, Grey to Sir John Harvey, 3 Nov. 1846.

8. *Ibid.*

9. P.A.C., Elgin Papers, M.G. 24, A10, Elgin to Grey, 27 Mar. 1847.

10. *Ibid.*, 13 July 1847.

11. T.P.L., Baldwin Papers, Hincks to Baldwin, 25 Mar. 1847. See also *ibid.*, 27 Mar. 1847.

12. P.A.C., Correspondence Chauveau, M.G. 24, B54, Drummond to Chauveau, 19 avr. 1847.

13. P.A.C., Macdonald Papers, vol. 209, Draper to Macdonald, 4 Mar. 1847.

14. Baldwin Papers, LaFontaine to Baldwin, 10 Apr. 1847.

15. Cornell, *Political Groups*, p. 100.

16. *Ibid.* Cornell lists 23 reformers at new parliament's opening, but notes that Hincks made the 24th when his opponent was declared unseated.

17. Baldwin Papers, Baldwin to LaFontaine, 25 Jan. 1848.

18. Cornell, *op. cit.*, pp. 6, 99-100.

19. In regard to the university question, it is noteworthy that John A. Macdonald had sponsored another attempt to settle it, in a bill he introduced in July 1847. But his measure to divide the public endowment among church colleges (King's College to receive double the annual income allotted) failed in the conservatives' weakness, and was withdrawn.

20. *Globe*, 10 Mar. 1847.

21. *Journals of the Assembly* (1848), p. 17.

22. Baldwin Papers, Baldwin to LaFontaine, 25 Jan. 1848.

23. It might be added that Taché, who had relinquished his assembly seat in 1846 to become Deputy Adjutant-General for Lower Canada, with the rank of Colonel, now was appointed to the legislative council. Henceforth as a cabinet minister he held his legislative place in the upper house. In 1849 he changed his ministerial office to that of Receiver General, a post he held until his retirement from the cabinet in 1857.

24. P.A.C., Macdonald-Langlois Papers, M.G. 24, B30, Baldwin to Sandfield Macdonald, 25 Jan. 1848.

25. *La Minerve*, 20 déc. 1847. These quotations came from Papineau's original address to his electors, here published (and soon known as "le manifeste Papineau"). For his supplementary manifestos, see *L'Avenir* (Montréal), 15, 24 mai 1848.

26. *L'Avenir*, 15 avr. 1848. It might be noted that the title of this journal suggested the affiliation of the *rouges* with the French anti-clerical democrat, Lamennais, whose own journal begun in 1830 was named *L'Avenir*.

27. A.P.Q., Collection Chapais, Correspondence Chapais-Langevin, Hector Langevin à Edmond et Jean Langevin, 8 déc. 1848.

28. Hind, *Eighty Years' Progress*, p. 291.

29. Tucker, *Commercial Revolution*, p. 70.

30. Elgin Papers, Elgin to Grey, 4 Jan. 1849.

31. The language question had finally been settled by an imperial measure of the year before that amended the Union Act of 1841 to remove its restriction on French.

32. *Journals of the Assembly* (1849), pp. 108-12.

33. *Ibid.*, (1846), Appendix X. Nelson actually claimed £23,109 for property destroyed, but deducted liabilities, leaving a claim on balance of £12,379.

34. *Examiner*, 21, 28 Feb. 1849; *Montreal Gazette*, 16, 19 Feb. 1849.

35. Elgin Papers, Elgin to Grey, 14 Mar. 1849.

36. *Montreal Gazette*, 28 Mar. 1849. The *Gazette* also wrote (16 Feb. 1849): "The bare proposal of the iniquity is a personal insult to every man who bore arms

in 1837 and a positive robbery of every man who was not a rebel against the Queen. But it is not a measure by itself; it is one of a chain long cherished in the Lower Canada Parliament and now revived under the union to put the Anglo-Saxon of Canada East particularly under the feet of the French . . ." *La Minerve* responded (3 mai 1849): ". . . c'est une guerre de race qu'ils veulent entreprendre, c'est notre nationalité qui est leur cauchemar . . ."

37. Quoted in *Examiner*, 21 Mar. 1849.

38. Montreal *Courier*, undated extract printed in Doughty, ed., *Elgin-Grey Papers*, I, 336.

39. *La Minerve*, 26 avr. 1849. See also Gérin-Lajoie, *Dix Ans au Canada*, p. 562.

40. Elgin Papers, Elgin to Grey, 30 Apr. 1849. Elgin added: "The whole row is the work of the Orange Societies, backed by the commercial men who desire annexation and the political leaders who want place."

41. Glazebrook, *Transportation in Canada*, p. 97.

42. Tucker, *op. cit.*, pp. 69, 82.

43. Elgin Papers, Elgin to Grey, 23 Apr. 1849.

44. *Ibid.*, 19 Mar. 1849.

45. Tucker, *op. cit.*, pp. 189-90. J. Monet, "French Canada and the Annexation Crisis," *C.H.R.*, XLVII, September 1966. 249-64.

46. Doughty, ed., *Elgin-Grey Papers*, II, 523, 4 Oct. 1849. *Ibid.*, 584, Elgin to Grey, 28 Jan. 1850.

47. For the text of the Annexation Manifesto of 1849 see Tucker, *op. cit.*, Appendix B, pp. 227-33.

48. *L'Avenir*, 18 mars, 6 juin, 17, 19, 25 juillet 1849.

49. J. M. S. Careless, *Brown of the Globe* (2 vols., Toronto, 1959, 1963), I, 98.

50. Doughty, ed., *Elgin-Grey Papers*, II, 572. "A Lover of Peace and Quietness."

51. P.A.C., R.G. 7, G5/35, Grey to Elgin, 9 Jan. 1850.

52. Longley, *Hincks*, pp. 167-75.

NOTES TO CHAPTER EIGHT

1. A. R. M. Lower, *The North American Assault on the Canadian Forest* (Toronto, 1938), pp. 98-101.

2. *Ibid.*, p. 108.

3. *Ibid.*, p. 116.

4. Hind, *Eighty Years' Progress*, p. 291.

5. *Ibid.*

6. Lower, *op. cit.*, p. 130.

7. Innis and Lower, *Select Documents, 1783-1885*, p. 481.

8. Lower, *op. cit.*, p. 134, diagram 4.

9. Tucker, *Commercial Revolution*, pp. 58-62, 209-11.

10. P.A.C., Elgin Papers, Elgin to Grey, 8 Nov. 1849, 10 Dec. 1849.

11. *Ibid.*, Grey to Elgin, 24 Oct. 1849.

12. *Ibid.*, Elgin to Grey, 6 Oct. 1850.

13. Lower, *op. cit.*, p. 122.

14. Quoted in D. C. Masters, *The Reciprocity Treaty of 1854* (Toronto, 1963: original edition London, 1937), p. 35, Crampton to Malmesbury, 6 Sept. 1852.

15. On the role of Andrews, see Irene W.

D. Hecht, "Israel D. Andrews and the Reciprocity Treaty of 1854, a Reappraisal," *C.H.R.*, XLIV, December 1963, 313-29.

16. Lawrence Oliphant, *Episodes in a Life of Adventure* (London, 1896), pp. 45-56. Oliphant, Elgin's private secretary, vividly describes the process whereby the treaty was "floated through on champagne." Elgin had been on leave in England since early in 1854, but returned to Canada via Washington first, to carry out this diplomatic mission.

17. *Montreal Gazette*, 6 June, 1854; *Globe*, 9 June, 1854.

18. Masters, *Reciprocity Treaty*, Appendix B, p. 147.

19. *Ibid.*

20. *Ibid.*, pp. 109-15.

21. Easterbrook and Aitken, *Canadian Economic History*, p. 295.

22. Lower, *op. cit.*, pp. 118, 171-75.

23. Longley, *Hincks*, pp. 220-22.

24. A. W. Currie, *The Grand Trunk Railway of Canada* (Toronto, 1957), Chapters 2 and 3.

25. Innis and Lower, *op. cit.*, p. 637.

26. J. H. Rose, A. P. Newton, E. A. Benians, eds., *The Cambridge History of the British Empire*, Vol. VI, *Canada and Newfoundland* (Cambridge, 1930), p. 338.

27. Innis and Lower, *op. cit.*, p. 660.

28. *Ibid.*, p. 601.

29. *Ibid.*, p. 610

30. *Ibid.*, p. 597.

31. *Ibid.*, p. 596. See M. Denison, *Harvest Triumphant* (Toronto, 1949), pp. 48-50.

32. D. C. Masters, *The Rise of Toronto* (Toronto, 1947), p. 64.

33. J. S. Hogan, *Canada* (Toronto, 1855), p. 66.

34. *Ibid.* T.P.L., "Memorandum on Materials and Labour in Canada for Commanding Officer R.E.," 1841, p. 97.

35. *Journals of the Assembly* (1856), Appendix 37.

36. J. S. Galbraith, *The Hudson's Bay Company as an Imperial Factor* (Toronto, 1957), pp. 35-36.

NOTES TO CHAPTER NINE

1. *Census of the Canadas, 1851-2* (Quebec, 1853), IV, 206.

2. *Journals of the Assembly* (1854-55), Appendix C.

3. Innis and Lower, *Select Documents*, p. 631.

4. Calculated from the census of 1851-2.

5. *Report of the Select Committee of the Legislative Assembly to inquire into Emigration* (Montreal, 1849). See also M. L. Hansen and J. B. Brebner, *The Mingling of the Canadian and American Peoples* (New Haven, 1940), pp. 123-28.

6. F. Morehouse, "Canadian Migration in the Forties," *C.H.R.*, IX, December 1928, 327.

7. *Census of the Canadas, 1851-2.*

8. *Globe*, 25 Nov. 1848.

9. On colonization roads, see Hodgetts, *Pioneer Public Service*, pp. 262-65, and A. R. M. Lower, "The Assault on the Laurentian Barrier, 1850-70," *C.H.R.*, X, December 1929, 299-302.

10. Jones, *History of Agriculture*, p. 99.

11. *Ibid.*, pp. 102-4.

12. Innis and Lower, *op. cit.*, p. 552.

13. *Ibid.*, p. 566.

14. P.A.C., Elgin Papers, Grey to Elgin, 2 Aug. 1850.

15. *Ibid.*, Elgin to Grey, 17 Sept. 1850.

16. Georges Vattier, *Esquisse historique de la colonisation de la Province de Québec, 1608-1925* (Montreal, 1927), pp. 42-46.

17. See the Ninety-Two Resolutions of 1834, resolutions 56 to 60.

18. M. Séguin, "Le régime seigneurial au pays de Québec, 1760-1854," *R.H.A.F.*, I, décembre 1947, 318-19.

19. W. B. Munro, *The Seigneurial System in Canada* (New York, 1907), p. 242.

20. *Mélanges Religieux*, 26 août 1845.

21. Glazebrook, *Transportation in Canada*, p. 164.

22. E. Parent, "L'Industrie considérée comme moyen de conserver la Nationalité Canadienne-française." Quoted in Monet, "The Last Cannon Shot," p. 239. See F. Ouellet, "Etienne Parent et le mouvement du Catholicisme social," *B.R.H.*, 1955, pp. 99-118.

23. *La Minerve*, 7 déc. 1846.

24. Monet, *op. cit.*, p. 245.

25. An Institut Canadien was also established in Bytown in 1852.

26. D. M. Hayne, "Sur les traces du préromantisme canadien," *Revue de l'Université d'Ottawa*, XXX (1960), 137-57.

27. M. Wade, *The French Canadians, 1760-1945* (Toronto, 1956), pp. 298-301.

28. Monet, *op. cit.*, pp. 461-65.

29. *Ibid.*, pp. 467-73.

30. The *rouge* anti-clerical criticism particularly attacked the tithing rights of the Roman Catholic Church in Lower Canada and its pervasive power over the educational system. Bishop Bourget in October 1849 anticipated a campaign for the suppression of the "dîmes" (tithes).

See Monet, op. cit., p. 693.

31. Ibid., pp. 698-705.

32. Chiniquy later (1858) left the Roman Catholic Church and became a Presbyterian minister in the United States. But he was in the forefront of Catholic missionizing zeal in the late 1840's.

33. Moir, Church and State, pp. xii-xiv.

34. S. D. Clark, Church and Sect in Canada (Toronto, 1948), pp. 332-35.

35. C. C. Taylor, Toronto "Called Back" from 1886 to 1850 (Toronto, 1886), p. 78.

36. C. Klinck, ed., Literary History of Canada, p. 147.

37. R. P. Baker, English Canadian Literature to the Confederation (Cambridge, Mass., 1920), p. 204.

38. John McMullen, The History of Canada from its first Discovery to the Present Times (Brockville, 1855), p. xiv.

39. Ibid.

40. Globe, 2 Jan., 20 Oct. 1847.

41. Ibid., 24 Aug. 1852.

NOTES TO CHAPTER TEN

1. P.A.C., Elgin Papers, Grey to Elgin, 12 Apr. 1850.

2. P.A.O., Clarke Papers, McDougall to Clarke, 20 Aug. 1850.

3. Examiner, 19 Sept. 1849.

4. Ibid., 12 Dec. 1849.

5. T.P.L., Baldwin Papers, McDougall to Baldwin, 9 June 1849.

6. Dent, Last Forty Years, II, 90.

7. Globe, 21, 23 Mar. 1850.

8. See North American (Toronto), Jan.-Feb. 1851.

9. Globe, 28 Mar. 1850.

10. P.A.C., LaFontaine Papers, Drummond to LaFontaine, 1 Mar. 1850.

11. Journal de Québec, 22 mars 1850, quoted in Globe, 2 Apr. 1850.

12. Elgin Papers, Elgin to Grey, 2 Aug. 1850.

13. North American, 21 June, 13 Dec. 1850.

14. P.A.O., Mackenzie-Lindsey Papers, Mackenzie to J. M. Kalida[?], 2 July 1850.

15. Ibid., Address from The Free and Independent Electors of Yarmouth, 29 Apr. 1851; D. McLeod to Mackenzie, 19 July 1851; W. Gibbons to Mackenzie, 23 Dec. 1851.

16. Journals of the Assembly (1851), p. 117.

17. LaFontaine Papers, LaFontaine to Ellice, 4 Nov. 1851.

18. Clarke Papers, McDougall to Clarke, 25 July 1851.

19. LaFontaine Papers, Cauchon to LaFontaine, 9 Sept. 1851.

20. Ibid., Dec. 1851.

21. Mackenzie-Lindsey Papers, Macdonald to Lindsey, 10 Jan. 1852.

22. Ibid., T. Tipton to Mackenzie, 21 Mar. 1851.

23. Ibid., T. Wiggins to Mackenzie, 24 May 1851.

24. Moir, Church and State, p. 38.

25. LaFontaine Papers, Drummond to LaFontaine, 1 Mar. 1850.

26. Careless, Brown of the Globe, I, 118-25.

27. C. B. Sissons, Church and State in Canadian Education (Toronto, 1959), p. 25.

28. Moir, op. cit., p. 143.

29. Globe, 9 July 1850.

30. A. Mackenzie, Life and Speeches of the Hon. George Brown (Toronto, 1882), p. 33.

31. La Minerve, 12 mai 1851. On the friction between Brown and Hincks see Careless, op. cit., I, 135.

32. Globe, 28 Oct. 1851.

33. North American, 22 Aug. 1851.

34. Montreal Gazette, 20 Dec. 1851.

35. Cornell, Political Groups, pp. 32, 103.

36. L'Avenir, 21 jan. 1852. It should be noted that publication was resumed in April, when friends raised sufficient funds, but the paper died again in November. Subsequently new owners acquired the name and property, and L'Avenir reappeared for a time in 1856-57, still as a "journal républicain," but

with less of its earlier eloquence and intellect.

37. C. B. Sissons, *Egerton Ryerson, his Life and Letters* (Toronto, 1937, 1947), II, 256. *Globe*, 8 June 1852.

38. *Patriot*, 23 Feb. 1853.

39. *Globe*, 12 Mar. 1853.

40. A.P.Q., Collection Chapais, Letellier à Chauveau, 28 fév. 1849.

41. *Journals of the Assembly* (1852-53), Part I, 539.

42. *Ibid.*

43. *Globe*, 26 March 1853.

44. *Ibid.*

45. Moir, *op. cit.*, p. 154.

46. *Ibid.*, p. 153.

47. *Globe*, 19 May, 2 Apr. 1853.

48. Moir, *op. cit.*, p. 154.

49. *Globe*, 16 June 1853.

50. On the Gavazzi riot in Montreal see R. Sylvain, "Le 9 juin 1853 à Montréal–Encore l'Affaire Gavazzi," R.H.A.F., 1960, pp. 173-216.

NOTES TO CHAPTER ELEVEN

1. *Globe*, 4 Nov. 1851.

2. Creighton, *Macdonald*, I, 197.

3. P.A.O., Clarke Papers, McDougall to Clarke, 17 Sept. 1853.

4. *Ibid.*, 4 Apr. 1854.

5. *Globe*, 2 Apr. 1852, 10 May 1853.

6. *Ibid.*, 14 July 1853.

7. *Ibid.*, 21 Dec. 1852, 18 Aug. 1853.

8. M. Ayearst, "The Parti Rouge and the Clergy," C.H.R., XV, December 1934, 391-93.

9. A.P.Q., Collection Chapais, Papiers Langevin, boîte 8, *Mores Porci*.

10. Wade, *The French Canadians*, p. 314. Cartier held the chairmanship of the Railway Committee from 1852 to 1867.

11. Collection Chapais, Letellier à Chauveau, 1 mai 1851.

12. *Montreal Gazette*, 18 Aug. 1853.

13. Mood, "Orange Order in Canadian Politics," p. 198.

14. P.A.C., Brown Chamberlin Papers, M.G. 24, B19, Macdonald to Chamberlin, 21 Jan. 1856.

15. *Ibid.*

16. P.A.C., Macdonald Papers, vol. 336, Macdonald to Strachan, 9 Feb. 1854.

17. *United Empire* (Toronto: the semi-weekly *Patriot*), 14, 17 Feb. 1854.

18. *Letters of James, Earl of Elgin to Mary Louisa, Countess of Elgin, 1847-1862* (London, 1864), p. 6. See also C.O. 42/594, Elgin to Newcastle, 22 June 1854.

19. *Journals of the Assembly* (1854), pp. 29-30.

20. P.A.C., R.G. 7, G12/66, Elgin to Newcastle, 16 June 1854.

21. A.P.Q., Collection Chapais, Cauchon à Chapais, 16 août 1854.

22. *Globe*, 19 Aug. 1854.

23. *Journals of the Assembly*, 1854-55, Part I, pp. 2-3.

24. Careless, *Brown of the Globe*, I, 191-92.

25. Explanations to the House by Hincks on his resignation, 8 Sept. 1854, quoted in Hincks, *Reminiscences*, p. 324.

26. This is frequently rendered as "railways are my politics," but the version quoted is the one more often seen in the press of the period.

27. See J. Garner, "The Franchise and Politics," Ph.D. thesis, University of Toronto, 1958, p. 265.

28. Macdonald Papers, vol. 336, Macdonald to Strachan, 7 Feb. 1854.

29. *Journals of the Assembly* (1854-55), Part I, p. 75.

30. Moir, *Church and State*, pp. 76-77.

31. *La Minerve*, 3 jan. 1855.

32. Cornell, *Political Groups*, pp. 61, 71, 106.

33. *North American*, 21 Feb. 1855.

34. *Journals of the Assembly* (1854-55), Part II, pp. 1286-87.

35. *Examiner*, 15 July 1855.

36. Brown Chamberlin Papers, Macdonald to Chamberlin, 7 Aug. 1855.

37. *Examiner*, 29 Aug. 1855; *Leader* (Toronto), 29 Aug. 1855.

38. *L'Avenir*, 4 jan. 1856.

39. C.O. 42/603, Head to Labouchere, 19 Feb. 1856.

40. *News of the Week*, 2 Feb., 6 Mar. 1856.

41. Moir, *op. cit.*, p. 162.

42. Careless, *op. cit.*, pp. 218-27.

43. *Journals of the Assembly* (1856), p. 538.

44. *Globe*, 27 May 1856.

45. *Journals of the Assembly* (1856), p. 555.

46. *Ibid.*

47. Dent, *Last Forty Years*, II, 346.

48. C.O. 42/604, Head to Labouchere, 26, 31 May 1856.

49. P.A.C., Head Papers, Head-Lewis correspondence, Head to Lewis, 9 June 1856.

50. *Montreal Gazette*, 16 Oct. 1855.

NOTES TO CHAPTER TWELVE

1. D. G. G. Kerr, "Edmund Head, Robert Lowe and Confederation," *C.H.R.*, XX, December 1939, 417-18.

2. C.O. 42/605, Head to Labouchere, 3 Sept. 1856.

3. P.A.C., R.G. 7, G1/140, Labouchere to Head, 4 Dec. 1856.

4. *Weekly Globe*, 14 Sept. 1855.

5. J. M. S. Careless, "The Toronto *Globe* and Agrarian Radicalism, 1850-67," *C.H.R.*, XXIX, March 1948, 17.

6. See particularly the series by "Huron" in the *Globe*, the first of which was published on August 19 and which ran onward to November 1856. There were numerous other North West articles also, both during August (from the first) and through November and December.

7. P.A.C., M.G. 24, B40. Brown Papers, Circular of 15 December 1856.

8. *Leader*, 5 Jan. 1857.

9. *Globe*, 21 Mar. 1857.

10. D. G. G. Kerr, *Sir Edmund Head: A Scholarly Governor* (Toronto, 1954), pp. 157-80.

11. *Journals of the Assembly* (1857), p. 142.

12. Cornell, *Political Groups*, p. 108.

13. A.P.Q., Collection Chapais, Taché à Chapais, 31 déc. 1857.

14. Ormsby, "Canadian Union, 1839-45," p. 219.

15. Hincks, *Reminiscences*, p. 322.

16. *Globe*, 27 May 1856.

17. Hincks, *op. cit.*, p. 322. See also T.P.L., Baldwin Papers, Hincks to Baldwin, 23 Sept. 1845.

18. P.A.C., LaFontaine Papers, Baldwin to LaFontaine, 16 Oct. 1845.

19. *Ibid.*

20. *Globe*, 27 May 1856.

21. *Journals of the Assembly* (1856), p. 562.

22. *Globe*, 4 June 1856.

23. *Le Canadien*, 11 juin 1856.

24. *Leader*, 26 Apr. 1856.

25. *Globe*, 6 Aug. 1856.

26. Monet, "The Last Cannon Shot," pp. 457-61.

27. Sissons, *Church and State in Education*, p. 135.

28. *Ibid.*, p. 17.

29. *Journals of the Assembly* (1852), Appendix EE.

30. Quoted in W. S. Wallace, *History of the University of Toronto* (Toronto, 1927), p. 75.

31. J. E. Hodgetts, *Pioneer Public Service* (Toronto, 1955), p. 36.

32. *Ibid.*, pp. 91-94.

33. *Ibid.*, pp. 96-104.

34. *Journals of the Assembly* (1856), Appendix 10.

35. R. B. Splane, *Social Welfare in Ontario* (Toronto, 1965), p. 35.

36. *Ibid.*, p. 36.

37. *Globe*, 15 Mar. 1853.

38. P. B. Waite, *The Life and Times of Confederation* (Toronto, 1962), pp. 110-11.

39. *Leader*, 10 Feb. 1857.

40. *Ibid.*

41. *Ibid.*, 7 Feb. 1857.

SELECT BIBLIOGRAPHY

NOTE: The bibliography has been updated for the 1972 edition.

MANUSCRIPTS

The two major sources of official correspondence for the period dealt with in this volume are the G Series (Record Group 7) at the Public Archives of Canada, covering dispatches from the Colonial Office to the governors of Canada, and C.O. 42 at the Public Record Office, London (microfilm copies available at the P.A.C.), containing dispatches and supplementary material sent from the governors of Canada to the Colonial Office. In G Series, G1 is the main file, but all are described in the P.A.C. Preliminary Inventory for Record Group 7, listing the records of the Governor General's Office. It should be noted that in addition to the volumes of C.O. 42, volumes 140-143 of C.O. 537 comprise material pertaining to the governorships of Bagot and Metcalfe. They, also, are available in microfilm copies at the P.A.C. Other relevant holdings of public documents at the P.A.C. include Record Group 1, covering the minutes of the Executive Council of United Canada, and Record Groups 4 and 5, containing the correspondence of the Civil and Provincial Secretaries of Canada East and West.

The Russell Papers, Derby [Stanley] Papers and Grey of Howick Papers, all on microfilm at the P.A.C., are significant as personal documents of leading Colonial Secretaries of the period. As for the Governors General, there are the very informative Bagot Papers and Elgin Papers (microfilm) at the P.A.C., along with lesser, more scattered holdings of Metcalfe Papers and Head Papers, of which the most useful part is the Head-Lewis Correspondence. While there is no similar collection of Sydenham papers, some valuable correspondence is found in printed sources (see below).

Among papers of prominent Canadian public figures, the following should particularly be mentioned: at the P.A.C., the Brown, Chauveau, LaFontaine, Macdonald, Merritt, Neilson and Viger Papers; at the P.A.O., the Clarke, Mackenzie-Lindsey and Hodgins Papers, the last largely containing Ryerson material; at the A.P.Q., the Collection Chapais (including the Papiers Langevin), the Collection Papineau-Bourassa, and the Papiers Taché; at the T.P.L., the Baldwin Papers. The Baldwin Papers and the LaFontaine Papers (handwritten copies at the P.A.C., the originals being in the Montreal City Library) are especially important for most of the period covered in this book. Unfortunately when it was being written relevant portions of the Papineau-Bourassa collection were not available for use, though the author was kindly permitted to see some transcriptions made previously. Other collections of private papers of less scope and weight have also been consulted, and references to them will be found in the Notes.

PRINTED SOURCES

The most generally significant are the government records published in the *Journals of the Legislative Assembly of the Province of Canada* and their *Appendices* (sessional papers). The Journals provide essential political information on the composition and votes of the house; the Appendices are a storehouse of data on economic activities and projects, population growth and social questions. On population trends and settlement patterns specifically, see the *Census of Canada, 1871,* Vol. IV (Ottawa, 1876), which summarizes the whole range of census reports from 1665 to 1871, and the detailed *Census of the Canadas, 1851-2* (Quebec, 1853).

There was no official Hansard for the period of United Canada, but parliamentary debates were fully reported in the leading newspapers. An unofficial *Mirror of Parliament* was also sporadically published, as in 1841 and 1846. Moreover, one now may look to a major project under way to compile an authoritative record for the Union period, *Debates of the Legislative Assembly of United Canada, 1841-1867*, Vol. 1 : 1841, edited by Elizabeth Nioh (Montreal, 1971). *Political Appointments and Elections in the Province of Canada from 1841 to 1865*, by J. O. Coté (Ottawa, 1866), is a valuable supplement for the study of public affairs under the union. Also important for their study is *Statutes, Treaties and Documents of the Canadian Constitution, 1713-1929*, edited by W. P. M. Kennedy (second edition, Toronto, 1930), which has not yet been superseded as a basic compilation of Canadian constitutional documents. Two other subsidiary documentary collections are *Canadian Constitutional Development, shown by Selected Speeches and Despatches*, edited by H. E. Egerton and W. L. Grant (London, 1907), and W. R. Manning ed., *Diplomatic Correspondence of the United States, Canadian Relations, 1784-1860* (4 vols., Washington, 1940-45). Instructive on economic development are *Select Documents in Canadian Economic History, 1783-1885*, edited by H. A. Innis and A. R. M. Lower (Toronto, 1933).

Several published collections of private papers should be noted. Volume 3 of *The Arthur Papers*, edited by C. R. Sanderson (Toronto, 1959), is useful on Sydenham's work in implementing the union. Still more so are *Letters of Lord Sydenham to Lord John Russell*, edited by Paul Knaplund (London, 1931). More of Sydenham's correspondence is found in G. Poulett Scrope's *Memoir of the Life of the Right Honourable Charles, Lord Sydenham* (London, 1844). Similarly, letters of Metcalfe not otherwise available are printed in J. W. Kaye, *Life and Correspondence of Charles, Lord Metcalfe* (2 vols., London, 1854). But most notable among printed papers for the period are *The Elgin-Grey Papers, 1846-1852* edited by Sir Arthur Doughty (4 vols., Ottawa, 1937), which offer an extensive collection of correspondence between Elgin and Grey, together with substantial enclosures. They should now be used in conjunction with the Elgin Papers, since made available, which contain additional letters from Grey, and also extend after 1852; but the published *Elgin-Grey Papers* remain a convenient, standard compilation.

PAMPHLETS AND NEWSPAPERS

The pamphlet literature extant is too large and varied to be detailed here. It includes, for example, items such as Egerton Ryerson's *Sir Charles Metcalfe Defended* (Toronto, 1844), *Manifeste du Club National Démocratique* (L'Avenir, Montréal, 1849), and *Statement, Reports and Accounts of the Grand Trunk Railway* (Toronto, 1857). Guides to this material are *Catalogue of Pamphlets in the Public Archives of Canada*, edited by Magdalen Casey (2 vols., Ottawa, 1931-32); *A Bibliography of Canadiana*, edited by F. M. Staton and M. Tremaine (Toronto, 1935); and *A Bibliography of Canadiana, First Supplement*, edited by G. M. Boyle (Toronto, 1959). Travellers' accounts such as Henry Taylor's *Journal of a Tour from Montreal thro' Berthier and Sorel to the Eastern Townships* (Quebec, 1840) provide another source of contemporary evidence, but they also are too numerous to mention. A helpful bibliography may be found in G. M. Craig, ed., *Early Travellers in the Canadas, 1791-1867* (Toronto, 1955).

The leading newspapers of the period, extensively consulted for this study, were the *Montreal Gazette* and the Toronto *Globe* in English Canada, *La Minerve* (Montreal) and *Le Canadien* (Quebec) in French Canada. Also very significant, and consulted for briefer periods, were the *Quebec Gazette*, the Montreal *Pilot*, and the *Patriot*, *Leader*, *Examiner* and *North American* of Toronto, *Le Journal de Québec*, *L'Avenir* and *Les Mélanges Religieux* of Montreal. Other papers, also briefly examined on specific issues, included the Kingston *Chronicle and Gazette*, the Toronto *British Colonist*, the Hamilton *Spectator*, *Le Fantasque* (Quebec) and *Le Moniteur Canadien*

(Montreal). The Canadian Library Association's continuing newspaper microfilm project, with its frequent mimeographed catalogues, provides an effective means of access to much of the press of the period.

SECONDARY AUTHORITIES

A. *General*

Though old, J. C. Dent's *The Last Forty Years: Canada Since the Union of 1841* (2 vols., Toronto, 1881) still has considerable value. Of similar character are J. P. Turcotte, *Le Canada sous l'Union, 1841-67* (Quebec, 1871) and A. Gérin-Lajoie, *Dix Ans au Canada, 1840-1850* (Quebec, 1888). See also relevant volumes in Sir T. Chapais, *Cours d'histoire du Canada*, vols. 5 and 6 (Quebec, 1932); in A. Shortt and A. G. Doughty, eds., *Canada and Its Provinces* (23 vols., Toronto, 1914-17); and in W. L. Grant, ed., *The Makers of Canada* (12 vols., Toronto, 1927).

Two modern works with their own particular themes but with broad significance for the union period are D. G. Creighton, *The Commercial Empire of the St. Lawrence, 1760-1850* (Toronto, 1937: republished as *The Empire of the St. Lawrence*, (Toronto, 1856), and Mason Wade, *The French Canadians, 1760-1945* (Toronto, 1956). See also M. Brunet, *La Présence anglaise et les Canadiens* (Montreal, 1958); Denis Vaugeois, *L'Union des deux Canadas, 1791-1840: Nouvelle Conquête?* (Trois-Rivières, 1962); and Chester Martin, *Foundations of Canadian Nationhood* (Toronto, 1955). And particularly see J. Monet, s.j., *The Last Cannon Shot: A Study of French-Canadian Nationalism, 1837-1850* (Toronto, 1969).

B. *Government and Politics*

1. *Union and Responsible Government*

For narratives by one of the leading contenders on these issues see Sir Francis Hincks, *The Political History of Canada between 1840 and 1855* (Montreal, 1877), and *Reminiscences of his Public Life* (Montreal, 1884) by the same author. Among older scholarly works, still with much significance for the subject, see J. L. Morison, *British Supremacy and Canadian Self-Government, 1839-54* (Toronto, 1919); W. P. M. Kennedy, *The Constitution of Canada* (Oxford, 1922); and Chester Martin, *Empire and Commonwealth* (Oxford, 1929). More recent scholarship is largely found in theses, biographies and articles; but see also G. P. de T. Glazebrook, *A History of Canadian Political Thought* (Toronto, 1966). More specifically on the union, see W. G. Ormsby, *The Emergence of the Federal Concept in Canada, 1839-1845* (Toronto 1969). See also V. Jensen, "Lafontaine and the Canadian Union," M.A. thesis for the University of Toronto, 1942, and G. Metcalf, "The Political Career of William Henry Draper, 1836-47," M.A. thesis for the University of Toronto, 1959.

Biographies include: Adam Shortt, *Lord Sydenham* ("Makers of Canada" Series, London, 1910); G. P. Scrope, *Memoir of Lord Sydenham* (see above); G. P. de T. Glazebrook, *Sir Charles Bagot in Canada* (London, 1929); J. W. Kaye, *Life of Lord Metcalfe* (see above); W. P. M. Kennedy, *Lord Elgin* ("Makers of Canada" Series, London, 1930); G. E. Wilson, *The Life of Robert Baldwin* (Toronto, 1933); R. S. Longley, *Sir Francis Hincks* (Toronto, 1943); A. D. DeCelles, *Lafontaine et son temps* (Montreal, 1907); A. Béchard, *L'Honorable A. N. Morin* (Quebec, 1885); R. Rumilly, *Papineau* (Montreal, 1934); C. B. Sissons, *Egerton Ryerson* (2 vols., Toronto, 1937, 1947).

Articles include: P. Knaplund, "The Buller-Peel Correspondence regarding Canada, 1841," *C.H.R.*, 1927, and "Some Letters of Peel and Stanley on Canadian Problems," *C.H.R.*, 1931; G. Metcalf, "Draper Conservatism and Responsible Government in the Canadas, 1836-1847," *C.H.R.*, 1961; W. G. Ormsby, "Sir Charles Metcalfe and the Canadian Union," *C.H.A.A.R.*, 1961; J. I. Cooper, "George Etienne Cartier in the period of the 'Forties," *C.H.A.A.R.*, 1938; V. Jensen, "Lafontaine and 1848 in Canada,"

C.H.A.A.R., 1948; J. Monet, "French Canada and the Annexation Crisis," C.H.R., 1966; F. Ouellet, "Denis-Benjamin Viger et le problème de l'annexation," B.R.H., 1951; W. G. Ormsby, "The Civil List Question in the Province of Canada," C.H.R., 1954.

2. Sectionalism and Party Changes

It should be evident that some of the political and biographical works named in the preceding section have relevance for this section also. In like manner, some of the books here listed for the 1850's bear on the 1840's as well. For example, P. G. Cornell, *The Alignment of Political Groups in Canada, 1841-67* (Toronto, 1962), while most valuable for studying the party changes in the mid-century years, is almost equally helpful for the preceding decade. Two other useful works for the 1850's are semi-autobiographical: Charles Clarke, *Sixty Years in Upper Canada* (Toronto, 1908); and vol. 1 of James Young, *Public Men and Public Life in Canada* (2 vols., Toronto, 1912).

Biographies include: D. G. G. Kerr, with the assistance of J. A. Gibson, *Sir Edmund Head: A Scholarly Governor* (Toronto, 1954); O. D. Skelton, *The Life and Times of Sir Alexander Tilloch Galt* (Toronto, 1920); D. G. Creighton, *John A. Macdonald, the Young Politician* (Toronto, 1952); J. M. S. Careless, *Brown of the Globe: the Voice of Upper Canada* (Toronto, 1959); J. Boyd, *Sir George Etienne Cartier, Bart: his Life and Times* (Toronto, 1914). See also A. Dansereau, *George Etienne Cartier* (Montreal, 1914); A. Labarrère-Paulé, *P.-J.-O. Chauveau* (Montreal, 1962); J. P. Merritt, *Biography of the Hon. W. H. Merritt* (St Catharines, 1875); and F. J. Audet, *Les Juges en chef de la Province de Québec* (Quebec, 1927), for A.-A. Dorion.

Some articles are: C. D. Allin, "The British North American League, 1849," O.H.S.P.R., 1915; G. M. Jones, "The Peter Perry Election and the Rise of the Clear Grit Party," O.H.S.P.R., 1914; M. Ayearst, "The Parti Rouge and the Clergy," C.H.R., 1934; F. H. Underhill, "The Development of National Political Parties in Canada," C.H.R., 1935; T. W. L. MacDermot, "The Political Ideas of John A. Macdonald," C.H.R., 1933; J. I. Cooper, "The Political Ideas of George Etienne Cartier," C.H.R. 1942; J. M. S. Careless, "The Political Ideas of George Brown," *Canadian Forum*, 1957; D. G. G. Kerr, "Edmund Head, Robert Lowe and Confederation," C.H.R., 1939.

3. Administration and Local Government

On administrative development see J. E. Hodgetts, *Pioneer Public Service: An Administrative History of the United Canadas* (Toronto, 1955); R. B. Splane, *Social Welfare in Ontario, 1791-1893* (Toronto, 1965); W. A. Langton, ed., *Early Days in Upper Canada* (Toronto, 1926); W. Smith, *The History of the Post Office in British North America, 1639-1870* (Cambridge, 1920). On local government see J. H. Aitchison, "The Development of Local Government in Upper Canada, 1783-1850" (Ph.D. thesis for the University of Toronto, 1953) and "The Municipal Corporations Act of 1849, C.H.R., 1949; and K. G. Crawford, *Canadian Municipal Government* (Toronto, 1954).

4. External Aspects

On imperial policy see O. A. Kinchen, *Lord John Russell's Canadian Policy* (Lubbock, Texas, 1945); W. P. Morrell, *British Colonial Policy in the Age of Peel and Russell* (Oxford, 1930); R. L. Schuyler, *The Fall of the Old Colonial System* (New York, 1945); C. P. Stacey, *Canada and the British Army, 1846-1871* (revised edition, Toronto, 1963); K. E. Knorr, *British Colonial Theories, 1570-1850* (Toronto, 1944). J. M. Hitsman, *Safeguarding Canada, 1763-1871* (Toronto, 1968).

On American issues see A. B. Corey, *The Crisis of 1830-1842 in Canadian-American Relations* (New Haven, 1941); L. B. Shippee, *Canadian-American Relations, 1949-1874* (New Haven, 1939); D. F. Warner, *The Idea of Continental Union, 1849-91* (University of Kentucky Press, 1960); J. B. Brebner, *North Atlantic Triangle* (New Haven,

1945); H. L. Keenleyside and G. S. Brown, *Canada and the United States* (New York, 1952).

Articles include: J. R. Baldwin, "The Ashburton-Webster Boundary Settlement," C.H.A.A.R., 1938; A. Watt, "The Case of Alexander McLeod," C.H.R., 1931.

C. Economic Affairs

1. Staple Enterprises

In regard to the staples, wheat and timber, and to the whole process of economic development, a good general account may be found in W. T. Easterbrook and H. G. J. Aitken, *Canadian Economic History* (Toronto, 1956). Another broad account, which deals with the social as well as economic implications of its subject, is R. L. Jones, *History of Agriculture in Ontario, 1613-1880* (Toronto, 1948). Still another, covering the other half of the union, is Fernand Ouellet's comprehensive study, *Histoire économique et sociale du Québec, 1760-1850* (Montreal, 1966). This outstanding work, which breaks new ground in the social history of French Canada, in addition to providing a detailed analysis of the Lower Canadian economy particularly related to price changes, was, regrettably, not published in time to be used in the writing of the present volume. However, articles by Professor Ouellet were utilized, some of them listed below, which embodied views and findings subsequently developed in his major book.

On agriculture, see further F. Ouellet and J. Hamelin, "La Crise agricole dans le Bas-Canada, 1802-37," C.H.A.A.R., 1962; R. L. Jones, "French Canadian Agriculture in the St. Lawrence Valley, 1815-50," *Agricultural History*, 1942; V. C. Fowke, *Canadian Agricultural Policy, the Historical Pattern* (Toronto, 1946); G. E. Britnell, *The Wheat Economy* (Toronto, 1939). On lumbering, see A. R. M. Lower, *Settlement and the Forest Frontier of Eastern Canada* (Toronto, 1936); also his *The North American Assault on the Canadian Forest* (Toronto, 1938) and "The Trade in Square Timber," *University of Toronto Studies, History and Economics*, vol. 6 (Toronto, 1933). See also H. A. Innis, *Problems of Staple Production in Canada* (Toronto, 1933); A. Shortt, "General Economic History, 1841-67," in vol. 4 of *Canada and Its Provinces* (Toronto, 1914).

2. Free Trade and Commercial Policy

A basic work still is G. N. Tucker's aptly-named *Canadian Commercial Revolution, 1845-1851* (New Haven, 1936, republished Toronto, 1964). There is good material illustrative of public opinion in C. D. Allin and G. M. Jones, *Annexation, Preferential Trade and Reciprocity* (Toronto, 1911). See also O. J. McDiarmid, *Commercial Policy in the Canadian Economy* (Cambridge, Mass., 1946); D. L. Burns, "Canada and the Repeal of the Corn Laws," *Cambridge Historical Journal*, 1928; G. W. Brown, "The Opening of the St. Lawrence to American Shipping," C.H.R., 1926; R. L. Jones, "The Canadian Agricultural Tariff of 1843," C.J.E.P.S., 1941.

On reciprocity, see D. C. Masters, *The Reciprocity Treaty of 1854* (London, 1937; republished Toronto, 1963), and his *Reciprocity, 1846-1911* (Canadian Historical Association Booklet No. 12, Ottawa, 1962); I. W. D. Hecht, "Israel D. Andrews and the Reciprocity Treaty of 1854, a Reappraisal," C.H.R., 1963.

3. Advances in Transportation

Most important, and comprehending roads, canals and railways, is G. P. de T. Glazebrook, *A History of Transportation in Canada* (Toronto, 1938, republished in 2 vols., Toronto, 1964). On railways, see also A. W. Currie, *The Grand Trunk Railway of Canada* (Toronto, 1957); G. R. Stevens, *Canadian National Railways*, vol. 1, *Sixty Years of Trial and Error* (Toronto, 1960); O. D. Skelton, *The Railway Builders* (Toronto, 1916); D. C. Masters, "T. C. Keefer and the Development of Canadian Transportation," *C.H.A.A.R.*, 1944.

On water transport, see M. J. Patton, "Shipping and Canals," in vol. 10 of *Canada and Its Provinces* (Toronto, 1914); R. B. Sneyd, "The Role of the Rideau Waterway, 1826-1856," M.A. thesis for the University of Toronto, 1965; W. Kingsford, *The Canadian Canals* (Toronto, 1865). On roads, see J. J. Talman, "Travel in Ontario before the Coming of the Railway," *O.H.S.P.R.*, 1933; G. W. Spragge, "Colonization Roads in Canada West, 1850-67," *O.H.*, 1957; E. C. Guillet, *The Story of Canadian Roads* (Toronto, 1966).

4. Other Economic Activities

On the fur trade, see H. A. Innis, *The Fur Trade in Canada* (New Haven, 1930); J. S. Galbraith, *The Hudson's Bay Company as an Imperial Factor, 1821-1869* (Toronto, 1957); E. E. Rich, *The History of the Hudson's Bay Company*, vol. 2, 1763-1870 (London, 1959). On industrial development, see S. P. Day, *English America* (London, 1864); H. Y. Hind *et al.*, *Eighty Years' Progress of British America* (Toronto, 1863); W. J. Donald, *The Canadian Iron and Steel Industry* (Boston, 1915); H. A. Logan, *Trade Unions in Canada* (Toronto, 1948); M. Denison, *The Barley and the Stream* (Toronto, 1955); H. C. Pentland, "The Lachine Strike of 1843," *C.H.R.*, 1948.

On banking, investment and currency, see R. C. McIvor, *Canadian Monetary, Banking and Fiscal Development* (Toronto, 1961); M. Denison, *Canada's First Bank: A History of the Bank of Montreal*, 2 vols. (Toronto 1966 and 1967); E. P. Neufeld, *Money and Banking in Canada* (Toronto, 1964); H. C. Pentland, "The Role of Capital in Canadian Economic Development before 1875," *C.J.E.P.S.*, 1950; A. Faucher, "Le Problème financier de la Province de Canada, 1841-67," *Recherches sociographiques*, 1960; D. C. Masters, "The Establishment of the Decimal Currency in Canada," *C.H.R.*, 1952.

D. Social and Cultural Development

1. Spread of Settlement and the Passing of the Frontier

General works that illustrate the increasingly intensive growth of society are S. D. Clark, *The Social Development of Canada* (Toronto, 1942) and A. R. M. Lower, *Canadians in the Making* (Toronto, 1958). See further, F. Ouellet, *Histoire économique et sociale du Québec*. On immigration, see H. I. Cowan, *British Emigration to British North America* (revised edition, Toronto, 1961); N. Macdonald, *Canada, Immigration and Colonization, 1841-1903* (Toronto, 1966); M. L. Hansen and J. B. Brebner, *The Mingling of the Canadian and American Peoples* (New Haven, 1940); C. Woodham-Smith, *The Great Hunger* (New York, 1962); F. Morehouse, "Canadian Migration in the 'Forties," *C.H.R.*, 1928; W. S. Shepperson, "Agrarian Aspects of Early Victorian Migration to North America," *C.H.R.*, 1952.

On the spread of settlement, see J. Spelt, *The Urban Development in South-Central Ontario* (Assen, The Netherlands, 1955); F. Landon, *Western Ontario and the American Frontier* (Toronto, 1941); J. H. Richards, "Lands and Policies . . . Alienation of Lands in Ontario," *O.H.*, 1958; and three works by R. Blanchard: *L'Est du Canada Français* (2 vols., Quebec, 1935); *Le Centre du Canada Français* (Quebec, 1947); *L'Ouest du Canada Français* (Quebec, 1953). On urban growth, see Spelt, *op. cit.*; D. C. Masters, *The Rise of Toronto, 1850-90* (Toronto, 1947); W. H. Atherton, *Montreal, 1535-1914* (3 vols., Montreal, 1914); J. I. Cooper, *Montreal: A Brief History* (Montreal, 1969); G. P. de T. Glazebrook, *The Story of Toronto* (Toronto, 1971). See also J. J. Talman, "The Impact of the Railway on a Pioneer Community," *C.H.A.A.R.*, 1955.

2. Other Aspects of Social Change

On the ending of seigneurialism, see W. B. Munro, *The Seigneurial System in Canada* (New York, 1907), old and subject to revision, but still a starting point.

Useful articles are, M. Séguin, "Le Régime seigneurial au pays de Québec, 1760-1854," R.H.A.F., 1947; F. Ouellet, "L'Abolition du régime seigneurial et l'idée de propriété," Hermès, 1954; M. Trudel, The Seigneurial Régime (Canadian Historical Association Booklet No. 6, 1960); J. P. Wallot, "La régime seigneurial et son abolition au Canada," C.H.R., 1969.

On changing class patterns and rising bourgeois and capitalist interests, see J. I. Cooper, "The Social Structure of Montreal in the 1850's," C.H.A.A.R., 1956; D. C. Masters, The Rise of Toronto; J. M. S. Careless, "The Toronto Globe and Agrarian Radicalism, 1850-67," C.H.R., 1948; F. Ouellet, "Les Fondements historiques de l'option séparatiste dans le Québec," Liberté, 1962; M. S. Cross, "The Lumber Community of Upper Canada," O.H., 1960. See also S. R. Mealing, "The Concept of Social Class and the Interpretation of Canadian History," C.H.R., 1965.

3. Religion and Relations of Church and State

General works are, H. H. Walsh, The Christian Church in Canada (Toronto, 1956); S. D. Clark, Church and Sect in Canada (Toronto, 1948); L. Pouliot, Mgr Bourget et son temps (2 vols., Montreal, 1955-56). Very useful on church-and-state issues over reserves, separate schools and universities in Upper Canada is J. S. Moir, Church and State in Canada West (Toronto, 1959). See also F. A. Walker, Catholic Education and Politics in Upper Canada (Toronto, 1955); G. A. Wilson, The Clergy Reserves of Upper Canada, 1791-1854 (Toronto, 1968). Articles include: L. Pouliot, "Les Evêques du Bas-Canada et le projet d'union (1840)," R.H.A.F., 1954-55; F. Ouellet, "Etienne Parent et le mouvement du catholicisme social," B.R.H., 1955; G. Carrière, "Le Renouveau catholique de 1840," Revue de l'Université d'Ottawa, 1954. See also M. Trudel, L'Influence de Voltaire au Canada (Montreal, 1945) and Chiniquy (Trois-Rivières, 1955); G. S. French, Parsons in Politics (Toronto, 1962).

4. Education and the Arts

On education, see J. D. Wilson, R. M. Stamp, L. P. Audet et al., Canadian Education, A History (Toronto, 1971); C. B. Sissons, Church and State in Canadian Education (Toronto, 1959), and also his Ryerson; J. D. Hodgins, ed., Documentary History of Education in Upper Canada . . . 1791 . . . 1876 (28 vols., Toronto, 1894-1910); L.-P. Audet, Le Système scolaire de la Province de Québec, vol. 6, La Situation scolaire à la veille de l'union, 1836-40 (Montreal, 1954). See also T. Matheson, "Les Origines de la surintend-ance de l'éducation au Bas-Canada, 1830-42," B.R.H., 1957; A. Maheux, "The Origins of Laval University," C.H.A.A.R., 1952; W. S. Wallace, History of the University of Toronto (Toronto, 1927).

On the arts, see C. F. Klinck, ed., The Literary History of Canada (Toronto, 1965); E. P. Baker, A History of English Canadian Literature to Confederation (Cambridge, Mass., 1920); P. Grandpré, Historie de la litterature française du Québec, vol. 1 (Montreal, 1967); J. R. Harper, Painting in Canada (Toronto, 1965); A. Gowans, Building Canada: An Architectural History of Canadian Life (Toronto, 1966); A. J. M. Smith, "Colonialism and Nationalism in Canadian Poetry before Confederation," C.H.A.A.R., 1944; J. S. Pritchard, "Some Aspects of the Thought of F. X. Garneau," C.H.R., 1970; E. Chartier, "La Vie d'esprit au Canada français: l'histoire et l'idée nationale, 1840-1925," M.S.R.C., 1934; D. Hayne, "Sur les traces du préromantisme canadien," Revue de l'Université d'Ottawa, 1961.

INDEX